James Randolph

PENNSYLVANIA
SONGS AND LEGENDS

PENNSYLVANIA
Songs and Legends

GEORGE KORSON
Editor

Philadelphia

UNIVERSITY OF PENNSYLVANIA PRESS

1949

Contents

Illustrations by Charles P. Allen

Introduction

by GEORGE KORSON

They are there, there, there with Earth immortal
(Citizens, I give you friendly warning).
The things that truly last when men and times have passed,
They are all in Pennsylvania this morning!*

Kipling may have had folklore as well as nature in mind when he wrote these lines. Certainly they describe Pennsylvania's oral popular traditions with uncanny accuracy—traditions that, through a persistent stability, remain alive when the conditions which inspired them and the people who created them have passed into history.

Pennsylvania is the Keystone State for more reasons than her location on the map. Within her borders there is "the memory of everything that America has been and the knowledge of what it may become." From the memory of her people great cultural wealth in the form of folklore may be recovered, just as fabulous material wealth has been extracted from her fertile soil and underlying minerals. Collected, classified, and put back into circulation for the people as a whole to enjoy, it can enrich every phase of Pennsylvania—and American—culture in much the same way as that other formerly wasted Pennsylvania raw product, coal tar, has become a source of far-reaching effect in modern medicine, in chemistry, and in industry.

* From "Philadelphia" from *Rewards and Fairies* by Rudyard Kipling. Copyright 1910 by Rudyard Kipling. Reprinted by permission of Mrs. George Bambridge and Doubleday & Company, Inc.

1

With the rest of the nation, Pennsylvania shares the common inheritance of English folk culture. In addition, she has other veins of folklore distinctively her own. The latter have sprung from the heterogeneity of her population and a rich diversity of industry growing out of her natural resources.

From the beginning of her history, Pennsylvania has been a place of refuge. The civil and religious freedom of the Quaker commonwealth appealed to the persecuted peoples of seventeenth- and eighteenth-century Europe. So did the prospect of a peaceful agricultural life on virgin acres in a "salubrious" climate. Even with all its advantages, the colony might not have attracted so many different groups of people in such large numbers had William Penn not combined business with noble ideals. Having millions of acres to sell, he was determined to stimulate immigration into his vast domain. His pamphlets glorifying the Quaker colony were printed in English, Dutch, French, and German, and distributed widely in Europe. As a good real-estate operator, he followed up his advertising copy with agents who carried his sales message directly to the dissatisfied and displaced peoples of Britain and the Continent. European peoples settling Pennsylvania in the colonial period included the English, Germans, Scotch-Irish, Irish, Welsh, Scotch, French, Dutch, Swedes, and Jews.

The presence of so many ethnic groups differing from one another in language, religious beliefs, customs, and traditions, and free to exercise their differences, gave Pennsylvania a colonial complexion described as "ring-streaked, speckled, and grizzled as any of Jacob's cattle." The English, the Germans, and the Scotch-Irish were the predominant groups, and remained so throughout her history. Their combined traits, good and bad, have given Pennsylvania her individual character as a state.

The settlers brought the folklore of their respective home countries. Instinctively preserved in their memory, it was transmitted to their children, who in turn handed it down to their children, in a continuous oral process from generation to generation. Further, each generation created its own folklore out of its experience and impressions which blended imperceptibly with its inherited background, for a creative vigor animated life in Pennsylvania as it did elsewhere in pioneer America.

Thus grew a great repertory of songs and ballads, tall tales and legends, folk speech, proverbs, superstitious beliefs, riddles, singing games, customs, fiddle and march tunes. This oral treasure reflects the spirit of Pennsylvanians, and their tastes and interests too. Moreover, it bears the influence of political, economic, and cultural movements within the commonwealth. A valuable record indeed for a full understanding of our people, past and present! "Toss out all the written records," suggests Duncan Emrich, Chief of the Folklore Section of the Library of Congress, "and you'd still find the juice of American achievement and the country's physical development in the folk music that passes from generation to generation, usually by word of mouth."

Pennsylvania was founded as an English community by the Quakers who followed Penn into the colony. Far more than the Germans and the Scotch-Irish, the English settlers were scattered all over the province, though most numerous in three counties in the vicinity of Philadelphia. English immigrants continued to come from the mother country, its dependencies and colonies in the New World, including Virginia, Maryland, New Jersey, and Connecticut. And so the most abundant source of Pennsylvania folklore is English in origin and influence. The only English settlers to remain aloof from the flourishing folklore movement were the Quakers, who proscribed "stage plays, cards, dice, May-games, gamesters, masques, revels, bull-baitings, cock-fightings, bear-baitings, and the like." They made other contributions to Pennsylvania, but folk minstrelsy was not their line.

The Scotch-Irish were the typical frontiersmen of colonial days. Proud, hardy, and daring, they were well fitted for the herculean task of taming the wilderness. The comparatively civilized eastern section of Pennsylvania did not hold them long. From Lancaster County and the present Dauphin County, they moved on to the Cumberland Valley, which, according to Wayland F. Dunaway, Pennsylvania historian, "became the headquarters of the Scotch-Irish not only in Pennsylvania, but also in America, the seed-plot and nursery of their race."

From the Cumberland Valley (the present Cumberland and Franklin counties) they pushed westward across the Alleghenies into southwestern Pennsylvania, where they formed another distinctive community of their own. Between periods of Indian fighting, fur trading, and farming, they contrived to carry on the tradition of Scottish Border minstrelsy. As in the old country, minstrels wandered from settlement to settlement singing traditional ballads.

Folk songs of English and Scotch-Irish inheritance will be found in Samuel P. Bayard's chapter on British folk traditions. As Professor Bayard points out, Pennsylvania, because of her geographical position, bridged the gap between the two great divergent regions of English folk-song cultivation—the Northeast (embracing New England and the Canadian maritime provinces) and the South. The folk songs of both regions mingled and crossed in Pennsylvania.

According to Dunaway, Pennsylvania served as an important population-distributing center during the colonial era. Thousands of English, Scotch-Irish, and Germans migrated from our state into the valleys of Virginia, Maryland, and the Carolinas, and some of them, like the Lincoln and Hanks families from Berks County, pushed on to Tennessee and Kentucky. Other thousands of Pennsylvania pioneers passed through Pittsburgh, "gateway to the West," into the Ohio Valley and farther west.

This mass migration was responsible for a wide diffusion of Pennsylvania-nurtured folklore. It would be futile to speculate as to the proportion of Cecil Sharp's informants, and the informants of later collectors, in the southern Appalachian region who were descendants of early Pennsylvania migrants. The amount of British folklore and folk music that filtered out of Pennsylvania with the migrants and was later recovered in the South may have been considerable. At any rate, the same type of material, and probably as abundant, was long kept alive by our own "contemporary ancestors." Colonel Henry W. Shoemaker early collected many fine Pennsylvania variants of Child ballads and other types of British song, and in more recent field researches Professor Bayard has recorded a large number of others. In beauty, variety, and in their state of preservation they compare favorably with any folk songs and ballads of British origin collected elsewhere in the United States.

The Germans—the so-called Pennsylvania Dutch—differed from the Scotch-Irish in their preference for the pastoral life, and from their Quaker neighbors in their liberal attitude toward amusements (excepting, of course, the Amish and other minority religious sects who were as austere as the Quakers). Some of their land was purchased from restive Scotch-Irish, but for the most part, following the trail of limestone soil and the walnut tree, they hewed farms out of the wilderness with their own hands.

The half-century or so after the end of the Revolutionary War was a period of prosperity for the Pennsylvania Germans. Revolutionary tension had eased and they were no longer called upon to contribute their sturdy young manhood to the Continental Army. Then, too, the Indians had been driven westward and no longer offered a threat to their security. Their industry was rewarded by abundant crops and overflowing larders. They developed their farms, built their homes of solid stone, and erected imposing barns. They raised their own flax, wove their own wool, and made their own garments.

It was during this tranquil period that the Pennsylvania Germans' native love of design and decoration began to assert itself, and led to the development of the individual Pennsylvania Dutch folk art. Dominated by geometrical balance and full of figures and motifs, principally peacocks, tulips, and pomegranates, the true meaning of which is lost in speculation, this folk art played an intimate role in their lives. Their *fraktur*—illuminated writing—an exquisite art form practiced with pencil, brush, and quill, and with lavish use of color, was carried on until the 1850's. But they continued using motifs in their handmade pottery, glassware, household furniture, needlework, quilts, and other useful products. About 1850 they began painting geometric designs over the distinctive red of their barns. Of uncertain symbolism, these signs may still be seen in eastern Pennsylvania.

The Pennsylvania Dutch made nothing that could not be used in everyday life; the embellishment of color and design was merely an expression of their buoyant spirit of creation.

What is true of their folk art holds equally for their folklore. Preserved in the Pennsylvania Dutch dialect were superstitious beliefs, proverbs, folk songs and ballads, nursery and counting-out rhymes, charms, riddles, and folk tales. These offered relief from monotony and boredom on the farm, especially during the bleak months between harvest and spring plowing. They were also the source of informal programs called "frolics" that accompanied the performance of communal tasks.

One of the most popular frolics was the apple-butter party, when neighbors gathered at a home to pare and quarter apples for the boiling, part of the process of making apple butter, the favorite Pennsylvania Dutch spread. Drudgery was taken out of apple cutting by the young people's approach to their communal effort. Coquettish repartee accompanied nimble fingers, and uninhibited laughter filled the house. There were riddles and parlor games which kept close to the love theme, storytelling, and individual and group singing of folk songs. When the apples had been prepared, the hostess served cider and cakes and pies, and the rest of the evening was given over to dancing. At one time or another these musical instruments were played at frolics: fiddle, banjo, bow zither, harpsichord, melodeon, and dulcimer.

The Amish held aloof from frolics and similar social functions featuring Pennsylvania Dutch folklore and folk music. Yet, as J. William Frey explains in his chapter, the Amish drew on folksong tunes for their church hymns. Parenthetically, the Amish represent a very small minority and are far from typical of the Pennsylvania Dutch, despite the popular notion to the contrary. They have attracted a disproportionate amount of publicity because of their quaint dress, strange customs, and anachronistic way of life.

Frolics gradually went out of fashion as technological improvements and more efficient methods on the farm and in the house reduced the need for communal tasks. Another factor in their disappearance lay in the social changes that affected the majority of the Pennsylvania Dutch and other rural groups. With the passing of frolics, Pennsylvania Dutch folk songs began losing their popularity until they were all but forgotten except by a scattered few traditional folk singers who preserved them in their memory.

In 1935 when organizing the Pennsylvania Folk Festival at Allentown, I had some difficulty at first locating traditional Pennsylvania Dutch folk singers for my program because of the general belief that none were alive. I learned otherwise, however, when I approached William S. Troxell, known throughout the Pennsylvania Dutch region as "Pumpernickle Bill." As dialect columnist of the *Allentown Morning Call,* Bill had (and still has) an immense following and many personal contacts. It was not surprising, therefore, that within a limited time he assembled a group of colorful traditional folk singers and dancers whose performance contributed substantially to the success of the folk festival.

This experience inspired Troxell to collect the folk songs and ballads of his people, and he soon teamed up with the Reverend Thomas R. Brendle, pastor of the historic Egypt Reformed Church in Lehigh County, a learned Pennsylvania German scholar with an unbounded enthusiasm for the lore of his people. The two men acquired a portable recording machine and with the occasional assistance of Paul Wieand scoured the region for Pennsylvania Dutch folk songs. Over a period of several years, they succeeded in recording more than two hundred songs which had been thought irretrievably lost. Their achievement surprised and pleased the whole region. However, except for an occasional song, Brendle and Troxell deferred releasing their collection to the public. They sought to study the individual items at their leisure and to wait for a proper time to make them available. Their chapter in this anthology, then, containing a representative selection of twenty-eight songs and ballads, marks the first publication of their collection.

Folklorists and musicologists will now have an opportunity to study this fresh and distinctive contribution to American folklore. German folk songs from time to time entered Pennsylvania from Germany and Switzerland contemporaneously with the British folk songs. Here on Pennsylvania soil the two great song movements met, mingled, and to a certain extent blended. We now have a basis for comparison between them.

Down to 1840, according to Professor Dunaway, "there still persisted with scarcely diminished vigor" distinctive sections of the three dominant colonial racial groups: the English in eastern Pennsylvania; the Germans in the area lying roughly between the Lehigh and Susquehanna rivers; and the Scotch-Irish in the west-central, southwestern, and northwestern parts of the state. A fourth section was comprised of the Wyoming Valley and the northern tier of counties settled by people from Connecticut and other northeastern states with traditions and social ideals patterned after those of New England.

In 1840, as the Industrial Revolution was developing in Pennsylvania, a new wave of immigration, larger than ever before, took on momentum. In the ensuing half-century, hundreds of thousands of immigrants poured in from the British Isles and Ireland, and from Germany and other northern countries. Irish immigrants far outnumbered all others. After 1890 the complexion of Pennsylvania's immigration changed. Immigrants from eastern and southern Europe came in much larger numbers than those from the British Isles and northern Europe. Polish, Russian, Czechoslovakian, Italian, and Austrian were the predominant strains.

The newcomers brought their folk culture into Pennsylvania as the early settlers had theirs. Each colonial immigrant group had been free to speak its native language, to follow its own folkways, and to make its own world out of the wilderness. Twentieth-century immigrants, on the other hand, found only a limited use for their mother tongue, and they had to conform to the new ways or starve. Peasant farmers, accustomed to a self-sufficient and hand-labor economy, they were catapulted into a technological environment where they were mere cogs of a complex industrial machine. Into coal camps, mine patches, and mill towns they came with their bundles and wicker trunks containing clothing, household tools, and other reminders of a material culture that was out of place in the New World.

Similarly, their folklore, bound up with their former peasant life and revolving around seasonal cycles, was anachronistic. Of what use was a harvest ritual when one worked in a coal mine or a steel mill? Torn from the old, not yet adapted to the new, they were caught in the middle of an interplay between two creative forces—their European heritage and the Pennsylvanian industrial environment. Their ordeal was harsh indeed, but the key to their difficult position was really transition. They were changing, and the changes lay in the direction of Americanization. But they never really forgot their imported folk songs, games, and dances, nor did they throw away their colorful native costumes. These

Booklet I   insert

were kept for special occasions, like weddings, saints' days, and church holidays, when countrymen met to celebrate.

When they had achieved what Mary Austin has described as a "complete saturation with a given natural environment," their folk creativity began to assert itself. Suiting their native tunes to texts reflecting their assimilated experiences, they began creating Pennsylvania folk songs and ballads. Until recently these have been overlooked by collectors because they were buried in foreign languages. The Slovak, Finnish, and Greek songs collected by Jacob A. Evanson especially for the present volume have beauty and rare emotional power. The outpourings of hearts deeply moved by ordeal and transition, they are valuable human documents.

Moreover, these beautiful melodies enrich our store of folk music. With other tunes imported into Pennsylvania, they form a source of musical culture that someday will be developed in terms of our modern American experience. Some of these imported folk songs are on the wane in their respective homelands, just as some English folk songs recovered in the United States are no longer current in England.

The minority groups also have a rich heritage of folk tales that are kept alive by oral tradition. Our American legendary giants— Paul Bunyan, John Henry, Mike Fink, and Jesse James—are matched in foreign tongues by superhuman folk heroes who accomplish the humanly improbable. In their own languages, but frequently drawing upon American idioms, Pennsylvanians of recent immigrant stocks amuse themselves with a retelling of these stories.

The invention of Joe Magarac by Slovak steelworkers of Pittsburgh typifies the process by which imported folk tales are being localized and Americanized. Only intensive research can determine how much narrative material lies hidden in foreign languages in Pennsylvania. over to Page 12 — mention other groups and give ex. German

One of the most hopeful signs of imperishable good in mankind is his habit of singing at his work regardless of its character. This unconquerable desire for beauty was early demonstrated by the Pennsylvania Dutch craftsman who hummed or sang to himself as he fashioned his artistic creations. Today it may be found even among the workers in the mass-production industries who turn out the stereotypes that have replaced the folk artist's individual creations. They may sing on the job or in their off hours, but what is sung bears a close relation to the social and economic conditions of the singers.

The Industrial Revolution with its far-reaching social changes in Pennsylvania life checked the continuity of that oral process by which the folklore of the colonial races was handed down from one generation to another. It compensated for this blight, however, by inspiring an entirely new body of folklore with many veins reflecting the pattern of living and working in industrial communities. The forest, the coal mine, the steel mill, and the oil well took the place of the farm as the focal point of community life. Folklore naturally sprang from industry because the essential elements for its growth were present. The lumberjacks in the northern woods, the miners in their mine patches and coal camps, and the steelworkers and oil-well drillers in their environments were as completely cut off from the main currents of Pennsylvania life as if they had been confined behind high stone walls. Even in urban areas, steelworkers were segregated more or less from the rest of the population, as, for instance, those living in the Soho district of Pittsburgh. In their isolation, the industrial workers achieved complete integration, acting and feeling as a group. When workers of the colonial stocks entered an industry, as many of them did, and merged with their fellow workers, they too participated in the new folklore movement. But on the whole, it was the immigrants who came after 1840—the Irish, Welsh, Scotch, Cornish, Germans, and the various national groups of the Latin and Slavonic races, as well as Negroes who migrated from the South to enter bituminous coal mines and steel mills—who created and disseminated industrial folklore.

Pennsylvania is unusually rich in this type of folklore because of her position as one of the nation's greatest industrial states. Underlying her fertile soil are such natural resources as iron ore, anthracite and bituminous coal, oil, limestone, sandstone, and slate, and clay deposits. In the northern tier of counties there once stood a vast virgin forest.

Pennsylvania long led the nation in the production of coal; her anthracite is duplicated nowhere else in commercial quantities. In the sixties she produced more lumber than any other state and continued to be an important shipper of pine and chestnut for many years thereafter. The proximity of Connellsville's coking coal to Pittsburgh's rolling mills helped make western Pennsylvania the world's greatest steel-producing region. As early as 1834, Pennsylvania had the greatest canal system in the world, with almost a thousand miles of these artificial waterways. Her railroads are among the most extensive in the country. Oil was first discovered in Pennsylvania; many of the mechanical devices and methods used by the oil industry originated here.

Throughout the years the people of Pennsylvania would, in the words of Samuel Johnson, "listen with credulity to the whispers of fancy and pursue with eagerness the phantoms of hope." Thus, there are in oral circulation a large body of legends and folk tales of all types. Each region usually leaves its distinctive stamp on universal folk-tale types, and these legends and tales, judging from those collected, preserve a generous slice of Pennsylvania living. Many are regional variants of stories as old as the human race. Their narrative motifs and structural forms are similar to those of other regions, and their appeal is to the same basic social and individual needs.

Take Pennsylvania Dutch traditional stories as an illustration. German folk tales of the type collected by the Brothers Grimm and published in their immortal *Kinder- und Hausmärchen* were brought over by early immigrants. Told and retold for generations in the Pennsylvania Dutch dialect, they were gradually localized in eastern Pennsylvania. In keeping with this oral process, Till Eulenspiegel, the fourteenth-century German rogue, is reincarnated in the folklore of the Pennsylvania Dutch as Eileschpijjel,* a beloved character. Eulenspiegel's practical jokes, often brutal, at the expense of the German upper classes established him in Germany and other European countries as a symbol of folk humor. In the cycle of Eileschpijjel stories collected by Brendle and Troxell in their book, *Pennsylvania German Folk Tales*, the local

* Also pronounced Eileschpiggel.

Mrs. Mary Brown
Mt. Morris
Lily Bell Dietrick
Morgantown
Thos. W. Galls-Mash
Perry Gump, Greene Co.

character is represented as a stolid farmhand of lovable qualities, the antithesis of his prototype. Eulenspiegel was a real person, but Eileschpijjel is a creation of the folk imagination. The latter is so vivid a folk character, however, that one informant told Brendle and Troxell, "Eileschpijjel often came to my grandfather's house."

The three legends comprising Colonel Shoemaker's chapter are typical of those that once relieved monotony and provided amusement in remote farmhouses and isolated mountain cabins in central and western Pennsylvania. Colonel Shoemaker was fortunate to have started collecting early enough to save many of them from extinction, and he has recorded them in his books, pamphlets, and in his Altoona *Tribune* folklore column.

Legends are also prevalent in other parts of the state. Indeed, there is scarcely a county that is without its local legends explaining natural curiosities; legends that have come down from the Indians and stories of Indian massacres and captivities passed on by the pioneer settlers; legends of lovers' leaps, of place names, of encounters with buffalo, bears, panthers, timber wolves, and wildcats that once roamed our forests; and legends of stirring local events that have gone unrecorded in the history books.

Among the Cornplanter Indians in Warren County there still survive many traditional Seneca myths and legends, according to Merle H. Deardorff. "Every ceremonial," writes Deardorff in his chapter, "has its body of legend, which is recalled each time the ceremony is performed."

The industries gave rise to their own cycles of legends and folk tales such as those found in Lewis E. Theiss's chapter on the canallers, Harry Botsford's chapter on the oil industry, and Freeman H. Hubbard's chapter on the railroaders. Steeling, lumbering, and coal mining were productive of many additional ones.

In Pennsylvania, as in the rest of America, the most characteristic form of traditional story is the tall tale. Americans early developed a flair for the big dimension in storytelling because they were so accustomed to doing things on a big scale. Extravagant dreams unrealized in brick and steel were mixed with bravado and humor and blown into gigantic balloons of fantasy. Storytellers with the most wind and the wildest imagination held their audiences longest. It needed but a kernel of truth—a stray item from

the local paper, a bit of township gossip, the opening of the
hunting or fishing season, or the beginning of spring plowing, to
launch soaring fancies and loosen facile tongues. Flavored with
the regional vernacular or idiom, or with the grotesque speech of
the backwoods, these tall tales enriched the folklore of the state.
While a certain amount of originality crept into them, the influence of Baron Münchausen was clearly discernible.

Not many traditional storytellers are alive today. Robert J.
Wheeler, author of the Pike County chapter, knew many of them.
Past seventy, Wheeler grew up in Pike County where tall-story
telling was as common as hunting, fishing, and bartering. As a boy
and later, when he returned to the county for fishing and hunting,
Wheeler listened to the best of the backwoods Münchausens. From
them he not only heard tall tales, which his own imagination later
embellished, but acquired the art of spinning a tall tale effort-
lessly, casually, and with a poker face. This art has been one of
his most potent assets as a businessman and politician in Allentown. In 1936 he won the state-wide tall-story contest held at the
Pennsylvania Folk Festival at Bucknell University.

Folk tales transcend boundary lines, racial differentiations, class
distinctions, and occupational pursuits. Thus various forms and
types of stories current among farmers, backwoodsmen, and mountaineers would also circulate orally among the state's industrial
workers—canallers, railroaders, coal miners, lumberjacks and raftsmen, steelworkers, oil drillers, and mill and factory hands.

Many of the traditional tall tales stem from the nineteenth
century, when a great deal of heavy labor in industry was still
performed by hand, and men delighted in their prowess and skill.
When mechanical power began displacing manual labor, causing
social upheavals and labor strikes, the workers poured their hearts
out into song but reserved the tall tale for their imagination—
their dreams. This medium with its saving grace of humor offered
relief from their pressing problems. By extolling man above the
machine, it gave them courage to continue the uneven struggle.
But, as John Henry's experience demonstrated, the gesture was
futile.

"I am reminded at this time of a little story," is usually the
preface to the telling of an anecdote for the purpose of creating

laughter. Simple in structure, with but a single narrative motif, the anecdote makes little demand either on the memory or skill of the narrator. Anecdotes by the thousands are floating about for use on appropriate or inappropriate occasions by all groups of society. Many of them may be collected in cycles revolving around a single character, real or synthetic. Howard C. Frey reminds us that anecdotes were preferred by the Conestoga wagoners because the hubbub and confusion in taverns along the Conestoga trail gave no encouragement to long-winded storytellers.

Another form of tale only now beginning to receive attention from students of folklore is the dialect yarn. Pennsylvania, with its diversified population, naturally would be expected to have this kind of funny story in great abundance. In the anthracite coal fields, for instance, gales of laughter have been produced among native American audiences by talented mimes imitating the immigrant's misuse of the English language. The dialect yarn spinners generally are Irish or Welsh who have lived in close proximity to immigrant miners and thus have acquired a good ear for grammatical errors, stock expressions, and intonations. These they reproduce with great effect. For their chief comic effects, they depend on sounds and funny situations, especially the misadventures of their characters with American mores. It is all done in good humor with no thought of offense in the mimicking.

An important influence in the dissemination of stories (and songs and ballads) from one part of Pennsylvania to another, and even beyond the borders of this state, were the wandering minstrels bred by the various basic industries. Though differing in occupations, they had a kinship with one another. They all had a certain amount of charm and shared human frailties, including a tendency to heavy drinking. Unfitted by temperament for the arduous or exacting labor of their respective crafts, they took to the road. Some of them led precarious lives subsisting on the free-will offerings of their audiences who adored them. Anthracite mining had its Con Carbon; steel labor its Philip Byerly; railroading its Harry Kirby McClintock, nicknamed "Haywire Mac," whose rambling experiences provided the material for his well-known song, "The Big Rock Candy Mountains"; and the oil industry its Gib Morgan.

Of the industrial folk minstrels, Gib Morgan, the gypsy driller, was the best known outside of Pennsylvania. His stories are repeated around the world wherever there is an oil derrick and the creak of a walking beam fills the air. Native son of Clarion County, brought up in Venango County, Gib Morgan was steeped in the folklore of western Pennsylvania, as indicated by some of his stories.

Harry Botsford, himself a native son of the Pennsylvania oil fields, had the good fortune of listening to Gib Morgan tell his stories. He has also heard others tell them, and recollects some of them in his chapter.

Similarly J. Herbert Walker, who writes of lumberjacks and raftsmen, grew up along the West Branch of the Susquehanna and knew many of the heroic men who had engaged in this thrilling but now vanished lumber industry.

I have tried to show how folklore has been in the making in Pennsylvania from one generation to another ever since colonial times. The oral process by which it was handed down might be likened to that of the Carboniferous age when successive growths of plants, flora, and fishes left their fossils and impressions in the rock strata of our coal mines. But it would be a mistake to view folklore as the fossilized remains of culture. This was the popular notion at one time, but folklore has outgrown its antiquarian phase. The modern concept stresses its living and dynamic aspects. The functional view of folklore, in which the "folk" receive equal attention with the "lore," is now generally accepted. "From the functional point of view," suggests B. A. Botkin, well-known scholar in the field, "folklore becomes germinal rather than vestigial, the 'germ plasm' rather than the 'fossils' of culture, and the study of folklore becomes a study in acculturation—the process by which the folk group adapts itself to its environment and to change, assimilating new experience and generating fresh forms."

The present volume was planned and carried through with the functional view of folklore uppermost in mind. My collaborators have understood from the outset that this was to be a work in which folk songs, folk tales, legends, and other oral popular traditions would be presented within the context of their environment. The relation between the folk and the lore they create is so intimate that the latter loses some of its significance and vitality apart from the former. So we give you a picture of the people who created and transmitted this folklore, and something, too, of the social, historical, and economic conditions out of which the material grew.

A very small portion of our material even reflects current problems, and this is not surprising inasmuch as folklore is a plastic medium that adjusts itself to changing times and new conditions. "For every form of folk fantasy," says Botkin, "a new one is being created, as culture in decay is balanced by folklore in the making." Every kind of social behavior and activity becomes of legitimate concern to the progressive folklore collector. Social groups in city neighborhoods and country districts alike—the educated and uneducated, every trade, every profession, every form of commercial life, every industry—are potential sources of folklore. This calls for a new interpretation of the term "folk," which no longer is restricted to those members of society who, because of geographical isolation, are cut off from change.

This volume marks the first attempt at publication of a comprehensive collection of folklore from the whole of Pennsylvania. It does not pretend to be encyclopedic, but offers a fair representation by charting the principal veins and types of Pennsylvania folk culture from colonial times to our own day.

We have tried to make a practical book, an authoritative book, an entertaining book. Read these stories and legends of Pennsylvania. We also invite you to sing these songs and ballads; they are presented in singable form; wherever necessary, they have been transposed to bring them within the average voice range.

Our primary appeal is to the reader who welcomes a chance to increase his knowledge of America's past to the end that he may form an intelligent understanding of our country's growth.

We wish to acknowledge our indebtedness to Ruth Crawford Seeger, our music consultant, for her valuable assistance which included the careful checking of the music proofs. Thanks are also due to Rae Korson, Reference Assistant in the Folklore Section of the Library of Congress, for her aid and counsel.

The British Folk Tradition

by SAMUEL PRESTON BAYARD

When the English-speaking settlers were colonizing what is now the Commonwealth of Pennsylvania, they came from different British regions and lands. Likewise, they entered Pennsylvania from various directions and at different times. But no matter who they were, or when or whence they came, the folk culture they brought with them was essentially the same heritage. There are some who still think that folk culture in any region must be independent and "homemade," and quite distinctive in all its features; but this is not the case with Pennsylvania or any other great region of America. What distinctive traits our oral tradition has are not due to its independence of Anglo-American folk culture elsewhere. The picture of Pennsylvania folk life and art on

17

which we are concentrating in this chapter is much more complex and fascinating than any purely local development could possibly be.

The folk culture of speakers of English is at the bottom the same, wherever encountered. Whenever or wherever the British colonists entered North America, they imported the identical elements of an old inheritance of customs, beliefs, story, song, and music.

This culture, strongly ingrained, survived the scattering of families, the mingling of peoples, and the readaptation to frontier conditions in a different climate. It throve in America, its growth encouraged by the fact that in the early agrarian days it was the only cultural resource of the folk. Cultivated for centuries in the old world, this lore was perhaps all the more intensely cherished in the new because it was something that no one could take away. It was the folk's one completely continuous link with its past. And, unlike the culture that is made with hands, this possession of the mind and heart could be carried wherever the people went.

The powerful hold that this strong, self-sufficient oral tradition had on the minds of our people is witnessed by the survival of folklore and art right up to the present. It has turned up plentifully and is still being recorded in surprising abundance. Even more surprising than their widespread survival is the evidence shown by recorded tales and songs of artistic handling by their preservers, of continual reinterpretation and revitalization.

Songs, tales, and tunes traveled over wide areas and were continually and selectively varied by countless folk artists. Tunes were shifted from song to song; stories relocalized and retold. The varied forms assumed by these traditions were handed down side by side and diffused in many different directions.

In these processes, shared by the entire country, in which the old tradition behaved like a living thing in the minds of its interpreters, the people of Pennsylvania were full participants. They undoubtedly gave and received in this complicated exchange of traditional goods. The aim of this chapter is to show something of the plenty of Pennsylvania's English folk inheritance, and its significance as an inseparable part of the whole immense national tradition.

In the eighteenth century, English and Scotch-Irish poured into the state from New Jersey, along with large numbers of German colonists; and they all penetrated westward, the Scotch especially making a marked impress on the western sections of Pennsylvania. While other English and Irish settlers entered Pennsylvania from Maryland and Virginia, more people of British descent, migrating from the northeast, moved across the northern areas of the state. Some of these settled permanently within its borders, establishing a New England culture in our northern counties.[1]

But in the eighteenth and early nineteenth centuries, Pennsylvania not only received settlers; she also sent them forth, being somewhat of a distributing center whence streams of migrants flowed into the South, into the Ohio Valley, and directly westward. Also, in modern times, a slow seepage of migration from the South into southwestern Pennsylvania has taken place, due to the industrial development of the commonwealth.[2]

In the mid-nineteenth century the great, famine-impelled Irish migration to this country began. Large numbers of Gaelic Irish settled in the northeastern counties of Pennsylvania and in the industrial regions of the Monongahela Valley, while throughout the century our state kept receiving new colonists from Scotland and England. Thus Pennsylvania has always been a crossing and meeting ground for the folk cultures of British peoples.

The notably musical Welsh likewise made extensive settlements within our borders; and while the British people were thus pouring in and mingling, the German colonists were diffusing themselves throughout the state, often becoming completely assimilated and adopting the British folk traditions in the process. Such cross-currents of population movement are the very things that transmit folklore in ways too complicated to trace.

But besides being the meeting ground for folk of different nationalities, Pennsylvania has also lain on the boundary of two great areas in which the original folk-song repertory of the English-speaking settlers has developed along noticeably different lines. In eastern North America there are two great regions of English folk-song cultivation: the Northeast (New England and the Canadian maritime provinces); and the South (extending from southern New Jersey southward, and indefinitely westward). Each region has developed in its own distinctive way a local form of the common English song. The two traditions of folk song show divergences from each other in repertory; in the relative popularity of certain types and versions both of songs and tunes; in the association of folk-song words with melodies; and in many small details of verbal and musical idiom that clearly identify versions of folk songs as northeastern or southern.

Pennsylvania is sandwiched in between these two important areas of folk-song cultivation in such a way that her oral song and music inheritance shares both traditions. Southern and southwestern Pennsylvania show a completely southern folk song similar to that known all over the region below the Mason and Dixon line. Northern Pennsylvania folk song, on the other hand, shows equally unmistakable affinities with that of New England and the whole Northeast. Let me cite a single example. Colonel Henry W. Shoemaker's collection from northern Pennsylvania indicates that many lumberjack songs characteristic of the Northeast have been popular also in our northern counties.[3] In the southwestern counties, however, we find no lumbering songs at all. To all appearances, they are simply unknown there, as is the case over the entire South.

We do not know what effects this entry of a double tradition into Pennsylvania has had on our folk-song development: our local traditions have been inadequately recovered. But from the lore that has been recorded to date, we can at least put together an intelligible (if imperfect) picture of the part played by nonmaterial culture in the lives of Pennsylvania settlers of British rearing. And the picture that emerges from the folklorist's inquiries seems to show that the preindustrial phase of our rural life has been a great deal more sociable, as well as more full and exciting, than many city dwellers today could imagine. What assures us of this is the stories told by the old folk, and the flood of tradition that inundates an inquirer when he encounters a person who retains a clear memory of country life in the last century. Let us allow the old-timers to speak for themselves by drawing on our records of their memories and lore.

In the first place, we know that aside from church gatherings—and I shall discuss our religious folk art presently—our rural forefathers had a somewhat greater variety of social get-togethers than many of their descendants have enjoyed, at least since the beginning of the present century. All the circumstances of early rural life impelled them to work and play together. Many important operations on the farms were done by coöperative community labor, and were often termed "frolics," presumably because of the sociability, music, dancing, singing, and general good cheer that were regular features wherever they were held. People held frolics for grubbing (clearing of land), house-raisings, manure-haulings, threshings, reapings, huskings, butcherings, and other such occasions. Women got together at quiltings and at times when a large amount of fruit and vegetables had to be put up. My grandmother has often told me how, in her girlhood days, she used to watch the reapers moving across a field in a slanting line, singing and joking and vying in skill with one another—while a jug of liquor stood at each end of the field to refresh their flagging spirits. All such affairs were part of neighborly life and were enjoyed accordingly.

The older folk can also draw out of their minds the recollections of numerous purely social and festive occasions: the "plays" in which dances were accompanied by song; the children's games; the big dances at weddings; the horse races along a straight track running the length of some "shelf" on a hillside; the turkey hunts, in which the birds were scared from hilltop to hilltop and shot at by those in wait there; the fox and coon hunts; the parades by bands of drums and fifes; the "literaries" and other reciting and singing contests; the house dances held so often; the music-making reunions of fiddlers and singers; the wintertime sleigh rides and overnight visits of family to family, characterized by profuse hospitality and all-night discourse and diversion; and other similar festivities that make the old people's accounts of rural life in the past century seem like narrations of events that occurred two or three centuries ago. Indeed, times are so altered that the world depicted in these reminiscences is far removed from the present scene. Yet, though the scene has vanished, the very oral traditions that informed and quickened its life are still lingering among us.

What did the people talk about at their gatherings, besides local events, theology, and current politics? Well, we know that because of their inherited folk beliefs their world was filled with mysterious action, and influenced by forces beyond those of the ordinary course of nature. The belief in magic and witchcraft is not yet dead. Every so often, in friendly conversation, one will be startled to hear the ancient, underlying superstitions force their way to the surface—either as articles of living faith or relics of a not-so-remote time when they were firmly believed in. Lately I have heard, from reliable informants, how only a half-dozen years ago a woman in Greensburg made a wax image, stuck it full of pins, and slowly melted it over a fire—thus bringing destruction on some enemy. Occasionally one encounters still more savage relics, as when I once heard an old woman mention that the way to get magic power was to tear the heart out of a living snake and eat it.

Ghosts and other spirits ("hants"or spooks) who walk and haunt certain places and appear at odd moments to various unfortunate mortals are still heard of frequently. Haunted houses may still be pointed out. A wealth of stories about appearances of strange animals on haunted roads or in mysterious hollows, about signs and omens of death or disaster, and about bewitched cattle and human beings can be gathered by anyone sufficiently interested in these old beliefs to listen to them with proper respect.

There is no doubt that until recently, if not up to this moment, there has been a lively belief in witches and their power among the Pennsylvania country people. In 1935 some real witch doctors (or, as they are oftener called, wizards or witch masters) were exercising their arts in Pittsburgh.[4] The often-heard stories of bewitched horses refusing to climb a hill, or of unfortunate sleepers roused in the dead of night and ridden with saddle and bridle by witches for incredible distances, may still be heard in the hills of Pennsylvania, as elsewhere in this country. Charms and recipes galore to induce love, dispel sickness, or learn the name of one's destined life partner can still be found by the earnest seeker after such lore. Whatever one may think of these beliefs, one must recognize in them some of the oldest and most enduring traits of folk culture everywhere. It cannot be denied that they quickened the imagination and heightened the emotional life of the unschooled rural folk in bygone days. Undoubtedly such things as these were often discussed about the stove or the open fireplace of a country home in the past—they still are, for that matter.

Whether or not the folk in Pennsylvania were given to telling the long and elaborate ancient folk tales that are among our most interesting relics of European peasant lore we cannot tell at present. But it is certain that numerous short stories, many of them humorous, some of them grim, were told and retold during long winter evenings in neighborhood or family gatherings. And most of them were old and widespread.

For instance, there was the familiar tale of the man who discovered, by cutting off the paw of an intrusive cat, that his wife was a witch; she was found suffering from an injury that proved to be a missing hand. One Pennsylvania version ends by narrating how the man choked the woman to death in some bedclothes after learning the truth about her. Another oft-relocalized story is the one in which a witch in the form of a cat or rabbit is pursued to her home. The house is burned over her, but she gets out, still in her changed form, and is shot with a bullet made of some silver object. There are still plenty of chances to hear changes rung upon the familiar anecdote of how a man shoots with a silver bullet the image of a witch he has drawn with charcoal upon a slab of bark or paper, and how, at the very moment of the shot, some crone in the vicinity falls over and inflicts upon herself a dreadful injury.

The humorous or grotesque little stories are varied, but seldom purely local. One of these is the old tale of how the man and wife argue over whether something was cut with scissors or a knife; the man insists on the knife, and the woman on the scissors. Finally, in exasperation, he drowns her, but she manages to have the last word; for in her final struggles, she puts a hand above water and makes the motions, with her fingers, of cutting something with a pair of shears. Another story concerns the great stone in the middle of the king's highway; it blocks traffic, but no one will exert himself to remove it. When one person finally does, he finds a store of gold beneath, the reward of his unselfish industry.

Another anecdote like the preceding one tells how a king sends out messengers all over the land to find a man who is truly boss in his own house. They always fail to find such an individual, for each time a man is interviewed on the subject and declares that he is master at home, his wife intervenes with "Oh, no, you ain't!" —and is never contested! Again, we hear of the sentimental girl who goes to the well to get her suitor a drink of water. She fails to return, and presently her mother goes to find out what is detaining her. The mother finds the girl in tears, and learns that her daughter has fallen into a reverie, in which she fancies that she has married the suitor, has had a child, and has seen the child fall down the well beside which she is sitting. The mother too bursts into tears at this point. When the father finally comes out to find the cause of their absence, he is drawn into their sorrow also; meanwhile the suitor leaves the house in a fit of pique.

Along with these, some short stories about exaggerated strength or size may naturally be found—like the one about the man who could toss a boulder the size of a cow over the barn roof and run around the building quickly enough to catch it as it fell; or about the aged blacksnakes that the first settlers found in the country: they had heads a foot broad, and dwelt by preference in berry briars thirty or forty feet tall. Merely to mention one of such miniature "tall tales" is sufficient to start a stream of them flowing, even in "these latter days."

At the frolics and dances there was plenty to eat and drink, and much singing and fiddling. Between dances the company might take turns at singing. Fiddlers who played for dances would often be plied with meat and drink in lieu of other payment. Often they played better, according to my informants, the more liquor they had in them; and they would never miss a beat or hit a false note, even when "they'd 'a' fell over if you'd 'a' throwed a rotten apple at them, you might say." Fiddlers held contests at which prizes might be anything from a jug of whisky to a good violin.

But there is also a darker side to the picture of the cultivation of folk arts. There was a great deal of fighting in the old days— at fairs and dances, when men got too much to drink, or when discussions of religion or politics got to a point beyond where the participants could master their feelings. People also fought for the mere fun of it, both in the country and the industrial towns. A newcomer to a community was likely to be matched with someone who seemed to be about his equal in weight and strength, and the crowd that egged the fighters on would enjoy the combat. Bullies were disliked, of course, but in general men were fond of fair play and a trial of strength and skill; matched tussles were frequent.

Dances and even camp meetings were sometimes spoiled by drunkenness and fighting. The individualistic back-country farmers and mountaineers got into frequent quarrels, and sometimes bloody fights, at their get-togethers. As time went on, fewer people cared to hold house dances that might end up in brawls and bloodshed; thus dancing and singing opportunities fell off perceptibly in some communities. But the old customs do not die easily, and they lived on right up to the present century in the rough yet stately hill country of Pennsylvania.

Such was the old agrarian life into which industrial development began to make inroads late in the last century. As we look back, trying to make out the course of events in the folk past, it seems as if the cultural effects of industrial civilization were so slight at first as to be imperceptible. We hear of Haas Wingrove of Fayette County, who sang continually and worked at quite a leisurely pace in the coal mines, but always got bigger pay than his fellows. The reason was that they were stopping so often to listen to his songs that they were losing many work hours. Agricultural workers simply transferred their labors to the mine or the mill, and their folk culture was undisturbed in the beginning. Indeed it was reinforced, for British mine bosses and millworkers who came over in the nineteenth century often brought along their share of traditional lore to add to what was already in full tide of cultivation here. Fifers, fiddlers, and singers from the old country found congenial surroundings in Pennsylvania. Fiddling for dances, indeed, has gone on continuously among mine and mill workers until today.

But little by little, as schooling and urban influence spread, and as conditions in industry changed, the old rural folk life began to decline. In a civilization increasingly dominated by special industrial problems and easily purveyed city amusements, the spontaneous, hitherto self-sufficient folk art of the countryside apparently could not hold its own. We see now that it was struck a series of blows from which it has never recovered, at least in Pennsylvania. The art of the folk singer was apparently the hardest hit. Sometime around the end of the last century or the beginning of the present, people simply ceased to pay attention to these old and vital songs—and the result has been that their singers have been steadily decreasing in number ever since.

Of course the physical changes that big industry brought into the districts where it developed were tremendous. The piece of verse that follows contains as vivid a picture of such alterations as I have ever read. This poem has a special interest because it is an absolutely genuine comment by a member of the old-time Pennsylvania folk on the industrial transformation of his native valley. Its composer, Eugene Gaines, who was eighty-six years old when he dictated this piece to me in August 1943, had lived all his life in the deep and steep-sided valley of Dunlap's Creek (a stream running into the Monongahela River at Brownsville) and had attended school only three months—during his seventeenth year. Those details of the changing scene that aroused his interest are illuminating to us in many ways. Gaines called his poem:

The Dunlap Creek*

A friend and I went walking
  Along the public way,
But things has changed so strangely
  From that of former days.
But the old Dunlap kept moving on
  And bubbling down the way.

Fish we used to have plenty,
  And turtles we had to spare—
But in the bowels of the old Dunlap,
  Not even a minnie there!

But the weeds have gethered on her banks,
  And the grass is bright and green;
But it seems so strange to relate the fact:
  Not a trace of a mushrat seen!

* All pieces marked with an asterisk are ones that I was enabled to collect through the generosity of the American Philosophical Society, which gave me grants in 1943 and 1946 for the collection of folk song and music in Pennsylvania.

We wandered to the old frog pond
   That is in our memory still,
But every stick and stone is gone
   Of that of Woods's Mill.

The little squirrels that used to play,
   The hawks and quails have fled,
But the old gray oak that sheltered us
   Was crumbled, dry, and dead.

They moved the mineral from beneath her boughs,
   And the earth throwed up in a freak,
And they pushed the old Dunlap aside
   In forms of little lakes.

The water came rushin' down the hill
   That filled 'em to the brim,
And the hearts of the children with rapture filled
   As they gathered there to swim.

A tunnel now goes through the hill,
   And a railroad on its side,
And a great train comes a-rushin' down
   That gives the valley pride.

A great train comes rushin' down
   To carry the mineral away,
And a dozen stacks and a thousand blazes
   On the spot we used to play!

A huge blacksnake lay quiet and still,
   That heightened all our fears—
That's the only thing that we could see
   Like that of seventy years!

Crude as this verse is, it still expresses eloquently the contrast between the interests of the old-time agrarian life and those of the oncoming age of technology and machines.

It is this clash of interests, I think, that mainly accounts for the decline of folk singing in rural Pennsylvania. The art of the folk fiddler kept its vitality renewed somewhat longer because the country violinists were in constant demand to perform at dances. Our folk song, on the other hand, seems to have been so indissolubly bound up with the old-fashioned pastoral and agricultural ways of living that it was unable to withstand the shocks caused by the intrusion of industrialized living patterns and the spread of general schooling. I have known men who had possessed a rich store of folk song acquired during their youth in farming communities, but forgot everything of this nature after a few years spent in the Pennsylvania oil fields. What they thus lost was not replaced by new song creations of the folk, but by popular pieces spread commercially from the large towns. In this way our ancient traditional song faded gradually away. Its remains are now found principally among the most conservative and economically depressed groups in the state.

Let me introduce a genuine old-time Pennsylvania folk singer, Mrs. Hannah Sayre, late of Washington County. Her father was a grubber, a fine singer, and a locally renowned witch master in Greene County. Consequently, she grew up surrounded by woods and fields, in a succession of log cabins and shacks back among the fastnesses of lonely hollows, and in an atmosphere filled with magic lore and old melody that she absorbed from both parents and from all her associates. She had scarcely any schooling and, for her way of life, needed none. Though she lived in the town of Washington for over forty years after her marriage, one might almost say that she was unaware of the twentieth century. Such things as electricity, factories, modern conveyances and conveniences, she practically ignored. Her memories—and, indeed, her whole mind and heart—were back in her half-wild girlhood. She thought and talked mostly of the shady streams with big, overhanging rocks where she had fished; of the woods where she had learned to eat various barks and berries; of the judgments she had seen visited upon sinners who had defied God; of the camp meetings, frolics, and dances she had attended; of the exploits of her father against the malice of witches; of the cures she herself had worked through her father's teachings. Her songs were especially valuable because of their uninhibited folk expression. In fact, people like her are altogether priceless to the seeker after the ways of the past, because, in a sense, they actually *are* a little bit of the past, preserved nearly intact.

The Cottage Door

(Sung by Mrs. Hannah Sayre in Washington County, 1943. Recorded by Samuel P. Bayard.) *

This song—the last one my old friend sang for me—is a characteristic old English love lyric, which she learned from her father.

1. As I walked out one May morn-ing For to
hear the lit-tle birds sing sweet, I set my-self down by a
lit-tle cot-tage door For to hear true lov-yers meet.

2. For to hear true lovyers meet, my dear,
   For to hear what they would say,
   That I might know some more off their minds
   Before I go away.

3. I never will believe what an old man says,
   For it's time they were gone;
   Nor a young man either, by the space of time,
   For they'll swear to a many off a one.

4. They'll swear to a many off a one, my dear,
   And a many a fine story they'll tell,
   But when their apron begins for to rise,
   It's my girl, fare you well!

5. There is a herb in father's garden,
   Some calls it maidens' rue:
   When figs they do fly like swallows in the sky,
   Then the young men they'll prove true.

6. I love to climb as high a tree,
   And rob as rich a nest,
   And 'turn down withal without ary fall
   And marry the girl I love best.

The Six Kings' Daughters

(Sung by Mrs. Hannah Sayre in Washington County, 1933. Recorded
by Samuel P. Bayard.)

This song of Mrs. Sayre's will be recognized by the ballad lover
as an old Scottish and English piece known over the entire country.
Her version is the form dominant in southern Pennsylvania and in
many parts of the South. She had no name for it; but Pennsylvania
knows it generally as "The Six Kings' Daughters," while to specialists in British folk song it is identified by the title of *Lady Isabel
and the Elf-Knight.*†

1. He fol-lered me up, he fol-lered me down, He
fol-lered wher-ev-er I lay; I
had no wings to fly— from him, Nor no tongue to tell him
nay, nay, nay, Nor no tongue to tell him nay.

2. Take some of your father's beaten gold
    Likewise of your mother's fee,
    And send two of the steeds out of your father's stable
    Where stands thirty and three, three, three,
    Where stands thirty and three.

3. She went and she took of her father's gold,
    And some of her mother's fee,
    And two steeds out of her father's stable
    Where there stands thirty and three.

† Henceforth, I shall give the scholars' "identification title" for a ballad in italics,
when such a title exists. Singers' own local titles are the ones that appear at the
heads of their versions.

4. She mounted onto the bony, bony black,
   And him on the di-pole gray,
   And they rode along through the merry green woods
   Till they come to the banks of the sea.

5. Light down, light down, my pretty *Polin,*
   I've something to say to thee:
   Six daughters of the king I've drownded here,
   And the seventh you shall be.

6. Take off, take off, that fine silk gown,
   And hang it on the tree,
   For it is too fine and too costly too
   To rot in the salt water sea.

7. And turn yourself three times around,
   And gaze at the leaves on the tree,
   For God never made sich a rascal as you
   A naked woman to see.

8. He turned hisself three times around,
   To gaze at the leaves on the tree;
   She picked him up so manfully-like,
   And plunged him into the sea.

9. Lie there, lie there, you false-hearted knight,
   Lie there in the stead of me—
   You've promised to take me to old Scotland,
   And there you would marry of me.

10. She jumped onto the bony, bony black,
    And led the di-pole gray,
    And she rode till she come to her father's own house,
    Three long hours before it was day.

11. Up bespoke the little parrot,
    Where in his cage it lay,
    Saying, Where are you going, my pretty *Polin?*
    You're traveling so long before day.

12. Hold your tongue, my pretty parrot,
    Tell none of your tales [lies] on me;
    Your cage shall be made of the yellow, beaten gold,
    And hung on the green willow tree.

13. Up bespoke the old man
    Where in his room he lay,
    Saying, What's the matter, my pretty parrot?
    You're pratteling so long before day.

14. The old cat come to my cage door,
    And swore she would worry of me,
    And I had to call on my pretty *Polin*
    To drive the bold pussy cat away, -way, -way,
    To drive the bold pussy cat away!

Lord Darnell

(Sung by Amos Riggle near Claysville, Washington County, 1943.
Recorded by Samuel P. Bayard.) *

Probably no English ballad remaining alive in this country can
excel the drama of *Little Musgrave and Lady Barnard*. The version
that I give here represents the way in which this stirring old song
was known in Greene County over sixty years ago.

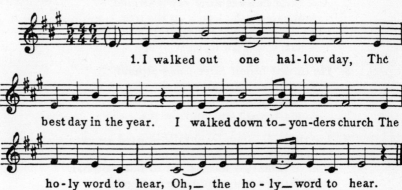

1. I walked out one hal-low day, The
best day in the year. I walked down to— yon-ders church The
ho-ly word to hear, Oh,— the ho-ly— word to hear.

2. Some come from the broad waterside,
   And some come from the hall;
   In len'th in came Lord Darnell's wife,
   The fairest of them all,
   Oh, the fairest of them all.

3. She lookéd high and she lookéd low,
   She lookéd high and low;
   In len'th she spied little Mathy Grove,
   And on him she fixed her eye, etc.

4. You must go home with me this night,
   You must go with me, she says,
   For of all the men that is living be,
   You are my heart's delight.

5. I cannot go nor I will not go,
   No, not for my sweet life,
   For by the ring that is on your hand
   You are Lord Darnell's wife.

6. Well, if Lord Darnell's wife I am,
   Lord Darnell's wife I be;
   Lord Darnell himself to the castle is gone
   King Henry for to see.

7. The little foot-page a-hearing this,
   He clapt to his heels and he run;
   He run till he come to the broad waterside;
   There he bowed his breast and he swum.

8. He swum till he come to the other side,
   Where there Lord Darnell he sees:
   Bad news, bad news, I bring to thee,
   Bad news I bring to thee!
   Little Mathy Grove is at thy house,
   In bed with the gay ladie.

9. If this be the truth that you do tell,
   Rewarded you shall be,
   But if it be a lie that you tell to me,
   You shall hang on the gallows tree.

10. He took his men at his command,
    He placed them in a row;
    He bid them not a word to speak,
    Nor not a horn to blow.

11. There was one amongst the rest
    Who thought well of little Mathy Grove;
    He placed his horn up to his mouth
    And he blew both loud and shrill.

12. I must git up, said little Mathy Grove,
    And in haste, and I must go,
    For if Lord Darnell living be,
    I heard his horn to blow.

13. Oh, no, my dear, lie still, she says,
    And keep me free from cold:
    For it's nothing but my father's shepherd boy,
    He's driving the sheep to fold.

14. So still they lie in sport and play
    Till they both fell asleep.
    Who was so ready to wake them up?
    —Was Lord Darnell, at their feet!

15. How do you like my bed, he says,
    Or how do you like my sheets?
    Or how do you like my gay ladie
    That lies in your arms asleep?

16. It's well I like your bed, he says,
    And better I like your sheets,
    But woe be to your gay ladie
    That lies in my arms asleep!

17. You must get up, says Lord Darnell,
    And put your clothing on,
    For it never shall be said when I am dead
    That I slew a naked man.

18. Must I get up, says little Mathy Grove,
    And fight for my sweet life,
    While you have got your two good swords,
    And I have nary knife?

19. Well, if I have got two good swords,
    They cost me deep in purse;
    I'll give to you the best of them,
    And I will take the worst.

20. And you may strike the first good blow,
    And I will strike the other;
    I could not do no more for you
    If you was my own brother.

21. Little Mathy struck the first good blow—
    He wound' Lord Darnell sore;
    Lord Darnell struck the next good blow—
    Poor Mathy could do no more.

22. He took his lady on his knee,
    He gave her kisses three,
    Saying, Which do you like the best,
    Little Mathy Grove or me?

23. It's well I like your cheeks, she says,
    And better I like your chin,
    But I would not give little Mathy Grove
    For you and all your kin!

24. He took his lady by the hand,
    He led her o'er the plains;
    He did not speak but a word or two
    Till he split her head in twain.

25. It's sweet-lye sings the nightingale,
    And sweet-lye sings the sparrow;
    Lord Darnell killed his wife today,
    And he'll be hung tomorrow.

A Gentle Young Lady

(Sung by Albert E. Richter at South Connellsville, 1946. Recorded by
Samuel P. Bayard.) *

Needless to say, the older ballads favored by Pennsylvania folk
singers were not all concerned with bloodshed and tragedy. From
Fayette County comes this version of a facetious old riddle ballad
known to scholars as *Captain Wedderburn's Courtship*. The
"preece and swarm" of stanza 10 is a corruption of "priest unborn."

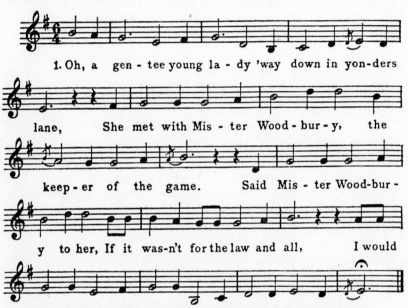

1. Oh, a gen-tee young la-dy 'way down in yon-ders
lane, She met with Mis-ter Wood-bur-y, the
keep-er of the game. Said Mis-ter Wood-bur-
y to her, If it was-n't for the law and all, I would
take this fair maid in my arms and roll her from the wall.

2. Oh, go away, you foolish man, and don't you bother me;
   Before you and I in one bed lie, you cook me dishes three.
   Three dishes you will cook for me, and I will eat them all,
   Before you and I in one bed lie, and I lie next the wall.

3. For my breakfast you cook for me a cherry without a stone,
   For my dinner you will cook for me a bird that has no bone;
   For my supper you will fry for me a bird that has no gall,
   Before you and I in one bed lie, and I lie next to the wall.

4. Oh, a cherry when in its blossom, it hasn't any stone;
   A chicken when in a egg, I know it has no bone.
   The dove she is a gentle bird, she flies without a gall—
   So jump into my arms, my love, and I roll you from the wall!

5. Oh, go away, you foolish man, before you me perplex;
    Before you and I in one bed lie, you answer questions six.
    Six questions you will give to me, and I will name them all,
    Before you and I in one bed lie, and I'll lie next to the wall.

6. What rounder is than my gold ring, what's deeper than the sea,
    What is worse than a woman's tongue, what's higher than the tree?
    What bird sings first, and which one best, and where does the
        dew first fall?
    Before you and I in one bed lie, and I lie next the wall.

7. Oh, this globe is rounder than your gold ring, hell's deeper than
        the sea,
    The devil is worse than a woman's tongue, heaven's higher than
        the tree;
    The lark sings first to which one best, and on the treetops dew
        first falls,
    So jump into my arms, my love, and I roll you from the wall!

8. Oh, go away, you foolish man, and don't you bother me;
    Before you and I in one bed lie, you get me articles three.
    Three articles you will get for me, and I will use them all,
    Before you and I in one bed lie, and I'll lie next to the wall.

9. First I want some farren fruit that in Car'lina grew;
    Next I want a silk dallman that never a warm male threw;
    Next I want a sparrow's horn, it will do us one and all,
    Before you and I in one bed lie, and I'll lie next the wall.

10. Oh, my father has some farren fruit that in Car'lina grew;
    My mother has a silk dallman that never a warm male threw;
    The sparrow's horns are easy found, there's one for every call
        [claw];
    Saint Patrick is the preece and swarm—so I'll roll you from the
        wall.

11. Oh, it's now to finish and conclude all these funny things,
    This couple now is married, and happy as can be.
    She's not so very handsome, nor not so very tall.
    But still he takes her in his arms and rolls her from the wall.

Fair Scotland

(Sung by Perry Gump in Greene County, 1929. Recorded by Samuel
P. Bayard.)

The very old tale of *Sir Hugh, or the Jew's Daughter* has always
been exceedingly popular in Pennsylvania. Though this piece is
a relic of false and atrocious medieval legends concerning alleged

Jewish sacrifice of children, I have never been able to perceive that present-day Pennsylvania folk singers associate this song with the Jewish people at all, or regard it as anything more than the sad story of a little boy's death at the hands of a cruel lady. Indeed, some singers say that the murderess was the "king's daughter." Popular as the story was in the Middle Ages, it survives today only on the lips of a few ballad singers in remote country places. The version I give here goes to a melody quite different from that to which it is usually sung in America. The first stanza is sung to the second half of the air.

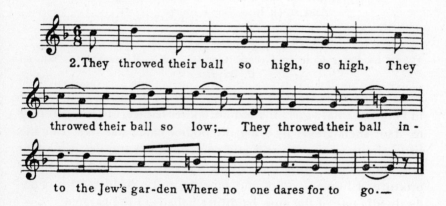

2. They throwed their ball so high, so high, They throwed their ball so low;— They throwed their ball in-to the Jew's gar-den Where no one dares for to go.—

1. There was some children in fair Scotland
   A-playing at school ball.

3. One of the Jew's daughters came out,
   Her doddle [sic] all dressed in green:
   Come in, come in, you little Sir Hugh,
   And get your ball again.

4. I will not do it, I shall not do it,
   Without my schoolmates all,
   For if I would, my mammy would whip
   Till the red blood down would fall.

5. She showed him an apple so round, so round,
   She showed him a cherry so red;
   And then she showed him a gay gold ring
   Which enticed this poor boy in.

6. She tuck him by his little hand
   And led him through the room,
   And then she led him in the kitchen,
   And there he saw his own dear nurse*
   A-cooking of a chicken.

7. And then she says, I'll do more for you
   Than any of your kin:
   I'll scour this basin of the bright silver
   To ketch your heart's blood in.

8. She laid him on her lap, her lap,
   And fed him sugar sweet,
   And then she laid him on her dressing board,
   And stuck him like a sheep.

There Was a Lady Lived in York

(Sung by Peter Cole in Greene County, 1929. Recorded by Samuel
P. Bayard.)

In *The Cruel Mother,* an ancient ballad formerly well known
in Pennsylvania, a girl kills and buries her babies, first endeavoring
to "lay" their ghosts by tying the bodies hand and foot. But the
little ghosts return to earth and confront their mother, who does
not know them until they speak up and denounce her. In its
mixture of human pathos and supernatural weirdness, this is undoubtedly one of the most haunting ballads in the language.

The singer of this version was one of the old-fashioned, un-
licensed farriers of the countryside, many of whom used music in
their treatments as well as knowledge and horse sense. To this tune
the ballad was most often sung in southwestern Pennsylvania.

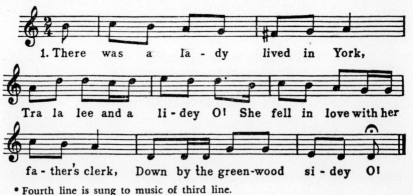

1. There was a la - dy lived in York,

Tra la lee and a li - dey O! She fell in love with her

fa - ther's clerk, Down by the green-wood si - dey O!

* Fourth line is sung to music of third line.

2. She leant herself against an oak,
   Tra la lee and a lidey O!
   And first it bent, and then it broke,
   Down by the greenwood sidey O!

3. She leant herself against a tree,
   And there she had her misery.

4. She leant herself against a thorn,
   And there's where these two babes were born.

5. She pulled out her little penknife;
   She pierced them through their tender hearts.

6. She pulled out her white handkerchief;
   She bound them up both head and foot.

7. She buried them under a marble stone,
   And then returned to her merry maid's home.

8. As she sat in her father's hall,
   She saw these two babes playing ball.

9. Says she, Pretty babes, if you were mine,
   I'd dress you in the silk so fine.

10. Say, dear mother, when we were thine,
    You neither dressed us coarse nor fine.

11. But you pulled out your little penknife;
    You pierced it through our tender hearts.

12. Then you pulled out your white handkerchief;
    You bound us up both head and foot.

13. You buried us under a marble stone,
    And then returned to your merry maid's home.

14. Seven years to wash and wring,
    Seven more to card and spin.

15. Seven more to ring them bells,
    · Tra la lee and a lidey O!
    Seven more to serve in hell,
    Down by the greenwood sidey O!

Old Jokey Song

(Sung by F. P. Provance at Point Marion, Fayette County, 1943.
Recorded by Samuel P. Bayard.) *

Of the widely known old humorous ballads in this country, the
one that students call *The Farmer's Curst Wife* seems to be by far

the most popular in Pennsylvania. The theme of the redoubtable wife who can worst the devil himself appears to be common in folk humor and is of incalculable age. The Fayette County version given here is set to the regular tune for the ballad in southwestern Pennsylvania.

1. It's off an old man, and he liv-ed poor, He
lived in a house that had but one door.

Chorus

Sing whack fa-loor-a, loor-a lay, Sing whack fa-loor-a, lad-die!

2. This old man he went out to foller the plow;
   'Long comes the old devil, saying, I'll have you now!

   CHORUS
   Sing whack faloora, loora lay,
   Sing whack faloora, laddie!

3. You shan't have me nor my oldest son,
   But my old scolding wife, take her and wel*come!*

4. He hobbust her up all onto his back,
   Like a pedlar packin' his pack.

5. He packed her along till he come to hell's gates;
   He hit her a kick, saying, Go in, you old jade!

6. And he packed her along till he come to hell's door;
   And he hit her a kick, saying, Go in, you old whore!

7. Now one little devil come and sit down by 'er:
   She up with her foot and she kicked him in the fire.

8. Oh, two little devils with rattlesome chains,
   She up with the poker, she knocked out their brains.

9. Then two little devils were lying in bed:
   She up with the poker, she killed 'em both dead.

10. Then one little devil run up the wall,
    Crying, Pap, take 'er out o' hell, or she'll kill us all!

11. Then he hobbust her up all onto his back,
    And like a danged fool he went packin' her back.

12. Then he packed 'er along till he come to hell's door;
    He hit her a kick, saying, Gwout [go out], you old whore!

13. Then he packed her along till he come to hell's gates;
    And he hit her a kick, saying, Gwout, you old jade!

14. He says, Now here's your old woman both sound and well—
    If I'd kep' her much longer, she'd lathered all hell!

15. She was seven years going and seven coming back,
    And she called for the mush that she left in the pot.

The Wee Cooper o' Fife

(Sung by J. D. Gordon and Mrs. Jennie Craven in Fayette County, 1943. Recorded by Samuel P. Bayard.) *

This humorous ballad, known to specialists as *The Wife Wrapt in Wether's Skin,* is of comparatively recent importation, having been brought to this country in the latter nineteenth century by a Scottish coal miner. This Scottish version differs greatly from the long-acclimated and widely known English form that Pennsylvania folk singers also remember.

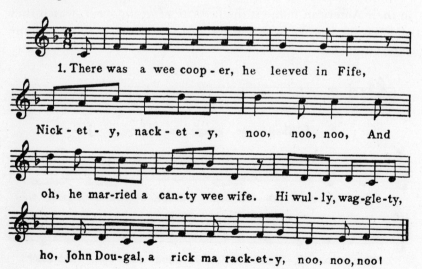

1. There was a wee coop-er, he leeved in Fife,

Nick-et-y, nack-et-y, noo, noo, noo, And

oh, he mar-ried a can-ty wee wife. Hi wul-ly, wag-gle-ty,

ho, John Dou-gal, a rick ma rack-et-y, noo, noo, noo!

2. She naither could bake and she naither could brew,
   Nickety, nackety, noo, noo, noo,
   For gaun aboot wi' her gentil crew.
   Hi wully wagglety, ho, John Dougal,
   A rick ma rackety, noo, noo, noo!

3. She naither could wash and she naither could spin,
   For gaun aboot wi' her gentil kin.

4. I'll awa' hame to my own sheepspark;
   I'll fetch hame a sheepskin, and I'll tie't on her back.

5. I leathered her but and I leathered her ben—
   Can I no' leather my ain sheepskin?

6. Noo she can bake and noo she can brew;
   She disne fash wi' her gentil crew.

7. Noo she can wash and noo she can spin,
   And she disne fash wi' her gentil kin.

8. Come a' ye young men that's got a bad wife,
   Noo just ye try the cooper o' Fife!

When Ye Gang Awa', Jamie

(Sung by J. D. Gordon and Mrs. Jennie Craven in Fayette County,
1943. Recorded by Samuel P. Bayard.) *

Another old Scots song that these same singers have preserved
in their American home is the favorite *Huntingtower,* which they
said was often sung by a boy and girl as a dialogue song at home
entertainments.

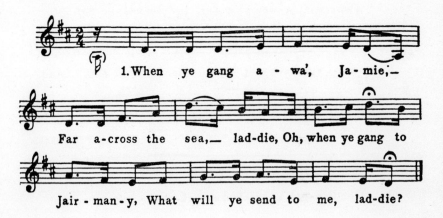

1. When ye gang a-wa', Ja-mie,— Far a-cross the sea,— lad-die, Oh, when ye gang to Jair-man-y, What will ye send to me, lad-die?

2. I'll send ye a braw new goon, Jeanie,
   I'll send you a braw new goon, lassie,
   And it shall be a sulken goon,
   Wi' flunces staunnin' roon', lassie.

3. That's nae gift ava, Jamie,
   That's nae gift ava, laddie;
   There's ne'er a goon in a' the toon
   I'll weer when ye're awa', laddie.

4. When I come back again, Jeanie,
   When I come back again, lassie,
   I'll bring to thee a gallan' ghie
   Ye're ain guidman to be, lassie.

5. Be my ain guidman yersel', Jamie,
   Be my ain guidman yersel', laddie;
   An' tak' me ower to Jairmany,
   An' dwell at hame wi' me, laddie!

6. I dinna ken hoo that would be, Jeanie,
   I dinna ken hoo that would be, lassie,
   For I hae wife an' bairnies three,
   And I'm no' share hoo ye'd 'gree, lassie.

7. Ye should 'a' tell'd me that in time, Jamie,
   Ye should 'a' tell'd me that in time, laddie,
   For if I had knew your falsie hairt,
   Ye'd never gotten mine, laddie!

8. Dry that tearfu' ee, Jeanie,
   My story's a' a lee, lassie:
   I have naither wife nor bairnies three,
   I'd wed nane but thee, lassie!

9 Think weel afore ye rue, Jamie,
   Think weel afore ye rue, laddie,
   For I hae naither gowd nor gear
   To be a match for you, laddie.

10. Little Drumkells are mine, Jeanie,
    And Huntingtowers are mine, lassie;
    Huntingtowers and hawthorn bovers
    And a' that's mine are thine, lassie!

The High Blanter Explosion

(Sung by Mrs. Jennie Craven in Westmoreland County, 1943. Recorded by Samuel P. Bayard.)*

Also imported recently, this song about a mine disaster is strongly characteristic of Anglo-Irish folk song in its continual references to a calamity that is never related in detail.

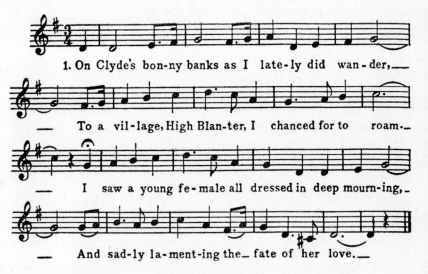

1. On Clyde's bon-ny banks as I late-ly did wan-der,—

— To a vil-lage, High Blan-ter, I chanced for to roam.—

— I saw a young fe-male all dressed in deep mourn-ing,—

— And sad-ly la-ment-ing the— fate of her love.—

2. I stepped up unto her, and said, My young woman,
   Pray tell me the cause of your sorrow and woe.
   I heard you lamenting the fate of some young man:
   His name and what happened I'd like for to know.

3. While sobbing and sighing, at length she made answer:
   John Murphy, kind sir, was my truelover's name;
   Twenty-one years of age, and of mild, good behavior,
   To work in the mines of High Blanter he came.

4. On the twenty-second day of October
   In health and in strength to his labor did go.
   On that fatal morning, without one moment's warning,
   Two hundred and ten in their deaths did lie low.

5. No more shall I walk with my lover
   With hand locked in hand on the banks of the Clyde,
   Where we told the long love tales and pulled the wild daisies;
   It was there I consented to be his bride.

6. But spring will return, and the flowers in blossom.
   On my truelover's grave I will transplant them there.
   With my tears I will water the wild little daisies—
   On my truelover's grave I will transplant them there.

Erin's Green Shore

(Sung by Mrs. Ethel M. Fox in Greene County, in the 1930's. Recorded by Samuel P. Bayard.)

Well-known over the entire country though relatively modern, "Erin's Green Shore" is cast in an old Irish form known as *aisling* (vision). Its tune is the usual one for the piece in Pennsylvania and the South.

1. One eve-ning so— late as I ram-bled On the banks of a clear, purl-ing stream, I sit down on a— bed of prim-ros-es And so gent-ly did fall in a dream.'Twas there I es-pied a fair fe-male, And her e-quals I'd ne'er seen be-fore, As she sighed for the wrongs done her coun-try, As she strolled a-long Er-in's green shore.

2. Her eyes were like two sparkling diamonds,
   Or stars on a clear, frosty night;
   Her cheeks were like two blooming red roses,
   And her teeth as the ivory were white.

She resembled the goddess of freedom,
    And of liberty the mantle she wore,
Bound round by the rocks and primroses,
    As she strolled along Erin's green shore.

3. Then I addressed this fair female:
    My jewel, come tell me your name,
For I know you're in a land of all strangers,
    Or I would not have asked you the same.
I'm a daughter of Daniel O'Connell,
    From England I've lately sailed o'er.
I've come here to awaken my brethren
    Who slumber on Erin's green shore.

4. In prospects of joy I awakened,
    And found I had been in a dream:
This beautiful damsel had fled me,
    And I long for to slumber again.
May the heavens above be her guardian,
    For I know I shall see her no more.
May the sunbeams of joy fall around her
    As she strolls along Erin's green shore!

Molly Banding

(Sung by Albert E. Richter at South Connellsville, 1946. Recorded by
Samuel P. Bayard.) *

"Molly Banding" is probably Anglo-Irish in origin, but has
long been known over the whole area of English folk song. From
northern Fayette County, it goes to a much-altered version of one
of its regular Irish airs.

1. As I was a-walk-ing, a-walk-ing a-long, As
I__ was a-walk-ing, a-hunt-ing for swan.

2. Molly Banding she was walking, she was walking along,
    Molly Banding she was walking when a shower it came on.

3. She stepped into some willows for the shower to shun;
    With her apron twine around her, I took her for a swan.

4. Oh, me being mistaking, and shooting through the dark,
   I swore by a lassie I would never miss my mark.

5. I then ran up to her and saw she was dead—
   A fountain of tears on her bosom I shed.

6. I ran to my father with the gun in my hand,
   Crying, Father, dear Father, I've murdered Molly Band!

7. It was not my meaning to render her sweet life;
   I intended for to marry her and keep her as my wife.

8. The old man to the window, his hair being grey,
   Crying, Jimmy, dear Jimmy, Oh, do not run away!

9. Stay in your old country your trial to stand,
   For I will not have it said that you murdered Molly Band.

10. Molly Banding next morning to her uncle did appear,
    Crying, Uncle, dear uncle, James Ransome you clear!

11. It was not his meaning to render my sweet life;
    He intended for to marry me and make me his wife.

12. All the girls in the city was placed in a row,
    Molly Banding in the middle like the mountains of snow.

13. All the girls in the city they seemed to be glad
    When they heard that Molly Banding this tiding were dead.

14. Come all you true lovers, take warning by me,
    Leave off your late walking and shun the willow tree.

15. Come all you late hunters who carries a gun,
    And watch where you're shooting between sun and sun!

The Battle of the Boyne Water

(Sung by F. P. Provance in Fayette County, 1943. Recorded by
Samuel P. Bayard.) *

In former times, one of the surest ways to make the Irish fighting
mad was to refer in their hearing to the defeat of James II at the
Battle of the Boyne in 1690. One had only to sing a certain
burlesqued and garbled fragment of the stirring Anglo-Irish piece
"The Boyne Water" to bring on a small riot if any Irishmen were
within earshot. But the popularity of the beautiful "Boyne Water"
air has not suffered from these unhappy associations, for many
favorite folk songs (including *Barbara Allen*) are set to versions of
the air in Pennsylvania and elsewhere.

They fought with clubs and they fought with stones, King
Wil - liam on his char - ger, He— says, Now, boys, don't
be dis-mayed At los - ing a com - mand - er.
Fierce and long the bat - tle raged, Till, crushed
by the fear-ful slaugh - ter, Ten thous-and micks got
killed with picks At the bat-tle of the Boy-en— Wa - ters.

I Wish in Vain

(Sung by F. P. Provance in Fayette County, 1943. Recorded by
Samuel P. Bayard.) *

F. P. Provance, like Mrs. Sayre, learned ballads from parents
and associates alike. His love lament is representative of what is
most genuine in our local English song tradition.

1. I wish, I wish, I wish in vain, I wish't I
was a maid - en a - gain! A maid I ain't, nor I
nev - er will be Through all this world and e - ter - ni - ty.

2. There is a tav'ren in yon town;
   He rides up and he sits himself down.
   He takes the strange girl on his knee—
   Oh, don't you think it's a grief to me?

3. A grief, a grief! I'll tell you why:
   Because she has more gold than I.
   But gold may sink, and silver may fly,
   But constant love will never die.

4. I would to God my babe was born,
   Sat smiling in his papa's arms,
   And I was dead and in my grave,
   And green grass growing over me!

5. Through the meadow this fair maid ran,
   Gathering flowers as they sprang.
   She plucked and pulled of every kind
   Until she got her apron full.

6. Then these green flowers was her bed,
   The heavens was her coverlid;
   And there she lies no more to say,
   Till wakened at the Judgment Day.

The Nightingale

(Sung by F. P. Provance in Fayette County, 1943. Recorded by
Samuel P. Bayard.) *

One marked characteristic that southern Pennsylvania folk
song shares with that of the whole South is a scarcity of songs
directly concerning marine life. We have many allusions to sailors
home from the sea or "plowing the raging main," but almost no
details in our songs about actual seafaring. Such a piece, then, as
"The Nightingale" is a decided rarity in inland Pennsylvania.

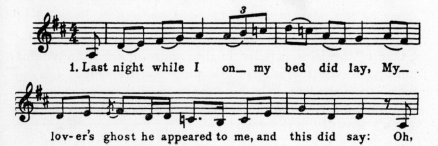

1. Last night while I on my bed did lay, My lov-er's ghost he appeared to me, and this did say: Oh,

weep, yes, oh, weep, but— you weep all a-vail, For your

true— lov-er's lost in the *Night - in - gale!* 2. On the

six-teenth day— of De - cem - ber— last, The—

wind did— blow a most hor - rid blast; Our

cap - tain says, My dear boys, look— brave, For

you— must ex - pect a— wat' - ry grave.

3. The wind did blow, and the sea did roll,
   And we prayed to the Lord for to save our soul;
   Our deck stove in and our timber did fail,
   And down to the bottom went the *Nightingale!*

Oh, No, No, Sir, No

(Sung by Mrs. Mary Brown in Greene County, 1929. Recorded by
Samuel P. Bayard.)

One of the most popular English songs in the Pennsylvania
countryside was the jaunty little piece usually called "Oh No
John," from the local title of a favorite version collected in England toward the end of the last century. This version is the first
which I recorded in the state.

1. Yon-der sits a love-lye crea-ture, Who she is I do not know;

I'll step up and court her fa-vor, Let her an-swer yes or no!

Chorus

Oh, no,— no, sir, no! Al-ways to an-swer the young men no.

2. Madam, I have come a-courting,
   And if your favor I can gain,
   And if you'll highly entertain me,
   Then perhaps I'll come again.

   CHORUS
   Oh, no, no, sir, no!
   Always to answer the young men no.

3. Madam, I have gold and silver,
   Madam, I have house and land;
   Madam, I have this world's pleasures,
   And all shall be at your command.

4. What care I for gold and silver,
   What care I for house and land?
   What care I for this world's pleasures?
   All I want is a handsome man.

5. My father was a Spanish merchant,
   Where he is I do not know;
   Before he left me, he made me promise
   To always answer the young men *no*.

6. Madam, if you were to live single,
   Say, perhaps, one year or two,
   Madam, would you be offended
   If I should offer my hand to you?

   CHORUS
   (emphatically)

7. As we sit together talking,
   The north wind began to blow;
   I saw the rising sun approaching,
   And I said, Dear madam, I must go.

   CHORUS
   (with fervor)

Harrison Brady

(Sung by Lily Bell Dietrick at Morgantown, W. Va., 1944. Recorded by Samuel P. Bayard.) *

Occasionally an American folk bard adapts some old British piece, with as little change as possible, to contemporary circumstances. The basis of this reckless ditty is plainly the old-world ballad of *The Gypsy Laddie,* once well-known in Pennsylvania but now exceedingly hard to find.

1. Go har-ness up my milk-white steed, My bon-ny brown is not so speed-y; I'll ride all night and I'll ride all day Till I o-ver-take my la - dy.

2. He rode as far as Pittsburgh, O,
   And there he spied his lady;
   With one arm around her baby, O,
   And the other around her Brady.

3. Oh, why did you leave your husband dear,
   Oh, why did you leave your baby,
   Oh, why did you leave your pretty little home
   To roam with Harrison Brady?

4. I never loved you in my life,
   I never loved your baby;
   I married you against my will,
   And I'll roam with Harrison Brady.

5. Last night I slept in my downy bed,
   And in my arms my baby;
   Tonight I'll sleep in the Pittsburgh jail
   In the arms of Harrison Brady!

Jackie Frazier

(Sung by Peter Cole in Greene County, 1930. Recorded by Samuel P. Bayard.)

This Pennsylvania version of an ever-popular song on the old theme of the girl who dresses as a man to follow her lover goes to a tune that I have not identified elsewhere.

1. There was a weal - thy mer - chant, in Lon - don he did dwell; He had a daugh - ter Pol - ly, and the truth to you I'll tell.

Chorus

And sing too - rul lun di ee doo, And sing too - rul lun di O!

2. She had both lords and squires, and courted day and night,
   But on none but Jack her sailor boy she placed her heart's delight.

CHORUS

And sing toorul lun di ee doo,
And sing toorul lun di O!

3. Her father being in a passion, and onto her did say,
   Good morning, Madam Frazier, since that's your truelove's name!

4. Father, here is my body, and it you may confine,
   But none but Jack the sailor boy can ever suit my mind.

5. Polly being at liberty, and money at command,
   She took a sudden notion to see some foreign land.

6. She went into a tailor's shop and dressed in men's array,
   And bargained with her sailor boy to carry her away.

7. It's now you are on shipboard, your name I wish to know,
   She, smiling in her countenance: They call me Jack Monroe.

8. It's now they have anchored and sailed far away;
   They landed at French Landing on a clear and pleasant day.

9. Your waist it is too slender, your hands they are too small,
   Your cheeks they are too rosy red to face the cannon ball.

10. I know my waist is slender, my hands they are but small;
    But my cheeks are *not* too rosy red to face the cannon ball!

11. So the drums did beat and rattle, and the fife did sweetly plav:
    She marched up to the enemy and bravely fought away.

12. The drums did beat and rattle, and the cannon balls did fly,
    When a ball from the enemy caused her darling down to lie.

13. She picked him up in her own arms, and carried him to the town,
    And left him with a surgeon to heal his bleeding wounds.

14. So now the war is over, and they'll sail back again;
    They landed at her father's house on a clear and pleasant morn.

15. Her mother being near them, and in some secret place,
    Says she, This young man's features resemble Polly's face!

16. I am your daughter Polly, from you I run away;
    I follered Jack my sailor boy to the wars of Germany.

17. I follered him over land, and I follered him over sea;
    I married him in the army, and I have him here with me.

18. So come all ye tender parents, and never part true love,
    For you're bound to see in some degree the ruin it will prove.

19. So now they are both married and living at their ease;
    So, parents, let your children get married as they please.
    And sing toorul lun di ee doo,
    And sing toorul lun di O!

The Sea Captain

(Sung by Thomas W. Gatts at Washington, Pa., in the 1930's. Recorded by Samuel P. Bayard.)

This old song, also about a clever girl who outwits a schemer, is known almost everywhere to forms of just one tune. The singer of this version was over eighty, musically gifted, and unlettered.

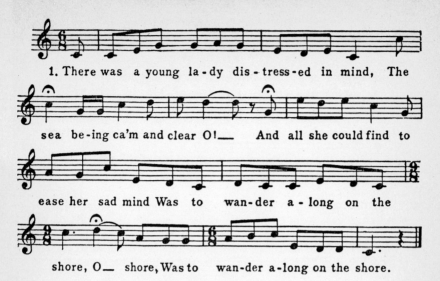

1. There was a young la-dy dis-tress-ed in mind, The
sea be-ing ca'm and clear O!— And all she could find to
ease her sad mind Was to wan-der a-long on the
shore, O— shore, Was to wan-der a-long on the shore.

2. There was a sea captain that plowed the main,
The sea being ca'm and clear O!
I shall die, I shall die, the sea captain cried,
If I don't get that young lady fair, O fair,
If I don't get that young lady fair!

3. Oh, what will you take, my jolly bold sea,
To bring her aboard to me O?
Some projict of love runs strong in her mind
For to wander along on the shore, O shore,
For to wander along on the shore.

4. After long persuading, on board she went,
The sea being ca'm and clear O!
The captain invited her down in the cabin,
Saying, Fare you well sorrow and keer, O keer,
Saying, Fare you well sorrow and keer!

5. I'll sing you a song if you think it is best—
The captain he set her a cheer O!
She sung so sweet, so neat and complete,
She sung captain and sailors to sleep, O sleep,
She sung captain and sailors to sleep.

6. She robbed them of jewels, she robbed them of gold,
She robbed them of costly-a ware O!
The captain's broadsword she used for an oar,
And she paddled her boat to the shore, O shore,
And she paddled her boat to the shore.

Dumb, Dumb, Dumb

(Sung by Peter Cole in Greene County, 1929. Recorded by Samuel P. Bayard.)

This song tells a story known also to Rabelais. As an English song this piece dates from the seventeenth century. Exceedingly popular in the eighteenth century, it has now all but died out.

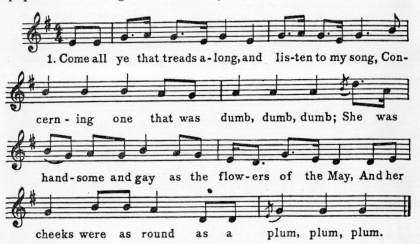

1. Come all ye that treads a-long, and lis-ten to my song, Concern-ing one that was dumb, dumb, dumb; She was hand-some and gay as the flow-ers of the May, And her cheeks were as round as a plum, plum, plum.

2. There was a country jake, and he courted this fair maid,
   Although she was young, young, young,
   And he loved her as his life, and he made her his wife,
   And he soon conducted her home, home, home.

3. To the doctor he did go, with his heart full of woe,
   Saying, Doctor, I am undone, -done, -done;
   Can you tell me of the part that is nearest to my heart:
   Can you cure anyone that is dumb, dumb, dumb?

4. So the doctor he did go, and he cured her, I know,
   For her tongue it began for to run, run, run,
   And next morning when she rose, she filled the room with noise,
   And it rattled through his head like a drum, drum, drum.

5. To the doctor he did go, with his heart full of woe,
   Saying, Doctor, I am undone, -done, -done:
   I am tired of her life, for she's proved a scolding wife,
   And I wish to my God she was dumb, dumb, dumb!

6. Go ye into the woods, and hunt the willow green;
   Be sure and pick for the young, young, young,
   And baste her body round till she fills the room with sound—
   That will make a scolding wife hold her tongue, tongue, tongue!

King William

(Sung by Lily Bell Dietrick at Morgantown, W. Va., 1944. Recorded by Samuel P. Bayard.) *

Pennsylvania game or play-party songs have served more than one purpose to our singers. They have been used in children's games and as lullabies and dance airs—both by those who had scruples about the righteousness of fiddling, and by those who simply couldn't find a fiddler when they wanted to dance. Professor Dietrick learned this old game song in her Butler County home.

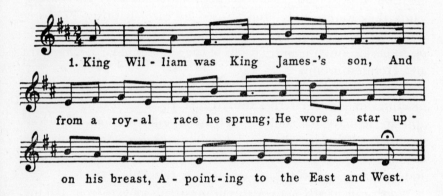

1. King Wil-liam was King James-'s son, And from a roy-al race he sprung; He wore a star up-on his breast, A-point-ing to the East and West.

2. Go choose your east, go choose your west,
   Go choose the one that you love best.
   If she's not here to take your part,
   Go choose another with all your heart.

3. Down on this carpet you must kneel,
   As sure as grass grows in the field;
   Salute your bride and kiss her sweet,
   And now you may rise upon your feet.

The series of religious revivals that swept over this country in the early nineteenth century did not pass Pennsylvania by. Here too there were camp meetings ("big meetings" or "bush meetings") in which a protracted effort would be made to redeem sinners amid scenes of the utmost fervor. People who recall these revivals consider that the true spirit of religion is now departed from the land. But although the big revivals are gone, they are not yet entirely forgotten; mingled with the memories are the remains of that abundant and moving religious folk song which was created in the back-country meetings and inseparable from them.

The Pennsylvania folk had a traditional religious song that was practically identical with that prevalent all over the South in the last century. It is still very much alive in some southern regions, but not so in Pennsylvania. Here, these "white spirituals" are now so far under the surface, and so different in quality from modern sacred song, that they stand little chance of being heard again in our country churches or rural valleys. Wherever the songs arose, or whichever sect was mainly responsible for their creation (they spread far and wide over the country), in Pennsylvania they were simply "folk": used by early Baptists, Presbyterians, and Methodists, and, when dropped by these sects, lingering on in back-country congregations of the Church of God, Christian, and Holiness groups.[5]

Despite the fact that Negroes used to hold great open-air camp meetings in southwestern Pennsylvania, the Negro religious song appears to have had only the slightest influence on our white spirituals. The latter are independently British-American, and used the old English-tradition folk music (with many modifications and rearrangements) to sing to the new religious texts.

Words can hardly convey the impression one gets from talking with the older folk about these ecstatic meetings and "sings"— with their inevitable shouting, jumping, falling on the ground, and all the other features that differ so strongly from staid services of today. Here, too, one feels oneself in contact with a whole cultural world that is a thing of the past. The singing of the folk hymns and spirituals certainly stimulated these actions; and the actions themselves were taken as infallible signs of possession by the divine spirit. Many people felt that the words of these songs were equal in authority and power to verses of Scripture. Many had special favorites among the spirituals, pieces that would never fail to move them strongly.

We cannot possibly compress in a few samples all the variety of this religious folk song. There were spirituals for all sorts of occasions and on numerous favorite religious themes, such as the dangers of sin and the pains of damnation; the joys of the righteous in the other world; the sweet prospect of seeing loved ones again "on the other shore," in "bright kingdoms" to come; and the question of whether one were fit to die and be translated to judgment.

I Want More Religion

(Sung by Hiram H. White in Greene County, 1930. Recorded by Samuel P. Bayard.)

Hiram H. White, who sang this characteristic spiritual to me, was the first traditional Pennsylvania singer I encountered, and one of the best.

I— want more re - li - gion, Lord, I want more re - li - gion, Lord, I want more re - li - gion to help me un - to God! Re - li - gion makes me hap - py,— and then I want to go To leave this world of sor - row and trou-ble here be - low.

How Will You Stand in That Day?

(Sung by Mrs. Mary Ann Rogers in Greene County, in the 1930's. Recorded by Samuel P. Bayard.)

This song is on a theme that was something of a favorite with old country singers: what will be our situation on the Day of Judgment?

1. For the sky it will be dark-ened, And the—
thun - der will be roll - ing,— And the—
light - ning will be flash-ing— In that day!—
Chorus
O fa - thers, And it's how will you
stand, And it's how will you stand— in that day?

2. For the earth she will be shaken,
   For the earth she will be shaken,
   And the rocks will be a-melting
      In that day!

   CHORUS
   O fathers, and it's how will you stand,
   And it's how will you stand in that day?

3. For the stars they will be falling,
   For the stars they will be falling,
   And the moon will be a-bleeding
      In that day!

(To continue, substitute "mothers," "brothers," and other words for "fathers" in chorus.)

Keep the Ark A-Moving

(Sung by Mrs. Hannah Sayre in Washington County, and Mrs. Mary Ann Rogers in Greene County, in the 1930's. Recorded by Samuel P. Bayard.)

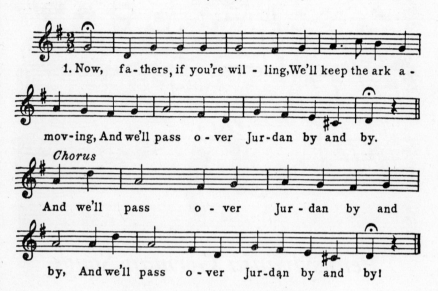

1. Now, fa-thers, if you're wil - ling, We'll keep the ark a-mov-ing, And we'll pass o-ver Jur-dan by and by.

Chorus

And we'll pass o - ver Jur - dan by and by, And we'll pass o - ver Jur-dạn by and by!

2. Where the streets is lined with gold,
   And the gates is set with pearl,
   And we'll pass over Jurdan by and by.
      CHORUS
   And we'll pass over Jurdan by and by,
   And we'll pass over Jurdan by and by!

(To continue, substitute "mothers," etc. for "fathers.")

---

1 See Wayland F. Dunaway, *A History of Pennsylvania* (New York: Prentice-Hall, Inc., 1935), pp. 74-80.

2 See Dunaway, "Pennsylvania as an Early Distributing Center of Population," *Pennsylvania Magazine of History and Biography*, LV, 134-69.

3 See any edition of H. W. Shoemaker, *North Pennsylvania Minstrelsy*. I have used the second edition (Altoona: Times Tribune Co., 1923).

4 See the *Pittsburgh Post-Gazette*, April 1, 1935, p. 5, col. 5; April 3, p. 15, cols. 6, 7; April 4, p. 1, cols. 1, 2.

5 The best over-all treatment of these religious revivals and the folk hymns and spirituals to which they gave rise is George Pullen Jackson, *White and Negro Spirituals: Their Life Span and Kinship* (New York: J. J. Augustin, 1943).

Pennsylvania German Songs

by THOMAS R. BRENDLE AND WILLIAM S. TROXELL

The Pennsylvania Germans, or Pennsylvania Dutch as they are popularly called, are descendants of German-speaking immigrants who settled in Pennsylvania in the eighteenth century. From southwestern Germany (the Palatinate, Baden, Alsace, Württemberg, and Hesse), Saxony, Silesia, and Switzerland, they came in such large numbers that in time they occupied one-third of the land area of Pennsylvania.

The early immigrants established German schools and printing presses, held their religious services in German, and read German devotional books or translations of English devotional literature. In doing so they were not motivated by a desire to isolate themselves in the new country or to preserve the integrity of the German language. It was simply that it was the only language they knew. From the very beginning they felt themselves an integral part of their new country. They and their descendants fought for America's liberties and contributed substantially to the country's economic, physical, and cultural development.

While the early immigrants used High German in their churches, schools, and newspapers, their spoken language was a Germanic dialect. Originally the prevailing dialect had come from the Palatinate except for a Swiss dialect used in Lancaster and York counties. The constant intermingling of the descendants of all the German immigrants resulted in the development of the homogeneous dialect known as "Pennsylvania Dutch" which is spoken today.

During the nineteenth century, English steadily displaced High German as the dominant cultural language in the Pennsylvania German counties. Today there are comparatively few Pennsylvania Germans conversant with High German, but the Pennsylvania Dutch dialect is still commonly spoken. Its persistence may be attributed to the fact that through the years it has been molded into a medium for expressing shades of thought and feeling for which English seems inadequate to the Pennsylvania Germans.

Pennsylvania Dutch customs and other phases of folklore are cradled in the dialect. For example, the month of December is called *Grischdmunet* (Christ Month), and Christmas Day is *Grischdåg* (Christ Day). A Christmas present is a *Grischkindel* (Christ Child), and the unseen bringer of the Christmas morning gift is *es Grischkindel* (the Christ Child). The Pennsylvania Dutch believe that on Christmas Eve, at the stroke of twelve, bees speak in their hives and cattle in their stalls; the Christmas flower rises up out of the ground in full bloom and disappears; a star brighter than any other appears in the heavens; and the dew which falls upon hay placed outside the barn that night will bring health to a farmer's cattle.

This lore has gathered around *Grischkindel,* and where Santa Claus has been substituted for *Grischkindel* the lore is in danger of being forgotten.

A revival of popular interest in Pennsylvania German folklore, and particularly in our folk songs, resulted from the meetings of the Pennsylvania Folk Festival at Allentown in 1935 and at Bucknell University in 1936 and 1937 under the direction of George Korson, and those of the Pennsylvania German Folk Festival at Allentown, 1936-1941, under the direction of William S. Troxell.

Up to that time it had been commonly believed that Pennsylvania German folklore, though rich in proverbs, quaint sayings, riddles, beliefs, and superstitions, was singularly lacking in folk songs.

However, snatches of songs heard here and there had given hope that traditional folk songs might still be recovered. This hope was strengthened by elderly persons in their accounts of singing at party games, corn-husking bees, quilting parties, and other social events of a bygone day. Then, too, it was reasonable to suppose that traditional songs would form part of the folklore of a music-loving people such as ours.

So for several summers we carried on an intensive field research. From time to time we were assisted by Paul Wieand of Allentown. Our first task was to find the persons who remembered traditional folk songs. When we located them it took much persuasion to overcome their natural reluctance to sing for strangers, and through the microphone of our recording machine. If the singer's home had electricity, we recorded there. Otherwise we drove the singer to a near-by garage or store where the recordings were made, sometimes in the presence of curious bystanders. Our best informants were elderly men and women who in their youth had sung in village choirs.

Our search was highly successful. We recorded more than two hundred songs, nearly all of which were unknown to students of Pennsylvania German folklore. We believe our collection would have been even larger if we had been able to continue our field researches during the war.

In our collection, the songs fall into four groups: first, those brought over from Germany and Switzerland and sung by generations of Pennsylvania Germans; second, those improvised within the state and sung to popular melodies—a small group of indigenous material; third, translations of English and American songs, the number of which is large; and fourth, variants of English and American folk songs and ballads found elsewhere in the state.

Just as the Pennsylvania Germans became integrated in the American population, so their folklore, originally from the Rhine Valley and Switzerland, has joined the stream of American folklore. Until now studies of every phase of Pennsylvania German folklore except folk songs have been made and published.

We feel that in this volume we can make no more valuable contribution toward a better understanding of our people than to present this selection of the most representative Pennsylvania German folk songs from our collection of field recordings.

The melodies were transcribed by Edwin B. Spaulding and his wife, Mary G., nee Brendle, of Parlin, New Jersey.

For the non-Pennsylvania German reader we provide translations of the song texts. These are line-by-line paraphrases designed to make intelligible the meaning of each stanza and thus enable the reader to grasp the central idea or story of each song.

In our spelling we have followed Lambert's *Pennsylvania German Dictionary*, the most authoritative work on the dialect. In the dialect, *b* takes the place of German *p* (*Babier* for *Papier*), and sometimes of German *pf* (*Blaschder* for *Pflaster*). Usually *p* takes the place of *pf* (*Pund* for *Pfund*, *gloppe* for *klopfen*, and *Dropp* for *Tropf*).

The German *t* has become *d* (*Dochder* for *Tochter*, *drinke* for *trinken*). In place of initial *k* in German *kl*, *kn*, and *kr*, we have *g* (*Gling* for *Klinge*, *Gnarre* for *Knorren*, and *Grach* for *Krach*).

Our *w* is not like the German *w*. "It is made with the lips in the position in which they are at the beginning of making English *w*, but the lips are not rounded as in making English *w*" (Lambert). It takes the place of medial German *b* (*Hawwer* for *Haber*, *dowe* for *toben*).

The long German *a* is rarely heard in the dialect, its place being taken by *a* as in English "ball," a sound not heard in High German. This sound is indicated by a circumflex.

Our *oi* takes the place of the German *ei*, *eu*, and *ai* (*Woi* for *Weihe*, *Hoi* for *Heu*, and *Moi* for *Mai*); *ei* of German *äu* (*Meis* for *Mäuse*), and *ie* for *ü* (*Hiet* for *Hüte*). In the ending *en* the *n* is dropped.

The diminutives are *li* and *che*, the former being heard mostly in Lancaster and York counties.

There are other differences, but enough have been noted to enable the reader with a knowledge of German to understand the dialect of these songs.

Wir reisen noch Amerikâ

(We Journey to America)

(Sung by Mrs. Jane Masonheimer at Egypt, Lehigh County, 1936. Recorded by Thomas R. Brendle and William S. Troxell.)

The wide currency in the Pennsylvania Dutch region of this "beloved song of the emigrants" is indicated by the different variants we heard in Lehigh, Northampton, Berks, and Northumberland counties. The song must have reached Pennsylvania soon after publication in Samuel Friedrich Sautter's *Collected Poems of a Poor Schoolmaster* (Karlsruhe, Germany: 1845).

In an article of the Reformed Church monthly publication, *The Guardian,* May 1888, describing a voyage from Philadelphia to Boston, W. M. Reily quotes the following stanza "from the familiar German song known as the *Bremer Auswanderers Lied*":

> *Und wenn das Schiff am Wasser schwimmt*
> *Un unsere Lichter an gezuendt*
> *Da fuerchten wir ken Wasserfall*
> *Denn Gott regieret ueberall.*

Compare with stanzas 4 and 5 of our recorded song, and note the dialect variations from the High German.

1. Jetzt is di Zeit un Schtun-de dâ, Wir reis-en noch A-mer-i - kâ; D'r Wâj-je schteht schun fa d'r Dier, Mit Weib un Kin - ner— zie-jen wir.

2. *Di Ferde sin schun eingeschpannt*
   Un alle die mit mir verwandt;
   Di Ferde sin schun eingeschpannt,
   Reich mir zum letschtenmâl di Hand.

3. *Ach Freinde, weinet nicht so sehr*
   Wir sehen einander jetzt nimmermehr,
   Ach Freinde, weinet nicht so sehr
   Wir sehen einander nimmermehr.

4. *Un wenn das Schiff aus dem Hâfen schwimmt*
   Do warren Lieder angeschtimmt,
   Un wenn das Schiff aus dem Hâfen schwimmt
   Do warren Lieder angeschtimmt.

5. *Wir firchten keinen Wasserfall*
   Un dencken Gott ist iwwerall,
   Wir firchten keinen Wasserfall
   Un dencken Gott is iwwerall.

6. *Un kommen wir noch Baldimor*
   Do schtrecken wir di Hende vor,
   Un rufen aus, "Victoriâ,
   Jetzt sin wir in Amerikâ."

1. The day and hour are here
   When we journey to America.
   The wagon stands ready at the door;
   We go with wife and children.

2. The horses are already hitched to the wagon,
   Now, kindred and friends—
   The horses are already hitched to the wagon—
   Clasp our hands in a last farewell.

3. Ah, friends, restrain your tears,
   Though we shall never see each other again;
   Ah, friends, restrain your tears,
   Though we shall never see each other again.

4. As the ship moves out of the harbor,
   Voices are raised in song;
   As the ship moves out of the harbor,
   Voices are raised in song.

5. We fear no disaster at sea,
   For God is everywhere;
   We fear no disaster at sea,
   For God is everywhere.

6. And when we get to Baltimore
   We'll stretch out our hands,
   And cry, "Victory,
   Now we are in America!"

Wann ich vun dem Land rei kumm

(When I Came to This Country)

(Sung by Marvin Wetzel at Crackersport, Lehigh County, 1939. Recorded by Thomas R. Brendle and William S. Troxell.)

This cumulative ballad was probably brought into Pennsylvania
by the early immigrants. We heard different versions in Lehigh,
Berks, Snyder, and Northumberland counties. A common varia-
tion is in the opening line, which gives the ballad its title. Two
of these are: *Wann ich in des Land bin kumme* and *Wann ich
noch dem Land bin kumme,* both meaning literally, "When I
came to this country."

1. *Wann ich vun dem Land rei kumm, No war ich en ârm-er*

Mann; No kâf ich mir en Hinck-el Un fang des Haus-en â.

Wann di Leid mich fro-je dee-de Wie mei Hinck-el heest,

Gick-er-i-gie heest mei   glein-es Hinck-e - lie.

2. *No kâf ich mir en End ___ Un fang des Haus-en â,*

Wann di Leid mich *fro-je dee-de* Wie mei End-li heest,

End - li Bend-li   Gick - er - i - gie   heest mei
heest mei End-li,

glein-es Hinck - e - lie.   - lie.

3. No kâf ich mir en Kuh
   Un fang des Hausen â.
   Wann di Leid mich froje deede
   Wie mei Kuh heest,
   Uff un Zu heest mei Kuh,
   Endli Bendli heest mei Endli,
   Gickerigie heest mei gleines Hinckelie.

4. No kâf ich mir en Genzel
   . . . .
   Schtumm Schwenzel heest mei Genzel,
   Uff un Zu heest mei Kuh, etc.

5. No kâf ich mir en Gaul
   . . . .
   Hawwer Maul heest mei Gaul,
   Schtumm Schwenzel heest mei Genzel, etc.

6. No kâf ich mir en Hund
   . . . .
   Immer Gsund heest mei Hund,
   Hawwer Maul heest mei Gaul, etc.

7. No kâf ich mir en Haus
   . . . .
   Rei un Naus heest mei Haus,
   Immer Gsund heest mei Hund, etc.

8. No grie ich mir en Frâ
   Un fang des Hausen â.
   Wann di Leid mich froje deede
   Wie mei Weiwel heest,
   Hell Deiwel heest mei Weiwel,

Rei un Naus heest mei Haus,
Immer Gsund heest mei Hund,
Hawwer Maul heest mei Gaul,
Schtumm Schwenzel heest mei Genzel,
Uff un Zu heest mei kuh,
Endli Bendli heest mei Endli,
Gickerigie heest mei gleines Hinckelie.

1. When I came to this country
   I was a poor man;
   Then I bought a chicken
   And began housekeeping.
   Should the people ask
   The name of my chicken,
   Gickerigie is the name of my little chicken.

2. Then I bought a duck
   And began housekeeping.
   Should the people ask
   The name of my little duck,
   End-of-the-String is the name of my little duck,
   Gickerigie is the name of my little chicken.

3. Then I bought a cow
   . . . .
   Open-and-Shut is the name of my cow.
   End-of-the-String is the name of my little duck, etc.

4. Then I bought a little goose
   . . . .
   Bobtail is the name of my little goose,
   Open-and-Shut is the name of my cow, etc.

5. Then I bought a horse
   . . . .
   Oats-Mouth is the name of my horse.
   Bobtail is the name of my little goose, etc.

6. Then I bought a dog
   . . . .
   Always-Well is the name of my dog.
   Oats-Mouth is the name of my horse, etc.

7. Then I bought a house
   . . . .
   In-and-Out is the name of my house,
   Always-Well is the name of my dog, etc.

8. Then I got a wife
   And began housekeeping.
   Should the people ask
   The name of my little wife,
   Hell-Devil is the name of my wife,
   In-and-Out is the name of my house,
   Always-Well is the name of my dog,
   Oats-Mouth is the name of my horse,
   Bobtail is the name of my little goose,
   Open-and-Shut is the name of my cow,
   End-of-the-String is the name of my little duck,
   Gickerigie is the name of my little chicken.

Was drâgt di Gans uff ihrem Schnawwel?

(What Does the Goose Carry on Her Bill?)

(Sung by Mrs. Emma Diehl at Freiburg, Snyder County, 1938. Recorded by Thomas R. Brendle and William S. Troxell.)

This is a Pennsylvania Dutch variant of a song found in several German collections. It was brought to Pennsylvania by German immigrants in the eighteenth century.

2. *Was drâgt di Gans uff ihrem Kobbfe?*
   En Schissel mit di Subbfe.

   CHORUS
   Un em Jaejer wâr di Gans,
   Un em Jaejer wâr di Gans.

3. *Was drâgt di Gans uff ihrem Halsee?*
   En Deller mit em Schmalzee.

4. *Was drâgt di Gans uff ihrem Bruschtee?*
   Brod mit em Gruschde.

5. *Was drâgt di Gans uff ihrem Flijjel?*
   En kind mit d'r Wiejjel.

6. *Was drâgt di Gans uff ihrem Bauchee?*
   En Schissel mit Sauergrâdee.

7. *Was drâgt di Gans uff ihrem Beh?*
   Wei Rewwerschtee.

8. *Was drâgt di Gans uff ihrem Schwenzlee?*
   En Deppich mit en Krenzlee.

1. What does the goose carry on her bill?
   A knife and fork.

   CHORUS
   And the goose belonged to the hunter,
   And the goose belonged to the hunter.

2. What does the goose carry on her head?
   A bowl of soup.

3. What does the goose carry on her neck?
   A plate of lard.

4. What does the goose carry on her breast?
   A crust of bread.

5. What does the goose carry on her wings?
   A child in a cradle.

6. What does the goose carry on her belly?
   A bowl of sauerkraut.

7. What does the goose carry on her legs?
   White river-stones.

8. What does the goose carry on her tail?
   A coverlet with a fringe.

Was wachst uff diesem Bâm?

(What Grows on This Tree?)

(Sung by Mrs. Jane Reitz at Himmel's Church, Northumberland
County, 1938. Recorded by Thomas R. Brendle and
William S. Troxell.)

1. *Schtamm-bâm in de Heeh, Hoch zwisch-en dem grien-en Wal-dee.*

Spoken: *Was is dann an dem Bâm?*
En wunderscheener Nascht.

Nascht âm— Bâm, Schtamm-bâm in de
(Repeat accumulated phrases
each time)

Heeh, Hoch zwisch-en dem grien- en Wal - dee.

2. *Schtammbâm in de Heeh,*
   Hoch zwischen dem grienen Waldee.
   Was is dann an dem Nascht?
   En wunderscheenes Blâd.
   Blâd am Nascht, Nascht am Bâm,
   Schtammbâm in de Heeh,
   Hoch zwischen dem grienen Waldee.

3. *Was is dann auf dem Blâd?*
   En wunderscheenes Nescht.
   Nescht uff em Blâd, Blâd am Nascht, etc.

4. *Was is dann in dem Nescht?*
   En wunderscheenes Oi.
   Oi im Nescht, Nescht uff em Blâd, etc.

5. *Was is dann in dem Oi?*
   En wunderscheener Vojjel.
   Vojjel im Oi, Oi im Nescht, etc.

6. *Was is dann an dem Vojjel?*
   En wunderscheenes Fedder.
   Fedder am Vojjel, Vojjel im Oi, etc.

7. *Was is dann an dem Fedder?*
   En wunderscheener Schpiggel.
   Schpiggel am Fedder, Fedder am Vojjel,
   Vojjel im Oi, Oi im Nescht,

Nescht uff em Blåd, Blåd am Nascht,
Nascht am Bâm,
Schtammbâm in de Heeh,
Hoch zwischen dem grienen Waldee.

1. Great lofty tree
   High in the green forest.
   What is there on the tree?
   A very pretty branch.
   Branch on the tree,
   Great lofty tree
   High in the green forest.

2. Great lofty tree
   High in the green forest.
   What is there on the branch?
   A very pretty leaf.
   Leaf on the branch, branch on the tree,
   Great lofty tree
   High in the green forest.

3. What is there on the leaf?
   A very pretty nest.
   Nest on the leaf, leaf on the branch, etc.

4. What is there in the nest?
   A very pretty egg.
   Egg in the nest, nest on the leaf, etc.

5. What is there in the egg?
   A very pretty bird.
   Bird in the egg, egg in the nest, etc.

6. What is there on the bird?
   A very pretty feather.
   Feather on the bird, bird in the egg, etc.

7. What is there at the feather?
   A very pretty mirror.
   Mirror at the feather, feather on the bird,
   Bird in the egg, egg in the nest,
   Nest on the leaf, leaf on the branch,
   Branch on the tree,
   Great lofty tree
   High in the green forest.

Was wachst in diesem Wald?
(What Grows in This Forest?)

(Sung by Mrs. Emma Diehl at Freiburg, Snyder County, 1938. Recorded
by Thomas R. Brendle and William S. Troxell.)

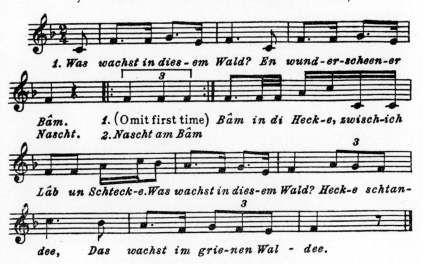

1. Was wachst in dies - em Wald? En wund-er-scheen-er
Bâm.   1. (Omit first time) Bâm in di Heck-e, zwisch-ich
Nascht. 2. Nascht am Bâm
Lâb un Schteck-e. Was wachst in dies-em Wald? Heck-e schtan-
dee,   Das wachst im grie-nen Wal - dee.

2. Was wachst an diesem Bâm?
   En wunderscheener Nascht.
   Nascht am Bâm, Bâm in di Hecke,
   Zwischich Lâb un Schtecke.
   Was wachst in diesem Wald?
   Hecke schtandee,
   Das wachst im grienen Waldee.

3. Was wachst an diesem Nascht?
   En wunderscheenes Heck.
   Hecke am Nascht, Nascht am Bâm, etc.

4. Was wachst an diesem Heck?
   En wunderscheenes Lâb.
   Lâb am Hecke, Hecke am Nascht, etc.

5. Was is in diesem Lâb?
   En wunderscheenes Nescht.
   Nescht im Lâb, Lâb am Hecke, etc.

6. Was is in diesem Nescht?
   En wunderscheenes Oi.
   Oi im Nescht, Nescht im Lâb, etc.

7. *Was is in diesem Oi?*
   En wunderscheener Vojjel.
   Vojjel im Oi, Oi im Nescht, etc.

8. *Was is an diesem Vojjel?*
   En wunderscheenes Fedder.
   Fedder am Vojjel, Vojjel im Oi, etc.

9. *Was is in diesem Fedder?*
   En wunderscheenes Bett.
   Bett im Fedder, Fedder im Oi, etc.

10. *Was wachst in diesem Bett?*
    En wunderscheenes Dâm.
    Dâm im Bett, Bett im Fedder, etc.

11. *Was wachst in diesem Dâm?*
    En wunderscheener Schatz.
    Schatz im Dâm, Dâm im Bett,
    Bett im Fedder, Fedder am Vojjel,
    Vojjel im Oi, Oi im Nescht,
    Nescht im Lâb, Lâb am Hecke,
    Hecke am Nascht, Nascht am Bâm,
    Bâm in di Hecke, zwischich Lâb un Schtecke.
    Was wachst in diesem Wald?
    Hecke schtandee,
    Das wachst im grienen Waldee.

1. What grows in this forest?
   A very pretty tree.
   Tree in the bushes,
   Among leaves and stems.
   What grows in this forest?
   Thicket of bushes,
   That grows in the green forest.

2. What grows on this tree?
   A very pretty branch.
   Branch on the tree, tree in the bushes,
   Among leaves and stems.
   What grows in this forest?
   Thicket of bushes,
   That grows in the green forest.

3. What grows on this branch?
   A very pretty twig.
   Twig on the branch, branch on the tree, etc.

4. What grows on this twig?
Very pretty leaves.
Leaves on the twig, twig on the branch, etc.

5. What is in these leaves?
A very pretty nest.
Nest in the leaves, leaves on the twig, etc.

6. What is in this nest?
A very pretty egg.
Egg in the nest, nest in the leaves, etc.

7. What is in this egg?
A very pretty bird.
Bird in the egg, egg in the nest, etc.

8. What is on this bird?
A very pretty feather.
Feather on the bird, bird in the egg, etc.

9. What is in this feather?
A very pretty bed.
Bed in the feather, feather on the bird, etc.

10. What lies in this bed?
A very pretty woman.
Woman in the bed, bed in the feather, etc.

11. Who lies with this woman?
A very handsome lover.
Lover with the woman, woman in the bed,
Bed in the feather, feather on the bird,
Bird in the egg, egg in the nest,
Nest in the leaves, leaves on the twig,
Twig on the branch, branch on the tree,
Tree in the bushes, among leaves and stems.
What grows in this forest?
Thicket of bushes,
That grows in the green forest.

D'r zwitzerich Danzer

(The Flashy Dancer)

(Sung by Marvin Wetzel at Crackersport, Lehigh County, 1939. Recorded by Thomas R. Brendle and William S. Troxell.)

This cumulative ballad about a young man proudly showing off his new clothes was probably brought over in the eighteenth century. German collectors have traced it to the seventeenth century. A number of variants circulated among Pennsylvania Germans. As he sings, the ballad singer points to the different articles of clothing he happens to be wearing at the time. The song has been adapted to modern dress, which accounts for the singer's using English terms to describe some of his wearables.

2. *Ei was hawwich so scheene Schtrimlicher â*
   Mit so scheene Schtreeflicher drâ
   Schtreefelle, Schtrimpelle,
   Bendelle, Schickelle, Schuh.
   Ei was bin ich so luschdicher Buh,
   Ei was kann ich so zwitzerich danze.

3. *Ei was hawwich so scheene Hesslicher â*
   Mit so scheene Gnebblicher drâ.
   Gnebbelle, Hesselle, Schtreefelle, etc.

4. *Ei was hawwich so scheenes Beltelle â*
   Mit so scheenes Schnallelle drâ.
   Schnallelle, Beltelle, Gnebbelle, etc.

5. *Ei was hawwich so scheenes Hemelle â*
   Mit so scheenes Breiselle drâ.
   Breiselle, Hemelle, Schnallelle, etc.

6. *Ei was hawwich so scheenes Jacketle â*
   Mit so scheenes Greewelle drâ.
   Greewelle, Jacketle, Breiselle, etc.

7. *Ei was hawwich so scheenes Reckelle â*
   Mit so scheenes Fliggelle drâ.
   Fliggelle, Reckelle, Greewelle, etc.

8. *Ei was hawwich so scheenes Hietelle â*
   Mit so scheenes Taselle drâ.
   Taselle, Hietelle,
   Fliggelle, Reckelle,
   Greewelle, Jacketle,
   Breiselle, Hemelle,
   Schnallelle, Beltelle,
   Gnebblicher, Hesslicher,
   Schtreeflicher, Schtrimlicher,
   Bendelle, Schickelle, Schuh.
   Ei was bin ich so luschdicher Buh,
   Ei was kann ich so zwitzerich danzen.

1. Oh, I wear such pretty little shoes
   With such pretty little strings.
   Little strings, little shoes, shoes.
   Oh, I am such a lusty boy,
   Oh, I can dance so flashily!

2. Oh, I wear such pretty little stockings
   With such pretty little stripes.
   Little stripes, little stockings,
   Little strings, little shoes, shoes.
   Oh, I am such a lusty boy,
   Oh, I can dance so flashily!

3. Oh, I wear such pretty little pants
   With such pretty little buttons.
   Little buttons, little pants, little stripes, etc.

4. Oh, I wear such a pretty little belt
   With such a pretty little buckle.
   Little buckle, little belt, little buttons, etc.

5. Oh, I wear such a pretty little shirt
   With such pretty little cuffs.
   Little cuffs, little shirt, little buckle, etc.

6. Oh, I wear such a pretty little jacket
   With such a pretty little collar.
   Little collar, little jacket, little cuffs, etc.

7. Oh, I wear such a pretty little coat
   With such a pretty little tail.
   Little tail, little coat, little collar, etc.

8. Oh, I wear such a pretty little hat
   With such a pretty little tassel.
   Little tassel, little hat,
   Little tail, little coat,
   Little collar, little jacket,
   Little cuffs, little shirt,
   Little buckle, little belt,
   Little buttons, little pants,
   Little stripes, little stockings,
   Little strings, little shoes, shoes.
   Oh, I am such a lusty boy,
   Oh, I can dance so flashily!

Di Lichputscher

(The Candle Snuffer)

(Sung by Mrs. Mabel Keeny at Rehrersburg, Berks County, 1937. Recorded by Thomas R. Brendle and William S. Troxell.)

This is a variant of the well-known *Schnitzelbank*. Mrs. Keeny told us she learned this version from an old schoolmaster who illustrated the ballad with pencil drawings.

1. Ei du schee-ne, ei du schee-ne,

Ei du schee-ne Lich-put-scher. Di Lich-put-scher.

Is des net des Hie un Her? Ja des is des Hie un Her.

Des Hie un Her.   *Un di Lich-put-scher.*

(Repeat accumulated phrases each
time in reverse order)

2. *Ei du scheene, ei du scheene,*
    Ei du scheene Lichputscher,
      Di Lichputscher.
    Is des net des Kaz un Lang?
    Ja des is des Kaz un Lang.
      Kaz un Lang,
      Des Hie un Her, un di Lichputscher.

3. *Is des net des Feierzang?*
    Ja des is des Feierzang.

4. *Is des net des Grum un Grâd?*
    Ja des is des Grum un Grâd.

5. *Is des net en Wajjerâd?*
    Ja des is en Wajjerâd.

6. *Is des net en Eijeschnawwel?*
    Ja des is en Eijeschnawwel.

7. *Is des net en Offegawwel?*
    Ja des is en Offegawwel.

8. *Is des net en Seijebock?*
    Ja des is en Seijebock.

9. *Is des net en armer Drobb?*
    Ja des is en armer Drobb.

10. *Is des net des Kaes un Budder?*
    Ja des is des Kaes un Budder.

11. *Ei du scheene, ei du scheene,*
    Ei du scheene Lichputscher,
      Di Lichputscher.
    Is des net di Hambargs Mudder?
    Ja des is di Hambargs Mudder.
      Hambargs Mudder, Kaes un Budder,
      Armer Drobb, Seijebock,
      Offegawwel, Eijeschnawwel,
      Wajjerâd, Grum un Grâd,
      Feierzang, Kaz un Lang,
      Des Hie and Her, un di Lichputscher.

1. O you pretty, O you pretty,
   O you pretty candle snuffer,
     The candle snuffer.
   Is this not a back and forth,
   Yes, this is a back and forth.
     Back and forth, and the candle snuffer.

2. O you pretty, O you pretty,
   O you pretty candle snuffer,
     The candle snuffer.
   Is this not a short and long?
   Yes, this is a short and long.
     Short and long,
     Back and forth, and the candle snuffer.

3. Is this not the pair of tongs?
   Yes, this is the pair of tongs.

4. Is this not the crooked and straight?
   Yes, this is the crooked and straight.

5. Is this not a wagon wheel?
   Yes, this is a wagon wheel.

6. Is this not an owl's bill?
   Yes, this is an owl's bill.

7. Is this not an oven fork?
   Yes, this is an oven fork.

8. Is this not a sawhorse?
   Yes, this is a sawhorse.

9. Is this not a poor devil?
   Yes, this is a poor devil.

10. Is this not the cheese and butter?
    Yes, this is the cheese and butter.

11. O you pretty, O you pretty,
    O you pretty candle snuffer,
      The candle snuffer.
    Is this not the Hamburg mother?
    Yes, this is the Hamburg mother.
      Hamburg mother, cheese and butter,
      Poor devil, sawhorse,
      Oven fork, owl's bill,
      Wagon wheel, crooked and straight,
      Pair of tongs, short and long,
      Back and forth, and the candle snuffer.

Der Jug hot en Loch
(The Jug Has a Hole)

(Sung by Henry Fink at Vera Cruz, Lehigh County, 1940. Recorded by Thomas R. Brendle and William S. Troxell.)

This ancient ballad was brought to Pennsylvania in the eighteenth century. The German version is listed by Erk and Böhme in *Deutscher Liederhort.* There are a number of variants in the Pennsylvania Dutch region, including *Liewer Heindrich* in the chapter on Conestoga wagoners. In some cases the dialogue is carried on by two men, but here the musical colloquy is between a man and a woman—Heinrich and Lizz.

The tune has been transcribed from Fink's recording, but the text is from the version published in *Proceedings of the Pennsylvania German Society,* Vol. XXIII. Repetitions of second and fourth lines in this version have been omitted as Fink's tune has only four lines in each stanza. The spelling has been retained.

2. *Mit was soll ich es aver zu stoppe,*
   Lieber Heinrich, lieber Heinrich,
   Mit was soll ich es aver zu stoppe?
   Lieve Lizz, ei mit Stroh.

3. *Wann's Stroh aver zu lang is,*
   Lieber Heinrich, lieber Heinrich,
   Wann's Stroh aver zu lang is?
   Lieve Lizz, ei hock's ab.

4. *Mit was soll ich es aver ab hocke,*
   Lieser Heinrich, lieser Heinrich,
   Mit was soll ich es aver ab hocke?
      Lieve Lizz, ei mit em Beil.

5. *Wonn's Beil aver zu stump is,*
   Lieser Heinrich, lieser Heinrich,
   Wonn's Beil aver zu stump is?
      Lieve Lizz, ei mach's scharf.

6. *Uf was soll ich es aver scharf mache,*
   Lieser Heinrich, lieser Heinrich,
   Mit was soll ich es aver scharf mache?
      Lieve Lizz, ei uf em Stee.

7. *Wonn d'r Stee aver zu drucke is,*
   Lieser Heinrich, lieser Heinrich,
   Wonn d'r Stee aver zu drucke is?
      Lieve Lizz, ei hole Wasser.

8. *Mit was soll ich aver Wasser hole,*
   Lieser Heinrich, lieser Heinrich,
   Mit was soll ich aver Wasser hole?
      Lieve Lizz, ei mit en Jug.

9. *Wonn d'r Jug aver doch en Loch hot,*
   Lieser Heinrich, lieser Heinrich,
   Wonn d'r Jug aver doch en Loch hot?
      Lieve Lizz, ei stopp's zu.

1. But if the jug has a hole,
   Dear Henry, dear Henry,
   But if the jug has a hole?
      Dear Lizzie, stop it up.

2. But with what shall I stop it up,
   Dear Henry, dear Henry,
   But with what shall I stop it up?
      Dear Lizzie, with straw.

3. If the straw is too long,
   Dear Henry, dear Henry,
   If the straw is too long?
      Dear Lizzie, cut it off.

4. How shall I cut it off,
   Dear Henry, dear Henry,
   How shall I cut it off?
      Dear Lizzie, with a hatchet.

5. But if the hatchet is too dull,
   Dear Henry, dear Henry,
   But if the hatchet is too dull?
   Dear Lizzie, sharpen it.

6. But how shall I sharpen it,
   Dear Henry, dear Henry,
   But how shall I sharpen it?
   Dear Lizzie, on a stone.

7. But if the stone is too dry,
   Dear Henry, dear Henry,
   But if the stone is too dry?
   Dear Lizzie, fetch water.

8. With what shall I fetch water,
   Dear Henry, dear Henry,
   With what shall I fetch water?
   Dear Lizzie, with a jug.

9. But if the jug has a hole,
   Dear Henry, dear Henry,
   But if the jug has a hole?
   Dear Lizzie, stop it up.

Schpinn, schpinn

(Spin, Spin)

(Sung by Aaron Rehrig at Lockport, Northampton County, 1939.
Recorded by Thomas R. Brendle and William S. Troxell.)

This is one of the Pennsylvania Dutch versions of the well-known German spinning song brought to Pennsylvania in the eighteenth century. Its motif is familiar in folk songs, and parallels may be found in many languages.

(Verses 1 to 5)

1. Schpinn, schpinn, mein-e liew-e Doch-der, No
kâf ich dir'n Frack. Ja, ja, mein-e liew-e Mam-mi, Un

Chorus

den mit ma Sack. Ich kann nim-mi schpin-ne, Mei

Fin-ger schwellt im-mer, Un'r dudd m'r weh, so weh.

(Last Verse)

6. Schpinn, schpinn, mein - e liew - e Doch - der, No

kâf ich dir'n Mann. Ja, ja, mein-e liew-e Mam-mi, Den

Chorus

brauch ich schun lang! Ich kann wid-der schpin-ne, Mei

Fin-ger schwellt nim-mi, Un'r dudd m'nim-mi weh, m'nimmi weh.

2. *Schpinn, schpinn, meine liewe Dochder,*
    No kâf ich dir'n Schatz.
    Ja, ja, meine liewe Mammi,
    Un den net zu kaz.

    CHORUS
    Ich kann nimmi schpinne,
    Mei Finger schwellt immer,
    Un 'r dudd m'r weh, so weh.

3. *Schpinn, schpinn, meine liewe Dochder,*
    No kâf ich dir Schuh.
    Ja, ja, meine liewe Mammi,
    Mit Bendel dazu.

4. *Schpinn, schpinn, meine liewe Dochder,*
    No kâf ich dir'n Kuh.
    Ja, ja, meine liewe Mammi,
    Mit ma Kelwel dazu.

5. *Schpinn, schpinn, meine liewe Dochder,*
   No kâf ich dir'n Gaul.
   Ja, ja, meine liewe Mammi,
   Mit em Hawwer im Maul.

1. Spin, spin, my dear daughter,
   And I'll buy you a dress.
   Yes, yes, my dear mother,
   And one with a pocket.

   ### CHORUS
   I can spin no more,
   For my finger keeps swelling,
   And hurts me much, so much.

2. Spin, spin, my dear daughter,
   And I'll buy you an apron.
   Yes, yes, my dear mother,
   And one not too short.

3. Spin, spin, my dear daughter,
   And I'll buy you shoes.
   Yes, yes, my dear mother,
   With shoestrings too.

4. Spin, spin, my dear daughter,
   And I'll buy you a cow.
   Yes, yes, my dear mother,
   One with a calf.

5. Spin, spin, my dear daughter.
   And I'll buy you a horse.
   Yes, yes, my dear mother,
   With oats in his mouth.

6. Spin, spin, my dear daughter,
   And I'll buy you a husband.
   Yes, yes, my dear mother,
   I've wanted one for a long time!

   ### CHORUS
   I can spin again,
   My finger swells no more,
   And no longer gives me any pain, any pain!

Nein un neinzich
(Nine and Ninety)

(Sung by Mrs. Alice Frankenfield at Allentown, 1937. Recorded by Thomas R. Brendle and William S. Troxell.)

This song continues down through the eighties, seventies, etc., repeating the chorus at the end of each stanza.

2. *Nein un achsich, acht un achsich,*
    Siwwe un achsich,
    Sexe, fimfe, viere, drei un achsich,
    Zwei un achsich, ein un achsich,
    Achsich.

CHORUS
Jâ, jâ, ich fiehle dass du mich liebe,
Es klopfet auf meine Bruscht.

1. Nine and ninety, eight and ninety,
    Seven and ninety,
    Six, five, four, three and ninety,
    Two and ninety, one and ninety,
    Ninety.

CHORUS
Aye, aye, I've a feeling that you love me,
There's a throbbing in my breast.

2. Nine and eighty, eight and eighty,
   Seven and eighty,
   Six, five, four, three and eighty,
   Two and eighty, one and eighty,
   Eighty.

In Poland schteht en Haus

(In Poland There Is a House)

(Sung by Mrs. Jane Reitz at Himmel's Church, Northumberland County, 1938. Recorded by Thomas R. Brendle and William S. Troxell.)

In German song collections, this is described as a children's game song, but whether our people in Pennsylvania ever used it as such we are unable to determine. The following version differs considerably from the one appearing in German collections; this is indicative of the molding process the song has undergone in our state. "Joe Keiser" probably is a corruption of some German phrase like *ho heisa*.

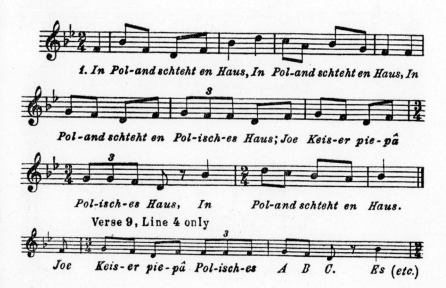

1. *In Pol-and schteht en Haus, In Pol-and schteht en Haus, In*

Pol-and schteht en Pol-isch-es Haus; Joe Keis-er pie-pâ

Pol-isch-es Haus, In Pol-and schteht en Haus.
Verse 9, Line 4 only

Joe Keis-er pie-pâ Pol-isch-es A B C. Es (etc.)

2. *Wer wuhnt dann in dem Haus?*
   Wer wuhnt dann in dem Haus?
   Wer wuhnt dann in dem Polisches Haus?
   Joe Keiser pie på Polisches Haus,
   Wer wuhnt dann in dem Haus?

3. *En Wadd wuhnt in dem Haus.*

4. *Was dutt ar in dem Haus?*

5. *Ar macht d'r Måd en Kind.*

6. *Was dutt sie mit dem Kind?*

7. *Sie schickt sel in di Schuhl.*

8. *Was lannt es in di Schuhl?*

9. *Es lannt des ABC.*

10. *Sie schrieb sel an di Wand.*

1. In Poland there is a house,
   In Poland there is a house,
   In Poland there is a Polish house;
   Joe Keiser pee paw Polish house,
   In Poland there is a house.

2. Who liveth in this house?
   Who liveth in this house?
   Who liveth in this Polish house?
   Joe Keiser pee paw Polish house,
   Who liveth in this house?

3. A landlord liveth in the house.

4. What does he do in the house?

5. He fathers a child for the maid.

6. What does she do with the child?

7. She sends it to school.

8. What does it learn in the school?

9. It learns the ABC's.

10. She writes that on the wall.

Des bucklich Mennli

(The Little Humpback)

(Sung by Mrs. Eva Roth at Egypt, Lehigh County, 1937. Recorded by
Thomas R. Brendle and William S. Troxell.)

Believed to have been inspired by a house spirit, this song was
brought to Pennsylvania in the eighteenth century. We have
collected five different versions.

1. *Mar-jets wann ich uff-schteh, Schau ich an di Wolk-e,*

Mud-der is di Subb ge-kocht? Sin di Kieh ge-mol - ke?

2. *Wann ich in mei kieh-schtall kumm Fa mei Kie-che mel-ke,*

Schteht des buck-lich Menn-li do Un fangt â su— schel-te.

3. *Wann ich in mei Gârde kumm*
   Fa mei Blumme blanze,
   Schteht des bucklich Mennli dadd
   Un fangt â zu danze.

4. *Wann ich in mei Keller kumm*
   Fa mei Millich seije,
   Schteht des bucklich Mennli dadd
   Un fangt â zu geije.

5. *Wann ich in mei Kichli kumm*
   Fa mei Esse mache,
   Schteht des bucklich Mennli dadd
   Un fangt â zu schaffe.

6. *Wann ich in mei Schtibbche kumm*
   Fa mei Schtibbche kehre,

Schteht des bucklich Mennli dadd
Un fangt â zu wehre.

7. *Wann ich in mei Schpeicher kumm*
   Fa mei Better mache,
   Schteht des bucklich Mennli dadd
   Un fangt â zu lache.

1. When I get up in the morning,
   I look up into the clouds.
   "Mother, is the soup ready?
   Are the cows milked?"

2. When I enter my barn
   To milk my cows,
   The little humpback is there
   And begins to scold me.

3. When I enter my garden
   To plant my flowers,
   The little humpback is there
   And begins to dance.

4. When I enter my cellar
   To strain my milk,
   The little humpback is there
   And begins to fiddle.

5. When I enter my kitchen
   To prepare my meal,
   The little humpback is there
   And begins to work.

6. When I enter my room
   To sweep it out,
   The little humpback is there
   And attempts to hinder me.

7. When I go upstairs
   To make my beds,
   The little humpback is there
   And starts to laugh.

Es wollte ein Jaejerlein jâje
(A Young Hunter Went A-Hunting)

(Sung by Mrs. Jane Masonheimer at Egypt, Lehigh County, 1936.
Recorded by Thomas R. Brendle and William S. Troxell.)

German collectors have traced this folk song to the sixteenth century. It was brought to Pennsylvania in the eighteenth century by early immigrants. Our singer, Mrs. Masonheimer, said that in her girlhood "Hei lie, Hei lo" was sung as a refrain. We heard parts of the same song in Schuylkill, Northumberland, and Snyder counties.

1. Es woll - te ein Jae - jer - lein jâ - je, Drei Vad - del Schtund vor Dâ - je, Ein Hasch - lein od - der ein Reh, ein Reh, Ein Hasch - lein od - der ein Reh.

2. *Es begejet ihn auf d'r Reise*
   Ein Medche in wunderschee Gleidche;
   Die wâr schee angethan, gethan,
   Die wâr schee angethan.

3. *'R deede sie friedlich frâje*
   Ob sie wollt mit ihm jâje,
   Ein Haschlein odder ein Reh, ein Reh,
   Ein Haschlein odder ein Reh.

4. *"Ach jâje, ach jâje, das mâ ich nicht,*
   *En andre Bliehe bescha ich nicht,**
   'S mag heissen was es will, es will,
   'S mag heissen was es will."

5. *"Schteh auf! Schteh auf! du fauler Jaejer,*
   Die Sonne scheint iwwer di Techer,
   Une Jungfrâ bin ich noch, ja noch,
   Une Jungfrâ bin ich noch."

6. *D'r Jaejer dutt sich bedriese,*
   'R wollte das Meedche erschiesse,
   Woll weje dem einzige Wadd, ja Wadd,
   Woll weje dem einzige Wadd.

* This line is a corruption of: *En andre Bidde versâ ich nicht.*

7. *D'r Jaejer dutt's widder bedencke,*
   'R wollt ihr des Lewe erschencke,
   Bis auf ein andres Mâl, ein Mâl,
   Bis auf ein andres Mâl.

1. A young hunter went a-hunting,
   Three quarters of an hour before daybreak,
   A little deer or a doe, a doe,
   A little deer or a doe.

2. As he went along he met
   A maiden in beautiful clothes;
   She was beautifully dressed, dressed,
   She was beautifully dressed.

3. He asked her kindly,
   Whether she would hunt with him,
   A little deer or a doe, a doe,
   A little deer or a doe.

4. "Ah, ah, hunting does not appeal to me,
   But I would not decline any other invitation,
   Whatever it might be, might be,
   Whatever it might be."

5. "Get up, get up, you lazy hunter,
   The sun already is shining over the rooftops,
   And a virgin I remain, remain,
   And a virgin I remain."

6. The hunter became enraged,
   He wanted to shoot the maiden,
   Merely on account of that one word, one word,
   Merely on account of that one word.

7. The hunter changed his mind,
   He would spare the maiden's life
   Until another time, another time,
   Until another time.

Wie kumm ich an des Grossvadder's Haus?
(How Do I Get to Grandfather's House?)

(Sung by Charles Christman at Strausstown, Berks County, 1936.
Recorded by Thomas R. Brendle and William S. Troxell.)

This charming lovers' trysting song goes back to sixteenth-
century Germany, according to *Deutscher Liederhort* by Erk and

Böhme, Vol. II, p. 282. It was probably brought to Pennsylvania in the eighteenth century. The following Pennsylvania Dutch version is one of three recorded by us, each having a different tune and chorus.

1. Wie kumm ich dann an des Gross - vad-der's Haus,
Mein ge-lieb-des Maed - lein? So gehscht du gleich di
Schtrooss hin-aus, No kummscht du an des Gross- vad-der's Haus.
Chorus
Un so mei Mae-del, so, so, so, Un so mei Mae-del, so.

2. Wie kumm ich dann zu d'r Dier hinein,
   Mein geliebdes Maedlein?
   Dadd vor d'r Dier, dadd liegt ein Schtein,
   Dadd schtellscht dich druff an gehscht hinein.

   CHORUS
   Un so mei Maedel, so, so, so,
   Un so mei Maedel, so.

3. Wu henck ich dann mei feiner Rock,
   Mein geliebdes Maedel?
   Dadd hinnich di Dier, dadd schteht en Schtock,
   Dadd hengscht du dran dei feiner Rock.

4. Wie kumm ich dann di Schteeg hinauf,
   Mein geliebdes Maedel?
   Duscht einen Fuss vorm andre naus,
   Dann kummscht du gleich di Schteeg hinauf.

1. How do I get to grandfather's house,
   My beloved maiden?
   Take the road and follow it
   And you will come to grandfather's house.

CHORUS
And so my maiden, so, so, so,
And so my maiden, so.

2. How do I get into the house,
My beloved maiden?
Before the door there lies a stone,
Step on it and enter in.

3. Where shall I hang my fine coat,
My beloved maiden?
Behind the door there is a clothes tree
Hang your fine coat upon it.

4. How do I get up the stairs,
My beloved maiden?
Put one foot in front of the other
And you will soon be up the stairs.

Willst du wiezen?

(Do You Want to Know?)

(Sung by Simon Wilhelm at Bernville, Berks County, 1937. Recorded by Thomas R. Brendle and William S. Troxell.)

Text and melody are Pennsylvania Dutch variants of a song that appears in German collections. The singer employs pantomime with the lines "And this is the way, etc."

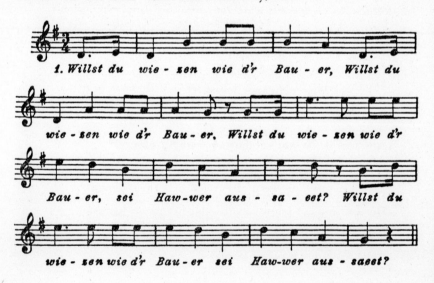

1. Willst du wie-sen wie d'r Bau-er, Willst du wie-sen wie d'r Bau-er. Willst du wie-sen wie d'r Bau-er, sei Haw-wer aus-sa-eet? Willst du wie-sen wie d'r Bau-er sei Haw-wer aus-saeet?

Un so dut d'r Bau-er, Un so dut d'r Bau-er, Un

so dut d'r Bau-er sei Haw-wer aus - sa-een, Un

so saet d'r Bau-er sei Haw-wer al - lein.

2. *Willst du wiezen wie d'r Bauer,*
   Willst du wiezen wie d'r Bauer,
   Willst du wiezen wie d'r Bauer sei Hawwer abmaehet?
   Willst du wiezen wie d'r Bauer sei Hawwer abmaehet?
   Un so dut d'r Bauer,
   Un so dut d'r Bauer,
   Un so dut d'r Bauer sei Hawwer abmaehen,
   Un so maeht d'r Bauer sei Hawwer allein.

3. *Willst du wiezen wie d'r Bauer sei Hawwer aufrechet?*

4. *Willst du wiezen wie d'r Bauer sei Hawwer aufbindet?*

5. *Willst du wiezen wie d'r Bauer sei Hawwer ausdreschet?*

6. *Willst du wiezen wie d'r Bauer sei Hawwer verkaufet?*

7. *Willst du wiezen wie d'r Bauer sei Geld nun verschpendet?*

8. *Willst du wiezen wie d'r Bauer dann endlich heimgehet?*

1. Do you want to know how the farmer,
   Do you want to know how the farmer,
   Do you want to know how the farmer sows his oats?
   Do you want to know how the farmer sows his oats?
   And this is the way the farmer,
   And this is the way the farmer,
   And this is the way the farmer sows his oats,
   And this is the way the farmer sows his oats all alone.

2. Do you want to know how the farmer,
   Do you want to know how the farmer,
   Do you want to know how the farmer mows his oats?
   Do you want to know how the farmer mows his oats?
   And this is the way the farmer,
   And this is the way the farmer,

And this is the way the farmer mows his oats,
And this is the way the farmer mows his oats all alone.

3. Do you want to know how the farmer rakes his oats?
4. Do you want to know how the farmer binds up his oats?
5. Do you want to know how the farmer threshes his oats?
6. Do you want to know how the farmer sells his oats?
7. Do you want to know how the farmer spends his money?
8. Do you want to know how the farmer finally returns home?

Drei Wochen vor Oschdren

(Three Weeks before Easter)

(Sung by Anson Roebuck at Sacramento, Dauphin County, 1938. Recorded by Thomas R. Brendle and William S. Troxell.)

These quatrains, each complete in itself and unrelated to each other, are sung to a common melody. Among Pennsylvania Germans they are known as *Schelmlieder* (roguish songs) or *Schtroosselieder* (street songs), and in Germany they are termed *Schnaderhüpfl* (rounds) because the type is believed to have originated with the *Schnitterdanz* (the reapers' dance). Creating these songs called for a considerable amount of improvisation, a process that came close to communal composition. In a gathering, a stanza would be sung by one singer who would be followed in turn by others singing either traditional quatrains brought over from Germany or those made up on the spot from experiences in the Pennsylvania Dutch environment.

1. Drei Woch-en vor Osch-dren Do geht d'r Schnee weck; Do heir-et mei Schet-zel, Do haw-ich en Dreck.

4. Ein ald-es Pâr Och-sen, En schwaz-e-braun-e Kuh, Des gebt mir mei Vâd-er Wann ich hei-râ-de du.

2. *Die hawwich geliebt,*
   Was hawwich dovun;
   Ball hawwich en Schetzel,
   Ball hawwich ebbes schunscht.

3. *Drei Rosen im Garden,*
   Drei Weglein im Wald;
   D'r Sommer is lieblich,
   D'r Winder is kald.

   (Return to the regular tune)

5. *So gebt ar mir sie nicht,*
   So heire ich sie â nicht;
   Un bleib bei meim Schetzel
   Un sâjes ihm nicht.

6. *Hab Hawweren gedrosche,*
   Hab Lintzen geseet;
   Hab manche schee Meedel
   Im Danz gedreht.

7. *En wadshaus dadd drowwe,*
   Dadd schteht einen Disch;
   No rabble di Glesser,
   No drincke m'r frisch.

8. *'S war âgenehm am Bedallje,*
   Dadd geht es luschdich zu,
   Do danze di Meedlen,
   No glabberen di Schuh.

1. Three weeks before Easter
   The snow melts away;
   Then my sweetheart marries
   And I am left in the lurch.

2. This one I loved,
   But what did I have thereby?
   Sometimes I had a sweetheart;
   Sometimes I had none.

3. Three roses in the garden;
   Three paths in the woods;
   The summer is lovely;
   The winter is cold.

4. A pair of old oxen,
    A dark-brown cow;
    These my father will give me
    If I marry you.

5. If he doesn't give them to me,
    I won't marry,
    But will remain true to my sweetheart
    And say nothing about it.

6. I have threshed oats
    And I have sown lentils.
    Many a pretty girl
    Have I swung in dancing.

7. A tavern on the hill
    And in it a table,
    There the glasses clink
    And there we drink anew.

8. Battalion Day was pleasant
    And merriment prevailed;
    The maidens danced
    And the shoes clattered.

D'r Guckgu
(The Cuckoo)

(Sung by Mrs. Jane Reitz at Himmel's Church, Northumberland County, 1938. Recorded by Thomas R. Brendle and William S. Troxell.)

According to German collectors, this song is known throughout Germany. In the Pennsylvania Dutch region it has been sung for many generations and probably was brought over in the eighteenth century. We have heard it sung in Lehigh, Dauphin, Schuylkill, and Northumberland counties.

1. D'r Guck-gu is en brâv-er Mann, D'r vazz-eh
Wei-wer an-neh-re kann. Guck-gu Guck-er-di-gu.

2. *Di erscht di drâgt des Hols ins Haus;*
   Di zwett di macht des Feier daraus.
   Guckgu Guckerdigu.

3. *Di dritt di drâgt des Wasser ins Haus;*
   Di viert di macht di Subbe daraus.

4. *Di fimft di macht den weissen Disch;*
   Di sext di drâgt gebrodene Fisch.

5. *Di siwwet di zappt des Bier un Wei;*
   Di acht di schprach, "Es kann net sei."

6. *Di neint di hockt im gentleman's Haus;*
   Di zehnt di schprach zum Fenschder raus.

7. *Di elft di macht em Harrn sei Bett;*
   Di zwelft di leid schun lang un schtreckt.

8. *Di dreizehnt hot ar in seim Ârm.*
   "Di vazzehnt, Gott, drum danck ich dir."

1. The cuckoo is an able man
   Who supports fourteen wives.
   Guckgu Guckerdigu.

2. The first wife carries wood into the house;
   The second builds a fire with it.

3. The third carries water into the house;
   The fourth makes soup out of it.

4. The fifth sets a white table;
   The sixth places roast fish upon it.

5. The seventh taps beer and wine;
   The eighth cries out, "Impossible!"

6. The ninth sits in the gentleman's house;
   The tenth speaks through an open window.

7. The eleventh makes the master's bed;
   The twelfth lies outstretched in it.

8. The thirteenth is in the master's arms;
   "For the fourteenth, God, I thank thee."

Unser Salwi hot en Kaldi

(Our Salome Has a Cold)

(Sung by Mrs. Flora Hankee at Northampton, Northampton County,
1937. Recorded by Thomas R. Brendle and William S. Troxell.)

This song is an example of vagrant stanzas hung together on a
common refrain. Stanza 4 is recited rather than sung. Common in
folklore is the mother-in-law motif of this stanza, which is a Pennsylvania Dutch variant of an old German folk song. Compare it
with the following High German stanza quoted from Franz Magnus Böhme's *Deutsches Kinderlied u. Kinderspiel* (Leipzig: 1924),
p. 204:

> *Eine alte Schwiegermutter*
> *Mit der krummen Faust,*
> *Sieben jahr in Himmel droben*
> *Kommt nun wieder raus,*
> *Is das nicht en dummes Weib,*
> *Das nicht in dem Himmel bleibt?*

1. Un-ser Sal-wi hot en Kal-di, Hot en hilz-ni Pisch-
tol;— Fan-ne Schallt si, hin-ne gnallt si, In d'r Mitt is si hohl.
Chorus
Lud-el lei lei, lud-el lei lei, Lud-el lei lei, lud-el
lei lei, Lud-el lei lei, lud-el lei lei, Lud-el lei lei lei lei.

> 2. *Wann ich geld hab kann ich Grundniss esse,*
> *Wann ich kens hab muss ich di Schâle fresse;*
> *Sis mar all eins, sis mar all eins,*
> *Hawwich Geld odder hawwich keins.*

CHORUS
Ludel lei lei, ludel lei lei,
Ludel lei lei, ludel lei lei,
Ludel lei lei, ludel lei lei,
Ludel lei lei lei lei.

3. *Meine Schwiejermudder is en Schindluder,*
   Hot di Damfnudle âgebrennt;
   Bin ich widderkumme hot si di Pannekuche,
   Mit dar Mischtgawwel rumgerennt.

(Spoken)

4. *Unser aldi Schwiejermudder*
   Wâr en aldes Dunner.
   Siwwe Jâhr wâr sie im Himmel,
   Kummt si widdar runner.
   Iss si net en Dunnersweib
   Ass si net im Himmel bleibt?
   Sedd mar net en Kuggel giesse,
   Un sedd si widder nuff schiesse?

1. Our Salome has a cold,
   Has a wooden pistol;
   In front an echo, in back a bang,
   In the middle it is hollow.

CHORUS
Ludel lei lei, ludel lei lei,
Ludel lei lei, ludel lei lei,
Ludel lei lei, ludel lei lei,
Ludel lei lei lei lei.

2. When I have money I eat peanuts,
   When I have none I eat the shells;
   It is all the same,
   Whether I have money or none.

3. My mother-in-law is a cadaver;
   She lets the noodles burn
   And turns the pancakes
   With a pitchfork.

4. Our old mother-in-law,
   What a terror!
   Seven years she was in heaven;
   Then she came down again.
   Is she not a holy terror
   Not to have stayed in heaven?
   Should one not mold a bullet
   And shoot her back?

Dadd driwwe
(Over There)

(Sung by David Paul and Mrs. Mabel Keeney at Rehrersburg, Berks
County, 1938. Recorded by Thomas R. Brendle and William S.
Troxell.)

Erk and Böhme, German folk-song experts, are authority for the
statement that this song, known throughout Germany, has been
traced to the sixteenth century. This Pennsylvania Dutch version
was brought to Pennsylvania by eighteenth-century immigrants.

Another version in our collection places the phrase "says he" at
the beginning of the line, like this:

> Says he, over there,
> Says he, on the hill,

And the refrain goes like this:

> *Ei di ie, ei di o,*
> *Wackel doch nimmi so.*

Still another version combines lines in this manner:

> Over there on the hill, says he.

1. Dadd driw-we, sâgt-'r, Uf 'm Bar-rick, sâgt-'r, Schteht-en
Haus sâgt-'r, Sis tzu arr-ick, sâgt-'r Uf d'r Seid, sâgt-'r, Hots ken
Wand, sâgt-r So en Haus, sâgt-'r, Is en Shand.

Chorus

Wir leb-en so wohl, Wir leb-en so wohl, Ken-na
Frank-reich nicht werd-en, Wir leb-en so wohl.

2. *Dadd driwwe, sâgt'r,*
   Uf em Barrick, sâgt'r,
   Schteht en Hasch, sâgt'r,
   Sis tzu arrick, sâgt'r.
   Un d'r Jaejer, sâgt'r,
   Schteht dabei, sâgt'r,
   Hot ken Bulfer, sâgt'r,
   Hot ken Blei.

   CHORUS
   Wir leben so wohl,
   Wir leben so wohl,
   Kenna Frankreich nicht werden,
   Wir leben so wohl.

3. *Dadd drunne, sâgt'r,*
   Uf d'r Brick, sâgt'r,
   Leid en Gaul, sâgt'r,
   Uf sei Rick, sâgt'r.
   Un d'r Saddel, sâgt'r,
   Uf em Bauch, sâgt'r,
   Un d'r Reider, sâgt'r,
   Hockt do auch.

4. *Dadd driwwe, sâgt'r,*
   Is d'r Schneider, sâgt'r,
   Macht di Hosse, sâgt'r,
   Eng un weid, sâgt'r.
   Un di Node, sâgt'r,
   Gut un schlecht, sâgt'r,
   Fa di Leid, sâgt'r,
   Wie ar's drefft.

5. *Dadd driwwe, sâgt'r,*
   Is d'r Singer, sâgt'r,
   Schpielt di Geig, sâgt'r,
   Mit di Finger, sâgt'r.
   Un di Node, sâgt'r,
   Weis un schwaz, sâgt'r,
   Un di Ruthe, sâgt'r,
   Lang un Kaz.

6. *Dadd driwwe, sâgt'r,*
   Is d'r Schreiner, sâgt'r,
   Macht en Gsicht, sâgt'r,
   Wie en Zeiner, sâgt'r.

Schiebt d'r Howwel, sâgt'r,
Hie un her, sâgt'r,
Macht en Gsicht, sâgt'r,
Wie en Ber.

1. Over there, says he,
   On the hill, says he,
   Is a house, says he,
   'Tis scandalous, says he.
   On the side, says he,
   Is no wall, says he,
   Such a house, says he,
   Is a shame.

   CHORUS
   We live so well,
   We live so well;
   Cannot belong to France,
   We live so well.

2. Over there, says he,
   On the hill, says he,
   Is a deer, says he,
   'Tis scandalous, says he.
   And the hunter, says he,
   Stands near-by, says he,
   Has no powder, says he,
   And no lead.

3. Down there, says he,
   On the bridge, says he,
   Lies a horse, says he,
   On its back, says he.
   And the saddle, says he,
   On its belly, says he,
   And the rider, says he,
   Sits there too.

4. Over there, says he,
   Is the tailor, says he,
   Sews the pants, says he,
   Tight and wide, says he.
   And the stitches, says he,
   Good and bad, says he,
   For the people, says he,
   All by luck.

5. Over there, says he,
   Is the singer, says he,
   Plays the fiddle, says he,
   With the fingers, says he.
   And the notes, says he,
   Black and white, says he,
   And the staff, says he,
   Long and short.

6. Over there, says he,
   Is the joiner, says he,
   Makes a face, says he,
   Like a gypsy, says he.
   Moves the plane, says he,
   Back and forth, says he,
   With a face, says he,
   Like a bear.

Â, Â, Â, d'r Winder der is dâ

(A, A, A, Winter Is Here)

(Sung by Mrs. Jane Reitz at Himmel's Church, Northumberland County, 1938. Recorded by Thomas R. Brendle and William S. Troxell.)

This is the Pennsylvania Dutch version of an ancient German folk song which was probably brought over early in the nineteenth century. Its melody antedates 1800. The German version appears in *Volksthümliche Lieder der Deutschen in 18 und 19 Jahrhundert* by Franz Magnus Böhme (Leipzig: 1895).

1. Â, Â, Â, d'r Wind-er der is dâ,

Herbscht un Som - mer sin . ver-gang-e; Un d'r Wind-er

an-ge-kom-men, Â, Â, Â, d'r Wind-er der is dâ.

2. *Ie, Ie, Ie, geht en reisend Schnee,*
   Blumme bliehe an di Fenschderscheiwe;
   Mudder un Kinner di Hende reiwe.
   Ie, Ie, Ie, geht en reisend Schnee.

3. *Ei, Ei, Ei, vergiss di Ârme nie,*
   Hot m'r nix sich zu zudecke,
   Wird d'r Froscht un Keld arschrecke.
   Ei, Ei, Ei, vergiss di Ârme nie.

4. *O, O, O, was sin di Kinner so froh,*
   Wenn des Grischtkindel dutt was bringe;
   Un di Engel hoch duhn singe.
   O, O, O, was sin di Kinner so froh.

5. *Eu, Eu, Eu, no weiss ich was ich du—*
   Grischtkindel lieben, Grischtkindel loben,
   Mit den scheenen Englen droben.
   Eu, Eu, Eu, no weiss ich was ich du.

1. A, A, A, winter is here,
   Autumn and summer are gone;
   Winter has come.
   A, A, A, winter is here.

2. E, E, E, a cutting snow is falling,
   Flowerlike frost is on the windowpanes;
   Mother and children are rubbing their hands.
   E, E, E, a cutting snow is falling.

3. I, I, I, don't forget the poor,
   Those who have no shelter
   Will be scared by frost and cold.
   I, I, I, don't forget the poor.

4. O, O, O, the children are happy,
   As the Christ Child is bringing gifts;
   And the angels on high are singing.
   O, O, O, the children are happy.

5. U, U, U, I know what I shall do—
   Love the Christ Child, praise the Christ Child,
   Even as the angels do on high.
   U, U, U, I know what I shall do.

D'r Schwiezemann hot Heisen â

(The Swiss Wears Pants)

(Sung by Mrs. Cassie Seyfert at Strausstown, Berks County, 1937. Recorded by Thomas R. Brendle and William S. Troxell.)

Mrs. Seyfert told us that in her girlhood she danced to this *Schnaderhüpfl* (round). A nonsense song, it was probably brought into Pennsylvania by early Swiss immigrants. The allusion is to the knee-length leather pants customarily worn by men in the mountain districts of Switzerland.

2. *D'r Schwiezemann hot Hosen â,**
   D'r Schwiezemann hot Hosen â,
   Mit lauder lederne Bendel drâ,
   Mit lauder lederne Bendel drâ.

1. The Swiss wears pants,
   The Swiss wears pants,
   With all the strings of leather,
   With all the strings of leather.

2. The Swiss wears trousers,
   The Swiss wears trousers,
   With all the strings of leather,
   With all the strings of leather.

* Second stanza sung in slower tempo.

Hawwer reche

(Raking Oats)

(Sung by Tilden DeLong at Egypt, Lehigh County, 1939. Recorded by Thomas R. Brendle and William S. Troxell.)

This is an old Pennsylvania Dutch game song, both text and tune being widely known. German authorities trace stanza 2 to a sixteenth-century German game called "Mowing the Oats."

This is how *Hawwer Reche* was played in Pennsylvania: "Couples form a ring around a single player and sing it; and at a certain period, each young man, and sometimes a girl, lets go of his or her partner's arm and takes the arm of the one in advance, at which time the solitary player endeavors to step into the line and cut one out" (*Proceedings of the Pennsylvania German Society*, Vol. XXIII).

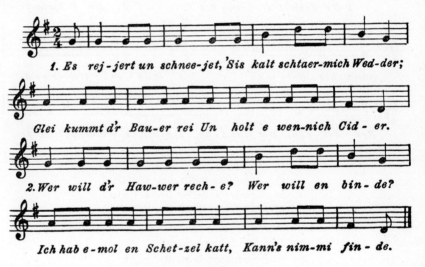

1. *Es rej-jert un schnee-jet, 'Sis kalt schtaer-mich Wed-der;*

Glei kummt d'r Bau-er rei Un holt e wen-nich Cid-er.

2. *Wer will d'r Haw-wer rech-e? Wer will en bin-de?*

Ich hab e-mol en Schet-zel katt, Kann's nim-mi fin-de.

1. It rains and it snows;
It's cold stormy weather.
The farmer comes into the house
And fetches a little cider.

2. Who will rake the oats?
Who will bind them?
I once had a sweetheart,
But I cannot find her.

Wu danze dann di Weiwer?
(Where Do Women Dance?)

(Sung by Mrs. Jane Reitz at Himmel's Church, Northumberland County, 1938. Recorded by Thomas R. Brendle and William S. Troxell.)

A quiz song found in Lehigh County also.

1. Wu dan-ze dann di Wei-wer? In di ald-e Schei-er; Wie eld-er ass di Schei-er is, Wie lie-wer ass di Wei-wer is.

2.   *Wu danze dann di Menner?*
     Auf di alde Schtenner;
     Wie elder ass di Schtenner sin
     Wie liewer ass di Menner is.

3.   *Wu danze dann di Buwe?*
     In d'r neie Schtube;
     Wie neier ass di Schtubb is
     Wie liewer ass di Buwe is.

4.   *Wu danze dann di Meedcher?*
     In di gleene Peedcher;
     Wie griener ass di Peedcher sin
     Wie liewer ass di Meedcher is.

5.   *Wu danze dann di Kinner?*
     Auf di alde Rinner;
     Wie elder ass di Rinner sin
     Wie liewer ass di Kinner is.

6.   *Wu danze dann di Greemer?*
     Auf di alde Eemer;
     Wie elder ass di Eemer sin,
     Wie liewer ass di Greemer is.

1.   Where do women dance?
     In old barns;
     The older the barn
     The better the women like it.

2. Where do men dance?
    In old vats;
    The older the vat
    The better the men like it.

3. Where do young men dance?
    In new rooms;
    The newer the room
    The better the young men like it.

4. Where do maidens dance?
    In narrow paths;
    The greener the path
    The better the maidens like it.

5. Where do children dance?
    On heifers;
    The older the heifer
    The better the children like it.

6. Where do peddlers dance?
    On old buckets;
    The older the bucket
    The better the peddlers like it.

Do wâr ich mol in Schtad Redding

(Once I Was in the City of Reading)

(Sung by Mrs. Annie Wright at Egypt, Lehigh County, 1936. Recorded
by Thomas R. Brendle and William S. Troxell.)

This indigenous ballad is widely distributed in the Pennsylvania
Dutch region under different versions. It is probably an adaptation and extension of the following vagrant quatrain:

> *Do wâr ich mol in Deitschland,*
> *Do wâr ich net bekannt,*
> *Do kummt en gleener Deitscher*
> *Un gebt mir di hand.*

Or of this quatrain:

> *Do wâr ich mol in Deitschland,*
> *Do wâr ich net bekannt,*
> *Do kummt d'r Cherli Schinnerhannes*
> *Un gebt m'r grâd di hand.*

1. Do wâr ich mol in Schtad Redd-ing,— Do
wâr ich net be-kannt; Do kummt d'r Bul-ly
Ly-an ____ Un grickt mich an de Hand.

2. No sâ ich, "Bully Lyan,
   Was hawwich dir gedu?"
   No sâgt d'r Bully Lyan,
   "Du bischt en wieschder Bu."

3. No fiert 'r mich ins Prison,
   Dadd, sâgt'r, misst ich nei;
   Dadd misst ich drei Jahr bleiwe,
   No werd ich widder frei.

4. Dadd kummt mei Frâ mich sehne.
   Sie hot so arrig weit,
   No sâgt d'r Bully Lyan,
   "Die is gewiss net gscheid."

1. Once I was in the city of Reading,
   Where I was unknown;
   Bully Lyon approached me
   And took hold of my hand.

2. Said I, "Bully Lyon,
   What have I done to you?"
   Said Bully Lyon,
   "You've been a bad boy."

3. He took me to the prison,
   And said that I must go in,
   And stay there three years,
   Then I could go free.

4. My wife came to see me.
   Because she had come from afar,
   Bully Lyon said,
   "This is surely a foolish person."

Di Matztown Cornet Band
(The Mertztown Cornet Band)

(Sung by Samuel Haas at Chapmans, Lehigh County, 1937. Recorded by Thomas R. Brendle and William S. Troxell.)

This is another indigenous ballad, still commonly heard in Berks and Lehigh counties. It was improvised a century or more ago in honor of a cornet band in Mertztown, a village in the northeastern section of Berks County. The ballad mentions various members of the band and satirizes their playing. Other bands took up the ballad and adapted it to their own purposes, substituting their own names, places, and allusions for those in the original version. Thus, in one form or another, the ballad attained widespread circulation. It was in the repertoire of many ballad singers. Note its use of Anglicisms and Americanisms.

1. In Matz-town meet un Cor-net Band, / Un sie be-zâh-le â ken rent; / Denn es Schul-haus is ge-we vor, / En Da-ler fier en gan-zes Johr.

2. Es sin jo fier un zwanzig Man
   Mit des Poea grosse John;
   Deel sin gross un deel sin dick,
   Deel sin Demokrât un deel sin Whig.

3. D'r Kuder teacht mit guder ârt,
   Mit seinem schwaze Backebârd;
   Ar teacht dennowed selli band
   Vor en Dâler dreissich cent.

4. D'r Billy Walbert blossd Bass
   Secht es wer f'r ihn ken Schpass;
   'R blossd sei Bass un guckd so bees
   Ass wie en Katz am grosse Kaes.

5. *D'r Allen Trexler ohne Schpass,*
   Selwer blossd der zwette Bass;
   'R hot verlohre sei Nodebuch
   D'r Nutteltauner Barrick nuff.

6. *D'r Milton Schubert, schquire sure*
   Seller schpielt d'r bar-a-toon;
   'R schpielt sei Hann noch guder Ârt
   Un hot noch gar ken Hâr am Bârd.

7. *Milton Warmkessel, ihr liewe Leid*
   Schloft auch schun bei seinem Weib;
   Seller schpielt den B trombone
   Macht en Gsicht wie en Raggoon.

8. *D'r Denny Webb geht â dazu,*
   Nau Buwe schpielt "Red, White, and Blue."
   'R schpielt sei tenor, O, so fei;
   'R gleicht die Kuche un der Wei.

9. *D'r Oliver Schubert, denck mol drâ,*
   Seller chap hot â en Frâ;
   'R blossd sei Hann uf un ab
   Un secht es wer en verdulder job.

10. *D'r Isaac Warmkessel, O my dear,*
    Secht die bandleit gleiche Bier;
    'R schpielt sei alto bei d'r band,
    D'r "Yankee Doodle," "Dixie Land."

11. *No is awwer noch des Keisers Frantz,*
    D'r greeschde Lacher in d'r band;
    'R an d'r D flat cornet schteckt
    Wie en Hâhne uf em Nescht.

12. *D'r Johnny Barley net juscht dumm,*
    Seller schpielt di gleene Drumm;
    'R is noch jung un 'r is noch glee
    Un gratzt di Meed schun an di Beh.

13. *D'r Peter Walbert gut gelannt,*
    Mit seinem Knibbel in d'r Hand;
    Seller schlackt di grosse Drumm—
    D'r Peter Walbert is net dumm.

14. *Der letschte is d'r grosse John,*
    For seller gewiss is allemol do;
    'R halt des band Haus in repair;
    Un war â mit noch d'r Kutztown fair.

15. *'R is d'r Mann mit em grosse Hud,*
    Di Weibsleid sâje 'r guckt so gud;
    'R geht fanne her darrich Schlapp un Dreck,
    Un scharrt di gleene Kinner weck.

1. A cornet band meets in Mertztown
   And pays no rent;
   For the schoolhouse is given for their use
   At a dollar for a whole year.

2. There are twenty-four men
   Including Big John Poe;
   Some are big and some are fat,
   Some are Democrats and some are Whigs.

3. Kuder teaches with ability,
   He has a black beard;
   He teaches the band this evening
   For a dollar and thirty cents.

4. Billy Walbert blows bass
   And says that it's a serious matter;
   He blows bass and looks as cross
   As a cat at a big piece of cheese.

5. Allen Trexler, without joking
   Blows the second bass;
   He lost his notebook
   While going up the Noodletown hill.

6. Milton Schubert, the squire,
   He plays the baritone;
   He plays his horn in good style
   Though he still lacks hair on his chin.

7. Milton Warmkessel, my dear people,
   Sleeps already with a wife;
   He plays the B trombone
   With a face like a raccoon.

8. Denny Webb also belongs to the group,
   Now, boys, play, "Red, White and Blue."
   He plays tenor, oh, so softly;
   He likes cakes and wine.

9. Oliver Schubert, think of this,
   He also has a wife;
   He plays his horn up and down
   And says it is a deuced job.

10. Isaac Warmkessel, O my dear,
     Says the band members like beer;
     He plays alto for the band,
     "Yankee Doodle," "Dixie Land."

11. Then, too, is Frantz Keiser,
     The greatest laugher in the band;
     He sticks to his D-flat cornet
     Like a rooster to his nest.

12. Johnny Barley, not a dope,
     He plays the little drum;
     He is young and small
     But already tickles the girls.

13. Peter Walbert, well learned,
     Takes his club in hand;
     And beats the large drum—
     Peter Walbert is not dumb.

14. Last of all is Big John,
     Who is always present;
     He keeps the band house in repair;
     He was along to the Kutztown Fair.

15. He is the man with the big hat,
     The ladies say that he looks good;
     He leads the parade through mud and mire,
     And keeps the children out of the way.

Du denkscht es dut mich reien
(You Think That I Regret)

(Sung by Charles Christman at Strausstown, Berks County, 1937. Recorded by Thomas R. Brendle and William S. Troxell.)

This song of unrequited love appears to be indigenous, but we have been unable to trace its origin in the Pennsylvania Dutch region.

1. Du denkscht es dut mich rei - en Dass du mei Schetz-el wârscht; O nee, sell muscht net

denk - en Was du hascht haw-wich â.___

2. *Was du vun deinem Vadder hascht,*
   Das hawwich â vum meim;
   So scheene Maedche wie du bischt
   So hatts doch iwwerâl.

3. *So scheene Maedche wie du bischt*
   So hatts doch iwwerâl;
   So hocke alli Pârche voll,
   So hot man doch di Wâhl.

1. You think that I regret
   That you no longer are my sweetheart;
   Oh, no, don't think that at all—
   I'm as well off as you are.

2. What you've received from your father,
   I've received from mine;
   And girls as pretty as you
   Are found everywhere.

3. Girls as pretty as you
   Are found everywhere;
   The porches are full of them,
   And one may take his choice.

In einem kiehlen Grunde

(In Yonder Lovely Valley)

(Sung by Mrs. Elizabeth Hoffman at Deer Run, Carbon County, 1936.
Recorded by Thomas R. Brendle and William S. Troxell.)

This love song has long been a favorite among Pennsylvania
Dutch lovers. An illustration of the oral process by which it has
come down to us from preceding generations is in Edith M.
Thomas' book, *Mary at the Farm and Book of Recipes*, originally
published at Norristown in 1915. On p. 93 of the first edition
appears this sentence: "Then Elizabeth Schmidt played and sang
a pretty little German song called 'Meuhlen Rad,' meaning the
Mill Wheel, taught her by her mother." The author quotes a few
lines of the song with an English translation.

In Einem Kiehlen Grunde arrived in the Pennsylvania Dutch region about 1830. It had a wide circulation in the Lehigh Valley as borne out by the number of variants that we heard. It was composed in Germany in 1814 by Joseph von Eichendorff and Friedrich Glück.

Our English translation is from *Concordia,* a collection of four-part songs for male voices (Philadelphia: Schaefer and Koradi, 1872).

3. *Ich mecht als Schpielmann reisen,*
   Weit in di Welt hinaus,
   Un singen meine Weise
   Un gehn vun Haus zu Haus,
   Un gehn vun Haus zu Haus.

4. *Ich mecht als Reiter fliehen*
   Wuhin der dunckle Klaft;
   Im schtillen Freien liegen,
   Im Feld bei dunckler Nacht.

5. *Haer das Miehlrâd gehen
Ich weiss nicht was ich will;
Am liebschten mecht ich schterben
Dann werd es auf einmol schtill.*

1. In yonder lovely valley,
The wild mill-waters roar.
My love, who dwelt there, vanished,
I'll see her never more,
I'll see her never more.

2. She gave me a faithful promise,
Gave me a gold ring, too;
But soon her vow was broken;
Then broke my ring in two.

3. I fain would be a minstrel,
And wander far away;
And sing in town and hamlet
My brokenhearted lay.

4. Where I a knight, I'd hasten
To join the bloody fight;
And by the campfire couching,
Seek rest in gloomy night.

5. That clatt'ring mill wheel's echoes
Strike woe into my breast;
I wish that I were dying,
Then all would be at rest.

Susanna Cox

(Sung by Mrs. Jane Masonheimer at Egypt, Lehigh County, 1936. Recorded by Thomas R. Brendle and William S. Troxell.)

This dirge, or *Drauerlied* as it is termed in the Pennsylvania Dutch dialect, represents a type of indigenous ballad once common in the Pennsylvania Dutch countryside. Invariably it was sung to a religious melody in harmony with the heavy moralizing tone of the text.

Murders, hangings, and other local events of violence or tragedy were commemorated in ballads printed on penny broadsides. Often the balladist himself sought to profit from his own creation. Ballads were sold in printing shops and bookstores. They were also peddled around the countryside by itinerant folk minstrels who sang their wares to stimulate sales.

Though sometimes taking poetic license with the facts, Pennsylvania Dutch dirges followed a familiar pattern: they recounted actual events, attributed the cause of violence or tragic events to godlessness, and admonished the unfaithful to obey God.

Dating back to 1810, "Susanna Cox" was sung in High German, the language of the broadside. There were two versions; one mentioned Susanna's betrayer, and the other did not. The English translation was made about 1845 by one Ludwig Schtark, a wandering poet well known in the Pennsylvania Dutch countryside, according to Mrs. Masonheimer.

One of the best of the traditional Pennsylvania Dutch ballad singers, Mrs. Masonheimer sang "Susanna Cox" clear through from memory—a remarkable feat! She took the thirty-two stanzas in stride and stuck close to the High German text.

Ein Trauerlied enthaltend Die Geschichte der Susanna Cox, welche in Reading wegen Ermordung ihres Kindes higerichtet wurde.

1. *Ach merk-et auf, ihr Mensch-en all, Nun wird's Euch vor-ge - sagt___ Von ein-em sehr be- trübt-en Fall, Von ein - e arm-en Magd.___*

2. *Sie hatte lang in Oley gedient,*
   Wohl bei dem Jacob Gehr:
   Ihr Name war Susanna Cox,
   Wie ich ihn hab' gehört.

3. *Sie hatte gar kein'n Unterricht*
   In Welt un geistlich Recht,
   Sie wuszt' den Willen Gottes nicht,
   Und auch nicht sein Gesetz.

4. *Das ist uns Menschen wohlbekannt,*
    Und geht so in der Welt,
    Wer von der Schrift hat kein'n Verstand,
    Der thut was ihm gefällt.

5. *Ihr Nachbar, der uns ist bewuszt,*
    Sein Name, der war Mertz,
    Hat sie verführt durch Fleisches-Lust,
    In Unfall sie gestürtzt.

6. *Ein Beispiel, gleich von Adam's Zeit,*
    Wie uns die Bibel lehrt,
    Wie jene Schlang', der Satans-Geist,
    Die Eva hat verführt.

7. *Durch die Verführung kam der Tod*
    Von Anfang in die Welt;
    So ging es der Susanna Cox
    Durch diesen Mannsgesell.

8. *Er achtet' die Gesetze nicht,*
    Er hielte nur für Spott
    Was uns die heil'ge Schrift verbiet't
    Im siebenten Gebot.

9. *Als Eh'mann er sie hat verführt,*
    Und sie gebracht in Noth,
    Wird es bereuen, wohl zu spät,
    Einmal nach seinem Tod.

10. *Sie hat es nicht geoffenbart,*
    Sie schämt sich vor den Leut',
    Darum es Niemand sollt' erfahr'n
    Vor der Gebärungszeit.

11. *Im achtzehnhundert neunten Jahr,*
    Den vierzehnten Februar,
    Des Morgens früh um halb fünf Uhr,
    Sie's Kind zur Welt gebar.

12. *Da diese arme Sünderin*
    Verblendet war so fest,
    Hat sie ihr neugebornes Kind
    In die Ewigkeit versetzt.

13. *Sobald es aber war entdeckt,*
    Das dieser Mord gescheh'n,
    So war sie in Arrest gesetzt
    Und sollte es gesteh'n.

14. Ein' Jury ward sogleich bestellt,
    Sie sollte es nachseh'n;
    Was dieser armen Sünderin
    Für Urtheil sollt' gescheh'n.

15. Sie hielt wohl bei derselben an
    Und bat für sich um Gnad',
    Doch klagten sie sie schuldig an
    Des Mords im ersten Grad.

16. Man führte sie in's Courthaus h'nein
    Wo der Herr Richter Spayd,
    Wo sie ihr schrecklich Tods-Urtheil
    Mit Weinen angehört.

17. Ein Jeder kann nun denken wohl,
    Wie es ihr war zu Muth,
    Da sie auf'm Richtplatz sterben sollt',
    Bedauernswerthes Blut!

18. Die Todes-Warrant man bald schrieb
    Für die arme Magd,
    Und ward zum Gouverneur geschickt
    Nach der Lancaster-Stadt.

19. Ein'n Mann, der sehr mitleidig war,
    Den hat sie selbst geschickt
    Zum Gouverneur in jener Stadt,
    Der hat für sie gebitt't.

20. Allein für sie war kein Pardon,
    Gehangen muszt' sie sein,
    Den zehnten Tag im Inni schon,
    Die Welt zum Augenschein.

21. Die Todes-Warrant ward geschickt,
    Ihr vorgelesen gleich,
    Da hat sie brünstig Gott gebitt't
    Um Gnad im Himmelreich.

22. Sie ward in ihrem Buszestand
    Besucht von Geistlichkeit,
    Und sie hat ernstlich Busz' gethan
    Und ihre Sünd bereut.

23. Sie ward aus der Gefangenschaft
    Um elf Uhr ausgeführt,
    Dann ging es nach dem Hinrichsplatz,—
    Bedauernswerther Schritt!

24. *Sie warnte alle Menschen treu,*
   Besonders junge Leut',
   Und sprach: "Nehmt ein Exempel Euch
   An meinem Schicksal heut."

25. *Sie kniete auf die Erde hin*
   Und rief den Herren an,
   Er möcht' vergeben alle Sünd',
   Die sie allhier gethan.

26. *Ihr Weinen war mitleidenswerth,*
   Wie sie lag auf den Knie',
   Die Thränen fielen auf die Erd',
   Viel' weinten über sie.

27. *Sie sprach: "Ich geh' zur Ewigkeit*
   In einem Augenblick;
   Ach Gott! nimm auf mich in Dein Reich,
   Zerstosz' mich Sünd'rin nicht!"

28. *Nach Diesem ward sie hingericht't,—*
   Mitleidenswerther Schritt!
   Nach siebenzehn Minuten ist
   Schon Leib und Seel' getrennt.

29. *Nach ihrem Tode ward mit Fleisz*
   Von Doktor'n viel probirt,
   Zu bringen sie zum Leben gleich,
   Jedoch es war zu spät.

30. *Wer dieses Liedchen hat gemacht*
   Und erstlich neu gedicht't,
   Der hat den Jammer mitbetracht't,
   War selbst bei em Gericht.

31. *Ihr Menschen all' auf Erden, hört*
   Nur dieses beispiel an,
   Wenn Jemand ist so ungelehrt,
   Wie's ihm ergehen kann.

32. *Sie lebte nicht gar lang in Freud',*
   Als sie im Unfall war;
   Bracht' ihre ganze Lebenszeit
   Auf vierundzwanzig Jahr'.

(A New Dirge Containing the History of Susanna Cox, Who Was Executed at Reading, Pennsylvania, for the Murder of Her Own Child.)

1. All ye who feel for others' woes,
    With hearts compassionate,
   Oh, listen to the woeful tale
    Of a poor damsel's fate.

2. Susanna Cox, a country maid,
    Young and of beauty rare,
   In Oley, as a servant, had
    Long lived with Jacob Gehr.

3. Ne'er had she been instructed in
    The course of human law;
   Nor did she know God's Holy Word.
    Which strikes the world with awe.

4. For every one must be aware,
    From what he daily sees,
   That whom the Scriptures don't restrain
    They'll do just what they please.

5. Her neighbor, well remember we,
    Mertz was his second name;
   He recklessly led her astray
    By lust's unhallowed flame.

6. An instance, which, from Adam's time.
    The race of man defiled;
   When Satan in a serpent's garb
    His helpmate Eve beguiled.

7. Death followed in seduction's train
    When first the world began;
   This happened to Susanna Cox
    Through that unworthy man.

8. What in His seventh commandment God,
    What sacred laws forbid;
   He wantonly trod under foot
    And laughed and scoffed at it.

9. Though married, to seduce this girl
    He did not hesitate;
   He'll rue it when he's dead and gone
    But then 'twill be too late.

10. Fear of disgrace prevented her
    From making known her state,
    Which she by every means concealed,
    Despair did indicate.

11. The eighteen hundred and ninth year,
    At half past four at morn;
    The fourteenth day of February
    The unhappy child was born.

12. So far misled this sinner was,
    So much bewildered she,
    That she her helpless infant's soul
    Sent to eternity.

13. As soon as rumor did at her
    Point as a murderess;
    Off was she hurried to the jail
    Her foul deed to confess.

14. A jury then impanelled was
    To investigate the case,
    And to decide accordingly
    What sentence should take place.

15. Although she supplicated hard
    To pardon her great sin,
    Of murder in the first degree
    They guilty brought her in.

16. Ere long she in the courthouse was
    Arraigned before Judge Spayd,
    While shedding many scorching tears
    She learned her awful fate.

17. Each one may easily conceive
    What her own feelings were,
    To think, O lamentable case,
    What end awaited her.

18. Then to the Governor was sent,
    Who lived in Lancaster,
    The warrant which contained her doom
    For his own signature.

19. A gentleman who pitied her
    Had by herself been sent,
    To supplicate the Executive
    Law's rigor to suspend.

20. But she no pardon could obtain,
      For she was to be hung,
    As early as the tenth of June,
      To warn both old and young.

21. The warrant was returned and read
      In her dark prison cell,
    When fervently she prayed to God
      To save her soul from hell.

22. The clergy oft did visit her
      In her repentant state,
    For earnestly she penance did
      Preparing for her fate.

23. Just as the clock did strike eleven,
      She straightway from the jail
    Was led to where the gallows was.
      O lamentable tale!

24. She faithfully admonished all,
      Young folks especially,
    "O let," said she, "my dreadful fate,
      To you a warning be!"

25. She humbly knelt upon the ground
      And called in her distress
    Upon the Lord, to pardon all
      Her sins and wickedness.

26. So piteous her crying was,
      Her anguish and her fears,
    That every heart was moved,
      And every eye shed tears.

27. She said, "I in an instant
      Shall go to eternity;
    O God! for my Redeemer's sake,
      Turn not Thy face from me."

28. She then was made to undergo
      The punishment of death;
    Scarce seventeen minutes had expired
      When she resigned her breath.

29. Although without the least delay
      Their skill the doctors tried;
    To bring her back to life again
      Was to their art denied.

30. He that composed this little song
    In mem'ry of the event
    Was present at the closing scene
    And did the trial attend.

31. Let all who live upon this earth
    By her example see,
    What dire disgrace may those befall
    Who are raised illiterately.

32. Short was and sad her pilgrimage,
    Her youth mere drudgery;
    Her age but twenty years and four,
    Her exit—infamy.

Amish Hymns as Folk Music

by J. WILLIAM FREY

The hymns sung at the biweekly worship service of the Old Order Amish of Lancaster County (and by the Amish in their various settlements in Ohio, the Middle West, and the Far West) constitute a unique and fascinating study in both American and European folklore.

Religious hymns are usually considered to be songs of praise, odes, or lyrics, such as were written and set to music during the Protestant Reformation of the sixteenth century, mainly in Germany and Switzerland. These hymns were composed by giants like Martin Luther and his contemporaries and followers who strongly desired to introduce congregational hymn singing into the worship service. Thus the ordinary Protestant hymnal of today contains hymns and tunes written by church leaders in various periods of church history, limited to a fixed melody (in a few cases an alternate tune or two may be found), accompanied by a rather fixed or traditional harmony, and very often assigned to a specific musical key.

The Old Order Amish hymns, on the other hand, differ in a number of ways from the worship songs of Luther and his champions. In the first place, these hymns are not odes or lyrics, nor are very many of them hymns of praise per se. They are for the most part martyr hymns, written by prisoners awaiting the death sentence. Hence the story they tell is sorrowful, awe-inspiring, and a true reflection of the deepest sufferings of a folk. In this respect they have some points in common with the sadder Negro spirituals. Then, too, the Amish hymns originally were not songs but poems, often epics, relating the story of the awful tortures endured by the Amish forefathers. These were adapted to folk tunes, Gregorian chants, or other melodies current in the early sixteenth century.

Until recently these Amish hymn tunes were not written down, but passed orally from generation to generation. Recent recording and notation of these interesting hymns have been done by scholars, not by the Amish, who still teach the time-tested hymns to their children by word of mouth. Unlike scored hymn tunes, the melodies used by the Amish may vary slightly from region to region or even in the various church districts within any given area. Although they are basically the same among all Amish congregations, their unwritten nature permits a great deal of individual expression and emotion when they are sung. Of course, they are not relegated to any fixed musical key but always follow the pitch set by the leader of the hymn. Thus we see that these Amish hymns are in every sense of the word dynamic folk songs.

Folklorists have long since discarded the old German romanticists' notion that a folk song more or less rises up out of the folk in various places simultaneously like a silky mist. They have definitely concluded that a true folk song is written by some individual (in most cases now forgotten); then it is passed along from mouth to ear and literally "sung to pieces"; that is, it is altered in tune and text by each succeeding singer until the variations seem almost unlimited.

The texts of the Amish hymns have not changed throughout the centuries because they appeared in printed form as early as 1564. The melodies, however, and the execution of them in the worship service, most certainly have changed during the passing generations of Amish folk. What better examples of true, heartfelt, soul-filled folk music could be found anywhere in the world than these sad hymns sung by the Amish in Lancaster County?

In an excellent article entitled "The Strange Music of the Old Order Amish" in *The Musical Quarterly,* July 1945, George Pullen Jackson has shown through a laborious process of tune matching and tune tracing that many of the Amish hymns are based on old German folk-song prototypes, as found in the huge and authentic collection by Erk and Böhme. Jackson has found that not a few, surprisingly enough, have borrowed their tunes from old American folk melodies:

The brace of American folk tunes in this list is significant. It is well known to hymnologists of this land that our own folk melodies have been all but completely rejected from standardized hymnals of today. And here we come upon the bearers of a different and largely alien melodic and linguistic tradition who for some reason have recognized the beauty of "Ortonville," "Rockbridge," "Babe of Bethlehem," and other hymnal-ostracized melodies, have fitted them to German verse, and thus incorporated them with their own song body. The case is deeply interesting.

It is interesting also to find that *any* American tunes—whether folk airs or creations of the gospel-hymnsters—made their way into this otherwise so exclusive environment. My guess as to the reason of such adoption is that the Amish came to realize, let us say 75 or 100 years ago, that they were lyrically undernourished and that, despite their conviction that all change is bad, they let in these elusive tunes (which they couldn't bar out like telephones and watch chains) just to relieve their song hunger.

In regard to the European ancestry of some Amish hymn tunes, Jackson has discovered that in one particular instance the Amish in America still sing a derivative tune of a song that in various forms is now at least 1,100 years old!

A number of popular and illustrated articles concerning the Amish people and their way of life has appeared in recent years,[1] but only a very few serious research studies have been made on Amish history and sociology.[2] We possess far too little material on their Pennsylvania Dutch dialect and their church-service German,[3] their hymnology,[4] and their beliefs, superstitions, and folkways in general. They make an intensely interesting group to study, not merely for the transient big-city newspaper reporter who comes with a candid camera and without any knowledge of Pennsylvania Dutch, but for the student who appreciates the real value and charm of folklore, and for the linguist, the historian, the theologian, the sociologist, the agriculturist, and the anthropologist. It will be the purpose of this chapter to point out some of the outstanding features of the history, content, and music of Amish hymns. But first a word about the people themselves, their background, their dress, their customs, their work, their religion, and their speech. Even a casual perusal of the more striking features of these people will go a long way in helping to understand the real nature of their hymns.

Contrary to popular belief, the Old Order Amish are an offshoot of the large group of Plain Sect people known as the Mennonites. At the time of the Protestant Reformation, when Luther, Zwingli, and Calvin were holding sway in Germany, Switzerland, and France respectively, there was a smaller group of reformers known as the Anabaptists *(Wiedertäufer)*, who felt that to break with the Roman Catholic church was to go all the way. They taught that all worldliness was wicked and the work of the devil, that one should lead a very plain, austere, and pious life after the manner described by St. Paul in his various epistles to the Middle Eastern churches, and that one should refuse to bear arms in the military. Their adherence to these basic beliefs, strict or lax throughout the centuries, has caused them undue persecution and suffering. Their most outstanding leader was Menno Simons (1492-1559), a former Catholic priest who renounced his first faith in 1536 and was baptized into the new teaching. These people believed in rebaptism because they felt that baptism into the faith should be reserved for early adulthood rather than given during infancy, since the individual cannot be intelligently sincere about the rite unless he can comprehend its meaning. They followed a rather rigid and literal interpretation of Paul's teachings as to matters of dress, speech, and faith. Thus the beard was encouraged, but the upper lip had to be shaved since the mustache was vain and worldly and flaunted by the military. A woman was not pious with her head bared, hence the wearing of the bonnet, which to this day is the common identification of all Plain Sects, liberal and conservative.

The followers of Menno Simons were called Mennonites (or Mennonists or *Mennischte*). They accepted the Dortrecht Confession (council held in Holland in 1632) after the death of their leader. Article 17 of the Confession strictly defines the so-called *Meidung* (the complete avoidance or shunning of an erring member), a ban that had been practiced by the early Mennonites, but about which they had grown lax through the years. A young bishop in the Mennonite church, named Jacob Amman (or Ammon), held to the strictest enforcement of the *Meidung,* and his dogmatic insistence upon its complete recognition and observance led to an important schism in the church. After much controversy, Amman and his followers broke away from the original group. Later they called themselves *Amisch* after his name, and today they represent the most orthodox of the Mennonite groups. They still practice the *Meidung;* a sinful brother or sister must eat at a separate table, have no conversation with friends or members of the family, and must ultimately do severe penance before the congregation to be readmitted to the church. It is interesting that the very thing that caused the original split in the early Mennonite church still persists today among the Amish as strongly as ever.

The first Amish to come to America probably arrived around 1714, and by 1727 Amish names began appearing frequently on the passenger lists. They settled in eastern Pennsylvania and have made a virtual paradise of farmland in Lancaster County. Some have moved to the Middle West and the Far West, more recently to St. Mary's County, Maryland. In all these places they have gained an outstanding reputation for their excellent farming, their neat, clean buildings, and, above all, their honest business dealings. The Old Order Amish are often called the House Amish because they hold services in the various homes of congregational members. In the Morgantown area there is a Church Amish group that holds services in a meetinghouse and even permits the driving of automobiles. Essentially, however, all Amish groups are alike in their thinking.

Social and religious behavior of the Amish is regulated by their interpretations of biblical precepts relating to discipline, unity, humility, nonresistance, adult baptism, unequal tie with non-believers, and, above all, nonconformity. Strong are the convictions of the Amishman, but he does not carry on missionary work. He does not force his views on anyone, nor does he approve of mixed marriages. The Amishman is peace-loving and refuses to bear arms, and only very rarely does he even resort to the law to defend his rights.

Today the whole picture of the Amishman can be obtained and understood in the light of his preference for nonconformity to worldly ways. It determines his plain garb, hooks and eyes, broad-fall trousers, broad-brimmed hat, and beard. It causes him to shun modern appliances and practices such as drinking intoxicants, smoking cigarettes, dances, card parties, movies, theaters, amusement parks, outdoor shows and centers of entertainment, radios, telephones, electricity in the house, modern plumbing, automobiles, tractors for plowing in the field, photographs or any other likeness, jewelry, cosmetics, perfume. In the home there are no curtains, wall pictures, decorative furnishings, or upholstered suites.

The Amish do not join political groups, community organizations, civic or social clubs, coöperatives, or government farmers-aid projects. Nor do they carry insurance. They have an agreement among themselves that affords them ample protection against loss from property damage; if a man's barn burns down, for instance, he bears only one-fourth of the cost toward a new barn. His Amish neighbors voluntarily raise his new barn in a single day, and this communal effort is crowned with an elaborate feast.

Among the Amish poverty is virtually unknown. At death they leave a substantial heritage to descendants, the farm alone being worth as high as $600 to $800 per acre. Their children attend school for only eight years, then follow the typical Amish life. Travel is by buggy—the open-top runabout for the young un-married men, the closed carriage for the family. In cases of necessity and emergency, the Amishman will gladly pay a neighbor to drive him to the city in a car. When visiting Amish settlements in distant cities, he will not hesitate to travel Pullman. Home medical cures are generally practiced, but when an illness is serious or an operation is necessary, the Amish desire only the best: a private room, special nurses, the most skilled surgeon. All bills, just as all purchases, are paid in cash on the line.

In keeping with their plain living, they have simple tastes in entertainment, such as Sunday night "singings" for young people, barn-raisings, quilting parties, a few religious holidays, weddings, and buggy racing on the side roads. Of course there is backsliding among some youthful Amishmen who smoke, play the guitar, mandolin, or harmonica, dance (chiefly clog and square dances), attend an occasional movie, play hillbilly records on the sly, and even drink. The youth problem among the Amish is, and always has been, serious, yet their life goes on very much as it always has. They are quite satisfied with their philosophy of *unser Sart Leit* (our kind of people). The Amishman may be wild and full of radical ideas in his youth, but when he grows older he settles down and forgets the reforms he had dreamed about in his adolescence. He has no thought of forsaking the fold and forfeiting the economic security promised him upon his early marriage.

Prosperous and frugal, these people continue buying additional land to keep the clan and the church districts close together. Although the average Amish grandfather at age fifty-five to sixty has forty grandchildren, everyone in the fold seems well provided for.

Additional evidence of the doctrine of nonconformity is the fact that the Amish use Pennsylvania Dutch exclusively in conversation among themselves. Anyone who has delved into the field of Pennsylvania Dutch soon discovers that he has actually three languages to contend with: the Pennsylvania Dutch (or German) dialect, which resembles Palatine German folk speech despite all exterior influences that have come in contact with it since 1683, the year of arrival of the first Pennsylvania Germans;[5] High German —that is, American High German, or more especially the brand spoken in this country during the last century and maintained in Pennsylvania chiefly through the then flourishing German press and the Lutheran and Reformed pulpits; and American English. It does not require a linguistic research expert, however, to discover this interesting philological trinity of the Pennsylvania Dutch. Naïve outsiders have frequently dismissed the matter of the Pennsylvania Dutch dialect by describing it simply as "garbled English in the mouths of ignorant farmers who speak with a heavy Dutch accent"! And the speakers of Pennsylvania Dutch themselves are well aware of their own bilingualism, though at times they are not quite sure whether a word or idiom is wholly German or English or a combination of both. Today most Pennsylvania Dutchmen cannot be called trilingual because American High German is known to them only passively; they have heard sermons or speeches in it or heard their parents read it aloud from the German Bible and hymnals and prayer books. They can no longer converse in any sort of German, however, except perhaps to repeat a few familiar scriptural passages.

The Old Order Amish are the important exception to this statement concerning trilingualism among the Pennsylvania Dutch. Here is one religious and linguistic group that can speak three somewhat distinctive yet intermixed tongues: Amish Pennsylvania Dutch, Amish High German, and Pennsylvania Dutch English. I speak of "Amish" Pennsylvania Dutch because their dialect has some unique characteristics, although in general it is typical of the whole region of "western" Pennsylvania Dutch dialects—that is, of Lancaster and York counties as opposed to the "eastern" variety found in Bucks, Northampton, Lehigh, and Berks counties. Amish High German is a survival from German-preaching days in Pennsylvania churches during the last century, but again there are some peculiarities in pronunciation that are typically Amish.

The English used by the Amish—this language is employed only on "forced" occasions such as talking with non-Amish in towns and cities, or in the public schools—has all the earmarks of the type of speech found among any other Pennsylvania Dutch group. It can be described briefly as American English built on a framework of Pennsylvania Dutch language patterns and interjected continually with whole or part loan-translations from the dialect. It is commonly believed in Lancaster County that the Amish do not speak English with as "Dutchified" an accent as do their Mennonite brethren or other Pennsylvania Dutch groups who may or may not speak the dialect. In all probability this is true because Amish children do not speak or even hear English until they enter school. Thus they avoid picking up much incorrect grammar and a thick accent. In school they learn a pure English, actually as a foreign language.

It might be well to say a word about the general features of the type of Pennsylvania Dutch and High German that the Amish speak, as their language is an integral part of their secular life, their religious life, and their hymnology. At the outset, I wish to point out the occasions when the Amish use their dialect and when their High German. The former is employed for all normal everyday conversation with members of the household, friends, and other Amish and Plain sectarians (such as Mennonites and Dunkers) whose acquaintances has or has not already been made; at meetings, congregational gatherings, and in the devotional service for secular announcements.

Amish High German is used mainly for preaching and praying. One can see at once that an Amishman speaks far less High German than Pennsylvania Dutch, and if he never holds a church office he may virtually never discourse in High German, except to quote from the Bible at home. On the other hand, the church officers must be fairly well versed in the Scriptures (largely in the New Testament and Psalms) and be able to read long passages aloud, offer "printed" prayers, and deliver lengthy sermons in High German. Two factors help preserve the active use of High German among all the Amish who are not church officers. First, Amish children receive some instruction in High German in the elementary school: the teacher may be asked by the congregation to teach the elements of reading and pronunciation during the lunch hour or at some other time outside the regular school hours; and the Amish bishop teaches the more advanced German of the Scriptures to school children. Second, all the Amish—men, women, and children—sing hymns in High German at least twenty-six times a year, as preaching service is held every other Sunday in different homes. Special occasions such as weddings, funerals, and the Sunday night singings for the young people help to keep alive the German language of the old or "slow" hymns and the new or "fast" tunes.

At the regular fortnightly *G'mee* (church service), the High German sermons, intermixed with dialect, consist largely of memorized scriptural passages and lengthy elaborations upon them. These passages are taken almost entirely from *'s Teschdement* (the New Testament) or the Book of Psalms; the Old Testament and apocryphal books are not read at a worship service. (The word *Biwwel* or *Biewel* [German *Bibel*] in the Amish dialect includes both the Old and New Testaments and the Apocrypha.) The prayers offered by the ministers during the service are lengthy liturgical prayers read from a small devotional book called *Christenflicht* (Christian Duty). This collection of prayers for different occasions and of instructions for the Christian life was first printed in this country in 1745.

Probably the most striking feature of Amish High German is that all the unstressed endings that have been weakened or dropped entirely in the dialect are still completely retained. The influence of scriptural German and hymn singing is very apparent here. Thus the adjective *deine* (your), for example, is simply *dei* in Amish Pennsylvania Dutch, but keeps its full pronunciation "dine-ay" in Amish High German. The orthographic symbols *ö* and *ü* in the German text are not pronounced with any rounding of the lips by the Amish, as they are in modern standard German. Thus, *fröhlich* (joyous) is pronounced "fray-lich," and *Füsse* (feet) is pronounced "feesa." The diphthongs *eu* and *äu* are consistently pronounced like "ei" in English "height"; thus, *Freud* (joy) is pronounced "fright" and *Häuser* (houses) is "heiser." All these peculiar pronunciations, however, are simply the regular American-German pronunciations that were prevalent in the eighteenth and nineteenth centuries among Germans in Pennsylvania. The *r* is an interesting case. The Amish have a strong tendency to pronounce the *r* in the American fashion; this is especially true in hymn singing. In fact, the Amish use this same type of *r* in their Pennsylvania Dutch to a greater extent than is heard in the eastern counties. In all probability the encroachment of strong American English environs is responsible for this linguistic situation.

It might be well to add at this point a word about the number of English loan-words used by the Amish. In their Pennsylvania Dutch they employ a great many (as is the case for the dialect on the whole), although in most of the popular and unsympathetic accounts of Pennsylvania Dutch the percentage of English loan-words is always grossly exaggerated. Amish High German, on the other hand, contains virtually no English words. There may be a few loan-translations or loan-constructions here and there, but the very nature of the subject excludes the use of borrowed words. At one of the services that I attended, only one English word was used during the entire four hours! It was the verb *kultivate-a* (to cultivate), a very expressive and highly important term to farmers.

In preaching, Amish ministers elaborate on the Gospel lesson in a combination of High German and dialect. They repeat memorized passages time and again and quote familiar verses such as the Twenty-third Psalm and John 3:16. Among the Old Order Amish, worship services are held biweekly and are rotated among the homes of the various members of a particular church district (called *Keer* in the dialect). Backless wooden benches are arranged for the congregation, whose members are seated in four separate groups: married men, married women, unmarried men, unmarried girls. A dinner of "schnitz" pies, pickles, cold cuts, beets, coffee, jelly, and bread is consumed by the congregation at the close of the service. The service itself averages about four hours, running in somewhat the following order: (1) sometime after 8 A.M. the congregation is seated, and the members sing a hymn or two; (2) after this, the ministers come from the *Abroot,* (council meeting) in another room of the house, and the *Lobg'sang* (Hymn of Praise) is sung; (3) one of the ministers rises and delivers the first discourse, from a half hour to an hour long, at the end of which he calls upon the people to pray; (4) all kneel and pray silently; (5) after arising, all remain standing while the *Aarmediener* (deacon) reads the Scripture lesson for the day; (6) members resume their seats and the main sermon, an hour or more in length, is delivered; (7) near the end of his sermon the minister sits down, and at its conclusion he invites the other ministers to give *Zeignis* (testimony), a brief statement of approval of what has been said; (8) here follows a lengthy prayer read from the *Christenpflicht;* (9) at the conclusion of the prayer the benediction is pronounced and there follows a short business meeting for church members only.

Sermons may be delivered with the "pulpit intonation" ascribed to ministers in general, but among the Amish they are often either "auctioneered" or chanted. By an "auctioneering intonation" I mean the type found among Pennsylvania Dutch auctioneers who raise their voices to a rather high pitch at the end of each phrase or unit clause. When a sermon is chanted, it is usually somewhat softer and generally follows the second Gregorian tone. An example of this sort of sermon chanting, with the phrase ending on the mediation, may be shown on the following four-line stave:

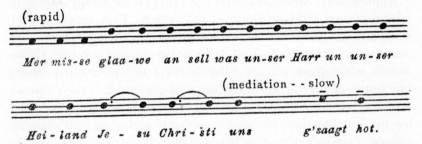

We must believe in that which our Lord and Savior Jesus Christ has told us.

Often an afterthought or repeated phrase is added in the mediation:

Yes, that is what He said.

And a thought may often end thus:

Yes, I believe that is right.

Sometimes there is a break in the midst of chanting the sermon, and the minister assumes again his natural voice at speaking pitch.

As noted previously, the Amish sing German hymns at their regular worship services, on special occasions, and at Sunday evening singings. All singing is done *a cappella,* as the use of musical instruments in the home or church service is strictly forbidden. The German hymns are of two types: the traditional slow tunes and the newer fast tunes. The latter are familiar to many Protestant groups and often are German versions set to widely popular hymn tunes, as for example: *Wo ist Jesus, mein Verlangen?* ("What a Friend We Have in Jesus"), *Du unbegreiflich höchstes Gut* ("Sweet Hour of Prayer"), *Herr Jesu Christ, dich zu uns wend* ("He Leadeth Me"). These newer tunes have a regular rhythm and can be represented in musical notation by systematic divisions through measures each having an equal number of counts or beats.

The slow tunes are by far the more interesting. They have their origin in the Gregorian chant or plain song, which was probably the only form of church music in existence down to the Reformation. They are practically impossible to represent by musical notation with regular divisions, since the rhythm of Gregorian chants is not subject to the laws of modern measure—that is, with uniform isochronous measures. It is curious that these tunes (tones or modes), originally composed for the singing of liturgical Latin and based on the Latin accent should have been adapted by the early Amish martyrs to their own peculiar Swiss-German dialect. It is also something of a miracle that these tunes have been passed down among the Amish from generation to generation for more than 250 years solely from mouth to ear! The only attempt to collect and transcribe all of the better-known hymns is the recent book by Joseph W. Yoder, *Amische Lieder,* containing some 115 pages of slow tunes, wedding songs, fast tunes, and rudiments of music designed to teach unaccompanied singing by shaped notes. Yoder has attempted to note down the slow tunes with measures of unequal count, but unfortunately no explanation of how these hymns are to be sung is given. I wish to acknowledge my indebtedness to him for permission to adapt scores from *Amische Lieder* for use in this chapter.

In "The Old Order Amish, Their Hymns and Hymn Tunes," published in *The Journal of American Folklore* in 1939, John

Umble told of the history and content of the Amish hymns and, to a slight degree, something about how they are sung: "The tunes of some of these hymns are reminiscent of the Gregorian chant; others, if they are speeded up somewhat, bear a close resemblance to German folk tunes." In this connection, it is noted that recordings of perhaps a dozen Amish hymns have been made and filed in the Archive of American Folk Song in the Library of Congress.

The texts to these old hymns are found in the Amish hymnal, the *Ausbund,* the first American edition of which was printed in 1742 in Germantown by Christopher Sauer. The fast tunes are contained in the *Unpartheyisches Gesang-Buch* (Nondenominational Songbook), the first edition of which was published in Lancaster in 1804.

At the congregational service, each line of a hymn is begun by a *Vorsenger* or *Vorschtimmer,* who sets the pitch by singing the first syllable of the line alone. On the second syllable the whole group joins in, all in unison, since harmonizing is not done by the Amish. The last syllable of a line is cut short abruptly, and there is a brief pause until the *Vorschtimmer* begins the next line alone, and so on. The hymns move along at an extremely slow rate, and everyone seems to know or feel where the succeeding note is. Although we do not speak of division into bars of this type of music, there is a noticeable pulse or beat between phrases, and the thesis and arsis of every line are quite clearly defined. Those who sing out of tune are younger members who have not yet mastered the melodies, or persons who have no musical ear. The *Vorschtimmer* need not be one special person; after a period of silence between hymns, any member of the congregation, if moved by the Spirit, may announce the number of a hymn and proceed to commence each line, thus setting the pitch.

Walter E. Yoder of Goshen College, who has made musical transcriptions of Amish hymns, said: ". . . when one hears an Amish congregation sing these tunes, he notes that there is freedom in the interpretation of the melody. One hears passing notes and embellishments in some voices, not all. This practice, no doubt, is a carry-over from the ancient method of singing plain song chants."[6] Joseph W. Yoder gave the following directions for the singing of the hymns:

All the notes between two consecutive bars are sung to one syllable. This necessitates slurring throughout the entire piece, and as slurring is one of the characteristics of these tunes, the marks indicating slurs are omitted, but understood. The whole notes represent a sustaining of the voice almost as long as a whole note in 2/2 time; the half note somewhat shorter; and the quarter note a quick swing of the voice, a mere touch of the voice to that note; and the double notes represent a rather long sustaining of the voice. A slight stress of the voice on the first part of each syllable is probably as near to the accent as we can come, as there is little if any accent.[7]

To give the reader an idea of this interesting music, the first stanza of the *Lobg'sang* is presented below. Remember that the division into bars does not indicate an equal number of counts in each measure in the conventional manner. It merely shows a sort of break between each musical syllable or phrase. At normal rate, it takes about thirty seconds to sing any one of these lines.

'S Lobg'sang
(The Hymn of Praise)

Library of Congress 1   Ausbund 131

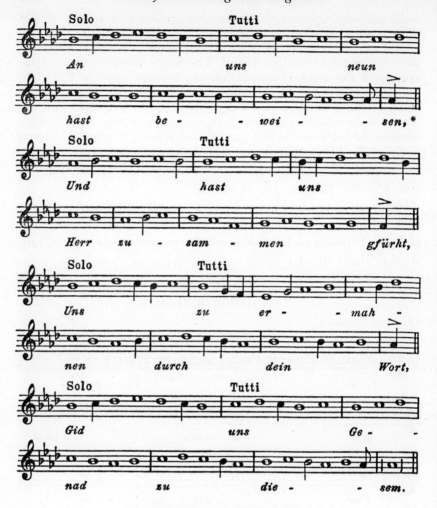

An uns neun

hast be - - wei - - sen,*

Und hast uns

Herr zu - sam - men gfürht,

Uns zu er - - mah -

nen durch dein Wort,

Gid uns Ge - -

nad zu die - - sem.

O, God, Father, we praise Thee,
And extol Thy many blessings;
That Thou hast, O Lord, proved
Thyself again so merciful to us;
And hast brought us together, Lord,
To exhort us through Thy word;
Grant us Thy mercy.

Joseph W. Yoder's aim in making his collection *Amische Lieder* was not to serve the ends of folklorists or musicians but merely to help preserve the music among and for the Amish themselves.

* Read: *bewiesen.* The error is copied here just as it appears in the *Ausbund.*

Therefore he presented all his tunes in the so-called "seven-shaped" notation, the famous Yankee-invented musical alphabet used for more than one hundred years by various sects in the American countryside from Pennsylvania southward and westward.

Yoder's task in recording these tunes was a hard one. Putting a simple melody into notes is, of course, not too difficult, but these were by no means simple melodies.

Amish reading in English is limited to a few popular county weeklies and farm journals. The Amish are most familiar with the German Bible (Luther's translation); the afore-mentioned prayer book, *Christenpflicht;* the *Ausbund,* which they always refer to as *'s dick Buch* (the thick book); and the *Unpartheyisches Gesang-Buch,* commonly called *'s dinn Bichli* (the little thin book). A few Amish in Lancaster County know, or know of, the little Amish paper in the German language, *Herold der Wahrheit* (Herald of Truth), published by the Mennonite Publishing House at Scottdale. Not a few of the Amish are familiar with and have read some portions of the famous *Martyrs' Mirror,* the tragic tale of Christian martyrdom and more than a century of Anabaptist persecution.

The *Ausbund,* however, is of chief interest in studying Amish hymnology because it contains the texts to the slow tunes. The nucleus of this book consists of a group of fifty-one hymns written by a number of Anabaptist prisoners from southern Germany and Switzerland who had been imprisoned for their faith between 1535 and 1537 in a castle in Passau, Bavaria; some of the prisoners were later put to death. About half of this original group of hymns was the contribution of two men, Hans Petz and Michael Schneider; the authorship of the rest is unknown. Being martyr hymns, written by condemned prisoners, one would naturally expect them to be permeated with a spirit of deep humiliation and an overwhelming sense of dependence upon God their deliverer. The dominant tone running through all of them is one of great sorrow and deep loneliness, of protest against the world of wickedness that puts forth every effort to crush the righteous. There is, however, no despair, but rather triumph and an unspeakable conviction that God will not forsake his own but lead them through sorrow and tribulation to everlasting life.

Hymn 125, for example, expresses the prevailing conviction that the world is hopelessly given over to corruption and sin:

> *Wo kommt das her O JEsu Christ,*
> *Dass all Welt so voll Falschheit ist?*
> *Wer jetzt nicht will das widerspiel,*
> *Derselbig wird verachtet viel.*
>
> *Gold, Silber, Geld und grosses Gut,*
> *Nur Geitz, hoch Pracht und Ubermuth,*
> *Ist jetzund wehrt auf dieser Erd,*
> *Der Fromm wird unbracht mit dem Schwerdt.*
>
> Whence cometh, O Jesus Christ,
> That all the world is so full of falsehood?
> He who will not combat it
> Will be much despised.
>
> Gold, silver, money, and worldly goods,
> Only avarice, splendor, and pride,
> Are of value on this earth;
> A pious man is executed by the sword.

The hymn continues in this vein through seventy-one stanzas, in the last of which God is praised for having sent a Savior to cleanse man of his sins. Many more of the hymns go on at great length about the wickedness of worldliness. It is small wonder then that humility is an Amish virtue, and pride is considered the cardinal sin. Each time an Amishman sings these hymns he reminds himself that it is worldly and sinful to be proud, to have any likeness made of himself, to have a whipsocket or dashboard on his buggy, or to display or even own any fancy gadgets on his farm.

Hymn 102 is typical of the group of hymns concerned with Christian doctrine. These hymns deal with the articles of the Nicene Creed, with love, infant baptism, communion, and the Trinity. In No. 102 we are told of all the good things and institutions that God has provided for man, as well as the great teachings of St. Paul, which the Amish strive to follow almost to the letter. In stanza 10 of this hymn, there is a reference to the characteristic beard which every Amishman must grow, if not upon joining the church, then without fail upon getting married:

> *Ein theil vom Haar hat er geschorn,*
> *Auf seinem Kopff ein Platte,*
> *Welches doch Gott mit hellem Wort*
> *Den Menschen hat verbotten.*
> *Den Bart solt er auch nicht abschern,*
> *Den thut er nicht behalten.*
> *Machts widerspiel, wie er nur will,*
> *Sagt, es thut Gott gefallen.*

> He sheared a part of his hair,
> And left on his head a tonsure,
> Which thing God had quite clearly
> Forbidden man to do.
> Nor should he shave his beard,
> Such a one He will not keep.
> If he opposes worldliness, as He wills,
> Why, then, God will be pleased.

Hymn 67 deals with regeneration and sets forth, in stanza 7, the essential religious practice of foot washing, which always accompanies the Amish *Grooss-G'mee* (communion service) twice a year:

> *Ein solcher mag recht werden gtaufft,*
> *Wenn er ist neu gebohren,*
> *Durch Christi Blut erlösst und kaufft,*
> *Sonst war es all's verlohren.*
> *Beym Brodbrechen wäscht man die füss,*
> *Wie Christus seine Jünger hiess*
> *Die Lieb einander reichen.*
> *Man wird darbey erkennen frey,*
> *Welches das Häufflein Christi sey,*
> *Lieb ist das einig Zeichen.*

> Such a one may be rightly baptized,
> When he is born anew,
> Redeemed and bought by Christ's blood,
> Or else all would be lost.
> At the breaking of bread there shall be foot washing,
> As Christ called upon His disciples
> To extend their love to one another.
> Through that, one can easily recognize
> Who make up Christ's little band,
> For love is the only true sign.

Of the 140 hymns in the *Ausbund* the most sorrowful are those which were written by the early Anabaptist leaders who later suffered martyrdom. Jörig Blaurock, Felix Mantzen, Hanss Hut, and John Huss, the pre-Reformation martyr of Bohemia, were among the contributors. A typical martyr hymn is No. 11, the detailed account of Jörg Wagner, who was burned at the stake in 1527. The first stanza introduces the story with the admonition that the true Christian must inevitably suffer persecution; the story proper is begun with the second stanza. In the next three, Jörg's severest test of his faith comes with the thought of leaving his family. Then in stanza 6 comes the usual attempt on the part of the ecclesiastical authorities to secure a recantation from the prospective martyr:

> *Zween Baarfüss-mönch in grauen Kleid,*
> *Jörg Wagner trösten in seim Leyd,*
> *Sie wolten ihn bekehren.*
> *Er wiess sie in ihr Klösterlein,*
> *Ihr Red wolt er nicht hören.*

> Two barefoot monks clad in gray,
> Consoled George Wagner in his suffering;
> They wanted to convert him.
> He sent them back to their cloister,
> Did not care to listen to their chatter.

But Jörg Wagner remains a true Mennonite, opposed to the Catholic beliefs, such as auricular confession, baptism, communion, and mass. In these things he does not believe. So, in spite of family ties and the knowledge of a terrible death at the stake, Wagner takes the consequences (stanza 26):

> *Man flocht ihn auf ein Leiter hart,*
> *Das Holtz und Stroh anzündet ward,*
> *Jetzt ward das Lachen theuer.*
> *Jesus, Jesus, zum virten mahl,*
> *Rieff er laut aus dem Feuer.*

> They bound him tightly to the rack;
> Wood and straw were set afire;
> But now their laughter was costly.
> "Jesus, Jesus," for the fourth time
> Did he call out loudly from the fire.

In stanza 27 we find a fitting close to the hymn:

> *Elias thut die Wahrheit sagen,*
> *Dass er in eim feurigen Wagen*
> *Fuhr in das Paradeise:*
> *So bitten wir den Heiligen Geist,*
> *Dass er uns unterweise.*

> Elias has spoken the truth,
> That he, in a fiery chariot,
> Would ride to Paradise.
> And so we bid the Holy Ghost
> To instruct us too.

In addition to the fifty-one hymns from the Swiss brethren and the martyr hymns already referred to, eleven were translated from the Dutch hymnbook *Het Offer des Heeren* (1563). A few were sung to original melodies, but nearly all of them were set to the popular religious and secular tunes of the day. Among those of a religious nature was the well-known Lutheran hymn *Ein feste Burg ist unser Gott,* which furnishes the melody for a number of the Amish hymns. The majority, as the *Ausbund* itself often suggests at the head of a hymn, and as Jackson has so ably shown in his tune-matching tables, was based on secular and popular folk songs. The most popular air, judging from the number of hymns that were set to it, seems to have been "By the Waters of Babylon." Also popular were: "A Flower in the Meadow," "I Stood in the Morning," "Lovely as a Rose," "The Maid of Britannia" (tune for "The Bride of Christ"), "The Forest Leaves Have Fallen" (tune for No. 27, which tells of the death of eighteen martyrs), "There Was a Time," "As You Sing to the King of Hungary," and "I Saw the Lord of Falkenstein." Sometimes some rather humorous combinations were made. The Fifty-fourth Psalm is sung to the tune of "In the Dawn I Heard the Cock Crow," and the death story of a martyr who was burned at the stake follows the tune of "There Went a Maiden with a Jug"!

The *Ausbund* went through numerous editions during the seventeenth and eighteenth centuries. The earliest we know of, one published in 1564, appeared without the name of the publisher to avoid confiscation as Anabaptist literature. Very few copies from the sixteenth and seventeenth centuries, therefore, have been preserved. As late as 1692 the government of Bern Canton placed the book on the proscribed list and ordered its confiscation when found.

The Palatines and Swiss brought this book with them to Pennsylvania in the early eighteenth century. It went through many American editions, not a few printed by the famous Sauer in Germantown. The book is still used by the Amish, but it was discarded by the Mennonites before the close of the eighteenth century. In the American editions the well-known Haslibacher Hymn, not found in the European editions, has been added. It is an old martyr hymn about Hans Haslibach of Bern Canton who was beheaded for his faith in 1571. In this hymn, No. 140, Haslibach prophesies that three signs would indicate to the bystanders his innocence at the time of his beheading: his head would jump back into his hat and laugh out loud, the sun would turn red, and the town well would run blood; all three predictions were fulfilled, according to the hymn. This hymn with its belief in the miraculous is still sung among the Old Order Amish, though not at their regular services, but strangely enough at such festive occasions as weddings and social gatherings. In an appendix to the American editions there also appear the following: a confession of faith; a brief account of the persecutions in Zürich, 1635-45, containing a number of Swiss names nearly all of which can be duplicated today among the Mennonites of Pennsylvania, such as Gut, Miller, Landis, Huber, Bachman, Schneider, Hess, Gochenauer, Weber, Baumgartner, and Schnebly; and six anonymous "beautiful spiritual hymns" which, curiously enough, contain the element of joy much more than is found elsewhere in the collection. The sixth hymn of this group, composed in 1540, is the interesting thirty-six-stanza tale of three Christian brothers who left Thessalonica to wander into the Upper Palatinate in search of their Swiss brethren, whom they joyously find.

The old *Ausbund* has never been revised, merely reprinted. The same archaic dialect (frequently the same as Amish Pennsylvania Dutch of today), spelling, and typographic errors in all the early editions have thus been perpetuated to the present day. The Old Order Amish would no more consider tampering with their *Aus-*

bund than revising the Bible. It is probably the oldest hymnbook in use in a Christian church anywhere in the world.

At social gatherings, such as on the afternoon and evening of wedding days, or at the Sunday evening singings, the Amish use an entirely different type of music. Seldom are the slow tunes employed on these occasions, but the hymns and songs are sung to what the Amish describe as the fast tunes. The book generally used for this purpose is the *Unpartheyisches Gesang-Buch* or *dinn Bichli*. Most of the singing is done in German, although now and then an English hymn or part of a hymn is used. In many instances the German text is simply set to the tune of a familiar English hymn. Thus, "Come, Thou Fount of Every Blessing" is rendered by

> *Jesu, Jesu, Brunn des Lebens,*
> *Stell, ach stell dich bei uns ein.*
>
> Jesus, Jesus, Source of all life,
> Stand, oh, stand by us now.

To the familiar tune of "What a Friend We Have in Jesus" are set the equally expressive words:

> *Wo ist Jesus, mein Verlangen,*
> *Mein geliebter Herr und Freund?*
>
> Where is Jesus, my desire.
> My beloved Lord and Friend?

"Jesus, Lover of My Soul" is *In der stillen Einsamkeit, Findest du mein Lob bereit* (In the peace of loneliness, Thou wilt find me ever ready to praise Thee); "Sweet Hour of Prayer" is the tune for *Du unbegreiflich höchstes Gut, An welchem klebt mein Herz und Muth* (Thou inconceivably wonderful blessing, To which my heart and my courage cling); "Home Sweet Home" forms the melody for *Mein Herz! sei zufrieden, betrübe dich nicht* (O heart of mine, be content and trouble not); the lively hymn "From Greenland's Icy Mountains" has an equally joyful counterpart in *Ermuntert euch ihr Frommen! Zeigt euer Lampen Schein* (Awake, ye pious Christians, And show the light of your lamps!); to the tune of "He

Leadeth Me" we find the words *Herr Jesu Christ, dich zu uns wend, Den Heil'gen Geist du zu uns send* (Lord Jesus Christ, please turn to us, And send us the Holy Ghost); "All Hail the Power of Jesus' Name" furnishes the tune for *Nun sich der Tag geendet hat, Und keine Sonn mehr scheint* (Now that the day has ended, And the sun shines no longer); and the Christmas hymn "Joy to the World" lends a fitting melody to *Mein Gott des Herz ich bringe dir, Zur Gabe und Geschenk* (My God, this heart I bring to Thee, As my offering and my gift). The famous Reformation hymn *Nun danket alle Gott* ("Now Thank We All Our God") remains the same in text but its tune differs slightly in the last four bars. Bachman points out one interesting instance in which the Amish use a portion of one of the hymns from the *Ausbund* (No. 125, stanzas 57-61), which they sing to the tune of "Beulah Land." After each stanza of this adapted version, the refrain of "Beulah Land" is sung in English. The first of the five stanzas may be found on page 155.

The favorite child's hymn "Jesus Loves Me" has as its first part the famous German version of "Now I Lay Me Down to Sleep," followed by a refrain that is a literal translation of the English. Here is the complete text as recorded by Bachman:

> *Müde bin ich, geh' zu Ruh,*
> *Schliesse meine Augen zu;*
> *Vater lass die Augen dein,*
> *Über meine Bette sein.*
> *Ja, Jesus liebt mich,*
> *Ja, Jesus liebt mich,*
> *Ja, Jesus liebt mich,*
> *Die Bibel sagt mir so.*
>
> Tired am I, go now to rest,
> And close my eyes;
> Father, let Thine eyes
> Watch over my bed.
> Yes, Jesus loves me,
> Yes, Jesus loves me,
> Yes, Jesus loves me,
> The Bible tells me so.

Popular ballads are readily adopted by the Amish at the young people's singings on Sunday night, often to the accompaniment of harmonicas which, though forbidden, are skillfully played by many young Amish lads. At the present time, Amish boys are thrilled with the mountain ballads and hillbilly songs of Roy Acuff, whose recordings they eagerly buy in the city and play on old gramophones which are kept well hidden under the hay or elsewhere in the barn. Some years ago, Bachman notes, the Amish invented their own concluding stanza to the popular ballad "The Death of Floyd Collins":

> Young people, oh, take warning,
>   Of Floyd Collins' fate;
> And give your heart to Jesus,
>   Before it is too late.
> It may not be a sand cave,
>   In which we find our tomb;
> But at the bar of judgment,
>   We too must meet our doom.

A selection of older slow tunes from the *Ausbund* follows, with the text to the first stanza of each hymn and with musical notation adapted from Yoder. The division into bars, as before, does not indicate an equal number of counts in each measure but merely shows the break between the syllables or phrases. The most famous Amish hymn, the *Lobg'sang,* has already been presented; it is No. 1 on the Library of Congress recordings. Among the hymns presented here are some others from these recordings, though sometimes with a somewhat different tune; their number will be indicated for reference.

Lebt friedsam sprach Christus
(Live Peacefully, Said Christ)

Library of Congress 4   Ausbund 134

Zu sei - nen Auss -
Und wollt sein Stimm

er - - kohr - - nen,}
gern hö - - ren.}

Das ist ge - seit,

zu eim Ab - - scheid

Von mir, wollt fest drinn

steh - en, Ob scheid ich

gleich, bleibts Herts bey euch

Biss wir zur Freud

ein - - geh - - en.

Live peacefully, said Christ the Lord,
To His chosen people;
Beloved, accept this teaching
And be glad to hear His voice.
This is said upon parting,
And it will stand fast by me;
Though I take leave soon, my heart will remain with you.
Until we enter into the joy of Heaven.

Es sind zween Weg
(Two Paths There Are)

Library of Congress 3   *Ausbund 125: 57-61*

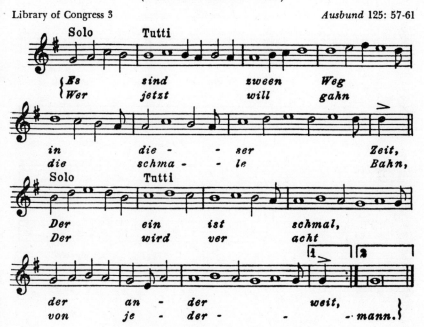

> Es   sind   zween   Weg
> Wer   jetzt   will   gahn
>
> in   die - - ser   Zeit,
> die   schma - - le   Bahn,
>
> Der   ein   ist   schmal,
> Der   wird   ver   acht
>
> der   an - der   weit,
> von   je - der - - - mann.

Two paths there are in these times,
The one is narrow, and the other wide;
He who follows the narrow road
Is despised by everyone.

Durch Gnad so will ich singen
(Through Grace Will I Sing)

(First Hymn at Preparatory Service)   *Ausbund 56*

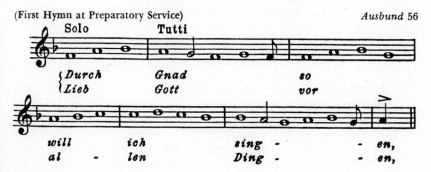

> Durch   Gnad   so
> Lieb   Gott   vor
>
> will   ich   sing - - en,
> al - len   Ding - - en,

In Gottes Furcht he -
Den Näch - - sten auch

ben an, } Das ists Gesetz
so schon, }

und Pro - phe - ten zwar,

Die sol - - len wir

treu - lich hal - ten, Das sag

ich euch für - - war.

Through Grace will I sing,
And raise my song in the fear of God.
Love God above all things,
And also thy neighbor;
That is the Law and the Prophets,
We should remain true to them,
Verily I say this unto you.

O Gott Vater ins Himmels Throne
(O God, Father, in Heaven's Throne)

(First Hymn at Communion)   *Ausbund 55*

{ O   Gott   Va - ter
{ Der   du   uns   hast

ins   Him - mels   Thro - - ne,}
be - reit   ein'   Kro - - ne,}

Solo   Tutti

{So   wir   in   dei - -
{Mit   ihm   hie   dul - -

nem   Sohn   be - - lei - - ben,}
den   Creutz   und   Lei - - den,}

Solo   Tutti

In   die - sem   Le - ben,

uns   ihm   er - ge - ben,

Solo   Tutti

Nach   sei - n'r   Gemein - -

schaft   all - zeit   stre - - ben.

O God, Father, in Heaven's throne,
Thou who hast prepared a crown for us,
As we, in the body of Christ,
Suffer with Him the cross and anguish,
Follow Him in this life,
Strive at all times toward His Kingdom.

*Von Hertzen wolln wir singen**
(Let Us Sing from the Heart)

* Tune: *Hildebrandlied;* cf. Jackson, *op. cit.,* p. 285, who claims that this tune
is at least 1,100 years old.

Let us sing from the heart,
In peace and in unison,
Let us strive toward perfection
With energy and sincerity;
That we might please God,
Which is what He wills of us;
Mark this, all ye pious,
And take it now to heart.

Einsmals spatziert ich
(Once, As I Went Walking)

(Sung after the Death of a Member)   Ausbund 48

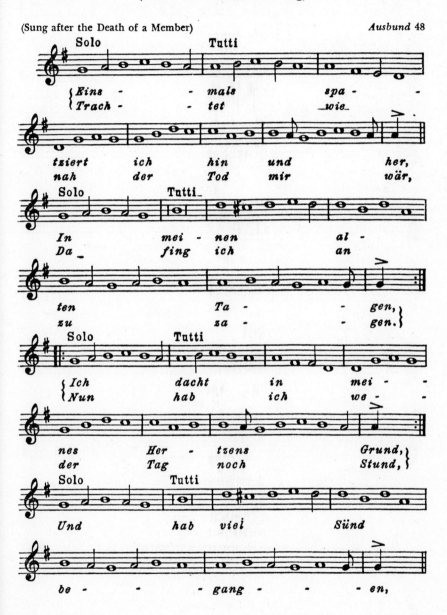

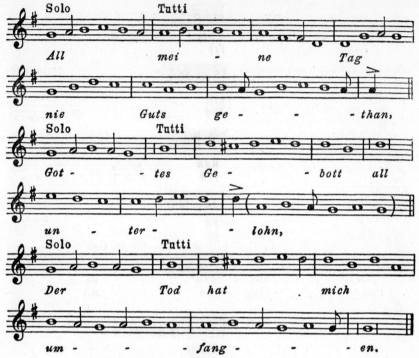

Once, as I went walking
In my old days,
I saw how close Death was to me,
Then I commenced to lose courage.
I thought deep down in my heart,
How not a day was left, not even an hour;
And how many sins I had committed,
And how I had performed no good deeds all my life;
How I had ignored God's Commandments!
By now Death had embraced me.

Gelobt sey Gott im höchsten Thron
(Praised Be God in the Highest Throne)

Library of Congress 2   *Ausbund* 122

Der uns hat aus - er - kohr - - en,
Hat uns ein schö - - nen Rock an - - thon,
Dass wir seyn neu ge - - bohr - - en.

Praised be God in the highest throne,
He who has chosen us,
Hath put a new cloak on us,
So that we are born again.

[1] See, among others, Jane Latta, "The Mennonites of Pennsylvania," *Coronet*, June 1947; Frederic Klees, "The Pennsylvania Dutch," *Holiday*, June 1947. Also the illustrated booklet by Dr. H. M. J. Klein, *History and Customs of the Amish People* (York: The Maple Press Company, 1946). The most satisfying popular book is C. S. Rice and J. B. Shenk, *Meet the Amish: A Pictorial Study of the Amish People* (New Brunswick, N. J.: Rutgers University Press, 1947).

[2] The most authoritative study of the Old Order Amish is *The Old Order Amish of Lancaster County*, by Calvin G. Bachman (*Proceedings and Addresses of the Pennsylvania German Society*, Vol. XLIX, 1942). At the time of publication, Bachman estimated that there were eighteen Old Order congregations in the Lancaster County section, with a total membership of about seventeen hundred. The religious census of 1936 stated that there were in that year one hundred Old Order congregations with nearly ten thousand members in the United States.

Three other reliable reference works are: Melvin Gingerich, *The Mennonites in Iowa* (Iowa City, Iowa: The State Historical Society of Iowa, 1939); C. Henry Smith, *The Mennonite Immigration to Pennsylvania in the Eighteenth Century* (*Proceedings of the Pennsylvania German Society*, Vol. XXXV, 1929); also by Smith, *Mennonites of America* (Scottdale: Mennonite Publishing House, 1909).

[3] Cf. J. W. Frey, "Amish Triple-Talk," *American Speech*, XX (April 1945), 84-98.

⁴ Cf. George Pullen Jackson, "Buckwheat Notes," *The Musical Quarterly*, XIX (Oct. 1933), 393-400; and "The Strange Music of the Old Order Amish," *The Musical Quarterly*, XXXI (July 1945), 275-88. Also John Umble, "The Old Order Amish, Their Hymns and Hymn Tunes," *The Journal of American Folklore*, LII (1939), 82-95; Joseph W. Yoder, *Amische Lieder* (Huntingdon: Yoder Publishing Co., 1942); Smith, *Mennonite Immigration*, Chap. XI, "Literature and Hymnology"; and Bachman, *op. cit.*, "Music among the Amish," p. 221.

⁵ For a general introduction to the study of the Pennsylvania Dutch dialect, cf. A. F. Buffington, "Pennsylvania German: Its Relation to Other German Dialects," *American Speech*, XIV (Dec. 1939), 276-86; O. Springer, "The Study of the Pennsylvania German Dialect," *Journal of English and Germanic Philology*, XLII (Jan. 1943), 1-39; and J. W. Frey, *A Simple Grammar of Pennsylvania Dutch* (Clinton, S. C.: 1942).

⁶ As quoted by Umble, *op. cit.*

⁷ As quoted by C. Henry Smith, *Mennonite Immigration*.

The Cornplanter Indians

By MERLE H. DEARDORFF

The Cornplanter Grant lies in Pennsylvania on the west bank of the Allegheny River about five miles south of the New York line. Only descendants of Cornplanter (the Seneca chief to whom Pennsylvania surveyed this tract in 1795) or other Seneca Indians to whom his heirs have sold may own any part of its 734 acres. In a measure intended to prevent whites from getting away with this last little piece of land, as they have at one time or another with everything else given Chief Cornplanter in recognition of his services to the commonwealth and the nation, Pennsylvania law has for a long time forbidden others to hold property on the Grant.

From Pennsylvania Route 346 on the east bank of the Allegheny, one sees across the river a small community backed by mountains that confine it to the stream margin. It looks like many others in this region. The roadside marker calls attention to the Cornplanter monument, a small white speck, to the north of which stands what is plainly a brick schoolhouse. Adjoining the school is the white-spired Presbyterian church. Some twenty houses show among the trees. They belong to the Lee, Bowen, Jackson, Bennett, Pierce, Redeye, Bucktooth, Gordon, Jacobs, Logan, and a half-dozen other families. In appearance the houses are much like those of the white neighbors. Each is adjoined by a garden plot for whose plowing the Quakers still provide, as they have for many years. With the express understanding that, when used of Indians, the word "permanent" does not mean "fixed" or "stable," as of this writing the Grant has a permanent population of thirty-eight. Next month there may be seventy-five—or fifteen.

Grant population has always been a variable quantity. When Brodhead, American commander at Fort Pitt, returned from his 1779 raid up the Allegheny against the Indians on and near what is now the Grant, he reported burning one hundred and thirty large houses and five hundred acres of fine corn. This argues between a thousand and fifteen hundred people. In 1798 the Quakers estimated that seven hundred gathered about Chief Cornplanter in his Grant town of Jenuchshadaga (i.e. *Dyononh' sadeege$^{n\prime}$*, "There a House Burned"—called "Burnt House" for short, in English). By 1814, however, a delegation of Friends who came to pay their respects to the old chief found only five or six families of his close relatives around him, with "the old town where all the first Councils between Friends & Indians were held . . . almost entirely deserted and so overgrown with young timber, as almost to conceal the place where it stood."

In 1845, nine years after Cornplanter's death, Schoolcraft counted fifty-one Indians on the Grant. The extra census of 1890 showed ninety-eight. Local lumbering activity stimulated rapid population growth in the 1890's; old folks who remember those days estimate that not fewer than two hundred and fifty residents might turn out of a summer's evening to watch Charlie Gordon's famous Cornplanter Town Silver Cornet Band parade down from his house over the mile-long boardwalk to the community center at the church.

No one thing accounts for these population fluctuations. Now almost all of the able-bodied find work elsewhere, since few can live on the Grant and hold jobs on the railroads and oil leases, in offices and shops. Except for a little lumbering and sawmilling work near by, employment easily accessible from the Grant is scarce. In winter and spring the one miserable road through the Grant may be impassable for weeks at a time, and the usual route over the river to the good road on the other side too dangerous to attempt. Some change in this situation, such as another depression, may again make the Grant popular. Cornplanter Indians have at least this one spot to which they may retire when things don't go well elsewhere. Most of them like it and would live here if they could.

The 1798 concentration around Cornplanter was due to the time's uncertainties for the Indians. Cornplanter stood high with the Americans, and he owned his grant in fee. A Seneca could feel safer here than on what were supposed to be lands reserved for him just over in New York on the Allegany and Cattaraugus Reservations and elsewhere. The whites were still making sheep's eyes at these lands, and one could never tell what would be left when they were satisfied. By 1822, when the census reported 597 Indians on the Allegany Reservation where there had been but a handful twenty-five years before, the Quakers' permanent establishment at Tunesassa, just over the reservation line near Quaker Bridge, New York, had pulled most of the Grant population up that way. Cornplanter's oldest son, Henry, had been among the first to move. The government had lavished much attention on Henry. It had educated him in schools at Philadelphia, New York, and Woodbury, New Jersey. He was useful as an interpreter for visiting whites. As an Indian, however, he was a bad one in his people's estimation. Handsome Lake, Cornplanter's half brother, had moved from the Grant to the neighborhood of Cold Spring, near Quaker Bridge. With him went a great many who believed in the validity of his claims as prophet of a new religion—a teaching that was really pretty much a throwback to old Seneca beliefs.

Handsome Lake at Cold Spring and the Quakers a few miles away at Tunesassa got along very well together. The Friends made no issue between "church" and "longhouse." They did not openly oppose the building of longhouses (those essential centers for all social and ceremonial activity in every community of "pagan"

Iroquoians) at Cold Spring and some twenty miles up the river at the other end of the Allegany Reservation.

Meanwhile, back at the Grant, the school that the Quakers had started in 1799 and abandoned when the people moved away was reopened under different auspices. The Presbyterians' Western Missionary Society, meeting at Pittsburgh, had resolved on March 7, 1815, to hire Samuel Oldham as schoolmaster "at the Cornplanter Town at $250 a year plus provisions & cost of getting his family up." Oldham and his wife were reported to be much esteemed by the Indians, and the school to be a success. It closed, nevertheless, in 1818 for reasons not specified in the record. Reverend Elisha McCurdy was delegated to fetch likely pupils to Pittsburgh to finish their educations there.

Also during this period, the Western Missionary Society saw to it that the Grant, at least, was regularly visited by missionaries, a service continued after the school's closing. To this day the Grant considers itself a "church" community, in contrast with Cold Spring, some thirteen miles above on the Allegany Reservation, which is called "pagan" or "longhouse."

These people are pagans only in the sense that the way they follow is considered to be false by the church people. The nonchurch people prefer to call themselves Handsome Lake people or longhouse people after their prophet or their characteristic institution. In the Seneca tongue, which is used exclusively in ceremonial affairs and is the common domestic speech, the word translated as longhouse means more than a long house. The bark-and-pole lodge was the usual Iroquoian dwelling, housing an entire family. The Seneca word for longhouse means literally "the extended lodge"—a bigger family home. The same idea was extended to cover the Iroquoians and their allies who came together in the League of the Iroquois. The League was conceived as a still more extended lodge, with all those sheltered in it one family. "Longhouse people," then, in its application to Cold Spring folk and other Iroquoians, means "old-fashioned folk," those who follow the "old way."

A passer-by might mistake for a Grange hall the only longhouse building left on the Allegany Reservation. It stands on New York Route 280 at Cold Spring. Its companion, toward the upper end of the reservation, was torn down some years ago and its timbers used to build an addition to the cookhouse at Cold Spring longhouse.

The longhouse way is exacting. It makes almost daily demands upon the time and attention of its followers, so the faithful must almost of necessity live near it. The longhouse half of the approximately nine hundred Indians now on the Allegany Reservation have, therefore, tended to gather around this building, in and near the small New York communities of Cold Spring, Quaker Bridge, Steamburg, and Red House. The church people are likely to be found toward the reservation extremities, near Ononville, and up around Salamanca, a city built on leased reservation lands.

Cornplanter Indians are in all of these places, on the other reservations in this country and Canada, and out in the white world from the Atlantic to the Pacific. Some are longhouse; some are church; many are neither. As bigotry is not a native Seneca virtue, church people often come to the longhouse ceremonies just as longhouse people go to church, without feeling out of place.

Since "Cornplanter Indian" has at least four distinct meanings, the term should be defined. The earliest sense is the broadest. Especially for the years after the Revolution, "Cornplanter Indian" was likely to mean any from the Upper Allegheny River and from the near-by towns on the Upper Genesee River. Commonly, it was extended to include those settled along Cattaraugus Creek in New York. The Cattaraugus Reservation (lying along that creek to its mouth at Irving on Lake Erie) joined many years ago with Allegany Reservation to make up the theoretically independent Seneca Nation of Indians. The Indians on these two reservations have always been much the same people. "Cornplanter Indians" as a name for the element that looked toward the Americans rather than to the British for its future is, of course, due to the fact that Chief Cornplanter (usually known to the whites as John Abeel, Abeal, Obeel, Obail) was by all odds the most conspicuous figure among them.

The narrowest sense is in current usage in the Grant's white neighborhood. There "Cornplanter Indians" means only those resident on the Grant at the time. Except as a locative, it is without real significance. "Cornplanter band" might be a better term.

To other Iroquoians, a Cornplanter is likely to be one who can trace descent entirely through a female line from Chief Cornplanter. Senecas count descent matrilineally. If one has a Seneca mother, he is a Seneca. If his mother is not a Seneca, he is not one. In this meaning, Cornplanter Indians number about two hundred today.

In white law, especially as our courts have applied it to cases involving Grant land titles, a Cornplanter Indian is one who can trace descent from Cornplanter through any line. His blood is recognized as coming down through three sons and three daughters. The latest occasion on which there was any official agreement generally accepted by the heirs as to what individuals were to be included in this group was some seventy-five years ago. In the meantime, the heirs have not been idle: best guesses put the number at upwards of five hundred.

This group includes many Indians who are not Senecas, and many individuals who do not consider themselves Indians. It had best be denominated "Cornplanter heirs," reserving for the purposes of this chapter "Cornplanter Indians" for those Senecas who would be so called by other Iroquoians—those who trace descent from Chief Cornplanter through a female line. Even though Cornplanter blood runs pretty thin in some veins, attachment to the Grant is strongest among this group wherever they may be. Here the heroic figures and events of the great Seneca days have a local habitation and a name.

Kai-a'sut-ha, for many years the Senecas' deputy on the Allegheny and the Ohio, died and is buried on the Grant. Through the period of the French and Indian Wars and Pontiac's War he controlled the comings and goings of dispossessed and migrant peoples of all Indian varieties, from east and west and south, who found temporary homes on the river, under Seneca jurisdiction. Here on the Grant lies, too, his nephew and successor as Seneca superintendent on the Allegheny, Chief Cornplanter (*Kai-on-twa'ko^n*, "By What One Plants"). The inscription on Pennsylvania's 1866 monument to him characterizes him as "one distinguished for talents, courage, eloquence, sobriety, and love of his tribe and race." The men who wrote these lines knew him well. Their words were not idly chosen.

Cornplanter was the outcome of a casual forest meeting between a young Albany Dutchman and a Seneca girl of influential family. The Albany Abeels were staid, respectable, substantial stay-at-homes. What cuckoo's egg in the family nest hatched out into their son John in 1722 they could never figure out. So in the family record John is written down as "a lunatic." To their way of thinking, his insanity showed itself in an early elopement to the woods in the disreputable business of Indian trader. He ranged far to the then West, among the Genesee-Allegheny Senecas, where few others dared go. That he was actually "mad but north-north-west" is evidenced by shrewd practices, such as the one credited to him by Sir William Johnson, who oversaw Indian affairs in the north for the King. Johnson credited Abeel and a partner with teaching the Canadian French how to make wampum out of manufactured beads, originally a counterfeit which later by reason of its general acceptance became legal tender in the Indian trade. Because John Abeel knew so much about so many Indians whom Johnson couldn't reach, Sir William could not get along without him. But neither could he get along with him. Many a hard Johnson word is broken over Abeel's stubborn Dutch head in that baronet's papers.

Cornplanter was born at Avon, New York, after 1740. A few years later his mother, hearing that Abeel had expressed some curiosity about the boy, sent him off to see his father. But, as Cornplanter said in his 1822 address to the Governor of Pennsylvania, John sent him away with no provision and with neither kettle nor gun. So Cornplanter grew up all Indian.

After the British, at Oswego in July 1777, had persuaded most of the New York Iroquois to climb down from their neutral perch and to join the British actively against the Americans, Cornplanter was made a war captain among his Senecas, much the most effective fighting force among the Iroquois. He fought through the Revolution for the British in that capacity. In one action he captured his father. John Abeel did not recognize his son, but Cornplanter knew his father and offered him the option of coming to live with him. Abeel was at the time living near Fort Plain, on the Mohawk River, where Abeel Island perpetuates the name. Indian activity thereabouts was strenuous, but Abeel elected to remain with his own people, and Cornplanter turned him loose.

The Revolution west of the Alleghenies was an almost entirely Indian-fought affair with Joseph Brant, Mohawk protégé of Sir William Johnson, as Britain's most influential agent among them. Formal suspension of hostilities between England and the colonies in 1782 settled nothing west of these mountains. The British may have been defeated on the seaboard, but the Indians had not been beaten. Far from it! In 1782 the Americans were shut up in Pittsburgh, their frontiers wide open. The Indians could not credit the word that the British had quit, and British officials among them were in no hurry to confirm the fact. If any Indian good will and trade were to be salvaged, they could not completely abandon their allies. A few Indians accepted their invitation to settle in Canada. Many more elected to stay where they were in order to resist American efforts to treat them as a conquered people. This resistance was so effective that not until the Treaty of Greenville, Ohio, in 1795 did American western advance acquire any substance.

During this post-Revolution conflict, the very able Brant continued to lead Indian opposition to the Americans. If not openly, he was at least strongly supported by the British from their Great Lakes posts which for various reasons they refused to turn over to the Americans. Brant's opposite number, for the Americans, was Chief Cornplanter. Neither was the tool of his white abettors. One considered that his people's future lay with the British; the other, that it was with the new nation. Brant was heir of a background that lay among the strongly Johnson-influenced, more easterly "League" element of the New York Iroquois; while Cornplanter's was in that western half of the Senecas who had always retained a large measure of independence in their Genesee-Allegheny home, deliberately remote from whites of all persuasions.

Brant walked out on the 1784 Fort Stanwix meeting, called by the Americans to let the New York Iroquois know on what terms peace might be had. He left the Mohawk Aaron Hill and the Seneca Cornplanter to speak for the Indians. Cornplanter had come to the meeting merely as representative of the six Allegheny-Genesee towns, expecting to take no prominent part, since he was only of the warrior class. He was genuinely surprised both at the news that the Americans regarded his as a beaten people, and at his own sudden prominence. He did the best he could. In the process, mutual respect developed.

Determination to throw his and his own Senecas' lot with the new country was, no doubt, influenced partly by realization that Brant and his party had left him holding a highly unpopular bag. The decision was fateful for America. Cornplanter's Senecas were in every way the strongest single element among the Indians with whom the Americans had to deal. Cornplanter's ability to hold them out of active participation in the next ten years' conflict was as negatively decisive for America as was the fact that he, their biggest man, was positively energetic in America's behalf.

In his pro-American course, Cornplanter had to contend not only with Brant and his pro-British Indians and with such Americans as New York's Governor Clinton, who suspected him, but also with strong opposition among his own people. When he told Washington in 1790 "that the Great God and not man has preserved Cornplanter from the hands of his own nation," he made a characteristic understatement.

During this period Cornplanter was constantly on the go. He and his friends moved down from the Genesee to the Allegheny, making headquarters at Jenuchshadaga. But they were seldom at home. Cornplanter's figure was a familiar one at Detroit, Sandusky, on the Au Glaize—wherever Indians met in council. He was equally at home with Congress and with Washington and his Cabinet at New York and Philadelphia. He could discuss religion and education with the Moravian John Ettwein and the Quakers at Philadelphia. With equal ease he could bear himself as the central, honored figure at a Tammany Society fete on the Schuylkill's banks. Since Indian problems were among the most acute of the day, no one was more sought after by the Americans in authority than Cornplanter.

A certain Miss Eliza Phile was commissioned by Philadelphia's Tammany Society to paint Cornplanter's portrait in 1786; he is reported to have sat for Gilbert Stuart. These pictures seem to have been lost; but the New York Historical Society has the fine one signed at New York in 1796 by F. Bartoli. Just who F. Bartoli was is not known; but his portrait of Cornplanter is said to be the earliest-known dated oil portrait of an American Indian made in this country. McKenney and Hall used it for their lithograph of "Ki-on-twog-ky or Corn Plant" in their popular series of Indian pictures, whence it became the often unacknowledged ancestor of most pictures of the Chief, none as fine as Bartoli's original.

It shows Cornplanter in mid-life, entirely Seneca in dress and feature. Forty years later, Justice Thompson of the Supreme Court of Pennsylvania visited him at his Grant home. He describes him as well over six feet:

Time and hardship had made dreadful impression upon that ancient form. The chest was sunken and his shoulders drawn forward. . . . I would say that most of his fingers on one hand were useless; the sinews had been severed by a blow of a tomahawk. . . . He had but one eye, and even the socket of the lost organ was hid by the over-hanging brow resting upon the high cheek bone. His remaining eye was of the brightest and blackest hue. . . . His ears had been dressed in the Indian mode, all but the outside had been cut away; on the one ear the ring had been torn asunder near the top, and hung down his neck like a useless rag. He had a full head of hair, white as the driven snow. His face was not swarthy.

The ragged ear noted by the judge was no battle scar. On an early visit to New York, Cornplanter and his party had walked as far as Shippensburg. Here their old friend General John Wilkins halted them while he called in the town tailor to make them suits of civilized broadcloth. Then he sent them on their way in a chaise. Near Philadelphia the horses ran away, and Cornplanter's vehicle overturned. His heavy ear ornament tore through the lobe and gashed his forehead. Bartoli shows the ragged ear; the scar he erased.

Some years before Judge Thompson's 1835 visit, Cornplanter had concluded that his election for his people had been wrong. The Americans had robbed both them and him. Only through the vigilance and diligence of Quakers and a few other devoted white friends had anything at all been saved from the greedy fingers of the chosen people.

As is still a good Seneca's wont, Cornplanter had a dream. He went about from one to another to find who could read it for him and what it imported. Henry York, a Cattaraugus Seneca, gave him the answer. It was time for him to quit—to lay aside white ways and associations and, by returning to his own people's, to attempt to redeem himself and them. Accordingly, Cornplanter discarded his old name and took a new: *O-no^hno,* "The Cold One." Uniforms, medals, swords, gifts of Washington, Adams, Jefferson, and the rest—he burned them all. He turned away the itinerant preachers and sent for a literate friend to write down his notion of creation as he had learned it from his Seneca mother. When he appeared at the longhouse thereafter, he came as an Indian participant in Indian ceremonies.

It is an eloquent commentary on something or other that, not long after Cornplanter's act of despair for his people's future with the Americans, his old opponent Joseph Brant turned away from the British and toward these same Americans in the vain hope that among them he might find what the British had failed to deliver.

The "old way" to which Cornplanter turned is still exemplified on the Allegany Reservation at Cold Spring longhouse. The folk who attend its observances include many Cornplanter Indians, though the Cornplanter band finds it too far away for any but very occasional visits. The longhouse people live, move, and have their being on two levels: white and red. They are organized with reference to their white men's jobs, but their real life is Indian. They are the local repository for the ancient wisdom. Their longhouse is at once the center of Handsome Lake religious observance and of the ceremonial and ritual expression of old customs and beliefs to which Handsome Lake did really little more than give a certain ethical content.

This Handsome Lake cult, which originated in 1799 on the Grant, binds the Allegany folk to the other longhouse groups in this country and in Canada, all of whom regard him as their prophet. This bond requires frequent travel of delegations from one longhouse to the others and makes for a certain continuum in belief and practice. It is quite possible, for instance, to see today at Cold Spring longhouse essentially the same observance of New Year's that the Jesuits reported over three hundred years ago of the Hurons, the first Iroquoians they knew intimately. There are differences, of course, but they are in incidentals rather than in

fundamentals. When, at a certain point in this nine-day ceremonial, Richard Johnny John stands in front of the longhouse
door and lets go at the sky with his shotgun, the instrument is a
modern substitute for shouts and arrow flights. But the act itself
at this point in the ritual is ancient.

Richard cannot explain why he does this particular thing in this
way at this time. The chiefs appoint him to perform a necessary
part of a ceremony, and he does so. His grandfather, Chauncey
Johnny John, knows, though, that Richard is scaring away a sky-
creature about to swallow the moon. It may be that Richard's own
grandson will just fire off a gun at New Year's, as an eastern Pennsylvania "shooter" does, for no reason whatever except that it's
good luck and fun to do so. What is with Chauncey's generation an
entirely rational act is with Richard's a religious formality. With
his grandson's it may be merely a superstitious gesture. Christians
of the Cornplanter band at the Grant fire off New Year's guns, too;
they gather on New Year's Day for a coöperative feast—vestiges but
still survivals.

At what point shooting ceases to be a reflective act and becomes
a folkway might be made a matter of considerable debate. One encounters the same difficulty wherever he turns among these people.
The past and the present are very close together. What is mere
knocking on wood with one Indian is a reasonable act with his
neighbor. Because of their relative isolation from the longhouse
and their long exposure to church and school, it may be said in a
general way that those in the Cornplanter band rationalize in
Indian terms fewer of the things they believe and do than do the
longhouse people. But what passes through the alembic of even a
Cornplanter band brain usually comes out looking much more red
than white. This shows up especially well in their stories about
their own heroes. Many of them were real people, but by the time
they have been worked over even a little by Seneca minds and
tongues they have become typical Seneca folk heroes rather than
historic figures.

In 1636 the Jesuits reported that among the Iroquoian Hurons
there were four classes of virtuous men: the shaman, the hunter,
and two kinds of "captain"—one for civil administration and the
other for war. Of the first class of captain they said that

those hold first rank who have acquired it by intellectual preëminence, eloquence, free expenditure, courage, and wise conduct. Consequently, the affairs of the Village are referred principally to that one of the Chiefs who has these qualifications and the same is true with regard to the affairs of the whole Country . . . [which] even bears his name . . . as if a good Chief and the Country were one and the same thing.

The Grant is identified with an outstanding Seneca hero in each category, around whom myth and legend cluster: Cornplanter, the statesman; Governor Blacksnake, the warrior; Handsome Lake, the shaman; Jim Redeye, the hunter.

Among Cornplanter Indians their eponymous hero naturally gets most attention. He is a true folk hero in the "father of his country" tradition, dominating every situation even if he is unable to control the event.

Here is one of the numerous variants on the Washington-Cornplanter theme so popular among the Cornplanters. There are scores of stories about the two, many with a kernel of fact concealed somewhere inside. This particular one, told recently by a Grant resident, is typical in that it is Cornplanter rather than Washington who dominates the story's situations:

That queen of England did more for the Indians, so they joined the English. The Cornplanter didn't want to take sides. He said it is just a fight between the father in England and his boys over here about which gets the Indians' business, and we ought to stay out. But he had to go with his people because then he was young and not a head chief. When the war was over, the English wanted the Indians to move to Canada and the Indians thought the Americans wanted to get rid of them because they had sent General Potter to New York to destroy them. But the Israel Jimerson and the Cornplanter didn't want to go to Canada. The Cornplanter thought the English had lied to the Indians and he told their general at Niagara that he wouldn't go with people who could wear such pretty red coats and gold braid and feathers in their hats and still say the Americans hadn't beat them, which everyone by that time knew they had. The general tried to make them go, but the Jimerson drove a bayonet into the neck of his horse and he and the Cornplanter ran back to Allegany as fast as they could go. They still didn't know whether the Americans would let them stay there, so the Cornplanter and twenty-six men went to Philadelphia to see the Washington. They waited on a hill outside while the Cornplanter and six men went in to see what would happen. The first guard let them through, but the second tried to stop them. The Cornplanter grabbed his gun and held it and told the others to go on in. The Washington heard the rumpus and came out and said, "What's going on here?" and told them to come in. He said the Indians had been beat and couldn't have any land.

"You are wrong," said the Cornplanter. "You beat the English, but you didn't beat us."

"Well," said the Washington, "then we'll have to beat you, too."

"All right," said the Cornplanter. "You and I will have to play and chase one another around the woods awhile." He meant they would have to fight.

So the Cornplanter went home and got together twenty-six hundred men. He went to the western tribes and got five hundred from them. They started to destroy the Americans' towns and to drive them into the sea. The Washington thought they had better quit, so he sent word to the Cornplanter to come down to Pittsburgh. He asked the Cornplanter whether he had any prisoners.

"Yes," said the Cornplanter, "and I'm going to keep them." Washington didn't have any prisoners.

The members of the Congress came in weeping and pleading with the Cornplanter to stop the war, as they didn't want to go back to England. The Cornplanter felt sorry for them. He said he would stop the fighting if the Americans would agree to let them stay in a good place forever. The Washington said he would; so the Cornplanter started out with fifty men to go among the Indian towns to tell them to stop. Some didn't want to stop. In one place they set out kettles of food for the Cornplanter's men to eat. The Cornplanter guessed it was poisoned, so he let only half his men eat at one time. Sure enough, they up and died; and only Cornplanter and the other half got away.

When they got as far as Franklin, the Cornplanter sent word to the Washington about the land. The Washington told him to bring the chiefs down. When they got there, the Washington took them in one at a time. All but the Cornplanter asked for money.

He just asked for land for his people and a little bit as big as the corner of his blanket for himself.

"You are a good man," said the Washington. "You and I can get along. These others who are supposed to be head chiefs looking out for the people don't even think about them. You do."

From then on the Washington and the Cornplanter were just like that!

A curious feature of Cornplanter legends is the accuracy with which certain details are recalled. It is, for instance, always just twenty-six men who accompanied Cornplanter to Philadelphia, no matter who the teller is. This may mean that the exact number is remembered or, much more likely, that as the story passes from one mouth to another certain quantities remain fixed—but not all. Another equally remarkable characteristic is the abandon with which they are put together with material from everywhere. There is vague recollection among the Cornplanters of such notable occurrences on the Allegheny as Céloron's planting of the lead plates for France in 1749 and Brodhead's expedition of 1779 against them, which burned Jenuchshadaga. But the plates are gold now; "Indian-Killer" Brady, the American scout, is substituted for Brodhead, and for almost every other white "villain" of that period. Here's what happened one time when Cornplanter and Brady met:

That Mister Brady was a smart man and killed quite a few Indians in his day, they say. When he captured one he would torture him. But in the end the Indians got even with him. The Cornplanter and some others snuk up on him one evening down towards Brady's Bend. They tied him up for the night. In the morning the Cornplanter went over to him and said: "Now, Mister Brady, we have you where you've had so many of us. But we are not going to treat you the way you treat our people. We are not savages, to do such things. We are going to cut your ropes, Mister Brady, and let you go free. But, before you go, there is a little thing to be done."

Then the Cornplanter took out his sharp penknife and he slit the skin loose from the soles of Mister Brady's feet, to make pockets. In these pockets the Cornplanter put some small pebbles and he sewed the skin together again.

"Now, Mister Brady," he said, "you may go free."

But the Mister Brady didn't get very far. He tried and he walked toward the river; but his feet hurt him so he knew he'd never make it far, so he just jumped off. And that was the end of the smart Mister Brady. You couldn't fool with the Cornplanter and last long.

(The sole-slitting is a common theme of legend and may have been actually practiced. The jump may be from vague rumor about Brady's fabled leap for life in Ohio. That Cornplanter and he ever met in a hostile way is extremely unlikely.)

Governor Blacksnake bodies forth the great warrior. He was Cornplanter's nephew; those of his descendants who don't like the name "Blacksnake" have taken "Nephew" as their English surname. Governor Blacksnake died at Cold Spring in 1859. A New York State monument there testifies to the high regard in which he was held. In the Seneca system, a warrior "stands behind" each civil chief as messenger, deputy, and general executor. Blacksnake actually bore this relation to his uncle for many years.

About 1845, under commission from Dr. L. C. Draper, the historian, a partly educated Seneca named Ben Williams took down what were supposed to be Blacksnake's recollections, and translated them into fearful and wonderful English with the title "Life of Governer Blacksnake In During the American Revolutionary." The valuable historic content was sifted personally with Blacksnake some years later by Draper, with the help of a better interpreter. Ben's manuscript is in the Wisconsin Historical Society at Madison. Its hundred or more pages are told in the first person, but what Ben actually turned out is not so much Blacksnake's autobiography as a folk epic about a golden age and its heroes. How much is Ben's and how much Blacksnake's is hard to say. Blacksnake had a high reputation for veracity; yet it is not impossible that the story is his, with all its embellishments, exaggeration, and evocation of attitudes and virtues from the traditional past to glorify himself and his companions in arms. Veracity is a relative thing, after all. It is quite possible that the story is Black-

snake's, being a unique written record in the "brag" style of storytelling so common among Indian warriors and expected of them.
An Indian audience would understand what Blacksnake was saying and would put the proper discount on it.

The relation between "Uncle" Cornplanter and Blacksnake in
this saga is not unlike that between King Arthur and Lancelot.
Blacksnake is the man of blood, slaying his thousands, deliberately
armed with something less than the jawbone of an ass to make it a
sporting affair. The battles are conceived almost as tournaments
rather than the rough-and-tumble dogfights they really were. The
following brief extract from Ben's account is concerned with the
period of 1777, immediately after the British at Oswego—with the
help of Brant, rum, "ostrik fethers and gingeling bells"—had persuaded some of the Iroquois to join them in an attack against the
Americans at Fort Stanwix, Rome, New York. Cornplanter opposed this move; but when the Iroquois made their decision he
acquiesced in it and the whole party set off with the British. At the
fort, a British officer went in blindfolded to treat for surrender but
really to spy out the American position. This excerpt gives the
authentic Indian flavor of Ben's story:

They let him out the gate, and let him come to us and form us that
the americas will not surrender and Rather fright an to given up they
fort or possessions. During this the america fire they cannon at us, and
the British party began to fire at them the same time.

But while maken the preparation for Battle the news come from
the enemies that we must wait till they are Ready about 2 Days. we
was notice that we not tak up the arms. there was Six Thusand men
arrived of americas to meet with us. So our head men make further
armament in preparing for Battle with them. our chiefs commander
and others officers concluded that we Should march about 3 miles off
from our camp to on the choice ground where and we must Shed our
whites Brothers and ourselves Blood over the Earth and the Bodies
of the Deade one will forever laid Down, for the sake (?) of obtaining
the British government. the most object of going off three miles from
the tents for to keep the Stinking the Dead Bodies off from the tents.
So all march out to the choice ground. when we got there, about the
second day morning from the time our British officer was Blindfulled,
before going into the fortstanwix—then we have met the Enemy at
the Place appointed Near a small creek, where had the Six Thusand
men that they 3 cannon and we have none, But Tomehawks and afew
guns amongst us. But agreed to fight with tomehawk & Skulling Knife.

As we approach to a fighting we had preparate to make one fire and Run amongst them. We so. No more to kill than the Beast, and killed most all the america army, only a few white men Excape from us there. I have seen many narrow places and close to be hand to be kill by the speare in the end of muskett that I had to defended myselfe By my hands. . . . Then I have seen the most Dead Bodies att it once that I never did see and never will again, I thought it at that time. the Blood Shed a Stream Runing down on the descending ground during the afternoon, and yet some Enemy crying for help. But have no mercy on to be spared for them. But as to the Distress of the Senecas, only 30 kill at that time and I have took prisoners at that time . . . but that they was kill by Clubing and Runing throught a certain distance an they were not one Excape . . . we never under take to Barrying them, So many of them.

Handsome Lake typifies the universal shaman. He was Cornplanter's half brother by a common mother. Without doubt, it was through her influence that he bore one of the two greatest Seneca federal chief names: *Gän-yo-dai'yo,* "Handsome Lake." In 1799 he was an old man worn out with disease and drink, living on the Grant with his daughter. Three young Quakers had come to work among these Indians the previous year. One of them, Henry Simmons, lived on the Grant and tried to teach a school there. Much of his evening time was spent satisfying Indian curiosity about the white man's heaven and hell. He did the best he could, but he was embarrassed and puzzled over what to do about the young bucks who reported visions in which they themselves had visited the places they had heard about from Henry. According to them, heaven looked just like a fine, big Indian town where one could eat, hunt, and tell stories world without end and no amen. As he lay on his couch, Handsome Lake must have heard all this. Perhaps it occurred to him that he was, after all, a great man who ought to be able to compete with these young fellows in the very important Indian vision business.

At any rate, one day in the middle of June 1799 (with Simmons fortunately on hand to write down what happened), he staggered to the door and fell down. His daughter thought he was dead and sent for Cornplanter, who was down by the river. Before he could come, Governor Blacksnake arrived. He felt Handsome Lake's cold body and detected a little warmth about the heart. So the people waited. When he waked from his trance, Handsome Lake reported that three angels had come to him, each with a berrybush under his arm. They had told him to pluck a berry from each bush and eat it. He would thus insure living at least another year, until those same berries ripened again. They then told him that there was a fourth angel who would not come until his end. In the meantime, Handsome Lake had been selected to receive from the three angels such messages as they had to give the people. Thus commissioned, Handsome Lake set out on the teaching career that ended at Onondaga in 1815, when the fourth angel called for him.

What Handsome Lake said from time to time was remembered and worked over by his disciples. Stories about him were incorporated with his teachings into a text, with the result that something like an oral authorized version was developed. This "Code" is recited in its four-day entirety several times a year at the longhouses, a feat perhaps equivalent to saying off by heart the Old Testament. The fact that longhouse people grow up in it from childhood tends to discourage departure from the accepted version in any particular longhouse. The additional fact that one longhouse customarily invites a Handsome Lake preacher from another for Code recitations at stated intervals has tended to keep the text much alike in all. The older preachers (like Cold Spring's Henry Redeye, who died in 1946) know it from memory so thoroughly that they can recite it in their sleep, if necessary. Amos Johnny John and other younger men at Cold Spring who are trying out for Henry's entirely unpaid but highly honored position know the Code, but they have had little practice in reciting it. Consequently, most of them keep hidden a "trot" in the shape of A. C. Parker's English translation, for reference and study. Parker secured his version from Edward Cornplanter, father of the Seneca artist and writer, Jesse Cornplanter. All agree that it is good as far as it goes, but that it does not square entirely with the versions currently heard at the longhouses. As long as the Code is entirely orally transmitted, such variations are bound to occur, of course. It seems certain, however, that the canon will be fixed eventually on the basis of the Parker translation. A Bible is in the making.

Handsome Lake's teachings were perfectly adapted to his people and excellent for them. He did really little more than take the

Indian beliefs and customs as he found them; ban those he considered bad, such as certain dances; and urge upon the people such virtues as sobriety, kindness to children, and a kind of marital fidelity. His general influence was conservative since he advocated a turning against white civilization and all its works. Even the Quakers could not take exception to his moral instruction. For some years they worked together for marked improvement of the Seneca lot. As Governor Blacksnake told a committee of visiting Quakers on one occasion: "Your young men tell us what to do. We ask our prophet whether it is right. If he says it is, we do it." Handsome Lake usually said "It is," since the Quakers were careful not to proselyte, taking as their guide rather "to find what good thing the *Indians* want to do, and then to help them do it."

Among the many stories about Handsome Lake in the recited Code is one that tells how he first tested his clairvoyant powers. Shortly after he had set his foot on the prophet way, a man and his son from Cattaraugus came through Jenuchshadaga bound down the Allegheny for the hunting season. After it was over, the son alone returned. Rumor ran that he had killed his father. Cornplanter called him in and questioned him. The boy said his father had lost himself. Cornplanter was not satisfied and took him off to Handsome Lake. Handsome Lake was hesitant because, he said, the angels had not as yet enabled him to "see." But he agreed to try. He called for a bullet, a knife, and a hatchet, which he laid on a blanket in the presence of the boy and the assembled chiefs. Handsome Lake said that if the boy had killed his father, the appropriate instrument would move when Handsome Lake spoke. He spoke. The bullet moved. Then "the diviner of mysteries" saw the whole thing: how the boy had shot his father and hidden the body in the top of a certain elm down near Oil City. A delegation from the Grant found it there, they say.

Handsome Lake reported George Washington to be the only white man he saw resident in the other world on his visits there. Washington lives in a house suspended between heaven and earth. Attended by a little dog, he spends his time pacing his veranda. Handsome Lake did meet Jesus on the heaven path one day. Jesus asked him how he was getting along. "Not too well," replied Handsome Lake. "Only a few believe in me and what I tell them."

"You're lucky if even a few believe in you," said Jesus. "When I was down there on the same job, nobody believed me."

Because of their church bias, the Cornplanter band has a little different feeling about Handsome Lake than do the longhouse Iroquois. It comes out in their stories about the relations between him and Cornplanter. Cornplanter is represented as having no faith in the prophet and as having driven him off the Grant. This is not altogether in accord with known facts. It is true that Cornplanter was skeptical at first, that he waxed wrathful over a witch-killing that seemed to have been inspired by Handsome Lake. It is true, too, that many followed Handsome Lake off the Grant to the Cold Spring vicinity shortly after 1800. But Cornplanter's reversal of face toward the whites and their works and his later conduct line him up squarely with the Handsome Lake party, with which Governor Blacksnake also was closely identified.

The fourth type of Iroquoian folk hero is the *good* hunter. The *good* hunter as distinguished from the good *hunter* is one who knows and observes the elaborate etiquette governing relations between animals and men. Animals do not at all object to giving their lives for human benefit, if it is done decently and in order.

Such a *good* hunter was old Jim Redeye, father of the Grant's Mrs. Charlie Gordon. He is in a fair way to become the red Davy Crockett of the Allegheny. When he was young, Jim divided his attention between hunting, and fighting his dogs and cocks. One day while he was having himself a nap he heard them talking out in the yard. His best rooster had the platform: "This business has got to stop. Jim makes us spend all our time fighting and killing our own people. They're all afraid of us. Even the hens and bitches take to the hills when they see us coming, and this bachelor life is getting doggone lonesome. Let's go in and tell him we quit."

So they filed in and lined up beside Jim's bed and put it up to him. Jim was a reasonable man, and he could see just how it was. Thereafter, he devoted himself entirely to hunting. His preference was for bear, the pursuit of which he made into a sport by entering combat armed only with a small single-bitted hatchet. He and the bears had a good understanding. True, Jim got himself considerably chewed up, but he was always fair to the bears; he always did

the right thing—so they were fair to him. He never lacked chal-
lengers when he went out looking for a bear fray. Around his
figure prodigious stories are gathering. Although he has been dead
only about thirty years, it is already hard to separate the real man
from his people's creation.

As it is with animals, so it is with plants. There is a code of
amenities that must be observed if one is to succeed with them.
The Grant is noted in all Iroquoia as the habitat of some of their
most esteemed specimens, both real and mythical. The manroot
(*Ipomoea pandurata*) grows better and more abundantly there
than elsewhere, as everyone knows; the large bifurcated roots look
not unlike the legs and body of a man. Only specimens found erect
in the ground are taken. Manroot is essential for certain longhouse
ceremonies. It is esteemed as a preventive of impotence much as
is the similar ginseng in China.

The mysteries practiced by the Little Water Company up at
Cold Spring, holder of the strongest of all Iroquoian magic "medi-
cines," originated in the legend of the *good* hunter. Long, long ago
this hunter was killed by a human enemy. He had so distinguished
himself in life by scrupulous observance of every letter of the law
governing relations with other living things that the plants, birds,
and beasts gathered round his corpse and decided to find a way to
revive him if they could. Each gave a sliver from his heart for
medicine. The restored hunter asked that he might take this medicine back to his people. It was given him on the usual condition
that his people always handle it properly. Thrice a year the company meets in all-night ceremonial to fulfill this obligation.

If and when this medicine runs out, those appointed to make
a new batch will have their lifework cut out for them. Hardest
of all to find will be three essential ingredients, seen by men
only when they are needed, and then only by individuals who have
made long ritual preparation: the Wild Cornstalk, the Wild
Squash, and the Wild Bean. Zeisberger, the Moravian, noted in
the diary of his residence on the Allegheny (1767-70) the excitement in the Indian towns near West Hickory when a report came
in that the Wild Cornstalk had been seen on a near-by mountain.
Old Alice White of Cold Spring claimed she had once seen its

picture in a Sunday rotogravure section. It is tall as the biggest tree, they say. It is a safe bet that any searcher would repair at once to the Grant as the most likely place to find these three "life-sustainers," such is its reputation.

Cornplanters are usually good herbalists. Dr. Owen Jacobs, who died not long ago, had a much more than local reputation in this line. Ezra Jacobs lives in his Grant house now and also follows herb-doctoring. Ezra observes the decencies in typically Cornplanter fashion: not all of them, only some. When he goes plant hunting he leaves the first specimen. He says please to the next and is careful to leave a little of it in the ground. His Cold Spring counterpart would, like Ezra, skip the first. Before the second he would burn a pinch of sacred tobacco (*Nicotiana rustica*) and explain to it why it is wanted, asking its permission. Like Ezra, he would leave some in the ground.

Presence of this native tobacco is what archaeologists call a diagnostic trait. If one sees it growing in the garden or about the house foundations, or drying over the kitchen stove, he may be sure that a longhouse follower lives there. Few are strong enough to smoke it. Old Henry Redeye, the longhouse Handsome Lake preacher, used to put it in his pipe when he ran out of Five Brothers; but Henry could smoke anything. Its real uses are ceremonial. As ceremony orders the daily life of an "old Indian" and is not relegated to Sunday only, he finds a good supply of sacred tobacco indispensable.

Since the Cornplanters on the Grant live so close to nature and are so dependent on it, it is not surprising that observation of its ways is keen. Ethnologists go there to study what is perhaps the last functioning survival among American Senecas of their old hunting economy. Frank Logan, for instance, supports his family almost entirely as his forefathers did—by hunting, trapping, and fishing, pursuits that he as a Cornplanter may follow the year round as a matter of reserved right. Naturally he must know his business. Most of the men work in the woods. The older ones were raftsmen in the old Allegheny lumbering days. Grant Cornplanters share with the groundhog a synthetic public reputation as weather wizards, manufactured by enterprising newsmen who make their predictions for them at space rates in the city papers. The Indians read in these papers what they have been made to say, and think it must be so because there it is in the paper.

The fact is that their interest in their surroundings is even more exclusively utilitarian than is that of whites in like situation. It expresses itself with a difference, of course. The white woodsman, for example, considers an ash tree with reference to its possibilities for Zelo Sheldon's ball-bat factory down at Kinzua. The Cornplanter thinks of its possibilities as a log out of which he may pound basket splints. A cattail flag is a parlor ornament among the whites in Corydon, the little town across the river from the Grant. At Cornplanter, its down is an absorbent for wound dressings and babies' diapers, ancient Indian uses. The old Indian corn varieties are still preferred to the newfangled because each is perfectly adapted to a well-known traditional use. They have not lost their native preference for saltless corn soup as the favorite Seneca food. At a Grant party a few summers ago to which several whites were invited, the long table in Windsor Pierce's yard was heaped with hot dogs, hamburgers, potato salad, delicious pies, and every other orthodox ingredient for a bang-up American picnic. A curious white man noticed that every so often an Indian slipped away into the kitchen, stayed awhile, and came out wiping a satisfied mouth. He investigated. There on the stove was a kettle of the ubiquitous corn soup. The hosts had figured that their white guests might not like it but that no Indian would count the feast a success without it, so they had taken care of the situation with characteristic courtesy and tact. Allowing, then, for differences in the way each values his environment, it may be said that the utilitarian nature lore of Cornplanters and their white neighbors does not differ greatly—except at one point.

Natural objects that figure in old Seneca legends and myths are recognized although others of the same order are little regarded. To illustrate: the goldfinch is common at the Grant. They call it *ga-nun'ee-das,* "He Eats Thistles." This bird's behavior is determined in a peculiar way by the ripening of the thistle, on which it depends for nesting material and food for its young. Its Seneca name embalms ancient observation of this. The

Cornplanters know the bird; they can translate the name. But they do not know what it signifies in terms of the bird's habits. They have no curiosity about it since it means nothing to them. On the other hand, mention of the chickadee, a less common and conspicuous bird there, at once evokes a smile and a story. Everyone knows the bird and its habits because everyone has heard the legend:

Once there was a woman who had a daughter she treated badly. The mother would be boiling corn soup and she would make the girl stir and stir. She would look in the pot and see it there and get hungry. But when she asked for some, the mother always said "Not yet." There never seemed to be a time when that corn soup was ready. The poor girl wished she could be a bird and fly away. Her wish was granted, and They turned her into a chickadee. That's why the chickadee always comes round when people have anything going on. It hopes they will give it corn soup. It follows you through the woods, too, when you go to cut logs or brush, thinking maybe you're going to build a fire and make soup.

It is almost axiomatic that when a Cornplanter evinces prompt interest in some bird or beast about which inquiry is being made, it is either because it is important to him for some reason or because he knows an old story about it. Others he disregards.

There are lots of snakes at the Grant. Chester Redeye just last fall watched a rattlesnake get ready for winter. It had its eye on a certain hollow log for residence:

That snake went downhill about fifty feet. He sighted back along his tail till he got it aimed straight at the hole in the end of that log. Then he started backing uphill, wiggling and screwing himself around in the dry leaves to get them between his body and his scales, until all you could see was leaves and no snake at all. He backed right into that log that way and I guess he's there now, snoozing away.

Chester's rattlesnake is not the only remarkable creature at Cornplanter. Up the Allegheny toward the state line a mountainside concavity, left long ago by a slide, faces the river. This is

Dyos-hais-de'on, "Where the Snake Slid Down." Once this mountain rumbled and shook and heaved. The very brave gathered on
the other side of the river to watch. Fire and steam issued from
the laboring hill. Out of the sky, *Hino,* "The Thunders," struck
at the Thing in the hill with his lightning sword until the
mountain was rent and the length of an enormous horned serpent
slithered down to the stream. It swam down the Allegheny, boiling
the river in its wake as it fled the strokes of *Hino.* Exact descrip-
tions (no two alike) of serpent and event may be obtained on
application to any Cornplanter, though none claims he saw it.
In 1825 Quaker Joseph Elkinton, working among these Senecas,
was troubled by the current prophet's threat to send another
horned serpent down the Allegheny if the people attended to
Elkinton's instruction.

The body of classical Seneca myth and legend is enormous.
Since it still functions, it still grows. Every ceremonial has its
body of legend, which is recalled each time the ceremony is performed. Sometimes a ceremony will dramatize its origin legends
explicitly in much the way the Last Supper is dramatized in the
Christian love feast. Little People, Flying Heads, Stone Coats,
Faces, Bushy Heads, Witches, Vampires, talking animals, minerals,
and vegetables, and all the rest of the natural and supernatural
paraphernalia of Seneca folklore still figure in Grant and Allegany stories. But there is a difference. "Old Indians" at Cold
Spring believe in most of these things. The typical Grant Indian
professes, at least, to take them less seriously.

New story-forms burgeon forth from the old stock. A common
mutational influence is the natural tendency of a narrator to
localize his tale, attaching to it familiar persons and places. For
instance, in the Cattaraugus version of the legend that follows,
Turtle's war party would be likely to set out from Versailles; in
the Allegany adaptation, from Wolf Run mouth. Turtle starts
from Cornplanter Run Cove, whence all Grant war parties em-
barked, in the story as it is told on the Grant:

Turtle watched a war party leave Cornplanter Run Cove, and
he was moved by ambition to do some like feat for the glory of
his pacifist race. So he thought himself up a personal war chant

and got himself a canoe. Thus equipped, he started off one day down the Allegheny, singing his war song as he paddled.

Down by Gowango, Wolf heard the song and knew that a war party was out. He called to Turtle from the bank, offering himself as a recruit.

"What can you do?" asked Turtle.

"I can run," said Wolf, and he gave a demonstration.

Turtle thought Wolf was a good runner all right; but he couldn't see the value of such an accomplishment except for retreat, so Wolf's offer was politely declined.

At Sugar Run, Skunk volunteered. Naturally he was at once accepted. In succession, Rattlesnake and Porcupine were taken on board.

The party paused for council at Kinzua Creek.

It was decided to attack "Old Man Geer" and his family, who lived at Big Bend in the first house on the west bank of Allegheny below Kinzua. The party would land at night and dispose itself for a morning attack, when the family got up. So on they went, leaving their canoe in a cove across from Tuttletown, a place on the river bank near *Geer-ne,* "Geer's Place."

Skunk hid himself near the back door, Porcupine at the woodpile, Rattlesnake in the kindling barrel, Turtle at the spring.

Came the dawn—and so did Mrs. Geer. As she opened the back door, Skunk let her have it. She fell on him and killed him. Her daughter, hearing the rumpus, dashed out the side door by the woodpile and received a flight of Porcupine's arrows in her legs. It made her so mad she picked up a chunk and killed him. Mrs. Geer got herself together and ran around the house to see what was happening to her daughter. As she passed the kindling barrel, she saw the shine of Rattlesnake through the staves, and she polished him off with a rock before he could strike.

Old Man Geer came out about this time, laughing at the trouble the women had got themselves into. He went to the spring for a pail of water. Turtle grabbed his foot. Geer hopped and howled and begged Turtle to let him go. Then he threatened to put Turtle in the fire.

"Good," said Turtle. "I have always liked fire. Let's go."

"Then I'll put you in the river instead," said Geer.

"Please, please! Don't do that. You'll drown me."

So Geer started for the river. He put his foot in. Turtle gave it a farewell bite and swam away. When he got to his canoe, he couldn't push it back up the river, so he just laid himself on a rock, put his hands behind his head, and thought: "Ah, well! Maybe I shouldn't have tried it. Turtles were never meant for warriors, I guess. Anyway, they don't need to be warriors to be great. Isn't it a Great Turtle that holds the world up? He's one of our boys; and there's no one else who can do that."

So he paddled back up to Cornplanter, and when he saw a war party start out from the cove he'd close his eyes, shudder, and say to himself, "That's not for turtles."

Oscar Nephew is an intelligent Seneca who lives at Quaker Bridge. He counts both Cornplanter and Governor Blacksnake in his ancestry, of which he is rightfully proud. Riding one day through the Allegany State Park over a dirt detour that gradually climbed a high hill, Oscar remarked to his companion: "We are getting close to the Indians' Fountain of Youth. Ever hear of it?"

"You mean one like that in Florida?"

"No, not like De Soto's. This isn't water. I'll show it to you when we get there."

He stopped the car at a certain place in the road where one could look back, and through the trees get a vista of mountaintops, one after the other, off to the horizon.

"That's it, that view there! I used to bring my old mother up here when I had a car. We came once a year to look at this. My father came too when he was alive. There's a story about why we Indians call a place like this the Fountain of Youth":

Once an Indian was shooting off his mouth about what a good runner he was. A Flying Head heard him and challenged him to a race. They agreed that the winner should kill the loser. The Indian thought he ought to have a little handicap, so the Flying Head said he would tell the Indian how to live forever if the Indian won. So they started. Each day they would race from one clearing to another, sleep there all night, and start out again. I don't know how many days they ran. Sometimes one was ahead;

sometimes the other. This went on till they came to the End of the World and they had to stop. The Indian got there first. The Flying Head felt bad but he was willing to keep his bargain. He showed the Indian two knives, one bright and sharp and the other dull and rusty. "One of these two will kill me; the other won't. Take your choice." The smart Indian picked the dull knife. The Flying Head's face fell. He thought the Indian would take the other.

"Well," he said, "you've got me. Go ahead and kill me."

"How about that secret of eternal youth you promised me?" said the Indian.

"Turn around and look behind you," said the Flying Head.

The Indian did so. As far as he could see, for miles and miles, there was a hill beyond a hill—just like that out there. It was all the country they had run over that he was looking at.

The Flying Head said: "As long as you look at this or anything like it, you will never grow any older. This is the Fountain of Youth for Indians."

So the Indian killed the Flying Head and stayed there for a long time looking at the hills. Finally he got lonesome and went home. When he got there, he didn't know anyone. All his friends had died long ago, and the people there didn't know him, nor would they believe him when he told them what had happened. But he said he could prove it. All they need do was travel to the End of the World. They would know when they got there because the Flying Head would be lying there. Some did. They stopped growing older from the time they started till they got back.

Wherever there are Iroquois, there are Little People *(Djo-ge'o^n)*. Those on the Grant live in that rock wall behind Charlie Gordon's old place. They aren't bad, just mischievous, with such monotony-banishing tricks as showering pebbles on the roof in the middle of the night to scare the life out of the sleepers. More than one boy playing around that rock wall has disappeared for a while. When they come back they tell how the Little People invited them in and what wonderful times they have. One boy couldn't stop talking about it. One day he disappeared again and never did come back. He's probably still with them.

White people can hardly understand the significance of dreams and visions to Iroquoians. What one sees with eyes closed has even more reality than does the visible world. Senecas were, in a sense, Freudians before Freud. Our "modern" concept of dreams as wish fulfillment is so old with them that some students feel it offers the best approach to elucidation not only of Seneca mythology and religion but of their whole social and ceremonial setup. Every longhouse Indian at Cold Spring knows what to do about a dream, of course. The business may be made a little clearer by the story of a rather unusual recent instance of an Indian who didn't.

John Jones (that is not his name) is of Seneca blood. However, he grew up as a white man and makes a prosperous living near Buffalo raising blooded cattle. He even doesn't look like an Indian and has always professed no knowledge of or interest in the ways of his people. A little over a year ago he had a dream. As he described it: "A dwarf no bigger than my thumb came and sat on my forehead and dangled his little feet in my eyebrows. He bore down so hard I thought my skull would burst. I woke up yelling. Next night he came again. I thought I was going nuts."

Luckily for him, his wife, of Cornplanter ancestry, had been brought up in the old ways at home. Her father when young was one of those who had spent some time with the Little People. Once a year, as long as he lived, he "put up" the Dark Dance for them. That is the Little Peoples' medicine dance. Mrs. Jones knew at once that the Little People wanted her husband to carry on the Dark Dance. So they packed up and went back to her mother's at Allegany, where people knew how to put on the dance. The Little People haven't bothered John since. He must, however, renew the feast at least annually, and he intends to. Once a year he will bow to his Indian ancestry.

Unless they live in longhouse communities, Cornplanters have little recollection of the hundreds of ceremonial and social songs and dances still functioning at Cold Spring. The great Seneca festivals are no longer observed at the Grant except, perhaps, in a token way. They do know and sing there the grand old Seneca language hymns printed for them years ago. Many have fine voices. The quartet that recently recorded some of these hymns for the Library of Congress was made up of Cornplanters. These songs are now most often heard at funerals of old persons, either Christian or longhouse. When Christian ministers permit, as some do, services are often conducted by both minister and longhouse speaker. This is especially so where the family is itself divided between longhouse and Christian. Any objection to such a joint arrangement will come always from the Christian side, never from the other.

White people fare none too well in their legends. There is no reason why they should. The Indian has mighty little to thank them for.

Many of the older Indians were trained, for a while at least, by the Quakers at their Tunesassa school. The building was torn down a few years ago. A white visitor remarked to an old Indian woman on the occasion that she must feel sorry to see her school go, as the Quakers had done a lot of good there for the Indians.

She replied: "Yes, I guess they tried to. But they didn't always do good. At that school they used to talk all the time about that William Penn and what a good friend he was to the Indians. But you know what he did, don't you? When he first met the Indians down there on the Susquehanna where he got off the boat, he told them he wanted to buy a little piece of land for himself. They asked how much he wanted.

" 'Just what I can cover with a bullhide,' the William said.

" 'If that's all you want, help yourself; take it free.'

"Then do you know what that William did? He cut up that bullhide into thin strings and he tied them together and he stretched the rope around nearly everything the Indians had down there. That's the kind of a friend William Penn was!"

This may not be fair to William Penn, but the story embodies a universal theme for legend and reflects the common attitude toward white men. Although the old woman was not at the time thinking of it, her story might as well have been inspired by the imminence of another event of greater significance for her and her people. If Pittsburgh, the United States Army Engineers, and some of the white communities on the Allegany Reservation have their way, her people on the Grant and on the Reservation below Salamanca are not long for this, their Indian world. The Allegheny Reservoir (Kinzua Dam) will cover the river valley to Salamanca, necessitating removal of the residents therefrom.

It is true that the Indians do not want to move. They reassure themselves by repeating over and over the promises of most solemn character under which they are guaranteed possession of these lands forever, unless and until they want to get out. But they do it all halfheartedly, knowing by long experience that seldom has a white government allowed sacred promises to Indians to block the "progress" of the master race.

If one regards only that element among them which behaves and believes like white people, it makes little real difference whether they live here or elsewhere—except, of course, that they want and are entitled to live *here*. With the longhouse folk it is a different matter, entirely. A community complete with long-house, with all of the clans and clan officialdom represented, with each member oriented from cradle to grave with reference to inherited or acquired community rights and duties without whose functioning the individual and the culture cannot "live," is nec-essary for their existence. Not all these longhouse people are aged, by any manner of means. It must signify something that veterans home from our latest war are, if anything, more ardent than ever for the status quo and the conservative way. It was they who, at the 1946 Seneca Nation election in November, organized a new party and carried a ticket on both Cattaraugus and Allegany Reservations dedicated to last-ditch resistance to the Kinzua Dam and all that it implies for them. The younger men feel, perhaps rightly, that their elders are by this time defeatists, too pessimistic from old experience for success in a struggle which they secretly feel they cannot win. Whatever their background, church or long-house, the young men are determined that their community shall not pass without a real fight for its existence.

If, as, and when it does pass, with it will go another microcosm of feeble folk who ask from us only that hardest of all boons for white people to grant, to be let alone.

Central Pennsylvania Legends

by HENRY W. SHOEMAKER

Many years ago I was driving with a companion along West Mahantango Creek when I saw Henry Rau, a typical mountaineer, standing in front of his cabin situated on a neck of woods that jutted into the creek. Always alert for folklore, I stopped the car and approached him. After a few minutes of conversation, he invited us into his cabin.

Around the old hunter's stove, we listened to his varied reminiscences of three quarters of a century of wilderness life. Old Rau was of the tall, gaunt type of mountaineer; in the army his comrades had dubbed him "Longstreet" because of his resemblance to that famous Confederate general. Despite his eighty years, he had a fine head of white hair, as wiry as Andrew Jackson's, and a flowing patriarchal beard. Stimulated by the presence of one of his old army friends, he was particularly communicative, especially about his favorite panther story, which is supposed to be based on a real encounter with a spook panther in the village of Penn's Creek, Snyder County:

THE PHANTOM PANTHER

A panther is harder to kill than a snake. A snake will die when the sun goes down, but not so with the panther; there are certain moonlight nights when he'll always come to life again. We old settlers thought we'd never rid this country of panthers; after we'd tracked and killed them, they always insisted on coming back in the form of ghosts.

These ghosts were harder to get rid of than the live ones. From Joe Knepp, Jonas Barnet, Johnny Swartzell, and other old hunters, I hear tell of panthers being seen in these mountains at the present time, but I think they are only the ghosts of the varmints we killed fifty years ago. But now as I grow older I realize that the panther wasn't so much of a varmint after all. He had his place in the order of nature. When we had plenty of panthers we had lots of deer, wild turkeys and pheasants and wild pigeons, coons and rabbits. With no panthers all we have left is a lot of no-good, half-tame game, not worth a real hunter's time to go out and shoot. Panthers ate all the sickly and weak game, animals, and birds; they left alive only the healthy active stock. There was no danger of a whole species being wiped out as there is now. Well, I mustn't get off my story of the spook panther.

Old Jake Sansom killed him the year I came back from the war, in '64; he caught him in the act of entering his chicken house, and shot him through the hindquarters. The animal backed out as best he could, and then young Dave Sansom shot him in the head. Old Jake was an antic sort of chap; he liked fun and nonsense. He took the hide, which was a very fine one and very dark in color, and stuffed it with straw and leaves. We did not know of taxidermists or glass eyes in those days, so the completed job looked rather uncanny with the great empty eye sockets. It measured a good nine feet from nose to tip of tail, and you can picture a pretty good-sized brute from that. After stuffing the hide, the old man set it up on the ridgepole of his woodhouse, which fronted on the public road leading to Centreville. You can be sure it was the nine days' wonder of the neighborhood. With the jaws propped open to show the enormous teeth, for it was a male, and with the tail high in the air, it looked almost as natural as life, and a damn sight more ugly.

Horses and even mules shied at it as they were driven past; dogs barked at it and tried to climb up on the shed. Children on their way to school would not go by it unless accompanied by grown persons. As a result the little folks forsook the highroad and made a path along Penn's Creek, but even there they complained of being scared by the playfulness of fish otters.

But one unfortunate feature of the case was that the dead panther had a mate. These animals are very devoted to one another, and if one is killed, the survivor hardly ever mates again. In this instance, the female kept coming to the edge of the dense brush at the rear of old Jake's garden, and howling pitifully on moonlight nights at the immovable carcass on the ridgepole. Some of the more timid neighbors urged him to take the carcass down. "It keeps the mate in the neighborhood, and our women and children can't have any peace at nights," they said. But Jake would only shake his hairy head and grin. "I'm going to get that mate some day. I'm only waiting for her to get real bold and show herself, then there will be two stuffed panthers on the roof of my woodshed."

He had killed the male about the first week in April, but summer was now on the wane, and he hadn't gotten a shot at the mate. A number of the boys who lived on adjoining farms were hoping she might elude him. If she did, they planned a big hunt with dogs as soon as harvesting was over. As it was, the dogs, whenever they were loosed, would take up the panther's scent, and make the nights horrible with their yelping. This was another reason why old Jake was urged to get rid of his stuffed panther. But the old man was stubborn; he was going to clean out the whole panther tribe, if given his way.

In August there was camp meeting in Emerick's Woods near New Berlin, and the number of rigs and travelers on horseback who passed the stuffed panther was well up in the hundreds. All stopped to look at it, for many of the younger people had never seen a panther; they were getting scarce outside the Seven Mountains. The night of the second Sunday of "camp," old Jake and his boys went off in their carryall, leaving his wife and their crippled daughter to mind the house. The old lady wasn't afraid; she said she could shoot straighter than her husband any time. It was a weird sort of night. Across the face of the full moon flew clouds shaped like panthers with long tails. There was a stiff wind, which rattled the loose palings on the front yard fence and sent the gate swinging to and fro. Bits of the garden, the orchard, and the creek were lit up by the moon; other places were dark.

"It's the kind of night we always saw the ghost of the Indian chief at the spring, when I was a girl," the old woman was telling her crippled daughter.

"Don't tell me that, Mother, it frightens me," said the girl, who was lying on a black haircloth lounge, and she pulled the patchwork quilt over her head.

"Don't be foolish," said her mother. "Ghosts are as much a part of this life as our daily breath. We cannot reckon without them."

"But I don't like to hear about ghosts," replied the girl. "I've always felt sort of uneasy ever since Daddy set up that ugly stuffed panther on the woodshed."

"My lands, girl," said the mother, "that's what I call an ornament! There never were any folks stopped to admire our premises until your father put that critter up there! They never noticed our hollyhocks and judas-bushes."

As she was talking, the patter of dogs' feet was heard on the kitchen porch. On opening the door, she saw six huge hounds running about and wagging their heavy tails. Two were her husband's, which he had freed before leaving for camp meeting, and four strangers. "Shoo, there," she shouted to them, striking at them with a broom handle. The animals ran off the porch and across the yard, where they began barking at the stuffed panther on the woodshed. The old woman looked out the kitchen window and watched them as they leaped wildly against the sides of the shed to get at the stuffed panther. Her eyes rested on the panther itself, and she recoiled in horror.

"What ails you, Mother? I thought you never got afraid," said the crippled girl sarcastically.

"I never do, but I didn't like the way that panther looked. That queer moonlight we have tonight was shining in his eye sockets, giving him an expression that would have scared the devil himself."

While she spoke the yelping of the hounds became fiercer than ever. It seemed as if they would demolish the shed in their fury.

"No wonder the neighbors complain they can't sleep," broke in the girl again. "Between that she-panther in the brush and the infernal carrying-on of the hounds, they might as well cut up their beds for kindling."

"I guess if we can sleep through it, they can too," said the old woman as she sank into her rocking chair by the window. For several moments she watched the frantic, howling dogs without saying a word. Then, as the noise increased, she screamed, ran to the door, and turned the key in the lock. Looking out the window again, she called to her daughter: "The hounds are up on the roof, they are pulling down the panther! My, but your father will lick them when he gets back." The poor crippled girl could stand the excitement no longer. Forgetting her fear and disability, she dragged herself to the window, holding on to her mother with a tight grip. Just as she reached the window, she saw panther and dogs come rolling off the shed roof into the yard. In an instant the angry brutes were on top of the carcass, intent on tearing it to pieces.

In the midst of their fury, something that seemed like a shadow cast by one of the long pantherlike clouds swept across the smooth-kept yard from the garden fence. It was no shadow—it was the drab form of the stuffed panther's mate. Taking the hounds completely off their guard, she plunged in among them, throwing them right and left. Yells of anger were followed by miserable, treble caterwauls of pain. Torn, bleeding, and helpless, the dogs lay about like sheep at a barbecue. With the last enemy dispatched, the pantheress sprang lightly to the side of the stuffed carcass of her mate. Pausing, she turned her uplifted head and ground her teeth in defiance at the terror-stricken women in the cottage window. A narrow streak of moonlight fell on the animal at that moment, setting out in bold relief the slim, lithe lines of her form. Crying softly, she began licking the eyeless sockets of the carcass. She rolled it over from side to side, now and then standing it on four feet, where it looked ready to take on life and speed with her to the pine forests. Suddenly she gave out an awful yell and, fixing her fangs tightly in the nape of its neck, she started to drag the carcass across the yard. When she reached the garden fence she had a hard time lifting it over, every muscle and sinew of her frame twitching.

Why the women stayed at the window all this time they could not tell themselves. It was a sight that, try as they might, they would never be able to forget.

It was just as the devoted pantheress, with her ghastly burden, was disappearing across the palings on the far side of the garden that, rifle in hand, I appeared on the scene. At that time I was living about half a mile up the road from the Sansom farm, nearer Centreville. My wife wasn't feeling well, so I hadn't gone to camp meeting that night. I had gone to bed early, but could not sleep for the hellish yelping of the hounds. It got so loud and kept up so long that I reckoned the female panther was abroad, and I meant to put a stop to her career, if possible. I was already on the highroad when I heard the pantheress let out that awful yell. Though I hurried, I reached the spot too late. I pushed through the gate, and across the yard, only to see the heap of dying hounds on the grass near the woodshed. Mammy Sansom saw me coming and ran out in the yard to meet me. She told the story as well as she could, but I could see she was half dead with fear. We looked at the dogs and found every one torn to pieces. A couple died as we were examining them, and I put the rest out of their misery with the butt end of my rifle. Turning to Mammy Sansom, I said, "I think I can get that pantheress tonight."

I had purposely left my dogs at home; they were only little rabbit hounds, so I hadn't wanted them to get mixed up in any mess. As I was going out the front gate on my way home after them, I heard the sound of a wagon down the road. When it came closer, I saw old Sansom and his boys. Quickly as I could, I explained what had happened. They ran into the yard to where the dead hounds were lying, while I jumped into the carryall and drove up the road. I leashed my little dogs and threw them into the wagon. Returning to Sansom's house, I found the old man and the boys waiting for me with their rifles. I put the dogs on the scent, and soon there was a lively tonguing.

The trail led us through the garden, across a pasture lot, and into the brushwood which stretched for half a mile to the beginning of the big pine forest that covered the slopes of Jack's Mountains. At the edge of the original pines was a spring. For some reason it had always been called Panther Spring; now it was to become doubly entitled to the name. The moon, which had been blacked out for a few minutes by long, slim clouds like panthers, suddenly shed its rays upon the spring. What had seemed to us like a couple of old rotting moss-covered logs turned out to be two huge crouching panthers, drinking. The smaller of the two raised its head at our approach, looked around, and ground its teeth at us. Then it quickly caught the other animal by the nape of the neck. When the larger brute wheeled, we noticed it had very imperfect eyes. We recognized it as the animated form of the stuffed carcass that for six months had been fastened to the ridgepole of old Jake's woodshed.

I had heard of buck fever hundreds of times, but I had never experienced it myself until I saw those two devilish panthers. I could not raise my rifle to my shoulder. My dogs, usually eager to attack anything big or little, cowered at my feet, shivering and shaking. Jake and his boys were stiff with fright. We stood there in the moonlight, as if hexed. I who had faced death at Malvern Hill and Chancellorsville allowed the two brutes to get away from me, without turning a finger to prevent it. The weak-eyed panther moved more slowly than his mate, for he was evidently being reanimated gradually. With any amount of sense, we could have shot them both, but it wasn't to be. When they were safely out of reach we woke up.

All of us started swearing at ourselves. Once I thought I'd whip my dogs, but I figured out if a thinking, reasoning human being like myself hadn't backbone enough to shoot, how could a pair of little rabbit hounds be expected to begin the attack. Sheepishly we all turned about and returned to our homes. It was the most unsatisfactory, cowardly night of our lives.

The story of the panther being torn off the shed roof and the mate coming to its rescue and killing the hounds became widespread, but our part of the adventure we kept dark. Many of the neighbors complained about two panthers being heard in the brush at night when the moon was full, for it was then they always wailed most mournfully. "That cursed panther of Jake Sansom's has brought two around to avenge it, instead of one," was their common talk. But Jake, his boys, and I knew that the second panther was none other than the stuffed carcass from the woodshed brought back to life.

*   *   *   *   *

"The Story of Altar Rock" was one of the first legends I collected. I obtained it in 1898 from Seth I. Nelson, then virtually the last survivor among Pennsylvania's famous big-game hunters. His life had nearly spanned the nineteenth century, as he was born in 1809. Rising above his mountain cabin near Round Island, Clinton County, was Altar Rock with a lone primeval white pine growing out of it. Nelson explained that the tree once had had a companion that was blown away by a strong wind. He then proceeded to tell me the following legend woven around those two white pine trees:

The Story of Altar Rock

In the first half of the eighteenth century, several bands of French trappers found their way from the trading posts on Lake Erie to the Elk Branch of the Sinnemahoning Creek. They followed this stream to the main run, where some of them went out the Bennett Branch toward Benezet, while another party of five built a camp and stockade on a high point at the great bend west of what is now Round Island station. The camp, which was christened Grande Pointe, and even the subsequent history of these French pioneers have been forgotten, although to this day the foundations of the camp can be located in the pine forest that has since grown up on the scene of this ancient fortification.

The French policy toward the Indians was to fraternize and be honorable in all dealings with them, and for this reason their trading and trapping enterprises were successful.

However, a few of the young bucks did not like the whites, especially after the building of the Grande Pointe camp, which seemed to indicate that they would live there permanently. But the squaws and less warlike of the braves, who bartered furs for undreamed-of fineries and liquor, were glad of the whites' presence in the neighborhood.

Of all the hostile braves, none carried a more bitter and uncompromising hatred than did the tall, spare young soothsayer whose name translated is equivalent to "Two-Pines."

A medicine man by descent, he visioned nothing but frightful omens of his people's annihilation at the hands of the pale-faced strangers. Still, the greed for barter and luxury was too strong in the majority of the tribe for them to give more than a passing thought to forebodings. They turned away, shaking their heads, when on festal days Two-Pines mounted Altar Rock for devotions; on this narrow ledge an Indian was supposed to bear a charmed life and be for the time invulnerable to poisoned arrows or javelins.

Altar Rock, which modern writers call Pulpit Rock, Chimney Rock, Steeple Rock, or Nelson's Rock, is one of the most remarkable natural wonders in Pennsylvania. Its diameter in no part being over ten feet, it rises like a graceful column to a height of sixty feet, where it is surmounted by a flat slab, the dimensions of which are about ten by twelve. The entire cliff is composed of brownstone and is undulated and fluted by the action of water in past ages.

On top of the flat slab stands a living white pine, forty feet tall; its gnarled roots clutch at the rocks in a grim effort to hold its place against the onslaught of the elements. There is no earth on Altar Rock from which the tree can gain sustenance, but it grows healthy and green in its barren home. There was once a second white pine, the exact counterpart of its mate, growing on the rock; but it was struck by lightning, lifted bodily from the roots, and blown into the valley below.

One bright September morning after Two-Pines, the soothsayer, had spent the night on top of Altar Rock in meditation and prayer, he heard the crack of a gun fired somewhere near the Sinnemahoning. A few minutes later he came face to face with a Frenchman, Pierre Le Bo, dragging the carcass of a bull elk to the river's edge to sink it until he might have time to prepare it for eating. Two-Pines' anger was thoroughly aroused. To see this intruder killing the beasts of the forest, which he thought belonged to the Indians, was too much for him. He struck the Frenchman a terrific blow on the head with a stone mallet, crushing his skull and causing instant death. Then he climbed back to his retreat on Altar Rock and prayed rapturously for the gift of strength to annihilate the white beings who defiled the valley of the Sinnemahoning.

It was in this attitude of prayer that he heard footsteps and whispering voices in the wood beneath. Nearer and nearer they came, until through the leaves, he saw four heavily armed French trappers. Two-Pines arose and stood erect. In the dignity of his titanic stature, and with arms folded across his breasts, he seemed to defy the avengers to slay him on his immortal pedestal, where poisoned arrows and javelins had less effect than drops of summer rain.

A little Frenchman named Lafitte leaned his heavy gun upon a snag, took careful aim, and fired at the defiant warrior. There was a loud report, and when the foul-smelling smoke had cleared, the dead body of Two-Pines lay upon Altar Rock.

An hour later the Frenchmen abandoned Grande Pointe with its valuable stores and started downstream in canoes. That night the camp was looted and burned by the Indians; whether the trappers succeeded in reaching a friendly refuge or were murdered on the way has never been determined. But from the flat top of Altar Rock two little pines with long silky needles sprouted slender and straight. Taller and taller they grew until, side by side, with their smooth-barked trunks and shapely tangle of dark green foliage, they resembled the figure of an Indian youth, the slain but defiant Two-Pines.

*   *   *   *   *

Crispin Fields on the side of Mount Jura of the Bald Eagle Mountains, setting of "Conrad's Broom," lie to the east of my home property at McElhattan. In my youth the fields were cleared so that they were visible for a long distance; now they are pretty well back in forest again. This is one of the best-known legends circulating in Wayne Township, Clinton County, where even school children whisper it in awe. I heard it originally a half century ago from a number of sources. After the disappearance of the hex girl in "Conrad's Broom," no blonde girls were born in Wayne Township. Now, of course, there are blondes among the daughters of the industrial population that has come into this locality.

Conrad's Broom

It is difficult to view the north slope of the lower Bald Eagle Mountain at McElhattan without catching a glimpse of the Crispin Fields. A great circular clearing carved out on the mountainside one-third of the distance from the summit, it is a conspicuous landmark for miles. At a distance it gives the impression of being well kept and smooth; but if you visit the ground, it will be found to be fast growing up with young *Pinus rigida,* sumacs, and blackberry vines. To all intents it is a part of the surrounding woods, for the fences have rotted or fallen down. A short distance below the western corner of the fields is famous Lower Gum-Stump Spring, a source of sweet pure water, which increases into a stream of no mean proportions, a much larger stream than that which flows from Main Gum-Stump Spring about a quarter of a mile farther west.

It was near Lower Gum-Stump Spring that William Crispin, a settler from New Jersey, said to be of English descent, erected his log cabin and commenced clearing the surrounding land. His former home was in the northern part of his native state, where mountains abounded. Hence his selection of a hillside plantation in central Pennsylvania when river-bottom lands could be purchased cheaply. On his way up the state (it was a tedious journey in those days when farming implements and household goods had to be transported in oxcarts or horse-drawn wagons over rocky or muddy roads), he met, wooed, and wed an attractive German girl whose home was near Weisersburg, afterwards called Selinsgrove. A good-sized family was born to them; all the children were handsome and healthy. The oldest son was named Conrad after the immortal Conrad Weiser, about whom Crispin's wife had heard so much in her youth.

The section now known as McElhattan was a wilderness even

in the early years of the nineteenth century; it has retained much of its delicious old-time flavor still, but then it was a primitive Arcadia. Once Conrad told his father that every morning a large black dog followed his three little sisters and himself to school. When it came too close and showed its teeth, they drove it away by throwing pine knots at it.

One morning after a snowfall the father accompanied the children to school; he himself wanted to see the dog. He was able to see it and shoot it. The familiar dog turned out to be a big black wolf. It was just when the hardy pioneer had got a nice farm tilled (he had to grub out and burn hundreds of trees to do so, to say nothing of piling up countless rocks) that he caught a heavy cold which developed into pneumonia; he died at the early age of forty-five.

Conrad, who was fifteen years old at the time, became the head of the household. He was a stout boy for his years, willing, alert, and cheerful. Aiming to leave nothing unfinished that his father had commenced, he took up the tasks with a vim. He was his mother's idol. By the time he was twenty he had the farm and livestock in good order, so much so that the sentimental German mother was continually saying, "Oh, if your father could only have lived to see all this!"

Chief among the stock was a large flock of sheep; it was told with especial pride that there had not been a single one taken by a wolf or panther since good William Crispin's death. This spoke volumes for the watchfulness of Conrad and his younger brothers. In the yard around the comfortable cabin were a goodly number of chickens of the old-time breeds, Creeleys, Bunties, Sprucies, Toppies, as well as brown ducks and white geese with black heads. The little girls vied with their brothers in keeping the foxes and weasels from destroying the fowl.

During the long winters Conrad practiced other accomplishments. He was an expert basket-maker with oak or willow withes, and grew some broomcorn back of the house, from which he made some excellent besoms. He also was proficient in carving out hickory ax handles. At the time of the young man's twentieth birthday there were about ten families living on the fertile plain

within the semicircle of mountains now included in the bound-
aries of Wayne Township. Most of the families were of Scotch-
Irish origin, but there were several mixed households where the
husbands were Scotch-Irish and the wives German.

On the sloping riverbank near the Big Bend and close to Spook
Hill with its crumbling palisade of Fort Horn, lived a German
couple named St. Galmier. While their name sounded more
French than German, they spoke the tongue of the fatherland,
in fact, could speak but a very few words of English. They were
probably of Huguenot extraction, coming from ancestors who had
fled to Germany from France during the St. Bartholomew's Day
massacre. They were past middle age and childless, when the
Crispins appeared and began clearing their farm near Lower Gum-
Stump Spring. Old Christ St. Galmier, it was said, was a butcher
by trade, but he had long since abandoned everything except til-
ling a small garden patch and eternally fishing for shad and sal-
mon. A few stalks of tobacco grew in his meager front yard; from
this he made his own smoking materials. He was an unsociable
fellow, sullen and uncommunicative; his wife, who was his counterpart, was further cut off from friendly intercourse by almost
total deafness.

Several years after the birth of the Crispins' first-born, Conrad,
old "Mammy" St. Galmier became the mother of a girl. At least
she said she did, and proudly exhibited a very beautiful infant.
Local gossips were limited to a few individuals in such a small
community, but they could not help doubting the baby's parent-
age. As Conrad Crispin grew sturdy and strong, the little St.
Galmier girl, who was named Elizabeth, developed slight, blonde,
and winsome. No such beautiful child had ever been seen in the
West Branch Valley; Vashti McElhattan of an earlier generation,
who ran off with an Indian, not excepted. Vashti was also a blonde
of much the same type. There have been no blonde girls in
Wayne Township since, not one.

At school and in the outdoor religious festivals, the mutual
fondness of Conrad Crispin and Elizabeth St. Galmier was noticed
and commented on. The St. Galmiers were pleased; but the
thought of it struck terror in good Mother Crispin. She had always
feared the elder St. Galmiers with their dark, mysterious past; in

her eyes, their supposed daughter, so ethereally beautiful, belonged to the world of black art.

Down at Weisersburg an old witch, who had the Black Book, the "sixth and seventh books of Moses," fancied she saw an affinity between the fair young girl and this awful old hex of long ago. What the resemblance was she never would tell, but she kept warning Conrad to beware, beware. This opposition only fanned his interest. As he was such a good boy in every other respect, his mother did not like to make it too hard for him. But when mother and son, sitting side by side on the doorstep and watching the sunset behind Mt. Pipsisseway, indulged in heart-to-heart talks, the demoniac origin of Elizabeth was never neglected. "That girl was not born to that old woman," the good mother would say. "She is a she-devil that took the form of a beautiful girl, deceiving the old couple and coming into this world to do mischief. You could not keep her if you married her, any more than if you tried to keep the snow on the roof from melting when spring approaches."

"How do you know all this, Mother?" the young man would plead.

"Never mind, Son, I know more than you think. Some day I will prove it to you."

Then, the sun having sunk behind the majestic peak, they would get up to go about their duties. But these words always threw a pall of gloom over Conrad's otherwise happy and hopeful nature.

Whisperings of Mother Crispin's opposition and the causes of it spread about the settlements, keeping many friends away from Elizabeth. It had an advantage to Conrad as no other lads noticed the exquisite girl. He did not have the annoyance of rivals, but if he had, he would have won out, as the girl cared for him alone. It seemed as if her destiny directed her to him.

Twenty years was a good age in the backwoods. As his twentieth birthday drew near, Conrad's mother asked him to name a wish, which she would grant if in her power.

"I'm going to marry Elizabeth some day, Mother," he replied. "I want you to really know her. Can't I have her here for supper on my birthday?"

The mother would almost as soon have entertained one of the black wolves from the forest, but she loved her son and thought he should have his way. Besides, the day of reckoning was drawing near. A wolf in sheep's clothing could only play the farce a certain length of time before blowing up like a bubble. Conrad invited Elizabeth in the presence of her parents. They beamed at this compliment to their strangely neglected beauty-child. "You will have a grand time," they said. "Conrad's mother is such a great cook."

Elizabeth, who had passed her sixteenth birthday two months earlier, was tall and graceful like a dryad, with hair of a peculiar golden tint and blue eyes kept ever at half-mast to hide the mystery of her soul. She had marked peculiarities for one so young. Even if there hadn't been a story of her ghostly origin, she was so different from girls of her age that during her brief school days her fellow pupils dubbed her "Cracky." The Irish schoolmaster, a drunken lout with a Dublin University degree, predicted she'd "go to the devil or marry the President." She would not learn, though she was naturally clever. There is much potential energy in such young persons, though the devil often inherits most of it.

Conrad's birthday dawned bright and clear, an ideal day in late summer. As the afternoon advanced, the Round Top and the lower McElhattan Mountain assumed the tone of dark heliotrope, and the air smelled like that exquisite flower. There was a pale gold mantle above the crest of Mt. Pipsisseway.

Mother Crispin outdid herself with the supper; it was ready for the arrival of the "ethereal" guest. Conrad seated himself on the doorstep and looked across the clearing for Elizabeth's approach. His mother came out, carrying one of the brooms that he had made the winter before, but never used.

"Let me sweep off the steps," she said. So the young man arose, and she swept industriously. He was leaning against the house, when he espied his sweetheart far in the distance. Mother Crispin saw her the same moment. "Conrad," she cried, "I told you that Elizabeth St. Galmier is a devil, a witch; now to prove it, put this broom under the steps, and you'll see she will not be able to walk over it."

"O Mother," protested Conrad ruefully, "how can you say such a thing? It would be awful to do that. You might as well scatter mustard seeds or put a sieve on the steps. If she were a ghost she'd have to count the seeds or the holes in the sieve before she could proceed."

"I am right, Conrad," said the mother forcibly. "I know that girl's secret; hurry, put this broom under the steps."

Conrad hesitated. "You do it, Mother, if you wish. I can't."

"It would not do any good if I put it there; a witch's lover must do it if the truth is to be shown."

Elizabeth was still too far off to see them, and there was a fringe of paw-paw trees along the fence which hid the cottage. There was time to make the test, to prove for all time the fair vision's innocence or guilt. Quickly seizing the broom from his mother's hand, he thrust it under the steps and ran down the path in the direction of his loved one. Both looked happy and beaming as they drew near the cabin. Mother Crispin was at the door to greet them. As they came in front of the steps, Elizabeth suddenly paused. For a bare instant the bright young smile vanished off her lips; her eyes never smiled as far back as anyone remembered. She stooped down and drew the new broom from its hiding place. "O Mother Crispin," said she, the old gaiety of her voice fully returned, "how did this fine new broom get under the steps?"

She rested it against the house, went up the steps, and inside the cabin, and the little supper party proceeded. But before grace was said, Elizabeth presented her lover with a pair of mittens and a pair of beaded deerskin moccasins she had made. Never had she seemed gayer or more witty. Conrad felt sick at heart, but he had to laugh at her jests. He could not be glum in the presence of such a radiant object. Mother Crispin was also in good humor, but hers was the elation of victory; the other children were joyous because they were young and the supper had tasted good. Altogether it was a most successful party. Joking and bantering, they sat at the table a good hour and a half. There were many sincere good wishes for Conrad's future happiness and Elizabeth's.

About ten o'clock, a late hour for mountaineers, the young girl started homeward, accompanied by her lover. There was a young moon with horns pointed to the east. "Don't they look like the devil's horns?" asked Elizabeth as they emerged from the wood,

Conrad thought that very strange talk, but said nothing. All was congenial and gay, and they kissed a long, lingering good night as they parted at the St. Galmier cabin. When she opened the door, her pet cat, a huge brindled creature with six toes on each foot, trotted out and rubbed against her skirts.

The moon, reflected horns downward, was dancing on the calm river when the young lover started back to the mountain. "Elizabeth, O Elizabeth, was there ever anyone like you in the world?" he kept repeating as he treaded his lonely way. A great horned owl perched in a white pine tree with supernaturally long branches insisted on answering, "No, no, no, no, no-o-o!" Whether from elation or the broomstick episode, Conrad could not sleep that night. Through the closed window he could still hear the owl reiterate, "No, no, no, no, no-o-o!" He dozed off a little while just before daybreak.

At six o'clock there was a knock at the door. Conrad opened it and found old Christ St. Galmier waiting outside. There had been a white frost, and the old man's face looked as ashen as the dew-enameled grass. "Elizabeth's very sick; she wants to see you at once," said the old man in German. Without waiting to find his cap, the young man followed him to the cabin by the riverside. He found the girl in bed, breathing heavily and only partly conscious. He could not be sure if she recognized him or not. All day and all night he remained with her, the old couple meanwhile plying her with herb remedies. By the following morning she seemed to improve and opened her droopy eyelids, smiling sweetly with her smooth, arched lips. But she never uttered a syllable. Conrad felt he should go home for a few hours, so taking advantage of her favorable condition, he started away.

When he was returning after dinner, he met old St. Galmier halfway. "Elizabeth's dead," the old man muttered. "She passed away suddenly fifteen minutes ago, just after she had begun talking to us so nicely."

"What were her last words?" asked Conrad.

"Oh, something about she wished you'd always believe in her."

The rest of the way, the two men walked in silence.

Conrad was ushered into the presence of the dead, but great was his surprise. Though life had vanished only a brief half hour, every

trace of her former beauty was missing. It seemed like the corpse
of an old weazened, wrinkled woman, and not a sixteen-year-old
girl. The bright gold hair had faded to an ash or silver color. Even
the teeth had fallen out. Conrad was shocked, but made no comment. In the ensuing hours he helped old St. Galmier construct
a coffin out of pine boards, which the aged man had recently
bought at young Billy McElhattan's water mill to build a bed.
Several neighbors called during the afternoon, and left, shaking
their heads after viewing the remains.

At nightfall the young man felt he ought to sit up with the dead,
but duty to his mother called him homeward. One of his good
friends, Hugh McMahon, offered to do the office for him. On his
way home a screech owl chasing a mouse scurried across the path
in front of him, flapping its big flat wings. He should have turned
back as it meant bad luck, but didn't. That night he slept, but
had troubled dreams. Though it was chilly he kept the window of
his room open. It seemed he saw a female figure astride a broomstick flying across the horned moon, a cat upon her back.

At dawn he started for the house of sorrow. Midway he met old
Christ, leaning on a staff and puffing for breath as he hobbled
along. "My God, Conrad!" he exclaimed. "Hugh went out for a
drink of water about midnight, and someone stole our corpse; the
pet cat, overcome with grief, has also disappeared."

Conrad turned white as the hoarfrost and trembled like an
aspen. The truth was now revealed, though he dared not offend
the old man by telling it to him. He hurried to the cabin and carefully examined the premises, but could see no earthly way that the
body could have been removed. Hugh McMahon, sobbing like a
child, sat on a log by the river; surely he was not to blame. The
only charitable thing to do was to say that the body had been stolen
by persons unknown. After consoling the grief-stricken couple as
best he could, Conrad returned home.

His mother met him at the door. "My God, Conrad son," she
said, when he had told her everything, "I knew it was so, and to
prove it that new broom has vanished." The young man made a
search, but it was nowhere to be found. Gone also were the moccasins and mittens that the dead girl had given him. "It must have
been Elizabeth I saw riding across the moon last night," he mused
sadly.

Pike County Tall Tales

by ROBERT J. WHEELER

Pike County, the most easterly of the border counties bounded by the Delaware River, is very hilly with many streams and beautiful lakes. In the old days when it was covered with a great stand of white pine, yellow pine, hemlock, spruce, tamarack, and all the hardwoods found in the eastern part of the United States, the county was full of good-natured storytellers. By nature the old-time Pike County resident was mild, reasonable, kind to his wife and other domestic animals, a good neighbor, and, occasionally, even a church member. But once he got well oiled with the brand of home-brew made in those hills he could tell the wildest yarns ever heard. The potency of those concoctions was unlike anything on earth outside of Pike County. Their effect on the victim's imagination was immediate and fabulous.

I shall always cherish those moments of my boyhood and youth when I sat at the feet of Pike County storytellers with open-mouthed awe as they spun their charm over me. Those backwoods Homers, who could keep an audience spellbound with their oral sagas of days gone by, provided the one type of entertainment available to all boys and girls. One of my boyhood homes in the county was what I call "The House by the Side of the Road," at Brink's Pond. The Milford road was crossed by the Bone Ridge road at our place, and so we had a lot of passers-by. In those days travelers walked, rode horseback, used a buckboard or heavy wagon. The roads were mere tracks between the stones, and the sound of a wagon falling from stone to stone could be heard a great distance. When a traveler approached near mealtime or when night was falling, it was the custom of the country to call him in for meals or accommodations, if he wished to stay overnight. We had so little contact with the outside world that a traveler was indeed welcome.

The most popular of our overnight guests was a neighbor named John Greening. John wore a heavy black beard. In cold weather he was dressed in a long black overcoat. His hairy appearance and his gruffness always made me think of a pirate. Whenever John Greening stopped at our house we begged him to stay overnight. This he was always willing to do. When the chores were done and supper dishes cleared away, John would sit in front of the fire and tell us wonderful adventure stories of Tom Quick, Pike County's great Indian fighter. John was a great romancer and could tell the most exciting hunting stories. At bedtime two scared little boys (my brother and I) would climb up to bed and be chased all night by Tom Quick's Indians or John Greening's bears.

Lige Pelton was another old-time storyteller I remember from my boyhood. He was our neighbor when we lived in Snufftown, a suburb of Hawley just across the Paupac River close to the Pike County line. On nights when we had built a big fire on the commons and were gathered around it, Lige would come out and tell stories.

Lige "fit in th' Civil War." With a couple of other Pike County boys, he held the Devil's Den and "liked to have licked Longstreet's hull army," as he would put it.

Lige was known all over Pike County for his yarns. At barnraisings, vendues, and political meetings, Lige regaled the boys with his hair-raising, bloodcurdling stories of Indian fighting. Most of his repertoire, however, consisted of tall tales, of which he had hundreds. He would tell them according to a formula all his own. "Storytelling," Lige would say, "is a lot like cookin'. Ye got to have a good experience. Now take me. I've told my share of yarns, and no one can say that Lige Pelton ever fell down on a story. It's a gift. But then, they is ways an' ye can l'arn 'em.

"One time a city feller came up to Hawley to rest. He wuz a storyteller himself an' got paid fur it, so he said. He used to poke around a lot an' him an' me went fishin' often. He liked me to tell yarns while we fished. He laughed a lot and always wanted me to keep on tellin' yarns. One day I told him about th' soft-soaped mule an' he liked that best. He used to make notes, an' that day, when he got back home, he gave me a paper that he had rit an' told me it wuz a receipt fur storytellin' like I told 'em. He said he made it up while he listened to me. But he said it wuz really my own way of tellin' 'em an' that no one could beat it. I have it here, just as he give it to me an' I'll give it to ye. Ye go to school a lot an' maybe ye can understand th' big words, Bob."

I took the paper and read:

"Lige Pelton's Recipe for Tall Stories"

"To make a tall story, you first take a modicum of fact; mix it with a lot of plausible circumstances; blend in plenty of descriptive words and well-rounded paragraphs; stir in times, places, characteristics, and psychological situations; flavor with quantities of highly-colored imagination; sweeten with a dash of moral observations and serve without apologies."

Lige Pelton was a charter member of a group of lovable old liars who used to meet at Bill McCarty's on the turnpike and, between swigs of hard cider, vie with one another in telling the biggest whoppers. I don't remember all their names any more. But there were John Greening, Big Bill Bradford, Charley Redding, Old Pap Curry, Tim Drake of Parker's Glen, Andy Mulligan of Matamorris, and, of course, Lige Pelton.

"The weather ain't like it used to be when I come to this country," said Bill Bradford, at one of these meetings. "Why, I mind one time when Bob Wheeler and me went fishin' on the ice at Big Pond (now Twin Lakes). We cut down two feet with the ax and then took the ice chisel and cut four feet more before we reached the water. The pressure on the water was so great that as soon as the hole was cut, the water spurted up into the air and froze as fast as it came out. Before you could say 'Jack Sprat,' there was a big hill of ice twenty feet high. We had to dump hunks of ice back into the hole or all the water in the lake would have squirted out."

"Yah, I seed it colder than that," said Charley Redding. "The first winter I lived on the Mitchell place it was colder than that. I got up before daylight to feed the stock and when I came back to the house, the flame in the lantern was froze stiff and I had to break it off to put the light out."

"Huh," snorted Old Pap Curry, "I've lived around here longer than enny of you fellers an' I mind one time when it was so cold that when the rooster got up an' came out to crow in the morning, his breath froze all the way from the barn to the house in a line, an' the wife came out an' hung up her wash on the line."

"Whin I come to Parker's Glen," recalled Tim Drake, "it was so cold that winter that th' wather froze in th' boilers av th' Erie engines whin they passed Parker's Glen an' stopped all th' trains from Port Jervis to Lackawaxen."

" 'Tis true," declared Andy Mulligan. "Th' same winter, whin I got up wan mornin' an' wan av th' b'ys wint by an' called th' house, an' I wint out to talk wid 'im, me words an' his, too, fell in a small pile at our feet, an' we had to carry thim in an' thaw thim out in a fryin' pan before we could understand a word we said."

"Wall," put in John Greening, "I mind some cold winters in Pike County. I wuz out b'ar huntin' one day an' I had only two loads fur th' gun. I didn't see no b'ar, so on th' way home I see a deer an' give it one load; then a cat jumps up an' I let it have th' other. By'n'by I see a whoppin' b'ar a-comin' right at me, an' I had nary a bullet. I wuz so scared th' sweat run off me in big drops an' froze as fast as it fell an' made a little pile at my feet just like bullets. That gave me an idea. I had a little powder left in th' pouch, an' I dropped it into th' gun, piled a lot of them big frozen drops in, an' just as th' b'ar stood up to swat me, I let him have it. It wuz so cold that when th' ice bullets came out, an'wuz turned into water by th' heat of th' powder, the cold froze th' water into a long, sharp icicle an' it hit th' b'ar right in th' eye an' went clean into his brain. Then the heat of th' b'ar's head melted th' icicle an' th' b'ar drapped dead from water on th' brain."

"Boys," said Lige Pelton, as he passed the hard cider, "I guess it's time we went home. But before ye go, I want to tell about one night when I wuz comin' along by Tafton an' th' Northern Lights came out an' it wuz so cold that they froze stiff an' stayed out until th' sun came out th' next day an' melted 'em."

The Self-Swallowing Blacksnakes

John Hobdy of Peck's Pond had lived all his life in Pike County. He was a mighty hunter and trapper, and in his day had seen about everything there was to be seen in the woods. Some of them were beyond belief, but old John Hobdy would swear on a stack of Bibles that they were true. He had a fifth sense in hunting. He did not have to see game; he simply sensed its presence. If he came within a hundred yards of a bear or a wildcat, he said he could just feel the critter in the vicinity.

"Yuh see, Bob," he would say. "It's this a-way. Yuh git to feel things. Somehow or other they is a sorta connection between me and th' wild critters. If I git close to a b'ar or a 'cat, th' hair back o' my neck appears to stand up an' I jest know th' critter is there."

Whenever I passed by Peck's Pond and found John home, I would go in to drink in his natural wit and wisdom. Over a period of many years I drew freely upon his store of yarns. I remember one of my visits. He was rocking on the porch of his little house overlooking Pinchot Island.

"Well, John, what's new?" I asked.

"Heh! heh! heh," old John chuckled. "Allus lookin' fur new ones, heh? Wall, I seed suthin' this mornin' I haint seed fur some time. I wuz just down th' road a piece, lookin' fur turtle eggs, when I seed two blacksnakes a-fightin'. They wuz big fellers, most of a size, an' when they ud fit a bit, th' one begin to swaller the other. He took him by th' tail an' kept swallerin' an' th' other took him by th' tail an' started swallerin'. By'n'by, both snakes got all th' way around an' th' heads met. Yessir, just met. An' by heck, while I stood there an' watched, they swallered each other. Yessir, swallered each other an' I come along home, thinkin' to myself, now if Bob Wheeler ud come along, there's a good one fur him to tell them folks down in Allentown."

A Pretty Big Blacksnake

Down Kimbles way a fellow lived on a little place close to the canal. One day he and a neighbor, each fortified with a bottle of homemade applejack, went squirrel hunting. After a morning of good hunting, during which many squirrels had been shot, the two men decided to sit down for their lunch. They found what looked like a nice big log, stood their guns alongside it, and began eating. One of the men took out his case knife to cut a piece of cheese. When he had cut off a hunk to give to his fellow hunter he stuck the knife deep into the log. And, believe it or not, the log moved swiftly from under them and disappeared into the brush. For, you see, it wasn't a log after all, but a big blacksnake.

When the hunters had recovered from their astonishment, they picked up their guns and went home. In moving up the road, the snake had left a big, wide track as if someone had dragged a big stovepipe over soft sand. The hunters followed the track to the point where it led to the brush and were fearful of going any farther. To quiet their nerves they began taking swigs out of their bottles. By the time they had drained their bottles of applejack, they recovered their courage. Their drunken state did not prevent their walking, but it seems the liquor had fired their imagination.

Walking homeward, they came to a farmhouse along the road. Just as they neared the house they caught sight of the big black-snake stretched across the road. They put down their guns and looked the snake over for size. It was the same snake all right. It reached from the field on one side of the road, across the road, and over the stone wall of the other field. And as they watched it, the snake raised its head about six feet off the ground on the other side. By this time they were so flabbergasted by the snake's great size, or by what the applejack made them think was the snake's size, that had the snake not taken advantage of their hesitation to move quickly away, they might have seen two heads, and thereby given Pike County another unbeatable snake story.

I heard about the incident some time after it had happened. One of those fellows said that he was saving the story for me and was not releasing it to the general public because of the tendency of some people to exaggerate Pike County snake stories. He said he knew that I would tell it just as it had happened.

When all the facts were in, this is how I reconstructed the incident:

The road was about five feet wide. Along both sides of the road there was a space of about three feet between the road tracks and the stone fences on either side. The stone fences were about three feet high and a foot wide. Now the snake was stretched across the fences and the road, with parts in each field and enough of it to enable it to raise its head up six feet above the fence.

I was very careful in calculating the distances, because even an amateur naturalist like myself must have his facts straight. I allowed about four feet of the snake on the one side in the field, three feet to the top of the wall, one foot across the wall, three feet down to the ground, three feet to the edge of the road, five feet across the road, three feet to the wall, three feet to the top of the wall, one foot over, three feet to the ground, about six feet on the ground, and six feet to the head of the snake as it looked over the wall at the hunters. The hunter checked up with me as I made these calculations. He set the figures down as I called them out. When we added them up, the snake was exactly forty-one feet. We checked and double checked, but the figures held. The old hunter was not entirely satisfied. He thought the snake was a bit longer, but I pointed out that he saw it after he had emptied his bottle. Then he admitted that he might have been a little too liberal in his estimate of the snake at that time.

HOOPSNAKES AND THEIR STING

There have always been hoopsnakes in Pike County. Maybe they don't have them in other counties. But then, maybe, they don't drink the kind of liquor made in Pike County.

Well, anyway, there are hoopsnakes in Pike County. Now a hoopsnake may be between five and fifteen feet long and may be colored blue, green, orange, pink, or white and black, according to what the observer has been drinking and how long he has been at it. Stories vary with the locality. In some parts of the county they make whisky out of apples; some sections make it out of rye; and in other settlements they make it out of radiator fluid.

But while Pike County citizens honestly differ as to the color and size of the hoopsnakes they have seen, everyone agrees that the hoopsnake has a stinger on its tail and that it rolls along by taking the tip of its tail in its mouth, which turns it into a sort of hoop. When it holds its tail in its mouth, the tip is covered with a deadly poison; when the snake sees a victim, it lets go of its tail and spears whatever it aims at with the poisoned tail.

Of course, there are a lot of skeptical folks who doubt this. But some people won't believe anything. Lots of folks don't believe that Jonah swallowed the whale, but that doesn't prove anything.

About the best hoopsnake story I ever heard was the one old Bill Durham used to tell. Bill was a raftsman in the days when they ran rafts down the Delaware. Rafts from up Hawley way were made into bigger ones at Lackawaxen and floated down to Philadelphia. While they were making up the rafts, the rivermen stayed at the Williams Hotel just below the point where the Lackawaxen River empties into the Delaware.

"Yeh!" said old Bill, "o' course, they is hoopsnakes. Why, they wuz a feller down to Matamorris who had a little field down close to the river. This feller wuz out hoeing corn one morning and along about nine o'clock he wuz a-leanin' on the hoe handle, restin'. He looked up the corn row, and there wuz a big hoopsnake rollin' right at him. All he could do wuz to stand behind the hoe handle, and when the snake struck at him, it hit the hoe handle close to the head. The feller wuz so scared he just ran for the house and left the snake stuck to the handle.

"Along about five o'clock, the feller started out to see what had become of the hoopsnake. He had heered that snakes what git into fights die at sundown, and it wuz nearing dark then. So he stole back to where he had the fight with the snake and, sure enough, there wuz the snake, dead as a last spring shad. But the pizen had swole the handle up until it was as big as a saw log. Now this feller wuz a thrifty cuss so he ran back, got his team, drug the log down to the sawmill, had it sawed up into shingles, and shingled his barn with them. But when the first big rain come, it washed out all the pizen and the shingles all shrunk up and fell off, or you could've seed it to this day."

THE FISHING COW

Long before my time there was a sawmill at Peck's Pond and a dam backing up water for miles. Old-timers told me that the pickerel in that water were so big and fierce that few people dared swim in it. In the passing years the people who had worked in the mill died or moved away, and no one lived there any more. The abandoned mill crumbled with age and the dam broke, but the old millpond remained. In its waters pickerel continued to thrive on frogs, turtles, young ducks, and, of course, on shiners.

Over on the Shohola a man named Hipe Rake found out about the pickerel in this pond. He went over to fish one day, and when the pickerel bit so fast he conceived the idea of catching them wholesale and selling them in Hawley.

Hipe built up a regular business, fishing every Thursday and selling his catch in Hawley on Friday. His business grew so fast, however, that he began to worry because he couldn't handle all of it by himself. He hesitated hiring an assistant because that would have given his business secret away. He could not fish two successive days because he could not keep his catch that long without their spoiling. So he worked just as hard as he could on Thursdays without being able to take care of all his customers. And he lost a lot of business.

Then a wonderful thing happened that solved his problem. Charley Hazen told me about it. Charley used to catch rattlesnakes at the High Knob den every spring and sell them to tourists in the summer. I was over to his place one day buying a yellow rattler when Charley told me all about it.

"Yeh," said Charley, "I mind th' time when Hipe had that cow. Real pert critter she wuz. Used to go over to Peck's Pond every day to graze an' stand in th' water round about noon an' fight flies. This here cow wuz standin' in th' pond one day, when Hipe wuz a-fishin', an' wuz a-swingin' her tail, a-fightin' th' deer flies. Everytime she swung her tail, th' end would drag in th' water. Now a pickerel is so fierce it'll jump at anything that moves. So when Hipe's cow drug her tail over an' back, th' pickerel got to jumpin' at it an' their big teeth got caught in th' end of th' tail. Th' old cow just swung an' swung, an' every time she swung, a big pike caught her tail an' she swung it right out on th' bank.

"Hipe wuz a-sittin' there fishin', an' he seed th' cow swing a big pickerel up on th' bank. He run over just in time to see her yank another one out. An' when he got close, he seed quite a pile of big pike a-jumpin' around. Well, sir, that cow chucked out more than enough fish for Hipe to haul home an' after that, he didn't have to work. Old Bossy caught all th' fish. They do say Hipe got to be right well off with th' fishin' cow."

MY WHITE-WHISKERED CATFISH

When I was a boy and lived on the old Merinton place above the Twin Lakes, I used to fish a lot. In the Big Pond, especially in the Merington Cove and around the big lily bed, catfish were most numerous, but the really big fish lived in the Little Pond.

We would keep our poles and lines piled up at our landing in the Little Pond. Pickerel and shiners were very numerous and often, when we came down to get water or to go out in the boat, we would see a pickerel chasing a shiner into the shallow water toward shore. On our side of the pond, the prevailing winds beat the water against the shore and the stones in the shallow water were worn flat and thin. Shiners, driven into the shallow water by the fierce pickerel, often were found partly under a flat stone. Sometimes we would catch the shiner, put him on a hook, and throw out and catch the pickerel that would be waiting for the shiner to come out.

One day I was at the landing when I saw a big shiner flapping under a flat stone in the shallow water. I quickly caught up one of our poles, put the shiner on, and looked for the pickerel. Evidently he had grown tired of waiting for the hapless shiner and had gone hunting farther down the pond.

There was a man fishing from a boat a short distance away and I started down toward him, still looking for the pickerel. Along this shore in the Little Pond, the water was shallow for about fifteen feet out, then it deepened to about twenty feet or more.

The water in this lake is very clear and one can see the white sand at the bottom. When I got opposite the boat, I looked under and there I saw a monster catfish swishing under the boat. At once I dropped my lively shiner in front of him, and he grabbed the shiner up. In my excitement, I pulled too soon and the result was I tore the shiner off the hook. When he felt the sting of the hook tearing out, he wriggled himself out of the catfish's mouth, dove under the monster, and fastened himself onto the catfish's tail. The big catfish whirled around once or twice, trying to rid himself of the fighting shiner. Then he drove right to shore and bounced out on the land with the fighting shiner fast to his tail.

When I got to him, the catfish was sitting up on his tail, with the big tears running down his face. Boylike, I felt sorry for the poor frightened fish and I unhooked the savage shiner from his tail and, taking him by one of his big fins, I led him to the water and let him get away. As he swam gratefully away, I noticed that he had one white whisker.

Years afterward I was fishing at about the same spot and I caught a monster catfish. When I pulled him ashore, I saw that it was my old friend, the white-whiskered catfish.

And, do you know, he recognized me. Yes sir, that white-whiskered catfish recognized me. He wriggled and gurgled with joy so glad was he to meet an old friend again.

And I thought what a beautiful thing is friendship. Even the dumb animals are moved by the sentiment of friendship. Here the white-whiskered catfish remembered me after all these years.

Of course, I could not keep him. I gently removed the hook and let him go again. I can still see him, gaily waving his tail as he swam away. Perhaps I shall meet him again sometime when I am fishing in the Little Pond. I'm sure that he would be as glad as ever to see me.

THE ANANIASAURIUS

In the good old days, a thrifty citizen of Pike County used to lay in a barrel of Jersey salt herring every fall to be eaten by his family after the sowbelly had given out.

One spring, when the herring barrel was empty and the man dumped out the brine, four large round objects like eggs rolled out. After being washed off, they were found to be white eggs of some kind. Puzzled, the man took them to the New York Museum of Natural History where he left them to be examined by scientists.

About a week later, the man received a letter from the curator telling him that the eggs were those of the "Ananiasaurius," a prehistoric mammal that lived in the swamps and streams of eastern Pennsylvania about two million years ago. "It is my belief," wrote the curator, "that if these eggs are planted in the mud of a warm lake, they might hatch out."

Well, a Pike County citizen will try anything once. The man took the eggs up to a lake high up on what they call High Knob above Peck's Pond and planted them in the warm mud on the east side of the lake.

A few years afterward, stories began to be told about some fearsome animal that lived in a lake up beyond High Knob. Finally, the stories reached the man who had planted the eggs. He got excited at once. Maybe the eggs had hatched out after all. "I'll go up and try to catch the damn thing," he said to himself. "Maybe I'll get something for it."

So one day the man took his gun and hied himself up to the lake beyond High Knob to look for the animal that might have hatched out of one of the eggs he had planted. It was a long distance and he did not get there until about four o'clock in the afternoon. When he finally broke through the swamp and reached the edge of the grassy lake, he was tired and a bit uneasy. It was a gloomy-looking place. The tall grass along the shore was all pressed down and when he went closer, he could see deep beaten paths worn along the lake side. It looked as though some great heavy animal had been dragging its body along through the grass. He could see clearly the imprints of immense, three-toed foot tracks in the mud. Slowly he followed the tracks that led around a bend in the lake.

The sun set behind the high mountain. Twilight spread over the lake. As he advanced along the path beaten down by the great three-toed animal, he began to feel a nameless fear. Strange prickling sensations began to run up and down his spine, "creeps" some folks call them; people always feel that way when they are about to run into some terrible danger. There was something around.

He felt it. Every sound in the woods seemed to him to be loud and startling as though there was something fearful hanging around just out of sight, waiting to grab him. Once a deer jumped away in front of him, and his hat lifted right up and down on his head as his hair stood up. In a word, he was scared.

All of a sudden he heard a terrific scream, a sort of cross between a locomotive and a steam calliope. His hair sprang up so straight that he never saw his hat again. There, right across the little lake, stood a great beast. Its body was a blood red, encased in a scaly armor. It stood upright about thirty feet tall. Its head was a brilliant blue, with great staring eyes ringed by a bright yellow circle a foot across. Its wide open sawtooth beak was a grass green. From the top of its head to its tail it must have been all of eighty feet. A ridge of sawlike teeth ran from head to tail. As it stood up and screamed at him it held its three claw feet close to its scaly breast.

Only an instant the man stood there. Then he turned and fled back to the forest as though the very devil was after him. He could hear the great beast leaping and plunging through the water behind him. Right in front of him as he neared the hardwoods stood a mighty pine tree. Without a moment's hesitation, the man swarmed up the branches of that tree just as the terrible monster came out of the swamp, screaming and snapping its great beak up after him. But the man had too much of a start and he was able to climb high enough to escape out of reach of the scaly horror.

Down below, the beast thrashed about, roaring and screaming. After a while its cries stopped. For a while the man heard nothing. Then he began to hear a funny, scraping sound. After a time, the big pine began to tremble strangely. Frightened, the man hurriedly climbed down until he could reach the limbs of a big oak tree that intertwined with those of the pine. Hardly had he reached the safety of the oak, when the big pine tree swayed and fell with a resounding crash. Now arose a mighty roaring and thrashing about on the ground below. It lasted for at least a half hour, then died away into heavy moans and groans, and then all was still.

The man climbed down lower until he could see the ground. To his amazement he saw that the Thing had actually sawed down the big pine with its saw tail and, in falling, the tree had pinned the mighty beast under it. Even as he watched its death struggles in horror, the Thing gave up and died.

When he got his wits again, the man climbed down from the tree and ran away from that spot as though the devil himself was on his trail.

Of course, when he related his experience, neither family nor neighbors believed his fantastic tale. But he insisted on organizing a party and the next day they reached the site of his encounter with the Thing.

The mighty tree was lying on the ground, as he had said, but alas! red ants had eaten the flesh of the Ananiasaurius and porcupines had gnawed up all its bones.

The Bear That Talked

Charley Smith and his family were hungry. All winter they had been subsisting on corn meal and sowbelly. The snow had been too deep in the woods to permit Charley to work. He had a hard time cutting enough wood to keep from freezing.

But now that the soft winds had banished the snow and ice, Charley had to go cut some railroad ties so that the family could have a change of food. Ties were sold in Shohola and only with money could one get groceries.

So Charley was out looking for ties. He worked hard. All about him spring was on the advance; brooks were burbling; buds were bursting; birds were singing. All nature was awake.

"How beautiful are all things here," mused Charley. The influence of spring in Pike County can make a poet out of any kind of a hick.

"Ah," sighed Charley, "how I love nature and th' wild folks. From now on I am a-goin' to be friends with everything."

Up along the hillside, a big mother bear came out of the brush and regarded Charley with amusement. "Listen to that big lug," she said to herself. "Only last fall he was looking for me with a gun. Now he loves everybody. Well, now, that gives me an idea."

The bear shuffled off into the brush to where she had planted her four cubs.

"Here's my chance to get a lift with this big family," she said. "I'm sure I'll not be able to bring up all these cubs in the manner which Pike County bear cubs are accustomed to. So I'll take a chance and plant one with this mug while his heart is soft. He loves everything."

So while Charley slashed at the trees, the old bear took her smallest cub and planted it in Charley's dinner bucket. Then she hustled the rest up behind a big bunch of laurel and waited.

By this time Charley had cut enough ties for the old team to haul; so he put on his coat, took up his bucket, and sauntered on home, well satisfied that he had done a worthy day's work: something remarkable for Charley. When Charley got home and the kids opened his dinner bucket to see if he had left anything, out popped the cutest little black bear you ever saw. He was black as coal and had the funniest little turned-up nose and jet-black eyes.

"Well, now, what do you think of that!" Charley said. "That damn old bear that lives in th' swamp planted this cub on me. Why, we can't afford another kid in this family. First thing you know I'll have to go to work in th' summer." And Charley vowed that he would take the cub right back in the morning. But when morning came, Charley was too tired from his exertions to get up right away and when he did get out, the kids were playing about the yard with the cub.

So that settled it. The woman and the kids set up such a howl to keep the bear that Charley agreed and the little bear became one of the family.

Now there must be something about the method of education in the backwoods that makes animals learn so easy. That cub got on to all the tricks the kids could teach him and actually learned to talk before the summer was over.

You don't believe it? Well, neither do I. But seeing is believing. That bear learned to talk and the next year he could read. Yes, sir, actually read.

He grew big over the summer and finally he insisted on going out with Charley. Wherever Charley went, the bear went too, and after people got used to him, they treated him like another person. And that's what started all the trouble.

Pike County folks are hospitable. When a neighbor comes over to call they always set out the drinks. Of course, the bear soon learned to drink. After that, the poor wife had two men coming home drunk instead of one. But she was not married to the bear, so she didn't have to stand for his monkeyshines. When he came home drunk one day and began to swear at the children, the wife chased him out of the place with the broom, and the poor bear, whose bad habits had now cost him his home, staggered off up the road to Peck's Pond.

Things might have been all right and he might have sobered up, but unfortunately he came to a summer cottage first. Nobody was home and the bear went poking about the garage and up on the back porch. He did not find anything there, so he loafed about the yard until he found the ground cellar. The summer residents had left the cellar unlocked; the bear lifted the door and went down. Inside the lower door, he found a long bottle labeled "Lehigh County applejack."

"Ha," said the bear. "I've heard Charley tell about this Lehigh County applejack. I'll try it."

Now they tell a lot of yarns about that Lehigh County applejack. One of the best is about the fisherman who used it to catch bait for pickerel fishing. That fisherman found it out accidentally. He used to bring a bottle along solely for defense against snakes. One day he was fishing along the lake and a pickerel took his bait off. The man looked around for a frog that he might use and he came upon a big water snake swallowing one that was just the size he wanted. So he stepped on the snake and tried to get the frog out of its mouth, but snakes have hooked teeth and this one hung on like grim death. Then the fisherman thought of the bottle of applejack he had in his hip pocket. He took it out, removed the stopper, and poured a drop or two into the snake's mouth. Choking, the snake spit out the frog, and the fisherman caught it and went on fishing. A little while later, as he was fishing from the end of the boat, he heard a sound, something slapping against the side of the boat. At first he thought it was waves playing against the boat, but the lake was perfectly smooth. Then he looked down and, believe it or not, there was the water snake with another frog.

Well, imagine the poor bear tackling such stuff. He was used to ordinary Pike County applejack, but the variety made in Lehigh County was something else again.

The bear in the summer cottage took one swig of the Lehigh

County applejack and jumped three feet in the air. Blowing the applejack out of his mouth, he ran down the road yelling, "Help! Help! Help! I'm poisoned."

And, do you know, no one ever saw that bear again.

THE SWAPPERS

In my Pike County boyhood, swapping reached the proportions of a major industry. How well I remember seeing the people sitting around and swapping at barn-raisings, vendues, weddings, funerals, and other occasions that drew them together! Those old-time swappers would barter anything from a jackknife to a farm. There was very little money in the county in those far-off days, and trading was about the only way folks had of meeting their wants in worldly goods. Sometimes it went to extremes. The story is told of a fellow down along the Delaware swapping his wife for a mule and a buggy. As the story goes, both got stuck. The woman was a redhead, and the mule had the blind staggers, while the buggy had only one wheel.

Many are the tales of the skill and ingenuity of the old-time swappers. One of the best I ever heard was told to me by Charley Smith, who himself had been a skillful trader. One day when I had nothing else to do, I drew Charley out on the swapping of those bygone days. He beamed, leaned back in his rocker, and reminisced as follows:

HOW A DOG MADE PETE ANDREWS RICH

I mind them old days right well. Them old boys used to be some punkins at swappin'. There wuz Lige Pelton, th' snake man. Lige was a great swapper. Why, he'd ruther swap than eat an' sometimes he just had to swap to eat. Lige wuz no great shakes at workin'. I mind one time Lige started out to cut some ties over on th' turnpike. Along th' road he met one of th' Greening boys. Th' Greenings wuz great swappers, too, an' Lige swapped his ax fur a hound pup. Th' Greening boys had lots of pups, but they needed an ax. So they swapped.

Lige must have been a little put out by th' swap after he done it, because he still needed to git some ties if he wuz goin' to eat that week. So he went on down th' road to Bill McCarty's place where he met John Hoffman. Now John Hoffman wuz a great dog man. He'd buy a good dog any time. Lige showed him th' pup. It wuz a nice pup. Th' Greening boys had good dogs. Hoffman wanted to buy th' pup, but Lige wouldn't sell. "Seems as though it's not fair to th' pup to sell him like he wuz a slave or suthin'," said Lige. "Now if ye wuz to say swap I'd take ye on."

"Tell ye what I'll do, Lige," said Hoffman. "I got a lot of ties down to my place that I'm countin' to take down to Shohola. I'll swap ye a small jag of ties for the pup." "Done," said Lige. So they swapped. Lige took th' ties to Shohola, bought a new ax, and had a load of groceries, an' that wuz that.

They wuz a lot of good swappers down our way when I wuz a boy. I mind one feller, name of Pete Andrews. This feller wuz so good that when he died a few years back, they had to hold an auction to git rid of all th' stuff. He had swapped all his life an' he started with only a yaller hound-dog fur capital. This feller started swappin' in his diaper days. They tell of Pete swappin' all th' rest of th' kids outen their Christmas presents, an' his pappy havin' to buy them all back from Pete. It never did no good though because Pete had them all back in a few days.

When Pete wuz goin' to th' Notch school, he had a pocketknife with a handle all pretty colored glass. Th' kids got all het up over that knife. A lot of them talked swap with Pete, so he swapped th' knife to one of th' Haas boys for a pair of skates. Pete made th' Haas boy believe that he could use th' knife the hull year 'round and th' skates wuz good only now an' then when th' Shohola Creek wuz froze over. It wuz a good swap.

On th' way home, Pete swapped th' skates to one of th' Shields boys fur a calf. When he got home with th' calf, his pappy swapped him a brood sow fur th' calf. Come spring th' brood sow had thirteen little ones an' Pete wuz set up in business.

Pete grew up and got married. He never needed no money. He had a lot of good stock then and a nice piece of land, all got by swappin'. He built a log house an' barn just by swappin'. Course th' neighbors helped with th' house an' barn at a raisin'. Pete swapped fur a team of mules an' some farm tools, an' give some of his stock in th' swap.

But th' best of all th' yarns about Pete swappin' I shoulda told afur, fur, after all, this is what set Pete up.

When Pete wuz about sixteen, his pappy brought home a yaller hound pup an' give it to Pete. Th' yaller pup grew up to be a big dog an' wuz just about th' beatenest hound-dog in the hull of Pike County. He wuz about the smartest dog I ever seed, an' Pete claimed that Old Sam, as he called him, could really talk, if ye could understand dog talk, an' Pete allowed he did. Anyway, this yaller hound-dog wuz Pete's capital. After he got past sixteen he wuz on his own an' he traveled around a lot with th' yaller dog, an' just swapped. But th' big thing wuz th' way Pete trained Old Sam.

In those days people put a sight of store by a good hound-dog. Pete's yaller hound wuz a good one an' th' hull county wuz always tryin' to swap Pete outen him, an' this give Pete his big idea.

So one day Pete got ready to go on a swappin' trip. Afur he started, he fed Old Sam a lot of mush an' other fixin's that dogs like. When Old Sam had swallered it all up, Pete fixed another lot but he did not let Sam eat it. He just let him see it and smell it, then he pulled him away and drug him off by th' chain. On th' way down th' road, Old Sam kept pullin' back, wantin' to git back to his dish, but Pete drug him along until he came to Joe Samson's place, a couple miles down th' road.

Joe wuz one of th' fellers who wuz always tryin' to git Old Sam. Him an' Pete talked a while, about swappin' as usual. Pete allowed he wuz not interested. "Got nothin' to swap just now," said Pete. "What about Old Sam?" said Joe. "Kind o' like to have Old Sam. Give ye th' little red heifer for Sam," said Joe. "Nope," said Pete. "Wouldn't swap Old Sam fur ary heifer ye got; 'sides, Old Sam wouldn't stay with ye. Run home th' fust time he got loose."

They talked a long time about swappin', an' finally Pete swapped Old Sam fur th' heifer, two shoats, an' a big goose. But Pete kept tellin' Joe that Sam wouldn't stay with him.

So th' next day Joe brought th' stock over an' took Old Sam home. Well, it turned out just as Pete told him. Old Sam come home th' fust time he got out an' made fur his dish, which Pete kept filled up, waitin' fur Sam to come home. Old Sam licked up th' food an' Pete kept fillin' th' dish up an' Old Sam et til he wuz fit to bust.

That afternoon, Joe come over to git Sam, all het up because th' dog had run away. Pete took it calm-like. "Told ye Old Sam wouldn't stay with ye," he said. "Wunt stay anywhere but to hum. Tell ye what I'll do, Joe. I'll give ye back th' heifer. Ought to have suthin' fur my trouble." Joe allowed that wuz fair so he took th' heifer an' went home, glad to git suthin' back.

After that, every time Pete went swappin', he filled Sam's dish an' drug him away when he had half et. This made Sam long to git back to finish th' good fixin's. Pete swapped Old Sam to a lot of fellers in Pike County afur th' trick got found out. Then he worked th' same trick over in Monroe County, an' along th' Wayne County side of th' Paupac, an' every time Old Sam came back. Pete got right smart rich with Old Sam before a rattlesnake bit the hound-dog an' he died.

THE SOFT-SOAPED MULE

About seventy-five years ago, the Collingswood Lumber Company began to cut timber in the Paupac River Valley marking the boundary between Pike and Wayne counties. Timber was cut in winter and floated downstream at flood stage in spring and summer.

When the first heavy cut of timber was made, the rivermen charged with floating the logs found that the main stream was lost when the river rose to a stage of six or more feet. Instead of floating toward the big sawmill at Wilsonville, Wayne County, the logs drifted all over the forest wherever vagrant streams carried them. Even when rafts were spiked together the stream could not be followed when the oxbow country was reached. Thus too many logs were lost.

Finally, the company rigged up a flat-bottomed boat with a paddle wheel at the stern propelled by a horse walking a treadmill. The boat made its way upstream and came back towing rafts of logs. The towboat worked all right at flood stage; but when the water receded and the river returned to its natural course, too much time was lost going around the oxbow loops through which the river wound its way down the valley. The worst place on the river was in front of the Schuman farm where the loops were so close they resembled a bunch of shoestrings folded together.

So a canal was dug across the loops to force the river to flow on a straight course. Then it was found that a horse could not take the hard work on the treadmill. Mules were substituted but they, too, failed to bear the strain. At length, it was suggested that only a canal mule, inured to long-sustained strains, could fill the bill. After a long search, one was located on a farm near the notch.

It was a big black mule answering to the name of "Old Satan." Old Satan had seen service with Sherman in the Civil War and had put in many years on the Delaware & Hudson Canal. The farmer had obtained it in a trade for a hog one dark night. Probably both traders had been stuck; the hog was one of those famous Pike County razorbacks and the mule lived up to its name. The farmer found Old Satan the blackest, ugliest, most ornery, and least desirable mule in Pike County. Old Satan fought off work and when put into the barn kicked everything to pieces. He would chase the dogs and scare the women and children.

The farmer in desperation was about to shoot Old Satan when one day a remarkable thing happened. The mule was in the yard kicking things around as usual when suddenly he discovered a half barrel of soft soap that the women had made and hidden under a few boards near the kitchen. Old Satan knocked the boards off and drank the soft soap to the last drop.

The soft soap worked a miracle in Old Satan. He now became mild, good-natured, gentle, and quite agreeable to work. He played with the children. The farmer rode him to town, and the women hooked him to the buckboard and drove to church on Sundays. Old Satan was soft-soaped for life.

The tough old mule became a great boon in a country where soap was scarce. One Sunday morning one of the hired hands could not shave because he lacked soap. Then he remembered that after each rain Old Satan broke out in a thick lather. The mule lathered so easily that the boys used to say, "The soft soap is coming out of him." So this hired hand took a cup of warm water, poured it over Satan, worked up a thick lather, and shaved with it. And then on Mondays the women stood Old Satan over a washtub, poured water over him, and did their washing in the soapy water.

Well, when the farmer was asked by the Collingswood Lumber Company to sell Old Satan, he agreed to sell at a good price. And so this remarkable canal mule put in several more years walking the treadmill of the Paupac River boat, towing rafts of lumber downstream to the Wilsonville mill.

When at last Old Satan became too old to work, the company sold him to a barber over at Shohola Falls. With the mule as a source of supply, the barber never had to buy any more shaving soap. Old Satan set the style for the shaving-brush tails that mules wear today.

OLD DAN AND HIS LITTLE BROWN JUG

One of the workers at the Wilsonville sawmill in the Paupac Valley was old Dan Roberts. A picturesque character, he stood six feet four inches when his powerful shoulders were not hunched; they say he had the strength of five ordinary men. He was a company blacksmith.

In the folklore of Pike County, Dan Roberts will always be associated with his little brown jug. He was by all odds the heaviest drinker in the county. The commercial brands served in saloons were too mild for his taste, and so in his little shack at Tafton he distilled his own brand of "snake pizen," as the natives labeled it, and it was mighty powerful stuff.

Wherever Dan went, his little brown jug, filled with this home-made liquor, was sure to go too. As he passed along the road, his black beard reaching down to his waist and the little jug in his right hand, children would sing and run away:

> Ha, ha, ha, you and me,
> Little brown jug, how I love thee.

Old Dan regarded them with a haughty disdain when he was not amused.

He would go to work carrying an immense dinner bucket in one hand and the jug in the other. The jug had its accustomed place on the floor close to his work. In the course of the day Dan drained its contents.

Some evenings after work he would walk the mile to Hawley and make the rounds of its saloons. When he entered a place he would set his little brown jug on the bar in front of him and imbibe from it. He was quite generous with his liquor, offering to pass the jug around, but none of the regular customers could be persuaded to drink the stuff.

Now and then, however, a stranger took a slug with dire results. There was one fellow from Lackawaxen who boasted that he could drink anything any other man swallowed. So he tried a swig from old Dan's jug. The poor fellow fell to the floor in convulsions. A man holding a lantern jumped to his aid, but when the lantern ignited the wretched victim's breath he had to be carried out in flames.

One Decoration Day many years ago, old Dan Roberts was in town for the parade. As usual he made the rounds of the saloons with his little brown jug. As it was a holiday, he made an exception to his rule and drank the commercial brands with the boys, but he washed out the bad taste with the contents of his jug. So he was feeling high.

Along about six o'clock, he crossed the Wilsonville bridge and started up the little hill in front of the Wheeley place. A rabbit hopped up the hill in front of him and dove under a little ledge. Putting down the jug, Dan started to pull out loose stones so as to reach in to get at the rabbit. Now in those days there was a rattlesnake under almost every ledge. When Dan put his hand in to feel around for the rabbit, a rattlesnake, resenting the intrusion of its privacy, promptly bit him.

The sting of the snake bite made Dan withdraw his hand instantly, but the rattler, unable to unhook in the narrow space, held on. When Dan saw what he had, he shook the snake off, casting it into the brush. Then he reached into the hole again, withdrew the rabbit, and killed it. Without the slightest concern over the snake bite, he continued on his way home.

But what happened to the poor rattler is something else again. An hour or so after the encounter, a traveler saw that snake on the road rolling convulsively in the dust, frothing at the mouth, barking like a dog, and, taking its tail in its mouth, rolling off into the woods like a hoopsnake.

The next day, Al Wheeley found a swollen dead rattler in his barnyard. When he got to the mill he learned that several other men had also found dead rattlesnakes.

The epidemic seemed to spread until the entire neighborhood was strewn with dead rattlers. A group of local characters who made a living selling snake oil and skins hired an expert from New York to advise them on how to check the plague killing off their means of livelihood.

Well, the New York expert arrived, examined the carcasses of the dead rattlers, and finally came to the sound conclusion that they were all dead. But as to the cause of death he gave no inkling.

And the mystery remained unsolved for a long time. I have given the matter considerable thought through the years and believe I have found the key to the mystery. Dan Roberts had trained on his own brand of "snake pizen" so long he had built up an immunity to every other kind of snake poison. The poor rattler, on the other hand, in biting Dan came in contact with a poison so many times more potent than its own that it went raving mad. It bit every other rattler it met. Each of these rattlers in turn bit others until nearly all the rattlesnakes in Pike County had been inoculated. And they all died of delirium tremens.

Well, the lumber is all gone and so is the big mill that stood on the banks of the Paupac at Wilsonville. Gone, too, are the old-time lumberjacks, raftsmen, and millworkers who were part of a colorful era in the history of Pike County.

But I have no doubt that the county's rattlesnakes still tell their children of old Dan Roberts as a warning against biting human beings. Perhaps this accounts for so few summer visitors to Pike County being bitten by rattlers.

Conestoga Wagoners

by HOWARD C. FREY

Long before the coming of the canals and railroads, Pennsylvania German farmers transported their products to Philadelphia in Conestoga wagons. These vehicles, drawn by four to six horses, had become the public freight carriers of the colonies by 1750. Until they were supplanted by canalboats and trains, three thousand of these white-topped wagons rumbled along the mountain roads between Philadelphia and Pittsburgh every day. On the westward trip they carried textiles, hardware, and other manufactured goods for western settlers. At Pittsburgh they were loaded with furs, skins, and farm products for the East.

The men who drove the wagons through the valleys and over the mountains of our state were a dashing, roistering group of young fellows who enjoyed a glamour not unlike that which in a later era surrounded cowboys in the West. They were a race apart, like the special breed of Conestoga horses they drove. Something of the romantic appeal went out of the Pennsylvania countryside when the Conestoga wagons gave way to the iron horse.

There were two classes of Conestoga wagoners—the regulars, whose only occupation was hauling freight, and the militia, who were farmers devoting part of their time to this work. Some of them were English, some Irish, and a few Negro, but by far the majority were Pennsylvania Dutch—short, stocky, and robust. Many belonged to Pennsylvania's Plain Sects, like the Amish.

These hard-bitten men, travel-stained and bronzed by exposure, were toughened to the point of despising comforts. They feared nothing. They were proud of their teams, their wagons, and their work. Though they indulged excessively in "Old Rye" and "Monongahela," they rarely allowed drinking to interfere with their duties. They carried gimlet bits and little brown jugs, and stole their supply of whisky from the barrels that made up part of their cargoes. Yet, paradoxically, some of them were so religious as to refuse to move their wagons on Sunday.

Rugged individualists, they competed ruthlessly for the business of the road and the right of way. Teamsters traveling in opposite directions frequently settled with their fists disputes over the high middle of the narrow turnpikes. Occasionally the man who could outshout the other or pour forth a greater volume of profanity and abuse was the winner. Now and then sheer bluff had the same effect.

The Conestoga wagoner wore a broad-brimmed hat, a beard or mustache or both, a blue cotton shirt, and a plain suit of homespun wool. Because of his hardiness (or contrariness), he frowned on underwear and stockings. His bare feet went into "stogy" shoes, which received their name from the wagon, or high leather boots. Shoe and boot soles were attached with square wooden pegs instead of nails; the cobbler made holes through the sole of the footgear with a round awl and then drove in these little pegs, clinching them against the last—literally "putting square pegs into round holes."

"Tough as nails" aptly describes the Conestoga wagoners. The work demanded prodigious physical strength. Each teamster manned a large vehicle hauling two to six ton loads, containing barrels of produce each weighing several hundred pounds. It is almost inconceivable that any man (for only one accompanied a wagon) could remove or replace the heavy endgate of a wagon with rear wheels six feet high—to say nothing of loading and unloading the cumbersome barrels of merchandise. Among the wagoners' feats of strength were these: lifting a hundred pound keg of nails onto the wagon by grasping the narrow edge of the keg between the fingers and thumb of one hand; unloading a six hundred pound barrel of molasses singlehanded; walking off with a half ton of pig iron to win a wager; handling a fifty-six pound weight with the ease of a gymnast throwing a dumbbell; and lifting a wagon off its four wheels by lying under it and pushing upward with both hands and feet.

A wagoner would demonstrate his ability to drive by word of mouth as he lay flat on his back in a field. By signaling to his lead horse, he would drive the six horses and wagon over him (straddling his body), turn them around, and have them pass over him again without getting off the flat of his back.

Teamsters, loyal to tradition, often refused shelter from the rain if their team had to remain unsheltered. On the other hand, there was the teamster who would hitch his laziest horse opposite the saddle horse and tie the horse's jaw to the end of the wagon tongue with a rope so that the horse had to pull or break his jaw.

At one time Conestoga wagoners were a power in Pennsylvania politics. In the gubernatorial campaign of 1835, Joseph Ritner, called "The Wagon Boy of the Alleghenies" because he had been a wagoner in his early days, was the teamsters' choice for the highest office in the state. At taverns and other places where the teamsters gathered, and while driving in strings along the pike, wagoners were heard to sing the following verse about their candidate for governor:

> *Wote nunner der Irisher*
> *Der Josef Ritner iss der Mann*
> *Der unser Staat regieren kann.*

> Vote the Irishman down!
> Joseph Ritner is the man
> Who this state well govern can.

Ritner was elected.

The majority of the **Conestoga wagoners** were honest, industrious, and thrifty. Old Jacob Givens, a Philadelphia-Pittsburgh teamster from York County, was on his deathbed when he remembered an unpaid debt. Calling one of his sons to his bedside, he made his last request: would he return a peck of salt the father had borrowed for his cattle? He wanted to die, he said, with no unpaid obligations to his neighbors. A few minutes later the son reported the debt had been paid. His slate now clean, Givens smiled wanly and passed to eternity.

The name "Conestoga" has been associated with almost everything from a shinplaster and a national bank to the modern freight-carrying airplane. Conestoga's origin poses an interesting problem for the student of etymology. One of the earliest references to a word similarly pronounced is "Onestoga," the name of a stream on Augustine Herrman's map of the lower Susquehanna Valley, which was dated 1665. The word "Conestoga," designating a tribe of Indians, a stream, and a manor in Lancaster County, antedates both the Conestoga wagon and the Conestoga horse. Tradition holds that both the horse and the wagon were named for the section of Lancaster County where they probably originated. Whether the wagon was named for the Conestoga breed of horse or vice versa is a matter of conjecture.

One of the earliest printed references to the Conestoga wagon is in the following advertisement in the *Pennsylvania Gazette,* Philadelphia, February 5, 1750: "Just imported and to be sold very cheap for ready money by Thomas White at his house in Market Street, between 4th and 5th, almost opposite the sign of the Conestogoe Wagon, etc." Just one week later the same advertiser used the term "Dutch Wagon" in a similar advertisement. In those early days the expressions "Dutch wagon" and "Conestoga wagon" must have been synonymous terms.

The Conestoga Wagon Inn was a well-known hotel in its day. Many notables, including Washington, were entertained there. Conestoga wagons must have been traveling to and from Philadelphia in large numbers during the first half of the eighteenth century to have earned the distinction of having a tavern named for them. The Philadelphia-Lancaster turnpike, formerly the old Lancaster Road, was called the Conestoga Road because it was the favored route of the Conestoga freighters.

When good roads were extended westward to Pittsburgh, the Pitt wagon came into existence. This vehicle was the large type of Conestoga wagon used almost exclusively for long-distance hauling just before the advent of the railroad era. It was the type of freighter used, not only on the two main arteries of travel into Pittsburgh, the old National Pike beween Cumberland, Maryland, and Pittsburgh, and what is now the Lincoln Highway between Philadelphia and Pittsburgh, but also for long-distance hauling to and from Baltimore. Naturally the Pitt wagon was built in the community in which it was most used. Therefore many wheelwright, blacksmith, and saddlery shops sprang up in western Pennsylvania for the making and equipping of this commodious type of Conestoga wagon. These big wagons were usually drawn by six well-matched horses.

No one seems to know exactly when or where the Conestoga wagon originated, but many believe that it was modeled after the old English covered wagon. Conestoga wagons were handmade and not built from a blueprint. No two of them were exactly alike. They were the product of individual blacksmiths and wheelwrights who were superb craftsmen with an artistic feeling for their handicraft.

To the average person, a Conestoga wagon means simply a covered wagon going westward. This is erroneous. The prairie schooner was a combined passenger and freight wagon, or rather an emigrant wagon, often containing not only a mobile kitchen but also provisions and beds. It was drawn by either horses or oxen with the driver and occupants seated within the wagon, and it was often followed by a primitive caravan of servants, cattle, sheep, swine, and dogs. It was a well-made vehicle, served its purpose nobly, and with its long train of concomitants made a picturesque scene.

The Conestoga wagon served an entirely different purpose. It was purely a freight carrier, and the driver did not ride inside the wagon. He rode his saddle horse, or sat or stood on a footboard (called the "lazy board") that slid out from the wagon bottom. One might note that a driver in a prairie schooner or other wagons and carriages sat on the right side of the seat, while the Conestoga horseman took the left side, just as the drivers of automobiles do today. Thus the Conestoga wagoners originated the American custom of driving to the right.

Certain sayings had their origin in wagoning days: for example, the expression "I'll be there with bells." Nearly all Conestoga wagon teamsters decorated their horses with sets of hame bells. It was the custom of the road for a teamster to forfeit his bells to another who pulled him out when his load became stuck or mired. If a teamster arrived at his destination with his bells, the assumption was that no trouble had arisen on the trip. Hence the expression "I'll be there with bells," literally, "nothing will hinder my coming."

Another expression, "Watch your *p*'s and *q*'s," originated in those days. Tavern keepers made a record of charges against their customers by writing on a slate that was kept behind the tavern bar in full view of all. When a pint of whisky was purchased on credit, the letter P was written on the slate, and when a quart was purchased, the letter Q was recorded. Some of the heavy drinkers would sometimes have too many P's and Q's entered back of their names, and the proprietor reminded them that their bills were getting too high by saying, "Watch your P's and Q's."

Originating in Conestoga wagon days, the stogie cigar was made especially to please the appetites of the long-distance teamsters. A writer gives the story of their origin:

Stogies were first made in the old turnpike days by George Black, a cigar manufacturer, in his store that was located in Washington at 116 South Main Street just north of the Reporter Building. The building is still standing. Drivers of the old Conestoga wagons on the National Road were as a rule inveterate smokers, and the government taxes on tobacco bore especially hard on them. Black came to Washington from Chambersburg in 1833 and made a cheap "roll-up" at four for a cent. He named these Conestoga cigars but they were soon universally called "stogies." Black manufactured them in the rear of his store from 1833 to 1853.

Picture in your mind those great wagons—manned by the proudest of all teamsters—traveling in strings, each wagon drawn by six well-matched horses of the genuine Conestoga strain, snorting, and champing their bits, clad in harnesses adorned with elaborately decorated sets of musical brass bells, and you will have a fairly accurate conception of the admirable vehicles that attracted the attention of our forefathers.

Conestoga wagoners took great pride in the appearance of their teams on the highway. They vied with one another in the adornment of their horses' harnesses. Among the traditional accouterments were: bridle rosettes, pompons, ribbons, tassels, and the musical brass bells with all their trimmings and adornment.

Bridle rosettes used on carriage and stage horses were varied in design and quite showy, but those used by Conestoga wagoners were merely a plain brass button. One hobbyist has collected four to five hundred different kinds of bridle rosettes ranging all the way from the small plain black ones used on buggy bridles by the Plain Sects of Pennsylvania and the brass rosettes of Conestoga wagons to the large and rather elaborate rosettes from the British royal carriages.

Tassels usually consisted of a bunch of horsehair or wool, six to ten or more inches long, dyed a vermilion red or pale blue. Sometimes these tassels were much longer and dyed several colors, making them quite artistic as well as expensive. The tassels were fastened by wire or a leather strap to the bridle under the rosettes and dangled beside the horse's head. Pompons sometimes adorned the strap of the bridle that crossed over the top of the horse's head, and often one or more pompons appeared on top of the bell arch. Colored ribbons were wrapped around the forehead and nosepieces of the bridle, and not infrequently the hair of the forelock was plaited and bedecked with ribbons the colors of our national emblem.

Much might be said about the attractive and musical brass bells that were suspended from the iron arch over the horse's shoulders. The bell arches were ornamented. They were covered with bearskin or some other fur, or with black and red cloth tied with dangling fancy ribbons. Six sets of bells were usual for a six-horse team, although many teamsters used only five sets because bells on the saddle horse interfered somewhat with driving. There frequently were five bells on the lead horses, four somewhat larger bells on the middle horses, and three still larger ones on the pole horses.

It is not known just how these bells originated. We do know, however, that the lead horse in a train of pack horses carried a bell, probably to warn approaching persons to move to the side and make way for passing on the narrow dirt paths that led through the wilderness. There is no manufacturer's name on these bells, and it is not known whether they were American-made or imported; nor does anyone know the significance of the customary 5-4-3 arrangement. The bells of different sizes produced not only noise but music as well, and were among the proudest possessions of the wagoners.

Nearly every teamster, whether he used it or not, carried a blacksnake whip. An indispensable part of every wagoner's equipment, it was about five feet long, thick and hard at the butt and tapering rapidly to the end, to which was attached a plaited lash, approximately eighteen inches long, with a cracker of silk or eelskin. The whip was made of one piece of leather with only one seam extending its entire length. The saddler did his work so skillfully that the seam was almost invisible; it was sewed from the inside and turned as it was stitched. The hand grip was usually marked with bands of plaited leather, or leather bands ornamented with small brass studs. A strap was sewed to the butt to hang up the whip when it was not in use.

The teamster's mattress was a simple homemade affair constructed in accordance with the design and whims of the owner. It was small and without elaborate covering; it was not filled with downy stuffing, since it was intended to be used by tough men who slept on barroom floors. During the day the wagoner's bed was rolled and pushed through the small end opening of the canvas cover at the rear of the wagon.

In intimate, vivid terms, H. L. Fisher's poem, "Wagoning," published in 1888, captured for all time the color and flavor of the Conestoga wagoners' picturesque way of life. A few of its thirty-odd stanzas are enough to give us a glimpse into that romantic era of Pennsylvania's transportation:

WAGONING

There were two classes of these men—
Men of renown, not well agreed;
"Militiamen" drove narrow treads,

Four horses and plain red Dutch beds,
  And always carried "grub" and feed;
Because they carried feed and "grub"
They bore the brunt of many a "rub."

The "Regulars" were haughty men,
  Since *five* or *six* they always drove
With broad-tread wheels and English beds,
They bore their proud and lofty heads,
  And always thought themselves above
The homespun, plain, Militiamen,
Who wagoned only now and then.

So were all goods transported then—
  By reg'lar or militia team—
And, though, a slow and toilsome way,
It was the best known in its day—
  Before the world had got up steam;
As, now, this steam-dependent world
Is round its business-axle whirled.

O'er mountain heights and valleys deep,
  Still, slowly on and on they move;
Along their tedious, rugged way
Some eighty furlongs in a day—
  Their stalwart strength and faith they prove;
And oft to their extreme delight,
Some old-time tavern looms to sight.

There, custom always called a halt
  To water, rest, and take a drink;
And, not unlikely, while they stopped,
A jig was danced, or horses swapped;
  And so, perchance, a broken link
The smith was hurried to renew,
Or tighten up a loosened shoe.

Meantime, the jolly wagoners stood
  And swaggered 'round the old-time bar—
The latticed nook, the landlord's throne,
Where he presided, all alone,
  And smoked his cheap cigar,
And reckoned up the tippler's bill
For whiskey, at a "fip" a gill.

There never was a rougher set,
  Or class of men upon the earth,
Than wagoners of the Reg'lar line—

Nor jollier when in their wine
  Around a blazing barroom hearth.
How did they fiddle, dance and sing!
How did the old-time barrooms ring!

They sat in all the different ways
  That men could sit, or ever sat:
They told of all their jolly days,
And spat in all the different ways
  That men could spit, or ever spat;
They talked of horses and their strength,
And spun their yarns at endless length.

Ten wagoners in a barroom—well,
  Say, twenty feet by scant sixteen;
A ten-plate stove, that weighed a ton,
Stood in a wooden-box spittoon—
  Which was, of course, not very clean—
'Mid clouds of cheap tobacco smoke,
Thick, dark, and strong enough to choke.

Reflections of their memory hangs
  And lingers 'round us like the air;
They haunt us in our waking dreams
And, often, in our sleep, it seems
  As if again, we see them, there;
But stern realities arise
While moisture gathers in our eyes.

The Conestoga wagoners participated fully in the processes by which Pennsylvania's oral traditions grew and were widely diffused. They not only evolved their own folklore but were active agents of folklore diffusion by virtue of their calling. They traveled far beyond the confines of their native Lancaster and York counties and constantly mingled with strangers, especially in Pittsburgh, gateway to the West. Just as their lumbering wagons exchanged the East's manufactured merchandise for the West's agricultural products, so did their hearts and memories swap traditional goods—songs and stories—with the people whom they met along the way and in Pittsburgh. After a century of this traditional process, they must have accumulated a vast store of folklore. It is all the more unfortunate, therefore, that no organized attempt to recover these oral treasures was made before the last of the wagoners had passed from the scene. What has been retrieved from the past has come from sons and grandsons of wagoners yielding family memories.

One of the wagoners' diversions, when they were around the blazing log fire in a wayside tavern, was exchanging tall tales, vying with one another to see who could tell the biggest "whopper." These tales invariably grew out of their personal experiences. One teamster told the same story so often he came to believe it himself. He said he drove over the Allegheny Mountains on a certain day in March when it was so windy seven men were required to hold his hat on.

Another traditional tall tale was the one of the teamster sitting on a log one day and eating an apple. After paring the apple he stuck his knife into the log, which turned out to be a blacksnake. It crawled away with the teamster enjoying a free ride on its back. One of the wagoners said that he hitched his lead horses to a tree one evening and gave them the word to pull; then he retired to a tavern. Returning in the morning, he found them with their traces taut and still pulling at the immovable tree because he had forgotten to give them the "whoa" signal to stop.

Because of the noise and hilarity in the taverns, long-winded storytellers found it hard to hold the attention of their listeners. So stories were brief and to the point. Jokes and puns were popular. Here are some examples:

A drinker would ask a tavern keeper, "Would you take my last cent for a drink?" If the tavern keeper said yes, the customer would lay a cent on the bar and demand a drink.

A wagoner, finding a blacksmith with a red-hot horseshoe gripped in his tongs, would say, "Give me a quarter and I'll put my lips against it." If the blacksmith handed over a quarter, the jokester would simply press his lips against the quarter and walk away with it.

Wagoners also had some beliefs and superstitions growing out of their calling. One of them was that horse chestnuts carried in the pocket helped ward off rheumatism. For good luck or protection, the farm bulldog sometimes was tied to the rear axletree of the wagon and taken along on a trip.

On January 27, 1807, Fortescue Cummings, an English traveler, recorded in his diary:

Four miles from Skinner's on Sidelinghill we stopped at a log tavern. It was a large half-finished log house, with no apparent accommodation for any traveler who had not his own bed and blanket. It was surrounded on the outside by wagons and horses, and inside, the whole floor was so filled with people sleeping, wrapped in their blankets round a large fire, that there was no such thing as approaching it to get warm, until some of the travelers who had awoke at our entrance went out to feed their horses, after doing which they returned, drank whisky under the name of bitters, and resumed their beds on the floor—singing, laughing, joking, romping, and apparently as happy as possible. So much for custom.

Yes, that was the custom. At nightfall the wagoners put up at one of the many taverns dotting the Conestoga trail. No matter how tired they were, they would plunge into the gaiety of the barroom. To the accompaniment of a fiddle, accordion, or banjo, and the pounding of mugs on barroom tables, they sang ballads and rowdy drinking songs, both German and English. Among the favorites were "Lauterbach," "Ach du Lieber Augustin," "The Arkansas Traveler," "Little Brown Jug," "O'Reilly," "Captain Jinks of the Horse Marines," "Zip Coon," "Turkey in the Straw," "Joe Bowers," and "Old Joe Clark." And many a stogy shoe sole was worn thin with dancing to the hornpipes and reels "spieled" by fiddlers.

In addition to singing traditional ballads, the wagoners made up their own songs to familiar tunes. Contrary to the antiquated theory, the modern view holds that folk songs are the original compositions of individuals known or forgotten. They are then changed, embellished, shortened or lengthened, and adapted to various tunes at the whim of the folk. No better example of this recasting process can be found than the songs lustily and boisterously produced from the whisky-soaked throats of the Conestoga wagoners. Their texts were often sheer nonsense, and some were profane and vulgar. Nevertheless they were the expressions of the folk, reflecting their moods, thoughts, and feelings. As the wagoners were bilingual, their made-up songs were sometimes horrible examples of English.

An interesting musical custom, imported from the Rhenish Palatinate of their forefathers, was *zersingen*, the process of "singing to pieces" as it is termed in English. This consisted of parodies improvised stanza by stanza in a competition. As it was carried on in the Conestoga wagoners' barrooms, a man would sing a traditional ballad. Then followed a free-for-all contest in which teamsters, using the same tune, would improvise stanzas of their own. Of course, improvisers were expected to stick as close to the original text as possible, but they seldom did. Their imagination would take them far afield, resulting in the creation of entirely new ballads. When the boys were really keyed up, their stanzas would go on interminably. Some of these improvisations were so good that the folk took them over and added them to the lore that was handed down from one generation to another.

Conestoga on the Jordan Road

This parody of "Jordan Am a Hard Road to Trabbel" is an example of the process of making new ballads out of old ones, as practiced by the Conestoga wagoners. The original chorus has been taken over intact, but the rest of the text was made up by the wagoners themselves.

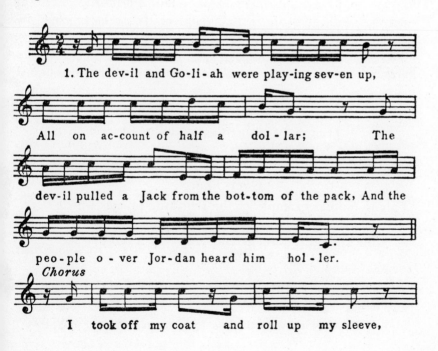

1. The dev-il and Go-li-ah were play-ing sev-en up,

All on ac-count of half a dol-lar; The

dev-il pulled a Jack from the bot-tom of the pack, And the

peo-ple o-ver Jor-dan heard him hol-ler.

Chorus

I took off my coat and roll up my sleeve,

Jor-dan am a hard road to trab-bel;   I

took off my coat and roll up my sleeve,

Jor-dan am a hard road to trab-bel I be-lieve.

2. Oh, I look to the North, and I look to the East,
And I see the old Con'stoga comin';
With six gray horses a-drivin' on the lead
To take us to the other side of Jordan.

CHORUS

I took off my coat and roll up my sleeve,
Jordan am a hard road to trabbel;
I took off my coat and roll up my sleeve,
Jordan am a hard road to trabbel, I believe.

3. Teamsters do some cussin' when they sing a song.
That's because they got no learnin';
But they're just about as honest as the day is long,
And they're trabbelin' to the other side of Jordan.

4. Their wagons are rust and their bodies dust,
So let's forget about their sinnin';
Their souls are surely with the saints, I trust,
For they're all on the other side of Jordan.

Over There

This is another example of the remaking process which I collected from descendants of the original teamsters. The parodied
song of the same title was current more than a century ago:

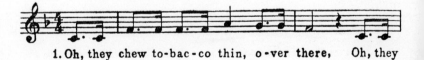

1. Oh, they chew to-bac-co thin, o-ver there,   Oh, they

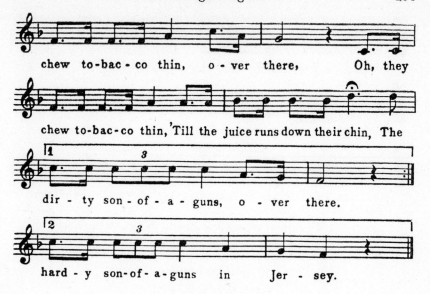

chew to-bac-co thin, o-ver there, Oh, they

chew to-bac-co thin, 'Till the juice runs down their chin, The

dir - ty son-of-a-guns, o-ver there.

hard - y son-of-a-guns in Jer-sey.

2. Oh, they eat the chickens small, over there,
   Oh, they eat the chickens small, over there,
       Oh, they eat the chickens small,
       They eat the feathers and all,
   The tickled son-of-a-guns, over there.

3. Oh, they wear their britches thin, over there,
   Oh, they wear their britches thin, over there,
       Oh, they wear their britches thin,
       And they let the wind blow in,
   They're hardy son-of-a-guns in Jersey.

The Farmer's Alliance

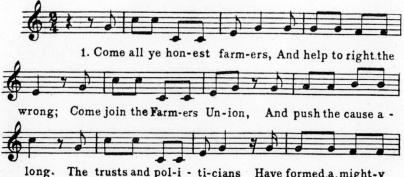

1. Come all ye hon-est farm-ers, And help to right the

wrong; Come join the Farm-ers Un-ion, And push the cause a-

long. The trusts and pol-i-ti-cians Have formed a might-y

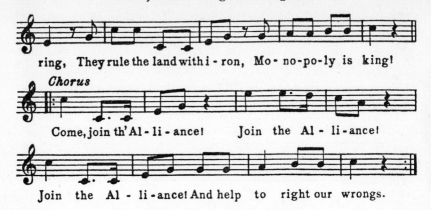

ring, They rule the land with i - ron, Mo - no-po-ly is king!

Chorus

Come, join th' Al - li - ance! Join the Al - li - ance!

Join the Al - li - ance! And help to right our wrongs.

2. From pine-clad Maine to Texas,
   From East and West and South,
   From Huron's heaving waters
   To Mississippi's mouth,
   Is heard a swelling murmur,
   A low, but ominous sound—
   The farmer hosts are gathering
   Upon the battle ground!

   CHORUS
   Come, join the Alliance!
   Join the Alliance!
   Join the Alliance!
   And help to right our wrongs.

3. Our fifteen million farmers
   Are rising in their might;
   They're girding on their armor,
   And training for the fight;
   They'll teach the politician
   In legislative hall,
   He must respect the farmer,
   Who clothes and feeds us all!

Liewer Heindrich
(Dear Henry)

(From *Der Pennsylvaanish Deitsch Eileschpiggel,* June 1945.)

Wagoners, riding or walking alongside their teams, whiled away
the long hours on the road singing to themselves. They had a
marked preference for the interminably long English ballads like

"Barbara Allen" and "Darby Ram." They also drew on their German repertoire, one of the favorites being the ballad "Liewer Heindrich," of which many variants have come down. The following version is in the form of a duet between Henry and his friend. The question "What shall I do?" is implied before each verse.

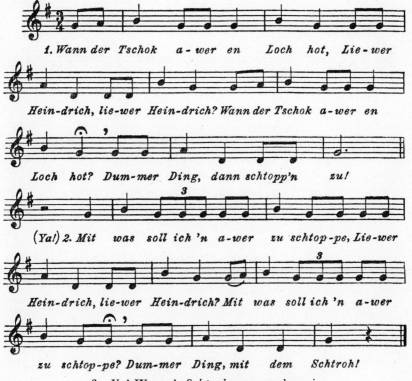

3. *Ya! Wann 's Schtroh awer zu lang iss,*
   Liewer Heindrich, liewer Heindrich?
   Wann 's Schtroh awer zu lang iss?
   Dummer Ding, dann hack 's ab!

4. *Ya! Mit was soll ich's awer abhacke,*
   Liewer Heindrich, liewer Heindrich?
   Mit was soll ich's awer abhacke?
   Dummer Ochs, mit dem Beil!

5. *Ya! Wann 's Beil awer zu schtump iss,*
   Liewer Heindrich, liewer Heindrich?
   Wann 's Beil awer zu schtump iss?
   Dummer Ochs, mach's scharref!

6. *Ya! Mit was soll ich's awer scharref mache,*
   Liewer Heindrich, liewer Heindrich?
   Mit was soll ich's awer scharref mache?
   Dummi Grott, uf dem Schtee!

7. *Ya! Wann der Schtee awer zu drucke iss.*
   Liewer Heindrich, liewer Heindrich?
   Wann der Schtee awer zu drucke iss?
   Dummer Ding, dann mach'n nass!

8. *Ya! Mit was soll ich 'n awer nass mache,*
   Liewer Heindrich, liewer Heindrich?
   Mit was soll ich 'n awer nass mache?
   Dummer Esel, ei, mit Wasser!

9. *Ya! Mit was soll ich awer Wasser draage,*
   Liewer Heindrich, liewer Heindrich?
   Mit was soll ich awer Wasser draage?
   Dummer Ding, mit dem Tschok!

10. *Ya! Wann der Tschok awer en Loch hot,*
    Liewer Heindrich, liewer Heindrich?
    Wann der Tschok awer en Loch hot?

Recite: *Dummer Ding, hab dir g'saat schtopp 'n zu!*
        Nau noch ee Mool,
        no gewwich dir eens uf der Kopp!

(Un do sin mer widder graad am naemliche Blatz, wu mer aag'fange
hen un sin net weit varschich kumme.)

1. If the jug has a hole in it,
   Dear Henry, dear Henry?
   If the jug has a hole in it?
   Stupid thing, then plug it up!

2. Yeah! What should I plug it up with,
   Dear Henry, dear Henry?
   What should I plug it up with?
   Stupid thing, with some straw!

3. Yeah! But if the straw's too long,
   Dear Henry, dear Henry?
   If the straw's too long?
   Stupid thing, then chop it off!

4. Yeah! What should I chop it off with,
   Dear Henry, dear Henry?
   What should I chop it off with?
   Stupid ox, with the hatchet!

5. Yeah! But if the hatchet's too dull,
   Dear Henry, dear Henry?
   If the hatchet's too dull?
   Stupid thing, then sharpen it!

6. Yeah! What should I sharpen it with,
   Dear Henry, dear Henry?
   What should I sharpen it with?
   Stupid toad, with a stone!

7. Yeah! But if the stone's too dry,
   Dear Henry, dear Henry?
   If the stone's too dry?
   Stupid thing, then make it wet!

8. Yeah! How should I make it wet,
   Dear Henry, dear Henry?
   How should I make it wet?
   Stupid ass, why, with water!

9. Yeah! But what should I carry water in,
   Dear Henry, dear Henry?
   What should I carry the water in?
   Stupid thing, in the jug!

10. Yeah! But if the jug has a hole in it,
    Dear Henry, dear Henry?
    If the jug has a hole in it?

Recite: Stupid thing, I told you to plug it up!
         Now if you ask me once more,
         I'll give you a good crack over the head!

(And here we are back at the same place where we began and haven't
made any progress.)

The Wagoners' Curse on the Railroad

This ballad dramatizes the Conestoga wagoners' plight when
the railroad doomed their calling. I first learned of it in the
twenties when a copy of the text came to me from an anonymous
correspondent in Lancaster County. An accompanying note explained that it was sung to the tune of "Green on the Cape." Later,
after a determined search for other versions, I located an old man,
the son of a miller who had done business with Conestoga
wagoners. He supplied the following text and tune:

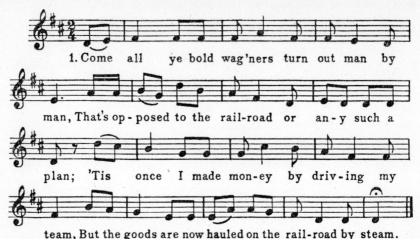

1. Come all ye bold wag'ners turn out man by man, That's op-posed to the rail-road or an-y such a plan; 'Tis once I made mon-ey by driv-ing my team, But the goods are now hauled on the rail-road by steam.

2. May the devil get the fellow that invented the plan.
   It'll ruin us poor wag'ners and every other man.
   It spoils our plantations wherever it may cross,
   And it ruins our markets, so we can't sell a hoss.

3. If we go to Philadelphia, inquiring for a load,
   They'll tell us quite directly it's gone out on the railroad.
   The rich folks, the plan they may justly admire,
   But it ruins us poor wag'ners and it makes our taxes higher.

4. Our states they are indebted to keep them in repair,
   Which causes us poor wag'ners to curse and to swear.
   It ruins our landlords, it makes business worse,
   And to every other nation it has only been a curse.

5. It ruins wheelwrights, blacksmiths, and every other trade.
   So damned be all the railroads that ever was made.
   It ruins our mechanics, what think you of it, then?
   And it fills our country full of just a lot of great rich men.

6. The ships they will be coming with Irishmen by loads,
   All with their picks and shovels, to work on the railroads;
   When they get on the railroad, it is then that they are fixed;
   They'll fight just like the devil with their cudgels and their sticks.

7. The American with safety can scarcely ever pass,
   For they will blacken both his eyes for one word of his sass.
   If it wasn't for the torment I as lief would be in hell,
   As upon the cursed railroad, or upon the canal.

8. Come all ye bold wag'ners that have got good wives;
   Go home to your farms and there spend your lives.
   When your corn is all cribbed up and your small grain is sowed,
   You'll have nothing else to do but just to curse the damned railroad.

About a decade ago, I took a group of descendants of York
County Conestoga wagoners to the Bucknell University campus
to participate in the Pennsylvania Folk Festival. Dressed in
wagoners' costumes, we sang some of the songs that make up this
chapter. By trying to revive the traditions of our forefathers, we
kept alive the memory of their deeds.

Canallers

by LEWIS EDWIN THEISS

What the canoe had been to the Indian, what the Durham boat, the keelboat, the ark, and the raft were to the earliest white settlers, and what the prairie schooner was to be to the pioneers of the West, the canalboat was to the sons of the settlers in the early nineteenth century.

The regions through which the Pennsylvania canals wound their way were still close to pioneer days, still in a primitive state of development, still reminiscent of the wild. Of the magnificent stands of timber that originally covered the state, relatively little had yet been cut. In effect, the commonwealth was a great forest. Held in check by hostile Indians, white men had made but slight penetration of the wilderness beyond the Blue Ridge until the end of the Revolution. Then came a rush of settlers who pushed far into the wilds; the more that came, the greater grew the need for that basic facility of civilization—transportation.

There is not space here to identify the many canals in the Keystone State. The Schuylkill, the Brandywine, the Lehigh, the Conococheague, the Conestoga, the Lackawanna, the Octoraro, the Delaware, the Chesapeake, and other streams all had canals paralleling their banks. The Susquehanna possessed artificial waterways from Athens on the North Branch and Farrandsville on the West Branch to Columbia on the main river. The Juniata was canalized from its junction with the Susquehanna at Clark's Ferry to Hollidaysburg. West of the mountains, the Conemaugh, the Kiskiminetas, the Allegheny, the Monongahela, and other streams were paralleled by additional artificial waterways. At Athens, the Pennsylvania Canal connected with a New York State canal. From Philadelphia, canalboats were towed up the Delaware to Bordentown, to connect with the Raritan Canal to New York. At Pittsburgh the Pennsylvania Canal connected with traffic on the Ohio and the Mississippi. In one way or another, all these canals were interconnected. Thus, a vast network of artificial waterways ramified throughout Pennsylvania to bring out its coal, its lumber, its minerals, its manufactures, the products of its agriculture, and to take back materials desired by its inhabitants.

The unique thing about the Pennsylvania Canal was the system by which canalboats were carried over the Alleghenies. The boats used on this route were built in two pieces that could be fastened together. Each half was mounted on a railway truck; these queer conveyances left Philadelphia at a given hour by railroad. The halves were drawn to Columbia on the Susquehanna, which was the end of the Pennsylvania Canal, the Tidewater Canal reaching the short distance from there to Havre de Grace, Maryland. At Columbia, the trucks were run down into the water, the two parts of the boat fastened together, and the craft was mule-drawn to Hollidaysburg on the Juniata. There a system of inclined planes, ten in number and powered by steam engines that pulled the boats by strong cables, drew the separate halves up to the mountain crest, an elevation of 2,332 feet, and let them down the western slope to the Conemaugh, where they were coupled together again, to continue on to Pittsburgh as a boat.

The canals were something absolutely novel in the life of the state. First, they offered employment in their construction; rugged indeed were the men who made them—rough and ready to fight at the lifting of an eyebrow. Secondly, the canals offered a chance for adventure, for travel, an opportunity for new experiences, for visits to distant parts. Farm lads, laborers, lumbermen, adventurers, bullies, pirates, and rough characters of all sorts swarmed to the canals, quite naturally frightening away more desirable persons. For many years canalboat men were considered little better than ruffians. Lack of home restraints, absence of customary observation by neighbors, the transitory nature of their calling, all tended to free the roving boatman from customary restrictions. Crime, rowdyism, feuds, and fighting were characteristic of the early canal days.

Nor were these objectionable characters all canallers. The frontier always has been the abode of brawny, reckless, savage men who lived by crime and plunder. The lumber woods and the mines were the frontiers of early canal days. They were filled with profane, reckless, hard-fighting men. The boatman who was to reach his destination with his cargo intact had to be equally tough and able to do battle, for Pennsylvania canals in the early days were as much infested by pirates as ever was the Spanish Main.

Unlike fast sailing ships that might possibly outrun an invader, canalboats practically invited invasion. They were bulky, lumbering craft, eight feet wide and between sixty and eighty feet long, the boats increasing in size as the canals were from time to time enlarged. Each had a blunt bow and stern, with a tiny cabin in the rear for the captain and crew, lighted by little windows. Many boats contained diminutive stables in their forecastles for the mules. The decks were practically flat, with large hatches through which cargo was loaded, and heavy hatch covers that could be fastened down tight when the boats were to enter sea water, as they did when traveling in the Chesapeake Bay. Drawn usually by three mules driven tandem, with the small boy driver plodding along beside them (although at times he rode the rear mule), these clumsy canal craft proceeded at a rate of two to three miles an hour when loaded, and a trifle faster when "light," or not loaded.

A quarter of a mile before the boat reached a lock, the steersman blew his horn to warn the lock tender to open the gates. Soon the mules ceased to pull and were cut loose from the boat, which then proceeded under its own momentum. It called for nice coöperation of the entire crew to get a boat neatly into a lock. The craft had to have just enough momentum to give it steerageway, but not sufficient headway to make it difficult to stop. The only way to stop a canalboat in a lock was for the bowsman to get the heavy snubbing line ashore, take a turn around a snubbing post, and bring the craft gently to a standstill with the snubbing rope. It sounds simple, but it was really a dangerous job, particularly in the dark, for sometimes the steersman was not able to send his craft squarely into the narrow lock, and it would crash violently into the lock wall. Even when the boat was barely moving, the shock was great. More than one bowsman was catapulted into the lock ahead of the entering boat. There was no room for the poor wretch in the close-fitting lock, and a terrible death was the usual result of such an accident.

There was much that increased the tendency to crime. One thing was an abundance of strong drink. In the early days, whisky sold for as little as a fip (6¼ cents) the half pint. Applejack sold for 25 cents a gallon, and it was deadly. "Black strap" (rum and molasses), at three or four cents a glass, was a favorite boatman's drink. At every canal basin and dock and sometimes at locks, there were places where drink could be had. There were floating saloons. At coal docks, where canalboats often lay for an entire week before they could be loaded, saloonkeepers did a thriving business; many men of the canal were hardly sober during their entire stay at a dock. Many canalside saloonkeepers were equipped with big stables. To attract boatmen, they offered free stabling to their customers. There were lewd women aplenty. They often traveled on the boats; not infrequently boatmen fought over them. In these and other battles of the canal, anything went. Fingers and ears were bitten off, eyes were gouged out, men were kicked in face and body. Frequently, the man attacked was left sadly maimed and battered, perhaps even dead.

In the early days, robbers infested the canals. Along the Schuylkill Canal, which penetrated the coal regions and brought black diamonds to the cities of the East, these ruffians were particularly bold and terrifying. Like wolves, they traveled in packs, usually attacking the defenseless or the easily overwhelmed. Townsmen as well as canallers were their prey. Like the Molly Maguires who terrorized the coal region at about the same time, these Schuylkill Rangers, as they were known, spread terror for miles along the canal. They came mostly from Philadelphia.

Ordinarily, it was useless to resist them. A canalboat crew of three—the captain, the bowsman, and the lad who drove the mules—had no chance against such a gang. Yet one Peter Berger, captain of the canalboat *Rattlesnake,* who was attacked when his boat tied up at Philadelphia, instantly drew an old pistol, shot two of the bandits dead, and drove the remainder to headlong flight. For this act the mayor of Philadelphia gave him a fine new revolver.

So bold did these Schuylkill Rangers become that once they even attempted to take possession of Schuylkill Haven, a large town along the Schuylkill Canal. Again they met their match. On another occasion, a large gang of these Rangers actually invaded Pottsville. That town, like Schuylkill Haven, was ready for them. The sheriff, with a large, well-armed posse, drove them off. The militia was called out; for some time these citizen soldiers were kept under arms, ready to march at a moment's notice.

Life on the canals, however, was not so violent everywhere; eventually it became more or less commonplace, even on the Schuylkill Canal. The Civil War was a factor in bringing about this change. During the struggle between the states, as in World War II, women took up jobs that men had had to relinquish. Then we were not the great industrial nation we are now; so there were few women who went into factories. But many of them took up tasks on the canals, just as some did recently on the railroads. Probably this was due to the fact that, although many boatmen were employed by canal companies and were known as "company men," there were many others who owned their own boats and operated them with hired boatmen; there was a third class of boatmen who both owned and operated their own craft. Indeed, there were many of the last. They were, by far, the best class of boatmen, for, with them, a canalboat was the source of livelihood for the family. Therefore, when the war drew large numbers of men of the last two classes into the armed services, women stepped into their places on the canals. Thus, it became an ordinary sight to see an entire family working on a canalboat. The woman not only did the cooking but she took her regular turn at the tiller. There were even a few girl mule drivers.

Canalboating was not limited to the carrying of freight. For the transportation of passengers, so-called "packets" were built. They were about eighty feet long and eleven in width. Right in the bow, carefully cut off from the rest of the boat, was a tiny cuddy for the crew. Immediately back of this came the ladies' dressing room and cabin, which was sometimes a separate room and sometimes was merely a space cut off from the main cabin by a red curtain. Next was the main cabin, thirty-five to forty-five feet long, which was a saloon and dining room by day and the men's dormitory by night. Back of this was the bar, and finally, at the stern was the kitchen. This was always presided over by a Negro cook who doubled as bartender.

Nor were freight boats and packets the only craft that operated on canals. There were also department-store boats, showboats, and missionary boats. Perhaps none was better known than Barnes's department-store boat. An advance agent, traveling along the canals, announced the dates at which this boat would arrive at different towns. This created much excitement. The boat's arrival was the big event of the year in many communities.

Canalboats' speed was limited by law to four miles an hour. This restriction was imposed to prevent damage to the canal banks by the waves that faster boats created. Despite speed regulations, packets often raced one another and thus exceeded the limits, but at best, they could make barely one hundred miles in a day.

Canalboating, which offhand may seem to have been a tame occupation after its turbulent early days, offered great attractions to those who loved adventure. True enough is the mental picture of a canalboat gliding gently at two to three miles an hour between lovely green banks or beside some rushing river, passing now in the shade of a towering cliff, now nosing noiselessly through somnolent stretches of sun-drenched canal, the very image of peace, serenity, and quiet, as it moved onward through scenes of striking beauty. This, however, is not all of the picture.

There were terrible storms to be encountered when rains poured down mercilessly, and times when the chill breath of late autumn froze the drops as they fell, making the towpath treacherous and slippery, and turning the towrope into an icy cable as hard and stiff as an iron rod. There were snowfalls that made the deck a treacherous thing to walk on, and glazed the towpath so that the mules could hardly keep their footing. There were tumultuous, treacherous winds that in a twinkling put life and limb in jeopardy. There were nights as dark as the interior of a closet, when mules and boats faced unseen and unsuspected dangers with breath-taking suddenness. There were cloudbursts and floods that put both the boat and its occupants in sudden dire peril. There were nocturnal collisions, born of the darkness, when the canalboat crashed into a lock, or splintered on some sunken rock in a stretch of slack water, hurling the bowsman into the stream, or worse yet, into the lock. Indeed, there was danger aplenty always at one's elbow.

There was an enormous traffic in coal between Nanticoke, on the North Branch of the Susquehanna, and Baltimore. From Havre de Grace at the end of the canal to Baltimore was an overnight journey. Boats left Havre de Grace at five or six o'clock in the afternoon and arrived at their destination eleven or twelve hours later, providing all went well. Lashed fast to one another, three abreast, with perhaps nine or twelve boats in the tow pulled by a single tug, the flotilla slowly breasted the waves. The different rows of boats were separated from one another by a few feet so that if a rough sea made the boats bob up and down, the stern of one boat would not crash against the bow of another immediately behind it. The three boats in a row were made as fast to one another as the hawsers would hold them. In the later days of the canals, boats were large enough to carry 180 to 200 tons of cargo. Thus, the dozen boats pulled by one little tug constituted a cumbersome and unwieldy tow. Yet the long journey to Baltimore was safe enough as long as no untoward situation arose.

One of the most menacing obstacles to navigation was a river flood. At many points along the canals, navigation was in the streams themselves after dams had been built to provide slack water. At places such as Northumberland and Clark's Ferry, the canal shifted from side to side of the river. Then the mules had to cross the stream on a bridge erected as part of the canal system. The mules actually traveled along on a little balcony or shelf built outside of the bridge proper, with a fairly high and exceedingly strong railing to protect them.

On one occasion a canalboat in command of eighteen-year-old Roy S. Wertz, who boated for his uncle, William Wertz, arrived at the Northumberland bridge when the West Branch of the Susquehanna was at high flood. Other boatmen feared to make the crossing, but this young man, saying that no flood could stop him, attempted it. It is a wonder that the mules were not dragged off the bridge, for the strain on the rope was terrific. When the full force of the current plucked the craft downstream, after the easing of the tension at the piers, the pull was so sudden and so powerful that the man at the bridge stick* could hardly keep it from being jerked from his grasp. The boat got across the river, only to miss the canal altogether and be sucked into the roaring flood.

Instantly someone cut the towrope to save the mules. The boat itself went shooting wildly down the raging river. The captain seized his conch shell and began to blow warning blasts. A little steamer, the *Ira T. Clement,* the captain of which saw the situation, pulled out from its pier at the foot of the cliffs, made fast to the runaway canalboat, and eventually dragged it back upstream and into the canal. The canal bank was deep under water, so the canalboat rode much higher than it normally would. When it shot under the Reading Railroad bridge, its wheelhouse was torn completely away.

* An instrument shaped like a large tennis racket with a vertical pin through its center. The towline was wrapped against the upper half of the pin. The lower half was held by the driver against the inner side of the bridge railing. This took the direct pull, instead of the mules.

The difficulty was that the canal now was truly "the raging canal"—in fact, it was a part of the rushing river. Swiftly the craft was swept along. At some distance below the steamer pier at the end of the Shamokin Dam was a lock. If the boat could get safely through this, it would be all right, because the canal level below the dam was not under water. Local rivermen pulled out in small boats to help. A snubbing rope was hastily tied about a tree, and an effort was made to stop the craft. The great hawser snapped like a packthread. The lock tender, never dreaming that any boat would come down the canal, was not on watch and did not open the gates. The runaway craft went charging into them. So great was the resulting damage that the boat owner lost an entire season's profit. He was fortunate not to have lost his boat as well.

Especially dangerous in time of high water was the Muncy Dam. It presented hazards that no other dam offered. The towpath was along the eastern shore. Along most of the entire four miles of slack water, the towpath was cut out of the solid rock, for towering cliffs rose sheer from the water's edge. Thus the towpath was really a long shelf cut back into the rocks and was very narrow. The boats were dragged in the river itself. Ordinarily, this was a satisfactory arrangement, but when the river was high and the current swift and treacherous, it was dangerous. A team of mules could easily have been pulled into the stream and drowned.

An added danger was the fact that in floodtime the Muncy Dam, about fifteen miles below Williamsport, the former great lumber manufacturing center, was filled with floating logs. If a boat were caught in a mass of logs in a rushing current, it could have become unmanageable, as the power of its three little mules was weaker than the force of the surging stream. Venturesome boatmen might get downstream by keeping their craft close enough to the bank to get into the lock, but few of them tried it because of the danger.

Charles F. Fortney of Williamsport, president of the Pennsylvania Canal Boatmen's Association, told me of a floodtime experience at the Muncy Dam, which he shared with his father many years ago. Their two canalboats, fastened together and traveling as a pair, could not be pulled beyond a certain point because of the strong current. Finding that they could not advance with two boats, father and son fastened the rear boat to bull rings and then applied the maximum mule power to moving the forward boat. After a hard struggle, they reached the lock and maneuvered their boat into the canal. Then they went back and got the second boat. Again they had a hard struggle. Once both boats were securely inside the canal, they were fastened together again, and the Fortneys resumed their trip.

Typical of what happened to more than one canalboat man whose boat had to travel in the streams was the experience of Captain Fred Gram. Failing to get inside the niggerhead* at the Nanticoke Dam in a flood, he and his boat were swept over the dam and down the raging Susquehanna. It was a wild trip. The boat had just been loaded with coal, so it floated low in the water. Fortunately there were no waves to sweep over the decks and further fill the hold. Had there been, this story would have ended almost before it began. But crosscurrents, treacherous swirls, and hidden rocks made the journey dangerous enough. The captain headed for the deepest part of the river. Luckily the fast water gave the boat speed enough to insure steerageway, and the flood was high enough to keep the boat off the rocky bottom. Gram managed to steer the craft downstream as it was hurled along by the water.

For fifty miles the craft went careening down the river, now shooting rapidly around the shoulder of a mountain, now rushing through the narrows, now plunging ahead in a welter of swirling waters, but safely passing every danger. One by one the towns along the river were passed—Shickshinny, Berwick, Bloomsburg, Danville—with people lining the banks to witness the exciting spectacle.

The craft neared Northumberland, where the two branches of both the canal and the Susquehanna unite. Rod by rod, the captain steered his craft closer to the shore. By the time he approached the boat basin at Northumberland, his boat was close to the bank. Boatmen were waiting to help him. Lines fast to the cleats of the boat were thrown to the shore. The shoreward ends were quickly passed around snubbing posts. Slowly the boat was

* Stone coping of the canal bank, on the downstream end of an entrance from river to canal.

stopped. Then a little steam towing craft that was used to shift canalboats put out into the river, made fast to Gram's boat, and towed it to the lock, where it was locked into the canal.

Storms and floods, however, were far from being the only dangers incident to life on the canal, even long after the days of the pirates. Before Ed Schrawder had reached his teens, he started one day from Port Trevorton on the Susquehanna for Newport on the Juniata. The canal followed the Susquehanna to Amity Hall, where there was a junction with the Juniata Canal. The little driver had been given some mules he had never seen before. No one said a thing to him about the new team, but it seems that one of the mules had the habit of rolling on its back the instant the harness was removed.

The boat traveled downstream as far as New Buffalo—some twenty-one miles—when darkness fell. The captain tied up there. The little driver took his team to a mule stable large enough to accommodate many animals. The stalls were bedded deep with fresh straw. Above one of the stalls hung a kerosene lantern. Young Schrawder proceeded to stable his mules. He lifted the harness from the mule that rolled and turned to hang it on a peg. Instantly the mule made a lunge and turned over to roll. In doing so it struck the lantern, which fell into the stall. In a second the barn was ablaze from end to end. The place was an inferno.

The driver's brother, also a boatman, was deep in the stable. The only way he could get out was to pass behind the stalls. There were only four mules in the barn, but all of them backed out of their stalls as far as their halters would permit and were plunging about in terror. The imprisoned canaller swiftly crawled beneath all four animals, miraculously escaping being kicked to death, and emerged like a flaming scarecrow with his clothing afire. He raced to the near-by canal and dived headlong into the water. Fortunately, he was not dangerously burned. The four mules perished.

But this was not the end. There was no telephone, no way of sending a message to the owner of the boat in Newport to supply more mules to power the boat. Before daybreak, young Schrawder started on a walk of many miles across the mountains to the

Juniata and Newport. He got three more mules. He said that
one of them, a white mule, was the meanest animal that ever
walked. He rode one of the mules and led the others. Hour after
hour the little lad fought that vicious white mule, but he com-
pelled it to come with him. It was long after dark before he got
back to New Buffalo. All this for five dollars a month and his food!

Canalboat fare was very poor, although in later years, when
so many women worked on the canals, it improved greatly. Bread
and flitch (bacon) with plenty of strong black coffee was usually
eaten at breakfast. At noon, crackers, cheese, bread, and molasses,
with more coffee, was a common meal. Supper might consist of
fried flitch with flour gravy, and more crackers and cheese. Good
homemade bread could be bought at some of the stores at the
locks. If women were aboard, there might be potpie, pie, and
other delicious foods. Lock keepers often gave boatmen fish they
had caught. If any stray chicken came within reach of a passing
boatman, it usually ended in a pot on the boat stove. But at best,
canalboat food was monotonous indeed.

On occasion, however, canallers were able to secure excellent
food. At Havre de Grace, while waiting to be towed through the
Chesapeake, they often had a little leisure time. Ed Schrawder
said that there one could buy a big sack of oysters for a dollar.
The boatmen would spread the oysters between layers of straw
or hay and keep the straw wet with salt water. Thus they had
fresh oysters for days. Herring and other fish could be had for
the taking. Fishermen seining for shad threw away most of the
other fish and were glad to give the boatmen all these fish they
wanted. Schrawder said that herring ran close to the canal bank
in such dense schools that he often took his wide-brimmed straw
hat and scooped out quantities of them. The boatmen fried them
crisp and ate bones and all.

Naturally there were boatmen who were none too scrupulous
about picking up extra food along the way. The story is told of
one who chased a farmer's chicken while the boat was passing a
farm. The farm wife came out and scolded him for trying to steal
her hen. "Madam," he replied unctuously, "I wouldn't think of
stealing your chickens. This fowl is one we had on board and it

got away." Thereupon the innocent farm wife helped the boatman to catch her own chicken. Tongue in cheek, he thanked her gallantly, and carried the loot to his craft.

On the five-mile level into Havre de Grace, a certain family lived by devious means, according to the late Marion Schoch's *Selinsgrove Times.* This family had all sorts of creatures that wandered unrestrained about the shabby homestead. One of them, a vicious gander, persistently attacked passing mule drivers, pinching them with its beak and slapping them with his wings. Little David Derr, a youthful mule driver who had suffered frequently in this way, feared this gander and usually rode past the place on his mule.

But once, on approaching this farm, he declared that if the gander attacked him that day, he would kill him. Derr got a strong piece of twine, fastened a stout fishhook to it, and baited the hook with corn. Instead of riding, he walked past the danger point. Sure enough, out came the belligerent gander, charging straight for David. The boy dropped his baited hook. The gander grabbed and swallowed it. David began to run, and the gander perforce followed him. Towed by the string, the gander went flapping and squawking down the towpath after David. The slatternly housewife, noticing the chase but unable to see the string, stepped out and yelled, "Don't run, little boy. He won't bite you." But David never stopped running until he was well around a curve and out of sight of the farmhouse. Then he grabbed his erstwhile tormentor and slit its throat. There was a real feast on the canalboat that night!

Not always did the boatmen make out so well, for not all farmers were as guileless as the woman who helped the canaller to catch her own hen. One farmer had a number of chicken coops standing temptingly near the canal bank. One time, long after dark, a foraging boatman entered one of these hen houses, only to be greeted by a tremendous uproar. He had invaded a pen of guineas, which are as infallible watchdogs as ever were the geese of ancient Rome. They instantly detected his presence and set up enough of an uproar to alarm the entire neighborhood. It was not due to chance that the guineas occupied the coop nearest the canal. The wily farmer had them there to serve as watchdogs.

Once a farmer tried to start an apple business with the canallers. As he could not stand and wait for boats to arrive, he put a bucket of apples on a canal bridge, with a sign reading: "Ten cents. Take apples and leave money in the bucket." The boatmen took the apples, all right, but failed to leave the money. When chided about it, their explanation was that boatmen could not read and so did not understand what was asked of them. Apparently all canalboat men were illiterate, for the farmer was soon forced to leave the apple business.

Farmers had a saying that the first three rows of corn in a planting along the canal were for the boatmen. Knowing the passing canallers would levy heavy toll on every bankside planting, they put out three additional rows in order to make sure they had enough corn for themselves.

In the early days, when there were no restrictions regarding hours of navigation on the canal, the boats usually kept moving day and night. They carried two crews and two sets of mules, each of which worked for twelve hours. It was a period when a twelve-hour day was common in industry. But as the social conscience developed and hours of labor were regulated in industry, a limit was set to a day's work on the canal. In 1890, or thereabout, the governor of Pennsylvania signed a regulation limiting the hours of navigation to the period between 4:00 A.M. and 8:00 P.M. This did not mean that all traffic ceased at eight o'clock; it meant that locks were closed at that hour, for boatmen pushed on fast to get through the lock immediately ahead, and then kept on until they reached the next lock. Thus, if a boat passed through a lock at eight o'clock and entered an eight-mile level, it would go on for eight miles more, at the rate of perhaps two miles an hour for a loaded boat.

What a day—from 4:00 A.M. to the following midnight—for a lad of seven or eight years, who thus walked almost continuously during the entire twenty hours! Although a driver rode the rearmost mule on occasion, it was customary to walk beside the mules, for just pulling the boats taxed the creatures. Twenty-five miles a day was a fair rate of progress. But on occasion an empty boat covered as much as forty miles with the weary little mule skinner often footing it every mile of the way, save when he was briefly aboard the boat eating.

At three in the morning the captain aroused his crew. While the "hair pounder" (mule driver) was feeding, currying, and harnessing his mules, the bowsman cooked something to eat, and a hasty meal was made. At four, the boat was on its way. In summer there would be enough light to see, but in the late autumn days it would be as dark as midnight. The nighthawk (a boat's large kerosene lamp) at the bow was lighted, the driver started his mules, and the day's journey had begun. From that moment until the craft tied up for the night, the boat never ceased to move, except, of course, when it was being locked from one level to another. About six o'clock the mule driver came aboard for another snack, and the bowsman relieved him on the towpath. When the captain ate, the bowsman took the tiller. The bowsman cooked, the captain ate first, the mule driver came last, and washed the few dishes before he returned to the towpath.

A light boat could glide up close to the bank, as the craft then drew less than a foot of water. When it was loaded, it had to stay well offshore in deep water. Then the little driver would drop on the deck as the boat passed under a bridge. If there was no bridge at hand, a gangplank was thrust ashore to get him aboard.

Innumerable bridges passed over a canal to permit farmers to cross from fields on one side of the canal to those on the other. These bridges were often so low that if a boatman was not watchful he would get a bump on the head. The driver was supposed to call out, "Low bridge!" when the craft came to one of these structures; that phrase has become a part of our vocabulary. From these low bridges persons could—and did—drop on passing boats. Sometimes these intruders were merely boys or others who wanted a little transportation. Boatmen never objected to them. But all too often the intruders were men bent on crime. They would wait until a lonely spot was reached, then beat and rob the captain and bowsman. The third member of the crew—the boy driver—never had any money. He was not paid for his services until the end of the summer's navigation.

The method of weighing canalboat cargoes is interesting. At the beginning of the season each boat entered a weighlock. The water was drawn off, and presently the boat was sitting on a huge scale. The weight was noted on the record; then the water was let in again and the boat floated out. During the entire season this weight was used in calculating the loads carried by the boat.

At a coal dock a canalboat was loaded by pouring coal down several chutes into the hold. At Beach Haven, on the way down the canal from Nanticoke, the boat would have to be weighed at the weighlock. If the weighmaster found that it was overloaded, he would order the crew to toss off the excess coal, which might amount to two or three tons.

Canalboat men hated the weighmasters and tried every trick they could think of to get ahead of them. Serving the same purpose as the Plimsoll lines on a steamer were horizontal markings on the hulls of canalboats; a properly loaded boat would float at a given level in reference to these lines. To fool the weighmasters, boatmen would chute the coal into their boat so that the craft did not ride on an even keel. The side opposite the weighmaster would be too far down in the water, but the side next to him would look all right. Weighmasters were not infallible and often passed a boat without really weighing it properly. A boat captain also had other tricks, for he was paid so much a ton for carrying coal to market, and it was to his advantage to overload the boat if he could get away with it. Eventually, the weighmasters detected all the tricks practiced.

On the way down the Susquehanna North Branch canal, the boats reached the "Onion House." Here a vessel would frequently be met by a rowboat full of attractive girls who smiled at the boatmen and joked with them. If the canaller knew that his boat was overloaded with coal, he would pick up a shovel and scoop as much coal into the girls' boat as it would hold. The girls would thank him with smiles and row the coal ashore. Thus, securing coal from one passing boat after another, they got an entire winter's supply at the price of a few smiles and a little good-natured joking.

Canallers were supposed to keep the lock tenders supplied with coal. Woe betide the lock tender who offended the boatmen, for there was never a spare ounce of coal on any boat when it reached his lock!

Evidently boatmen matched wits with many persons besides lock tenders and weighmasters. At Stoneytown a good-natured dealer in odds and ends bought rope from the boatmen, paying for it by the pound. Before reaching Stoneytown, a canaller with rope to sell always soaked the rope so that it would weigh a lot. In after years, a former boatman, perhaps troubled by his conscience, stopped to chat with the old rope buyer and confessed the trick he had played on him. The buyer merely smiled. "That was all right," he said. "I had my scales adjusted to take care of such little things."

Even the boat yards had to keep an eye on boatmen. A private yard that was a little off the canal, like the one in Lewisburg, probably did not suffer to any extent. But at Espy, near Bloomsburg, there was a considerable boat-building industry right on the canal. Here company boats were repaired. Boatmen had a different feeling about company property, for they levied a heavy toll on this yard. Observers remarked that it was surprising how many canallers' homes were made of exactly the same sort of lumber which went into canalboats, and that it was very odd how all these homes were painted with precisely the same kind of paint which covered the canalboats. Farmers' fences along the canal also suffered surprisingly, sometimes even disappearing entirely. Chestnut fence rails made first-class firewood.

Many odd things happened on the canals, but perhaps the case of the Fortney mules was unique. Fortney said that his father had a mule driver who curried the mules well, but when he was done with the job, the mules looked peculiar. In some unaccountable way, the driver managed to produce a ridge in the mules' hair, which stood up with startling effect. Captain Fortney spoke to the driver about it and asked him why he did it. The driver replied that he was left-handed and couldn't curry any other way. That did not satisfy Captain Fortney. Thereupon the driver suggested that he curry only one side of each mule and young Fortney should curry the other side. The more conventional result pleased the captain.

When Fortney was driving mules in his early days on the canals, he had a mule that would give a lightninglike kick on whichever side it was touched by the whip. As its aim was perfect, it was highly dangerous to be anywhere near this animal when it was necessary to use the whip. The young driver thought this situation over carefully. Then he got a barrel hoop and cut out a part of it so that the remaining portion of the circle would come down fairly on each hip of the mule. He fastened a long pole to this hoop, and thereafter, when it became necessary to touch up the animal, he brought the barrel hoop down evenly on the creature's rump. That puzzled the mule so much that it didn't know where to kick.

At times, the mule driver rode the rearmost of his three mules. With his long lash, he could easily reach the foremost mule. Some drivers became so proficient with that implement that they could literally flick a fly from the leading mule's ear. It was the startling crack of the long lash that spurred indolent mules. Seldom were the animals whipped severely. Drivers employed different expedients to hasten the somnolent creatures. Sometimes the mere shuffling of the drivers' feet on the towpath did the trick.

In many ways, canal mules gave evidence of real intelligence. Newton Baker's father had a gray mule that was always hitched in the lead. This mule showed every indication of realizing the importance of being the lead mule. When it came time to stop for the day, it would begin to neigh protestingly. Baker owned this mule from the time it was two and a half years old until it was twenty-four. The manner of the mule's death was almost dramatic. On the day it died, the boat started from McKees Half Falls and traveled all the way to Baker's home, a forty-five-mile haul. When the boat reached its destination, the mule promptly lay down and died. It had pulled to the last minute.

Most drivers were fond of their mules; probably the mules were fond of their drivers. It was a natural relationship between animals and boys. Often the timid youngsters snuggled up against the mules as they walked in the dark. They had no one but their mules to love them, at least in the early days of canalling. Eventually, this situation led the youthful canallers to cultivate pets. Without them life would have been even harder than it was. Dogs, of course, were prime favorites. One of the most amazing pets on the canal was a little dog that belonged to Charles F. Fortney. For sixteen years the two were inseparable companions.

Exactly where the dog came from Fortney never knew. He first saw it on a dark night when his father's boat lay in the shadow of the Brooklyn Bridge after they had taken a load of coal to New York. Late in the night a peculiar noise was heard on the deck. As the region was infested with "wharf rats" (river thieves), the boatmen went on deck to investigate. Strong metal strips were bolted over the wooden bumpers at the bow of the craft. One of these strips had become unbolted and had sprung away from the boat. There was a dog, a brown fox terrier, with one foot caught between this loose metal strip and the bow itself. They released the creature and took it into the cabin.

Day after day, mile after mile, the dog, which had been given to young Fortney and named Tippy, would walk with its new owner as he drove the mules. The dog watched the towrope with absolute attention. If the towrope became slack enough to dip into the water, Tippy would bark and nip at the mules to start them up. It would grab the rope in its teeth and pull on it savagely in an effort to get it up out of the water. Young Fortney, as full of mischief as the next boy, would give the mules a sharp cut with the whip at such a time, and the mules would spring forward, tightening the rope so suddenly that the dog would be shot high in the air.

At times the dog rode at the bow and watched the rope through the long hours. If the rope slackened and touched the water, the dog barked. Then it would run to the steersman, Captain W. C. Fortney, and bark excitedly until the rope was again taut and free from the water. When the craft stopped, the dog would dash for the hook to which the rope was attached and grasp the line in its teeth, pulling it free.

Through the years, Tippy usually walked just ahead of the lead mule. When Tippy's eyesight began to fail, it could hardly keep out from under the mule's hoofs. Yet the mule never stepped on it. If Tippy were too slow, the mule would hold its foot in the air until the dog moved on. There was a striking comradeship between these animals on the Fortney boat.

When, after sixteen years of faithful service, Tippy finally died, Fortney made a little coffin which he lined with sheepskin and covered with a sheet of thick glass. Then Tippy was buried appropriately at West Nanticoke, not far from the coal dock where the boats had so often been loaded. It was an appropriate resting place for such a good little navigator.

Snakes were everywhere. W. L. Derr, an old-timer who lived near Girty's Notch on the Susquehanna, said the Susquehanna Canal was a paradise for snakes. He said they would even bite the mules. Thus, a driver had to be very watchful. Once Newton Baker was driving on the McCall's ferry level when his animals suddenly stopped. No amount of urging would budge them. Young Baker hopped off the mule to investigate. Not far ahead of the team was a huge snake about ten feet long, slowly crawling out of the canal and up on the towpath. Not until the snake had disappeared into the bushes did the mules budge.

Snakes might have been more pleasant companions than some boatmen. There was, for instance, one canalboat captain who found it absolutely impossible to keep a mule driver even though he paid the highest wages on the canal. High wages could not offset his brutal treatment of the little hair pounders. He whipped, cursed, and generally abused them. When he came to the Nanticoke lock, he always chained his driver to the boat lest the lad run away, as he undoubtedly would have, had he been free.

When a captain could not keep his helpers—and many a captain could not—it was almost always his own fault. There was one captain, known as "Dumplin' Jim," who was forever losing his bowsman. The reason was that he compelled the bowsman to cook him dumplings every day. Canallers also associated the same word with the name of John Neitz, who cooked dumplings until he got tired of it. Once he made a lot of apple dumplings, but before serving them he made the crew all sit down close together on the canal bank. Then suddenly he pushed them all into the canal. It was indeed a day of rough jokes.

Sometimes jokes miscarried, especially if the perpetrator was physically unable to take care of himself. The little steamboats that shifted boats on the canals had a great attraction for youthful mule drivers. When Charles Christman of Bloomsburg was twelve years old and working on a canal boat, he had an inspiration one cold, snowy day: if he put some snow down the chimney of the cabin stove, causing steam to rise, the boat would look like a steamer. Charles scooped up some snow and dropped it down the chimney. Volumes of steam began to ascend—the effect was magnificent! Charles put more and more snow down the chimney. More steam came up, but the snow eventually put the fire out. When this happened, the wrathful captain rushed up to the deck and gave Charles what Paddy gave the drum.

Quite naturally, certain practices and customs arose on the canal. Decoration Day, as Memorial Day was long commonly called, was a well-observed holiday on the canals. In particular, boatmen were accustomed to tie up at McKees Half Falls for a feast of May suckers, wilted lettuce, potato salad, and other dishes that canallers relished. It was also a custom for farm girls from far and wide to make their way to the canals for the first swim of the season. Sly canallers used to slip to the points where the girls had left their clothes, and take them away. Memorial Day was thus suddenly turned into "September Morn." In the same spirit, boys were accustomed to seek out the clothes of their friends who were swimming, and tie hard knots in the garments, even soaking them to make them harder to untie.

The Fourth of July was also celebrated on the canals. The canals were usually closed in early November, thus making it impossible to observe Thanksgiving or Christmas there. Although canals were drained of water for the winter, there was always enough water left in low spots in the canal beds to make ideal sliding and skating places. Mothers, knowing their children were in no danger, permitted them to play there to their hearts' content.

Perhaps canallers never heard the term "tall tales," but they delighted in them nevertheless. Menacing the canals were muskrats, which burrowed into the canal banks and on occasion caused leaks that threatened to destroy near-by sections of the bank. So it was necessary for men to patrol the canal regularly, just as trackwalkers nowadays patrol railways. The canal patroller carried straw or hay and a few implements. If he detected a hole in the bank, he twisted up some hay, stuffed it into the hole, perhaps pounding down a stake to hold it tight, and hurried for help. In consequence of this danger, the canal company, through its lock tenders, offered bounties on muskrats.

One of these bounty-giving lock tenders was Sam Holt. He had a cat that could talk—at least, Sam said so. One night the lock tender heard his name called, "Sam! Sam! Sam!" Sam hopped out of bed, opened a window, and asked: "Who is it and what do you want?" Then he saw that it was his old cat. The cat replied at once, "Sam, put down a pole. I have a muskrat for you."

"I put down the pole," said Sam, "and up came the cat with a nice big muskrat. It's a fact, because I turned in the skin and got the bounty from the company."

A favorite tale was the one about the stuttering lock tender on the Susquehanna Canal. A boatman going upstream asked the lock tender how far it was to Liverpool.

"I-t-t-t-t's tw-tw-two—Aw hell! You can g-g-g-get there b-b-b-before I c-c-c-can tell you," replied the lock tender.

Another story that canallers liked to tell to newcomers was the one about a small mule in a team of three. The owners put him in the middle of the team, which was evidently contrary to custom. Hidden by his larger companions, the little mule could hardly be seen by the driver. On one occasion these boatmen tied up for the night at the end of a level. They were off again in the early morning before it was light enough to see. On they went until they came to a mule bridge where they had to pay toll for each mule crossing it. The driver paid for three mules, as a matter of course. The bridgekeeper looked puzzled. "Where's the third mule?" he asked. The driver looked at his team. "By George!" he exclaimed. "We forgot little Jerry!" Thereupon he headed back for the missing mule. When little Jerry saw the driver coming to get him, he laughed and laughed, "Heehaw! Heehaw! Heehaw!"

Tall tales like these were the most common type of story exchanged by canallers. In a day when most people feared the dead and believed in spirits, legends also sprouted on the canals. Legends sprang from local tragedies; startling and curious shapes of scenery passed along the way; the presence, in early times, of Indians; and, of course, the canallers' own superstitions.

There was, for example, the legend that grew up around a bachelor named Daddy La Grange, one of the most talked-of characters on the Pennsylvania Canal. He had been the tender of the northern lock at Liverpool, in which the canalboat *Seven Stars* was stranded by the draining of the canal about fifty years ago.

The story goes that Daddy La Grange took possession of this boat and each year until his death he would celebrate Christmas Eve by setting a table for thirteen persons.

Somehow he had acquired many fine things, and the table was set with precious linens, Stiegel glasses, beautiful silver, and all the other trappings for a regal party. But Daddy La Grange was the only diner who ever sat down to the feast. The other twelve places were set for "twelve girls who had gone sour on him." Daddy La Grange claimed that the girl he liked best, "the dark 'un," came back and spooked around. Her spirit would frisk about the deck of the *Seven Stars,* peer down the hatches, and appear at other points, but would never come closer. At midnight Daddy La Grange brought the festivities to an end. After that hour, he had a "handout" that was really a feast for any passing tramp or wanderer who would join him.

There is another Daddy La Grange legend involving little Rebekah Blackfair. Apparently she lived in Centreville with foster parents who treated her harshly. One day she disappeared, and her absence during Allhallows month led to suspicion and superstitious excitement.

Meanwhile on the Pennsylvania Canal, miles away, a small October flood had raised the river, and a flock of stormy petrels was following the swollen stream and the canal up from the sea. Boatmen were greatly troubled, for they regarded petrels as birds of ill omen.

One of the craft passing up the canal was the *Castle Wheel.* The petrels followed closely under its stern. When the craft entered the lock at the northern end of Liverpool, where it was shut in on all sides, the petrels rose in a body and began to circle endlessly around it, and to flit above it. So alarmed were the canallers that it was difficult to keep the crew aboard the *Castle Wheel.* Daddy La Grange declared that something was wrong, that perhaps there was a dead person aboard the boat. There was talk of shooting the petrels. He advised against it, saying that if they were killed, ill luck would be doubled. He suggested that the canalboat be unloaded in an effort to discover why the petrels stuck to it so persistently.

The craft, filled with bags of plaster, was en route to Plymouth on the North Branch of the Susquehanna. The crew tied up to the bank and laboriously removed hundreds of bags of plaster from the boat's hold. The toolbox was uncovered. Someone raised the lid. Inside was little Rebekah, unconscious. As soon as she was revived, the petrels disappeared.

It subsequently developed that Rebekah had gone to the Centreville store to do an errand for her foster mother. There the driver of a freight wagon had offered her a ride to Harrisburg, which she immediately had accepted. She had relatives there, but she had not been able to find them. She had seen the canalboat at the wharf, slipped aboard, and hid herself in the toolbox. Workmen, unaware that anyone was in the chest, had covered it over with bags of plaster when they had filled the hold.

When the story was finally unraveled, and the child protested that she just could not go back to her cruel foster parents, the boatmen took her with them to Plymouth. Daddy La Grange promised them that if any trouble arose, he would fix things with the overseers of the poor who properly had jurisdiction over Rebekah. But no trouble arose, and Rebekah, thanks to the petrels, grew to womanhood.

On the canals, as elsewhere, freshmen had to undergo some hazing. Canallers took great delight in telling young mule drivers the most frightening tales about ghosts, serpents, and other fearful things. The hours of darkness were frequently periods of mental torture for these youngsters.

Newton Baker told me about his experience at the Broad Creek lock. Having started on the canals at the age of seven, he was still a little fellow when this incident occurred. Already he had had his fill of ghost stories. Broad Creek, he said, was a very bad place for back swells. One frightfully dark night the boat got a very nasty back swell and ran into the gates with a terrific crash. In an instant, it seemed to young Baker, a terrible tall white ghost appeared on the lock wall. The ghost had white whiskers, its face was white, and it was wrapped in a white winding sheet. It stood there as though it believed the Day of Judgment had arrived. The apparition was terrifying, but the situation was relieved when the figure cried out and demanded to know what the boatmen were trying to do. It was the lock keeper in his nightshirt. He said that the crash had knocked him clear out of bed.

Old-timers tell about another superstition. Hemp for calking boats was grown near Drumore, and in the village itself there developed a trade in sickles, which were used to cut the hemp. Years before, a peddler had evidently been murdered in the near-by region of Prowell's Hollow, and this peddler's ghost was said to appear after dark. In consequence, little boys were frightened half to death when they had to pass through Prowell's Hollow at night with bundles of sickles. Another tale arose when some boys declared that they had seen the ghost of Arsène Lupin, the local schoolmaster and a Huguenot immigrant, who fell off a little bridge when he was crossing a creek, broke his neck, and died.

The Hog Pen lock, located between High Spire and Marietta, was very deep. One night a man was killed in a mule stable near by. Of course, the usual ghost legend promptly arose. A mule driver later approached the place and was scared half out of his wits because he thought he heard the ghost whistling. He was absolutely afraid to fetch water for his mules.

Not all these spirits were those of boatmen. There was the ghost of Demosthene Antoine Durang, who was supposed to have been a member of Napoleon's bodyguard. He settled at Hummel's Wharf, just below Sunbury. There he earned a living by carving figureheads for canallers, for many canalboats, like old-time sailing ships, carried these images at their bows. He became very fond of a sweet little girl whose foster father beat her to death and threw her body into the canal. Durang was beside himself. He recovered the body, and before burying it used the face as a model of a figurehead for a boat named the *Wooden Child*. When Durang died, the only valuables he left behind him were his bust of Napoleon, his tools, and the child's figure he had carved. The *Wooden Child* was believed to hold the ghost of the little girl. By burning the boat, the ghost was finally driven off.

When he was a little hair pounder, he was always warned to "look out for Albright's ghost at Girty's Notch," Schrawder recalled. This spot, where cliffs rise almost sheer from the water's edge, is well-known to motorists on the Susquehanna Trail. Here there was a very sharp curve in the highway that produced numerous other ghosts until the State Highway Department improved the road. The place got its name because Simon Girty, the notorious renegade of Revolutionary days, was said to have had a hideout in the cliffs there.

At any rate, long, long ago a girl who lived in this region had two lovers. One, named Miller, from Harrisburg, came to visit her; Albright, the other suitor, shot him. Then the killer took refuge in the cave that Girty had once occupied. Later, word went out that a body was found in the cave and that it was Albright's. Still later, it was said that friends, trying to help him get clear, stole a body from a graveyard, "planted" it in the cave, and declared it was Albright's. Whatever the truth about the matter, the legend grew that the slayer's ghost haunted the region. All youthful canallers were regularly warned to be careful lest Albright's ghost get them, like the goblins in the poem. Evidently such a legend arose at every place along the many canals where a tragedy had occurred. The poor little mule drivers had a terrifying time of it as they trudged along in the darkness.

Legendry was carried over into ballad-making, as shown by the following song, picked up by Colonel Henry W. Shoemaker, about a phantom boat on the Schuylkill Canal:

The Cruise of the Bouncing Sally*

The boat has slipped her moorings,
  The mules have whisked their tails,
While the captain grasps the tiller
  As the spray flies o'er the rails

Of the trim-built *Bouncing Sally,*
  On the waters free and bright;
Where the Schuylkill flows in beauty
  Through the starry, cloudless night.

We were bound for Penn's fair city
  With a cargo from the mines,
And the crew were staunch and steady
  With "Chief" Bangs to hold the lines.

O'er the leader gay and frisky
  On the towpath winding fair,
While the mule bells' drowsy tinkle
  Sang a ditty strange and rare.

* Used by permission.

"Chief" was a sunburned towboy,
　　Aged ten, or thereabouts;
And his looped and windowed apparel
　　Flapped lazily in and out.

Sometimes he slept in the saddle,
　　Sometimes by the leader's side,
He woke and slept alternate,
　　Nor recked he of time or tide.

The mellow sound of the boat horn
　　As it rang from the mountainside,
Echoed from crag to valley,
　　Or in lingering cadence died.

The twang of the tightened towline,
　　The watery drops that gleamed
Like gems in the glistening sunlight,
　　Or in filmy radiance beamed,

Seemed to come from a phantom vessel
　　On the waters free and bright,
Where the Schuylkill flows in beauty
　　Through the starry, cloudless night.

With a phantom crew to man her
　　And a phantom captain bold,
With a phantom sunburned driver
　　Who cared not for storm or cold.

And this phantom boat went drifting
　　O'er the waters free and bright,
With the phantom mule bells tinkling
　　Through the clear and silent night.

It is a well-established fact that most occupations develop their own distinctive folklore and folk songs. The canal industry was no exception. That more indigenous Pennsylvania canal ballads have not survived may be attributed to two factors: first, the comparatively short life of canalling; secondly, the fact that no systematic attempt was made to collect the songs a generation or two ago when many elderly canallers were still living. Most of the canal ballads that have been collected are about the Erie Canal, and some of them may have been adapted and sung, along with Pennsylvania ballads, on the canals in our state.

We do know, however, that minstrelsy flourished on the various

Pennsylvania canals. Not a few of the canallers carried fiddles, accordions, banjos, mouth organs, and other musical instruments on their boats. After a long haul they would relax and have fun. There was much merriment on Sundays and holidays, and on weekdays when their boats were laid up to be loaded, or on account of damage to the canal, or because some obstacle blocked navigation. On these occasions they loved to get together, perhaps in a canalside saloon, to play the fiddle or some other musical instrument and to sing their ballads. There were also those who entertained with jig dancing.

Elderly informants have told me that the indigenous canal ballads were often crude and vulgar and without much sense, but they reflected the canallers' life nevertheless. After the Civil War when women took up the occupation, canaller-bards improvised only in the saloons or other shore places as the women would not stand for vulgarity on the boats.

One type of indigenous ballad reflected the intersectional rivalry and jealousy among canalboat men. Those from Liverpool, location of an important lock of the Pennsylvania Canal along the Susquehanna, were nicknamed "Barnburners," after an epidemic of barn fires in that region. Juniata men were called "Poor Souls," because the Juniata division of the Pennsylvania Canal was smaller than the others and required narrower boats. Tidewater canallers for some unexplained reason were known as "Rock Jumpers." These were no mere teasing nicknames. They were terms of opprobrium calculated to cause a fight every time they were hurled at one another. And that was frequently.

Intersectional bitterness was also expressed in singing rhymes that boatmen improvised and sang "against" each other. Always sure to start a fist fight, if not a riot, was the following rhyme sung in a sneering tone by Susquehanna North Branch canallers when they met the West Branchers at the river junction town, Northumberland:

> West Branch drivers
>   They think they are so nice;
> They sit on the saddle mule
>   And pick off the lice.

Another type was a round like the well-known "Row, Row, Row

Your Boat." One about John Dobbin was sung endlessly by jolly boatmen. Fortney recalled these lines:

> John Dobbin he knew
> That his father lived well;
> His father he knew
> That John Dobbin lived well.

The canallers' belligerence was reflected in a ballad published in Colonel Shoemaker's *Mountain Minstrelsy of Pennsylvania:*

> I hired a shawny boat, a dollar forty-nine;
> If you don't work for this cap, you'll never get your time.
>
> I went down in the cabin to draw a pint of cider,
> There I saw a bedbug scrapping with a spider.
>
> CHORUS
> Backing, backing, then you needs the backing—
> When you wants to have a fight, then you needs the backing.*

"If you don't work for this cap, you'll never get your time" was an ominous warning. Some canalboat captains were unscrupulous enough to cheat their drivers out of their pay in this manner. They even tried to cheat older employees if they thought they could get away with it. A boy who had driven mules for an entire season might earn sixty to eighty dollars, drivers' wages varying between five and ten dollars a month. Payments were due at the end of the season in the fall. More than one little mule skinner went home brokenhearted when the captain, on one pretext or another, refused to give him his season's wages.

A favorite singing place of canallers was Cameron Furnace on the North Branch of the Susquehanna where the high cliffs acted as a sounding board. Farmers on the flats across the river delighted to listen to their singing and often spoke to the canallers about it appreciatively. Another well-known rendezvous for singing was the coal docks at Nanticoke where the men passed the time while their boats were being loaded with anthracite coal. A boatman named Benjamin Walker, who possessed a good voice, sang with gusto "I Took My Girl to the Ball One Night." Another of his songs was "Pretty Little Mary, Keeper of a Dairy."

There were a few Negroes on the canal; by nature, they were

* Used by permission.

good singers. Often a colored man carried a guitar. He was a valued member of a boat crew, for his music offered much diversion at the end of the day. One Negro used to sing a sort of spiritual that ran like this:

> The sun do move, the sun do move,
> That's what the colored preacher preaches,
> Way down souf, upon his knees,
> He will say that the sun do move.

Popular on the Schuylkill Canal was a Pennsylvania Dutch–English parody of Felicia Hemans' famous poem based on the experiences of the French naval officer, Louis Casabianca:

> Der mule sthoot on der canalboat deck,
>   Fer de towpath he wouldn't dret,
> Un dey tied a halter round his neck,
>   Un racked him on der het.
>
> Bud obstanade un braced he sthoot,
>   As do der scene to rule,
> A cretuer of der holtback brude
>   A stubborn, stheadfast mule.
>
> Dey curshed and shwore, but he wouldn't go
>   Until he felt inclint;
> Un do day dundered blow on blow,
>   He altered not his mint.
>
> Der boat boy to der shore gomplaint,
>   "Der varmount's bount to sthay";
> Sthill upon dat olt mule's hite,
>   Der sounting lash mate play.
>
> De captain from de shore replied,
>   "Der boat's apoud to sail.
> As utter means in wain you've trite,
>   Suphose you thwist his tail."
>
> De boat's prave boy who dared not fail,
>   De captain's orders heard,
> Den nearer trew mit oudstretched hant,
>   To make dem thwist awail.
>
> Den game a kick of dunder sount.
>   Of dis boy you needn't botter.
> Ask off der wafes dat far aroundt
>   Behelt him in de watter.

Old-time canallers cherish the memory of their tall tales, legends, songs, and ballads just as faithfully as they do thoughts of the days when the canal was in its heyday.

Nor are these former boatmen the only ones who experience a feeling of regret at the passing of the canal. For truly, those days,

> When the boatman's horn he'd blow,
> Waking echoes as he'd go,

were picturesque days, colorful days, delightful days of youth and hope and faith, when the new nation was just beginning to find itself. With their passing something went out of the life of the nation that we shall never quite replace. Gratified as we may be to have exchanged the pace of the canalboat for that of the railway train, nevertheless the shriek of a locomotive whistle will never have the appeal to sensitive minds that came from the haunting strains of the captain's conch,

> As his horn he'd blow
> Waking echoes through the vales, yo ho!

Railroaders

by FREEMAN H. HUBBARD

For many years a bitter feud between railmen and canalmen centered around Columbia, western terminus of the old state-owned Philadelphia & Columbia Railroad. Here on Front Street, once reputed to be the state's busiest thoroughfare outside of Philadelphia, the rival modes of transportation met and clashed, the Pennsylvania Canal hauling traffic to and from the west, the railway to and from the east. Here, too, the hardy raftsmen tied up their craft before navigating farther downstream.

Columbia was then so rough, tough, and rowdy that a single block had as many as four grog shops. In these hangouts "hair pounders" (drivers of canalboat teams) fought it out with rail-faring men amid much rancor and some bloodletting, because the rails had already begun to absorb the canal business. The raftsmen backed their canal cousins, and many a local Casey Jones went down to the barroom floor under the cleats of a rafts-man's heavy boots; many a canaller, too, howled at the resounding sting of a hickory brake club. As years slipped by, the canal, once extolled as an indispensable artery of traffic, gradually fell into disuse, vanquished by the iron horse. Peace came to Columbia, but it was a peace that led to stagnation when the town lost its importance as a transportation center.

Although the Pennsylvania Canal Commission had reported to the legislature in December 1831 that "Canals are from two to two and a half times better than railroads for the purposes required of them by Pennsylvania," the legislature chartered another railroad company, the Strasburg in Lancaster County, the following month. This road is now regarded as America's oldest existing short line. Ross H. Rohrer, who, as a boy, lived at Strasburg in the 1880's, recalled:

> My grandfather would send me to the Strasburg Railroad with letters for the engineer to mail at the other end of the four-mile line, Leaman Place, where it connected with the Pennsy—and still does. I would hand up the letters to the engine cab with a long cleft stick while the train was running, if you could call it such, at a leisurely pace. The line cut through several cow pastures. As they rambled along, the crew not only had to watch out for cattle but would stop now and then to remove fence bars from across the track and put them up again.

Undoubtedly it was from some such practice, maybe even from the Strasburg itself, that the locomotive pilot acquired its familiar term "cowcatcher."

In 1833, when railroads still had wooden rails, a mass meeting was held in Waynesburg to decide whether or not to allow the Baltimore & Ohio to build through Wayne County. At first, public opinion favored the railroad. Then a local spellbinder turned the tide by declaring: "Fellow citizens, corporations ain't got no souls. Why, if they broke one of their rails they wouldn't think nothing of going and stealing one off your fence!" The B. & O. was forced to reroute its line.

Four decades later the people of Waynesburg again voted on a railroad proposition. This time the plan was to build a narrow-gauge road between the Wayne and Washington county seats. Although there was some opposition on the ground that it would frighten livestock, otherwise inconvenience farmers, and ruin the market for horses, the ayes carried the motion. Tradition records that the hopeful young surveyor who led the way for the Waynesburg & Washington narrow-gauge line, affectionately called "The Waynie," was paid by the mile, for he laid out a twenty-eight-mile route with 174 curves, a route that the builders conscientiously followed. A homing pigeon in flight between the two terminals would cover only seventeen miles. Of the sinuous Waynie, someone wrote:

> It wiggles in, it wiggles out,
> It leaves the passenger still in doubt
> Whether the man who built the track
> Was coming in or going back.

The line has its Mule-Shoe and Pony-Shoe curves, and a lone pine tree that every train passed three times on a single trip. Locomotive firemen attempting to toss shovelfuls of coal into the firebox were said to have hit the headlight instead of the firebox. A humorist passenger gave vent to the following:

> In all my travels on the wide, wide earth
> I've never seen a more circuitous girth
> Than the Waynesburg-Washington Railroad, my dear,
> Where you can reach out and shake hands with the engineer;
> But I didn't know where to bestow my feet,
> So I curled all up and put them on my seat;
> When the next curve came—I am writing my best—
> My head was going east but my feet were going west.

As long ago as 1832, the year before Waynesburg townsmen's first vote on a railroad project, sheet-iron coal cars were being used elsewhere in the state on the Philadelphia & Reading. Some little five-ton cars had dump bottoms which developed a tricky habit of opening unexpectedly and dropping a trainman under the rolling wheels; so the men learned how to run along a twelve-inch catwalk fastened to the dump car's edge, instead of risking a jump into bottomless cars at night. It is said that anyone mastering this technique could have qualified as a tightrope walker. Before cabooses were invented, the flagman on a coal train usually rode the last hopper; sometimes when the weather was bitterly cold he built himself a small fire in the bottom of an empty car to keep from freezing.

Among the curious rules that governed pioneer railroading in this state were these two issued to Reading conductors in 1851: "Do not let your brakemen throw pieces of coal at anyone passing on the road" and "Signal men [flagmen] are not allowed to use fence rails to mark their last car; the lamp is the proper signal."

Prior to the use of telegraphy in dispatching trains, single-track operation was marked by frequent delays and confusion, according to the Reading's former secretary-treasurer, Jay V. Hare, who stated:

Ordinarily the coal trains were started out at certain times of day in groups of two or more. The last one leaving would carry a white circular signal, called the "ball," which had to be prominently displayed at all times and shown to each station and train that was passed, thus indicating that the track was clear for trains to proceed in the opposite direction. . . . Trains standing on sidings, after waiting the prescribed length of time for trains in the opposite direction to appear and pass, were permitted to run on the main track and proceed on their journey by running the curves—that is, one of the crew would run afoot at least a quarter mile ahead of his train around every curve in order to avoid a collision.

W. A. Gray of Pittsburgh, a veteran locomotive inspector for the Pennsylvania Railroad, said some years ago:

My father was a Pennsy engineer. He began his rail career on the old Portage lift, a state-owned enterprise that the P.R.R. took over in 1857. I also had eight uncles who lost their lives while blazing the iron trail in this state. When I was a boy I didn't have to read adventure stories; I heard them told by my father and uncles. Theirs was not fiction but real tales of the night express, the excitement of wrecks and blockades, of floods, blizzards, and runaway trains.

The Allegheny Portage Railroad to which Gray referred was perhaps the oddest transportation system of its day—a peculiar blend of canalboats, cars, rails, inclined planes, stationary engines, mules, and horses. Altogether there were thirty-three changes of motive power during a single trip between Philadelphia and Johnstown. On this line was bored at Staple Bend, four miles east of Johnstown, the first railroad tunnel in America. It is still there, deserted, overgrown with vegetation, and a bit spooky. No train has rolled through it since 1852. Locally it is believed to be a haunted tunnel. For years an inclined plane, operated by a stationary engine, was regarded as the simplest and cheapest method of getting trains over a hill. One of them, near Girardville on the Reading, was built in 1862 by the estate of Stephen Girard. The first load of coal hoisted to its top was presented to the mayor of Philadelphia for fuel in a soup kitchen that fed Civil War volunteers on their way to the front.

About eight years before the Civil War, Pennsylvania had a little war of its own. This was brought about by a move to standardize the gauges of the various railroads that formed a New York–Chicago connecting line, thus eliminating the inconvenient transfer at Erie. Local merchants, draymen, hotel owners, and other business interests fought the project. They sought to compel through travelers to stop over in Erie and spend money there. On December 7, 1853, an old bell from a British warship, which Commodore Perry had captured in the battle of Lake Erie some forty years earlier, clanged loudly in the Erie courthouse cupola. Most of the city's population gathered in the public square to hear Mayor King denounce the Erie & North East Railroad, one of the links in the long chain, for its "villainous work against the prosperity of our city." "Erie's destiny," he proclaimed, "is to become a powerful rail and water terminal! No railroad shall make it a mere hamlet by the wayside!"

This demonstration led to a series of bloody, occasionally fatal, fights between the railroad faction, dubbed "Shanghais," and the "Rippers," who ripped up tracks, cut telegraph wires, seized the E. & N. E. station and general offices at Erie, destroyed bridges and company records, and assaulted railroad officials. By removing rails, the Rippers made the suburb of Harbor Creek an eastern terminal village, leaving a six-mile gap between it and the Erie & Mad River Railroad that entered the city from the west. Travelers endured acute hardships in traversing that icy stretch in the dead of winter with cold winds howling across the big lake. They called it "crossing the isthmus." Many were afflicted by severe frostbites. One old man was actually frozen to death. Drivers of cabs, omnibuses, and drays solicited their trade, but most of the embittered railroad passengers ignored them. Stumbling through the snow afoot and dragging their luggage, they preferred to suffer rather than patronize local conveyances. Protests arose all the way from

New York to Chicago. Horace Greeley editorialized in the *New York Tribune,* "Let Erie be avoided by all travelers until grass shall grow in her streets!" Finally, the disputed section of railroad was taken over by the state, tracks were relaid under the protection of bayonets and two cannons, and an Erie union station was erected; but the feud dragged on, with sporadic outbreaks, until it was eclipsed by the larger issues of the Civil War.

Ephraim N. Jones, an engineer who claimed to have operated in Harrisburg the first yard engine on the Pennsylvania Railroad, recollected that by refusing to obey military orders on the night of September 12, 1863, he had saved not only his own life but also the lives of a Union army general, a governor of Pennsylvania, and many other people. As Jones related, he was running a munitions train and had lain on the ground beside his locomotive at Chambersburg to snatch a little sleep when he was awakened by an overbearing army officer who commanded him to transport Major General Joseph J. Reynolds and his staff to Hagerstown, Maryland. This the engineer declined to do, saying he was not subject to any orders except those from his immediate superior, Sam Potts, military superintendent of the railroad.

"Besides," he inquired pointedly, "how do I know what's moving between here and Hagerstown?"

As the road was single-tracked, it was quite evident to Jones, as it would be to any other railman, that if he tried to run a train to Hagerstown without authorization from the dispatcher he would risk colliding with another train that might be on the line.

But the officer ignored this point. "You're under arrest," he snapped. "I'll get someone else to take us through. We must get there in a hurry."

Other officers entered the argument, but they all suddenly fell silent when they heard an engine whistle and realized that an extra was pounding the rails. As the train hove into sight Jones turned to the officer who had arrested him, saying: "Now you see what would have happened if I had obeyed your orders. We'd have met that fellow head-on down the line!"

Later, the engineer learned that this extra had been carrying Governor Curtin of Pennsylvania, other state officials, a few army doctors, and some wounded Federal soldiers.

"Now," he chuckled, "every time I visit Gettysburg and see General Reynolds' statue I say to myself, 'General, if I hadn't disobeyed your orders at Chambersburg, your statue probably wouldn't be standing here today.' "

By the same token, if Governor Curtin had been killed in a head-on collision, he would not have sponsored the movement to dedicate the Gettysburg battlefield as a national cemetery two months afterward. It is just conceivable that, but for the obstinacy of Engineer Jones, the world might never have heard Abraham Lincoln's best-loved address.

To the end of the Civil War, railroad men were often paid with "shinplasters" (folding money) in bills ranging from two cents to one thousand dollars, issued by various transportation companies. Nearly seventy railroads in Pennsylvania alone are known to have sponsored such currency. Some shinplasters were fine specimens of the engraver's art; others were turned out on primitive presses by homespun printers. A dollar note with a nicely etched scene of surveyors at work, dated 1875 and bearing the imprint of the Philadelphia, Newtown & New York Railway (now in the Reading system), is the only paper currency familiar to numismatists that any railroad company has isued since 1864, when the National Bank Act virtually stopped the private printing of money.

Some roads used wooden tokens about the size of a quarter with which enginemen bought cordwood at points along the line for their wood-burning locomotives; others passed out scrip redeemable by local merchants. In order to prevent employees from resigning without due notice, still other railroads issued coupons that enginemen and trainmen could not exchange for cash until they had made a certain number of trips over the road. A retired engineer, James Deegan, recalled: "At least one turkey trail that has since become part of the Pennsylvania system used to pay with skins. A cowhide was equivalent to three dollars in wages, a sheepskin one dollar, and rabbit pelts small currency."

The pay-car no longer runs in this state except in the memory of old-timers. It vanished around the turn of the century. Earl Franklin Baker, sometimes called "the poet laureate of the rails," likes to talk of the long ago when he worked as water boy and timekeeper for the Pennsy section gang his stepfather bossed. He remembers the eagerness with which they all greeted the "money wagon":

> We fellers used to count th' days,
>   Like circus, when we knowed
> Month's end would bring th' old pay-car
>   A-gleamin' down th' road.*

"A-gleamin' " is the right word, for the pay-car boasted a piano-rubbed finish, gold-leaf striping and lettering, windows clear as crystal, and rear-platform railings that shone like pure gold. A remodeled coach, it had one platform removed to make robbery more difficult, and the interior partitioned off for sleeping, cooking, eating, and office space. In early days the pay-train generally included a boxcar loaded with tools and supplies for men along the route, and sometimes a third car for distributing signal oil, kerosene, and coal to section houses and stations. At one time it also dispensed rations to hungry trackmen, work-train crews, and bridge and building gangs, for the traveling bank served remote branch lines as well as busy terminal yards.

The pay-car, when not attached to a local passenger train as it sometimes was, had a flexible schedule that permitted the engineer to stop wherever he spied a section crew. At every stop the car was a center of drama and excitement. It carried a safe, of course, but the "Grand Lama" (paymaster) picked up additional funds at certain banks he passed on his route. A dignified figure he was, seated like the archangel Gabriel before a mammoth ruled pay-roll ledger that each employee had to sign, surrounded by trays of gold, silver, and lesser currency, and protected by a wicked-looking pistol near his elbow.

For greater protection, the pay-train ran only in the daytime, had a picked crew, and was guarded by "company bulls" (railroad police). The engine crew also had weapons, which usually rusted for want of use. Although the pay-train was on the go most of the time, it seemed to the average railroad employee to head into some fabulous region like the Big Rock Candy Mountains and stay there until the third of the month, or seventeenth, or whenever it was that he got paid.

* Used by permission of *Railroad Magazine*.

John S. Atherton, assisted by his brother Thomas, served for years as the Delaware & Hudson paymaster. Their engine, No. 184 (later rebuilt and renumbered 380), was popularly dubbed "The Reindeer" because of its Santa Claus implication. On the Lehigh Valley line the "family disturber" (pay-car) rode behind No. 371, which was named *J. H. Wilhelm* for the paymaster himself. And on the Pennsy's Philadelphia division the Grand Lama, J. Milton Meshey, made his rounds in a chariot wheeled by the elegant No. 929. The 929 was a privileged character. Trimmed with burnished brass and copper, she reflected so much sunlight that she appeared to be afire. This beauty could not be stabled with ordinary iron horses. She occupied a private boxed stall, apart from the others, in the old Seventh Street enginehouse at Harrisburg. Her reign was glorious, but it ended with the Pennsy's selling her to the Strasburg Railroad. Oliver S. Sprout said he last saw her in a Lancaster junk yard "with no hint of gold-leaf striping on her wooden pilot."

A series of landmarks in the Susquehanna River at Harrisburg, plainly visible from car windows of westbound Pennsylvania Railroad trains, are the stone piers of a projected bridge, originally a score or more, which have stood there since 1883 but have never carried a superstructure. More than one sermon has been based on that unfinished bridge. A leaflet issued by a religious tract society likens it to human life and the need for immortality: "It was meant to reach the further shore."

These piers represent the starting point of an ambitious venture, the South Pennsylvania Railroad, better known as the South Penn or Vanderbilt's Folly. Much construction work was done on that dream road in 1883, '84, and '85 at a total cost of ten million dollars. In brief, the South Penn is the story of a bold attempt by William H. Vanderbilt, New York Central president, to thrust a main line through the mountains and valleys of this state as a counteroffensive to the invasion of his Hudson River domain by the Pennsylvania and J. P. Morgan. In this campaign Vanderbilt was backed by the Philadelphia & Reading Railway, a rival of the Pennsy, and Andrew Carnegie, the steel king, who sought cheaper rates on the hauling of Pittsburgh steel to the seaboard. Before the South Penn could be completed, however, the financial titans came to terms; many years later the Pennsylvania Turnpike Commission built a motor super-highway over the abandoned route.

In Bradford County may still be seen traces of another phantom railroad, the Pittsburgh, Binghamton & Eastern, on which more than a million and a half dollars was spent. The project started out as a local trolley line. Then capitalists from Boston and Albany became interested and put over the idea of changing to a steam line between Towanda and Canton. Later, Tioga County residents came into the picture, and it was decided to extend the road from Canton to Newberry near Williamsport, and westward to Binghamton, New York, to connect with the Delaware & Hudson. Much land was bought; grading was done between Towanda and Cedar Lodge; some expensive rock cuts were blasted; and three bridges were built. Concrete abutments still standing indicate the start of a fourth bridge. However, the company went bankrupt; the state purchased the right of way and built on it a Towanda-Canton motor highway. Thus, this railroad dream ended the same way as had the South Penn.

No splinter is left of the granddaddy of all Pennsylvania railroads, the wooden-rail line sixty yards long that Thomas Leiper laid in September 1809 near the old Bull's Head Tavern in Philadelphia. Weeds cover the remains of the second railroad built by Leiper a month later for three quarters of a mile between his rock quarries on beautiful Crum Creek and a point in what is now Ridley Township.

Two of the very few wooden-covered railway bridges left in America are located in Pennsylvania on the Reading lines. Both were built in 1869, one over Fishing Creek a mile west of Outwood, the other spanning Manatawney Creek near Colebrookdale. Upstate, the Reading is called "The Dutch," and with Dutch thrift it never seems to wear anything out—machines and men alike keep on going. Great black breakers and culm banks are as much a part of the Reading as are locomotives and cars. In regions served by this road there are a host of pink-cheeked Pennsylvania Germans and much that appears quaint, old-fashioned, and home-made.

Reputedly the country's oldest brick depot is the Erie station at Susquehanna, west of which stood a famous caboose, No. 4259, that the Erie had presented in 1898 to Captain Robert E. Peary, U. S. N. This caboose served as deckhouse on the staunch ship *Windward,* but when the ship got stuck in the ice off Grinnell Land, the caboose was hauled ashore and there was occupied by Peary as his headquarters. After discovering the North Pole, Peary gave the caboose back to the Erie. It remained on exhibition near the old brick depot until the spring of 1941 when, rotted by weather, it was torn down.

Another old relic is the station standing at Darlington, Beaver County, on the Pittsburgh, Lisbon & Western. A fine old cut-stone building erected in September 1802, it originally housed the Griersburg Academy for boys. Among its alumni was John Brown of Harpers Ferry raid fame.

According to tradition, the Mauch Chunk, Summit Hill & Switchback Railroad was distinguished for the earliest use anywhere of the surveyor's level, in 1818, and for the first installation of iron rails on this continent, four-foot segments imported from England. Although it stretched over the mountains for only nine miles, the Switchback began operation in May 1827 as the country's longest and most important railroad. It started as a coal carrier near the spot where in 1791 anthracite had first been discovered by a hunter and trapper. As Summit Hill is about one thousand feet higher than Mauch Chunk, a train of from six to fourteen loaded coal cars could make the nine-mile run in about half an hour. The return trip by mule power took five times as long. Eventually two inclined planes and stationary engines were built to haul back the empties; in 1870 the system was converted to a roller-coaster passenger line. The Switchback was America's oldest existing railroad at the time it ceased operating in 1933. Four years later it was junked. At the height of its popularity as a vacation resort, the Mauch Chunk region was known as "The Switzerland of America" and vied with Niagara Falls as a honeymooner's paradise. Souvenir stores there sold a locomotive and tender model carved from solid anthracite as well as other novelties made of coal.

In the 1836-37 winter, when the Mauch Chunk Switchback

was only nine and a half years old, the country's first sleeping car was introduced on a Cumberland Valley (now P.R.R.) train running between Harrisburg and Chambersburg. Like the troop sleepers in World War II, it boasted three tiers of bunks. The car was heated by a wood-burning stove and lighted by tallow candles. A solitary basin and towels were placed at one end. There was no bed clothing. Weary travelers, fully clad, reclined on rough mattresses with overcoats or shawls drawn over them. An ancient cartoon entitled "Convenience of the New Sleeping Cars" showed a timid gentleman in one of the upper berths listening to this conversation:

Brakeman: "Jim, do you think the Mill Creek bridge is safe tonight?"

Conductor: "If Joe cracks on the steam, I guess we'll get the engine and tender over all right. I'm going forward."

One day in the 1890's a Pullman porter on a Buffalo, Rochester & Pittsburgh express rushed excitedly into the coaches just after they had left Johnsonburg, exclaiming to the conductor, Max J. Moore: "Max, come with me! A woman in one of the sleepers is going to have a baby!"

Max replied, "Great God, Bill, I'm not a doctor!" He persuaded a lady passenger to act as midwife. Unfortunately the infant was stillborn. At Bradford the mother was driven to a hospital, where she made a normal recovery.

Until shortly after the turn of the century, white served as the "clear" signal indication on all American railroads. The change in color indications was brought about largely as the result of a wreck that occurred on the Pittsburgh, Fort Wayne & Chicago (now P.R.R.) on the murky night of March 3, 1901, according to Harry K. McClintock, railroader and minstrel, who was braking for the road at that time. Evidently a signal near Baden had been set at "stop," but the red lens had fallen out of its frame and the engineer was thus given a white light, which meant "go ahead." Today, yellow or amber signifies "caution," regardless of whether it is caused by light shining through a yellow roundel or an empty socket. Another factor in the railroad's abandonment of the white clear signal was the increasing use of electricity and the growing number of white lights both off and on the right of way.

Four years later a foggy-night accident on the Pennsylvania had the effect of helping to make railroading safer. J. C. Clouser, a boomer trainman, recalled having seen the wreckage caused by the derailment of a carload of dynamite on a freight train pulling out of the Harrisburg yards on May 11, 1905. A fast passenger train had hit the derailed car; the ensuing explosion, plus the fact that the coaches were wooden and equipped with Pintsch gaslights, had made a ghastly funeral pyre of the express, with a heavy casualty list. Public reaction to this accident, Clouser reported, helped to bring about the enactment three years later of national legislation to regulate the shipment of explosives. It may also have influenced compulsory legislation regarding the use of all-steel passenger coaches, the Pennsy's first appearing voluntarily in 1906. However, all-steel baggage, express, and postal cars predated the Harrisburg wreck, and there were several thousand all-steel passenger coaches in operation years before their use was made mandatory.

According to old-timers, most of the Philadelphia & Reading trainmen of the late 1860's and early seventies wore beards, a practice they had acquired in the army during the Civil War. Beards were common enough all over America, but it seems that on the Reading they were almost obligatory. Came the panic of '73; wages were slashed and railway men were laid off in large numbers, but being unorganized, they could do little about it. Then the Reading management made a slip. A new "brass hat," brought in from the outside, took a gander at the passenger trainmen's foliage and issued an order requiring them to show up for duty clean-shaven.

This interference with personal liberty enraged the trainmen. "He wants us to look like priests," they protested, embroidering their remarks with terms that no priest would be likely to utter. They walked out in a body and tied up the road for twenty-four hours. Not only that, but they took with them the coupling links and pins and the engine side rods! A drawbridge over the Susquehanna River was said to have been so full of cars without links and pins that the span could not be opened for traffic. Company officials ran around in circles trying to settle the strike, but as there was no union they could not find an authorized spokesman with whom to make terms. Holding one session after another at various points, they had to organize the trainmen on a temporary basis to end the walkout. The ban on whiskers was lifted.

A relic treasured by Joseph Smeck, retired locomotive fireman, is a quaint old shaving mug into which is baked a picture of Reading engine No. 482 with Smeck himself as fireman for his engineer-father, Amos Smeck. The custom of keeping individual shaving mugs developed in Civil War days, but its popularity waned with the safety razor's arrival. Mugs belonging to railmen displayed designs varying from a caboose, lantern and flags, an engine, a boxcar, or even a handcar, depending upon the customer's branch of service. Barbers ordered them from supply companies, which usually imported blank cups from Europe and had their own decorators hand-paint on each the prospective owner's name and a picture showing his occupation or some other distinguishing pattern. The mugs were then fired to fuse the illustration with the chinaware.

Just north of Pottstown, a gnarled and ancient apple tree that flourished for years was said by local tradition to have been planted by Johnny Appleseed in the early 1800's on the only trip he made to southeastern Pennsylvania. The tree grew so near the Philadelphia & Reading southbound track that sometimes it just touched passing trains. An engineer named Bill regularly piloted a coal drag between Mount Carbon and Port Richmond, going through Reading late in the evening. Bill never seemed to get enough "shut-eye," so he devised a scheme of his own to catch up on sleep with the aid of that tree. After he had left Reading he would comfortably adjust himself in the cab with his legs projecting out of the window to nap for an hour or so while leisurely covering the eighteen-mile stretch to Pottstown. When he neared Pottstown the apple-tree boughs would brush his feet as a gentle warning (not unlike the telltales that hang suspended over tracks near bridges and tunnel entrances) that he was approaching the depot. Unfortunately for Bill, either Johnny Appleseed's tree was cut down or else General Superintendent G. A. Nicholls discovered his dozing propensity. Bill did not remain in P. & R. service long enough to draw a pension.

Time meant little in those halcyon days. There is the anecdote of an Erie conductor on local freight who asked his engineer while they were making setouts and pickups: "What time have you, Mike? Shure, I came away this mornin' forgettin' me watch."

Mike pulled out his "turnip," looked at it, shook it, held it up to his ear, and then said in disgust: "O the divil! The dom thing's stopped."

So the conductor sauntered over to the section house and asked the foreman's wife for the time.

"Well," she told him, "it do be half past tin, but Dinney says this ould clock is a half-hour fast. But whin No. 1 went by it was a half-hour slow, so I dunno what time it is."

"All right, Mike," the conductor yelled to the engineer, "set your watch by Mrs. O'Brien's clock an' get the hell outa town. You have plenty of time on No. 2." And he headed for the caboose.

The freight trainman's affection for his little red caboose, especially in the old days, can readily be understood from the fact that, besides being the place where he worked, it was literally his home for the most active part of his mature life—unless he was promoted to passenger service. The "crummy" or "hack," as it was nicknamed, had housekeeping facilities. There the trainman could sleep on a bed; cook tasty meals on a pot-bellied coal stove and eat them at a table; write his reports on a desk; change his clothes; relax while the flagman washed dishes and swept the floor; smoke in peace; sometimes enjoy a dog's companionship; and, in fact, do most of the things he did in the house on Railroad Avenue, Elm Street, or wherever else he lived while off duty. The caboose, however, was, and is, strictly bachelor quarters. Since adoption of the eight-hour day it has become less homelike and more utilitarian.

Many old-time railroaders believed that sweeping out a caboose after dark would bring bad luck. Other occupational superstitions include: Accidents usually occurred in series of three; a locomotive involved in one or more wrecks was jinxed; engines with 9 or 13 in their numbers were unlucky; September, the ninth month, was the fatal month in railroading; it was bad luck to take a reconditioned

locomotive out of the shops on Friday; no locomotive should be
turned to the left when taken from the roundhouse onto the turn-
table; it was an evil omen to step into the engine cab with your left
foot first, or to kick your foot in a switch frog, or to trip over a tie
or rail.

Harking back to vanished yesterdays, Ervin W. Reiter, a retired
telegrapher now living at Quakertown, said:

Remember the time the freight-house man found a barrel full of
porter among the empties, and you buried it in the coal pile and had
free liquor for three weeks afterward? The station agent could not
understand why you always smelled of booze, yet did not leave the
place.

Remember the redheaded country girl you kept hidden in the ticket
office while the superintendent was pacing back and forth past the
office window? What he didn't know wouldn't hurt him. Remember
when that same super called you on the phone one night and told
you to look for an important package on the next train and bring it
over to his house, and when he opened it there was a quart of whisky
and a box of Havana cigars? He didn't give you a nip of the Scotch
but he did offer you a smoke. And that evening when somebody threw
a railroad cop out of the signal tower while a little booze party was
going on? You claimed you'd been busy and had nothing to do with
it, but the very same super who had given you a good cigar a couple
of weeks before socked you with a load of brownies [demerits] and
ten days without pay, remember?

And how about the time you were washing a dirty mess of lamp
globes at a small jerkwater station and someone cheerfully greeted
you with, "Hard at it?" and you cursed a blue streak before looking
up, and then did your face get red? It was the village parson!

Most railroaders in the old days respected the parson and had
deep religious instincts that cropped out in the moralizing in
some of their songs and doggerel; but because trains were operated on the Sabbath as on other days, the engine bell often took
precedence over the church bell. To train and engine crews, not
to mention dispatchers and other railroad men, running a train
safely and on schedule was almost part of the Ten Commandments.
But they did go to church when they could. H. O. Moser
of Mount Carmel recalled that during his boyhood at Delano,
some of the Lehigh Valley employees there would regularly ride
a handcar to Mahanoy City and back on Sundays, pumping the
car themselves, to attend divine worship.

Speaking of railroaders in his county during the 'eighties and 'nineties, Oliver S. Sprout of Lancaster reminisced:

Those fellows were all God-fearing, if not God-serving, and for a reason. Most of their ancestors had come here to escape religious persecutions in Europe and consequently took time to be holy. The later generations in many cases slipped away from the religious practices of their forebears but, paradoxically, continued to hold those ideas sacred. Today at Columbia there are several large old stone churches, debt-free, that were well filled while the town was a rail center but now have congregations only one quarter their former size. These edifices were built and paid for almost entirely with railroad money. In pleasant weather, Bible study groups also met on the Pennsylvania Railroad Y.M.C.A. lawn under the direction of George C. K. Sample. The railroad men sat, sang, and prayed in their shirt sleeves, many of them enjoying a cud of tobacco at the same time.

An incident stood out vividly in Sprout's memory:

A brakeman had been seriously injured one winter day in the Columbia yards. He was laid on a hastily removed car door to be carried to a doctor's office. He asked somebody to pray for him. An engineer, Abram Meckley, who was a Quaker, crawled down off his engine, removed his hat, knelt down in the snow, and offered a prayer that I am sure the brakeman never forgot.

Train crews in those days carried "forty-eight-hour buckets," according to Sprout, a member of the fifth generation of a railroad family. These were capacious lunch pails about a foot square and fifteen inches long, filled with food for a long trip over the road; these trips often kept a man away from home for three days at a spell. The Columbia men were nicknamed "flitch eaters" and the Harrisburg crews "mackerel backs," on account of the kinds of foods predominating in their lunch boxes.

In an average train and engine crew of five men, one would be buying a modest home through a building and loan association; two fellows, paying rent, would be living in more pretentious quarters; and the other two might be eking out a precarious existence in the slums with their women and children undernourished and ill-clad because the men were spending much of their money in bars along the railroad tracks. It wasn't necessarily the engineers and conductors, the crew men in the upper wage brackets, who became homeowners. Brakemen and firemen often lived better and took more adequate care of their families than did the top-ranking crew members.

Railroad men's homes a generation or two ago were like average American homes. They lacked numerous comforts and conveniences that are now regarded as necessities. A typical home consisted of a parlor, a "middle room," and a combined kitchen and dining room downstairs; two or three second-floor bedrooms; an unplastered attic; usually a cellar for storage space; and an outhouse. The large coal range not only kept the kitchen warm, but also supplied a little heat to the rest of the house. It was supplemented by a heater with isinglass doors, which made the middle room cozy and even sent some warmth to the arctic regions upstairs.

Except for an outside hydrant, there was no running water on the premises. When it was needed, the distaff side of the family generally heated water in kettles. If a trainman or engineman was out on the road and was expected in at night, a supply of water was drawn and set on the range, with a washtub set near-by for his convenience, as baths were taken in the kitchen. Winter clothing included long-sleeved, long-legged underwear because houses and trains alike were insufficiently heated and outdoor trips were usually made afoot. Second-hand military overcoats were much in demand by brakemen, who often had to ride freight-car tops in severe weather. They tried to protect themselves with multiple layers of clothing, which, at times, hampered their movements and led to their being injured.

Most of the railroad families in the latter part of the last century paid as they went, but not a few lived by the book for whatever credit they felt they needed from local tradesmen. They kept a strict account of the charged items in a little book and settled once a month on the day the pay-car rolled around. Children delighted to accompany their fathers on this important day, for at such times the genial grocer would give them each a bag of hard-to-get-rid-of candy.

The simple pleasures of rail-faring men and women in bygone days included picnics and balls sponsored by the various brotherhood lodges. Many a slow freight was speeded up almost miraculously so the crew could arrive somewhere in time for a social affair. Telegraphers marooned at sleepy little stations in the hinterland would board a train, or maybe cajole some generous section boss into the loan of a handcar, in order to get to town on the big night, which was any evening when a shindig was scheduled within reasonable traveling distance.

Moser stated that his railroading father occasionally played the fiddle at informal parties held in Delano: "Possibly his greatest triumph as a fiddler was when he was called one evening to furnish the music for one of those impromptu dances at the home of A. P. Blakeslee, then division superintendent. For a mere fireman, still in his twenties, that was something."

Payday invariably brought revelry to the section gangs. "That night in the outfit cars on the spur track west of the pumphouse," reminisced McClintock the minstrel, "there were kegs of beer and roaring choruses of lusty song and heavy brogans stomping to accordion music."

Rule G in the standard code forbade drinking by railroad employees while on duty. This was broadened to include being seen in a saloon just before reporting for duty. "Erv" Reiter recalled having seen a telegraph operator report wearily for the night trick after an all-day picnic, "staggering off the front end of the train, in fine shape to handle a station."

An old custom was for engine crews to decorate their locomotives for Fourth of July, Memorial Day, and Labor Day excursions. Moser recollected watching his father, then an engineer, "spend hours at night cutting out stars and other figures from gold and silver foil, to be used for pasting on stack, sandbox, and dome. Great quantities of bunting, flags, and rosettes gave the engine a gala appearance."

Another engineer's son, Creedin A. Kruger of Carlisle, said:

Life was a picnic when dad ran the only steam engine on the Pennsy's Dillsburg branch. Between runs the crew might shoot rabbits, pick berries, or go to his cousin's farm for luscious hunks of pie. Once, by sad accident, they ran over a turkey. To make the best of their hard luck they cleaned the bird, had mother roast it, and ate it on the road. Dad's engine was the old 3-Z. I will always remember the thrill I got from tugging at her throttle whenever I went down to the railroad with dad's dinner pail.

Fast engineers were tabbed "ballast scorchers." They liked nothing better than to race trains of competing roads when their trains used parallel tracks at the same time and in the same direction. Heydorn E. Schleh recalled the nightly races between Reading train No. 70 and the Pennsy's evening train, both scheduled to reach Williamsport at about 10:30 A.M. The engineers would wait eagerly for each other at Montgomery station and then race side by side to Muncy, while passengers in the coaches would lay wagers on the outcome. As a rule, the Reading ten-wheelers were able to get under way before the Pennsy's Atlantic-type engines could hit their stride. Shenanigans of this kind violated company rules, but brass hats are said to have winked at racing as long as their own trains did not fare too badly.

In the early 1900's the Reading–Jersey Central Queen of the Valley used to put on quite a show. Guy H. Peifer, who then lived in Harrisburg, recalled:

The run was often handled by an engineer with a flair for the dramatic. The track from Paxtang to the state capital slanted through a stone cut downgrade to the station. Upon entering this cut, the man at the throttle, like the old-time stagecoach driver who "saved a gallop for the Avenue," would tie down his whistle cord to let the world know he was coming into town. You could hear it for miles. That piercing wail, plus the glow from the open firebox, was indeed exciting. Night after night my girl friend and I would walk over to the Thirteenth Street bridge in Harrisburg to enjoy the spectacle.

Some engineers were expert at "quilling" (playing tunes on their locomotive whistles) and reputedly could make a whistle say its prayers or scream like a banshee. A typical quill artist was W. H. "Whistling Bill" Wardoff, a Reading engineer who was born near Wilkes-Barre and died in 1941. J. Alfred Undy recalled Whistling Bill's prowess:

I often heard Bill play "Home, Sweet Home" on the whistle of his old camelback engine while he was pulling freight for the Atlantic City Railroad, a Reading subsidiary. Bill loved children and they loved him. Sometimes his engine cab was alive with kids. During the First World War he ran into Cape May on the Jersey seacoast, where an army training camp was located. His nostalgic tune made the rookie soldiers so homesick that their commanding officer asked the railroad management to instruct Bill to cease tooting "Home, Sweet Home" within earshot of Cape May.

More colorful than the kindred Western Union messenger and often pinch-hitting for him was that human bloodhound, the callboy of yesteryear, whose stock in trade consisted of a little black book, a pencil stub, a trainman's lantern, a wizardlike memory, shrewdness, and the persistence of a bill collector. The railroad industry could not have got along without him. Decades ago, before Alexander Graham Bell's invention became popular and the swivel-chair crew dispatcher succeeded him, the callboy with his rusty bicycle was as familiar a figure in railroad towns as was the cigar-store wooden Indian. There was something professional, like a doctor or priest, in the discreet silence he kept in regard to other folks' business. Now and then while on his rounds he barged into scandalous secrets that might have disrupted the town's social life, but a callboy could be trusted to keep his lips buttoned. William F. Knapke, a retired conductor, put it this way:

A callboy knew the favorite hangout of every man who had worked in that terminal a week. He was familiar with every light switch, ceiling bulb, and kerosene lamp in every rooming house in a city of 20,000 and he could put his hand on any of them in the dark. He also knew every loose stair tread and seemed to take a fiendish joy in stepping on it extra hard to evoke a nerve-racking screech. And in a certain quiet street just off the main business center or in a shabby district across the tracks, where dim red lights shone through transom and drapery, he knew whether it was Ruby or Gladys or Blanche he would have to find to contact the railroader he was looking for.

Did you ever try to hide out on a callboy? Brother, it couldn't be done. Say you're in that back room on the third floor of the Commercial Hotel. You've just picked up a picture that made it a full house instead of two pairs. Just then at your elbow appears a glim [lantern] plus the callboy saying, "Wancha for—" Did you ever try to lay off on the callboy and think up a perfectly swell excuse to hand him? Well, he knew the answer to that one—and a lot more you had never heard of. It generally was "no."

The callboy of Grandpa's day usually came from a railroad family and regarded his work as a necessary steppingstone to a seat in the engine cab or caboose, or perhaps he aspired still higher to the throne of yardmaster or division superintendent. He often got there too. *Who's Who in Railroading* is replete with the names of officials who started out with a scarred bike and a little black book, the autograph album of trainmen and enginemen, but came to know the right people and gradually climbed the ladder. There are, of course, some callboys still left in this state; not all of them are called crew dispatchers. To ease the manpower shortage in World War II, there were even a few call-girls, a very few.

A legend developed from the holdup of P.R.R. train No. 39, the Pittsburgh and Northern Express, in the early morning darkness of August 31, 1909. The scene of the crime—a wilderness gorge in the Alleghenies miles from the nearest house—had been well chosen. On one side of the track ran a rutted state road, the Pennsylvania Canal towpath, and the bluish-green Juniata River; on the other, a mountain wall. Between 1814 and 1820, this ravine had been terrorized by Dave Lewis' "merry men" who preyed on the stagecoaches and Conestoga wagons that rattled along the highway between Philadelphia and Pittsburgh.

Number 39, westbound, was regarded by railroaders as a treasure chest because of the tempting sums of money it carried nightly. On the night of the robbery, the first car held a little safe containing newly minted coins and bullion; in the second were five big strongboxes from Washington, all crammed with crisp new bank notes, roughly half a million dollars.

At about one thirty A.M., a series of torpedo explosions on the rail caused Engineer Samuel Donnelly to "wipe the clock" (make an emergency stop) at the foot of Black Log Mountain. Peering into the deep shadows, he and his fireman were startled to see neither a landslide nor a washout but a grotesque figure wearing a black slouch hat draped with gunny sack that covered most of his short, stocky body. The stranger flourished a revolver in each hand. He ordered them back to the first car, lined up several members of the crew, had them fill a burlap sack with small bags of currency until it weighed about seventy pounds, and forced them to lug it for him part way up the slope. Then he released the crew; the train sped away. The bad man inadvertently had passed up the half-million dollars and taken a mere $65 worth of shiny new Lincoln pennies.

Most of the pennies were found later, but the desperado was never apprehended. Even the pack of bloodhounds, borrowed from the Baltimore & Ohio, which picked up the scent a few hours afterward whimpered and turned back. Folks said that a wraith had frightened them off. As time went on, railroaders believed that the ghost of the outlaw kept walking along the track or lurking behind the jagged rocks and underbrush of Black Log Mountain in search of the half-million dollars.

The legend of the missing freight car pops up now and then and seems to have had its inception on the Erie some time before the automatic coupler was invented. The story goes that on a winter's night a livestock train in charge of Conductor Coe Littleton rumbled out of Susquehanna and reached its destination, Port Jervis, New York, with one car peculiarly lost from the middle of the train. Scrutiny revealed a broken link-and-pin coupler at the spot where the car should have been; the rear link, twisted like a hook, held the train together. Littleton was nonplused. He swore that before leaving he had checked all the cars by their waybill numbers, as was his custom. No hijacker could have stolen the car without his knowledge and certainly not without a complicated switching operation.

Hours later, the Erie agent at Shohola reported an empty cattle car standing in a snowy field near the station. This proved to be the missing equipment, but how it had landed there was a seven days' wonder. Railmen reasoned that maybe the coupling had snapped on a descending grade, the car being derailed and sliding down the low embankment while its fellows had closed the gap and the pressure had converted the torn link into a hook that recoupled the train. As for the cattle, they may have kicked open the door or it may have been shattered by the derailment. In either event, the cows swam the ice-filled river but were all eventually rounded up unhurt. Recent versions of this recital have cropped up on other roads, like the mythical presence of Kilroy and the signature of J. B. King scrawled on boxcars, but are modified by the modern automatic coupler.

Among the quaint rules on the old North Pennsylvania Railroad (now part of the Reading system) in the 1850's was one requiring a southbound train to wait at Fort Washington fifteen minutes, if necessary, for an expected excursion special; if it did not appear, the southbound engineer was to proceed slowly and

send ahead a man on horseback to warn the excursion of his
train's approach. If this practice had been followed scrupulously,
Philadelphia today would probably not have a suburb known as
Ambler, nor would John Gibb Smith, Jr., grandson of a Philadelphia & Reading president, Charles E. Smith, have among his
keepsakes the following entry in his grandfather's notebook:

July 17, 1856—A frightful accident occurred this morning on the
North Penna. RR. about 12 miles from Phila. (3rd and Berks Sts.)
in which 66 lives were lost and many wounded. Those so affected
belong to St. Michael's R. C. Church, Kensington, and were upon an
excursion to Ft. Washington, 16 miles from Phila. Engineer Henry
Harrison was killed, as was Rev. Daniel Sheridan, a priest of the
church. Albert Hoople, conductor of the up train, was wounded and
arrested in Montgomery County for murder. The conductor of the
down train, Vanstavoren, poisoned himself that very day, fearing he
would be arrested for causing the accident.

William S. Lee, engineer of the mixed train that rammed the
excursion special, admitted at the hearing that he was a dentist
by profession, that he had not been sure of the right time when
he left Fort Washington, and that he had failed to send ahead a
horseback rider to warn the northbound train. The result was
a head-on collision and fire that set a new high mark in American
railroad casualties. Amid the charred wreckage moved a local
Florence Nightingale—Mary Benjamin Ambler, widow of Andrew
Ambler and proprietor of a fulling mill at Wissahickon. She hurried to the scene with first-aid supplies, and all through that hot
July day ministered to the suffering victims, without stopping for
food or drink herself, tradition says, and afterward nursed some
of them in her own home. For this the railroad company showed
its gratitude by giving the name "Ambler" to the station at that
point. And Ambler it has been ever since.

Another Pennsylvania town owes its name to an excursion-train
wreck on the Lehigh Valley, but for a different reason. The tenth
of October 1888 was a gala day in Hazleton. All morning, train-
loads of visitors had been arriving from various points in the coal
region. The excursionists were mostly miners and their families,
members of temperance societies. Twenty thousand of them, all
wearing badges, paraded the main streets in honor of the Reverend

Theobald Matthew, the famed Irish teetotaler. Brass bands emitted lively airs. One group, St. Paul's Pioneer Corps, swung along with military precision, shouldering little broadaxes with heads that flashed like torches in the afternoon sun.

That night the tired picnickers began rolling homeward in eight sections. Each train had eight to a dozen cars pulled by two engines over the mountain grades. The trains left on ten-minute headway. At eight P.M. the sixth section passed Mud Run station, located in a remote stretch of woodland midway between Penn Haven Junction and White Haven; it rounded a curve, its engine headlight shining for one terrible second squarely into the rear end of the fifth section, and then telescoped the last three cars! A few passengers lolling on the back platform leaped to safety. The rest were trapped like deer in a corral.

Slaughter and panic followed. St. Paul cadets hacked valiantly at the wreckage, striving to free the imprisoned victims, but their light parade axes were useless in the emergency. Of the sixty-four persons killed that night, twenty-nine had come from the same village, Pleasant Valley, six miles from Scranton. The name was so ironic, in view of the tragedy, that grief-stricken survivors changed it to Avoca.

Apropos of names, this state has a town called Railroad (the only post office in America so named), but, oddly enough, without railroad trackage; on an Erie single-track branch is the country's only Whistletown, a one-house hamlet. Another Erie stop worthy of mention is Masthope. Its unique name was derived from the fact that a group of Philadelphians seeking a special kind of mast for the good ship *Constitution* journeyed as far as Lackawaxen without success. Natives told them that they could find such a tree a few miles farther on. They started, saying, "This is our last hope." But they found it and designated the spot Masthope.

The Erie station at Corry, originally an oil-boom settlement, was named for Hiram Corry by General Superintendent Hill of the Atlantic & Great Western because of Corry's liberal terms in selling the railway a piece of land. This crossroads hamlet originally had been called Atlantic & Erie Junction; pioneer oil shipments had been teamed into it from Titusville. A depot on the Waynesburg & Washington bore the name "Judge Chambers," later shortened to "Chambers." The story is that a Judge Chambers had granted right of way over his land on condition that the company build a station at that point, stop every passenger train there, and give a station call each time.

Whoever figured out the names of three towns on the Cambria & Indiana, a fifty-mile coal road in the Keystone State, must have gone on an etymological spree. Colver, the line's headquarters, has a peculiar composite name formed from the first three letters of Coleman and the last three of Weaver, those being the patronymics of the company's promoters. The other terminus is Manver, the last three letters of the same two names; at the end of a C. & I. branch is the small community of Revloc—Colver in reverse.

The site of the present Pennsylvania Railroad yards near Harrisburg was at one time so devoid of society that a lonely telegrapher christened the place Enola (spell it backwards). Enola it is today. The state-owned Philadelphia & Columbia located its main shops at Parkesburg because the Parke family, politically influential, induced the state to buy some of their land and establish shops on it. One of the arguments put forth was that Parkesburg, as a quiet rural community, was free of the city temptations that were considered harmful to sober, industrious, God-fearing craftsmen.

Tyrone, scene of a circus-train disaster in 1893, got its name from the fact that William Patton, railroad builder, was proud of having been born in County Tyrone, Ireland—at least, that claim is made by his great-grandson John D. Denney, Jr., research editor of the National Railway Historical Society's *Bulletin*. Fearsome tales of wild beasts lying in wait around Tyrone persisted for years after the wreck at McCann's Crossing, just outside the city. A seventeen-car train bearing the Walter L. Main Circus from Houtzdale to Lewistown was speeding down a mountain to make up lost time when the engine toppled over, and upset the cars. From the first car came the trumpeting of frightened elephants, from others, a bedlam of screams and howls. On the death list were six human beings, many trained animals, some ferocious menagerie beasts, and sixty-nine horses.

The horror of the wreck was described by James Vincent of Towanda:

William LaRue, a performer, stepped from a Pullman to be faced by a tiger and three lions, all loose and on the rampage. Dangerous reptiles slithered out of broken cages onto the right of way. One roustabout saw a tiger attack a zebra, then a sacred Indian cow. It was shot several hours later at sunset while stalking a milkmaid on the farm of Alfred Thomas. Circus men and posses rounded up as many of the creatures as they could and killed others. Until about the turn of the century, hair-raising tales were told of jungle beasts roaming the district.

Two New York Central stops in this state, Amasa and Stoneboro, perpetuate the memory of Amasa Stone, formerly prominent on the Lake Shore & Michigan Southern board of directors. Sayre, predominantly a railroad town, was named for Robert H. Sayre, the Lehigh Valley's first chief engineer. One of the very few trains ever named for railroad men is the semi-streamlined Asa Packer, which pays homage to the Mauch Chunk judge who helped to found the Lehigh Valley line. Packer Hill at Mauch Chunk also was named for him.

An engine was christened Advance to signify Alexander A. Mitchell's approval of the Emancipation Proclamation. Mitchell, who lived at Delano, was the Lehigh Valley's first master mechanic as well as an avid abolitionist. To draw attention to his beliefs, he adorned the locomotive with a cast-iron sculpture of a Negro's head so arranged that while the wheels were turning, it bobbed slightly in what observers said was a lifelike manner.

The record for misnaming seems to have been held by the Lancaster & Reading Narrow Gauge Railroad, which never had a foot of narrow-gauge track and never went anywhere near Reading. Actually, it ran in a different direction, from Lancaster to Quarryville, and was standard gauge from the very first. Built in 1875, it was absorbed into the Pennsylvania system in 1899.

Railroad trade-marks have a certain fascination. Shortly after the great railroad strike of 1877, Thomas E. Watt, the Pennsylvania's Pittsburgh district passenger agent, was preparing a folder to describe low-rate overnight excursions to Atlantic City. According to well-founded tradition, he decided to illustrate it with an adaptation of the Keystone State's emblem. It seems probable that this pamphlet, no copy of which is known to exist, was the first railroad literature to show the keystone insigne. It originally appeared with the road's complete name, then with variations of it, until finally in 1921 it became the present interlaced P.R.R. monogram.

The Reading, whose boast "America's Largest Anthracite Carrier" is backed by comparative tonnage figures, and the Lehigh Valley, whose crack train, the Black Diamond, rolls through the anthracite region, use the widely accepted coal symbol of the black diamond as their motifs. The Lackawanna utilizes a portrait of the mythical Phoebe Snow, who was created to symbolize the cleanliness of travel on that line in the days (now departed) when its locomotives burned Pennsylvania anthracite instead of the sootier bituminous coal used by other roads.

Long before railroad emblems were born, nameless trackside graves, of which the Keystone State has its share, had begun to be scattered over the country. A few miles west of Malvern, near Frazer, several laborers succumbed to cholera about 1830 while helping to build the Philadelphia & Columbia line. They are sleeping out eternity on the south side of the P.R.R. main stem, their rest undisturbed by trains that thunder overhead night and day. Section men keep "God's half-acre" neat and trim. And six miles from Pittsburgh the borough of Aspinwall is situated on land bought by a Mr. Darlington from an Indian chief, Guyasuta, for a barrel of whisky; when the old redskin trailed to his happy hunting grounds in about 1800, he was interred there beside the Allegheny River on General O'Hara's farm. For years the faithful members of his tribe made periodic pilgrimages to his tomb. At length the Pennsylvania Railroad bought that section for its Sharpsburg yards, and the ancient chief's remains were sent to Carnegie Institute in Pittsburgh. Today the former burial spot, a few hundred yards east of Guyasuta station, is covered by "hot" railroad tracks.

In a Pittsburgh cemetery stands a tombstone sculptured with a bas-relief of locomotive No. 105 of the Pittsburgh, Fort Wayne & Chicago and this epitaph:

HUSBAND
CHARLES A. HAGGERTY
BORN AUG. 2, 1870
KILLED IN WOODS RUN WRECK
APRIL 7, 1897

In the latter half of the last century many an engineer's gravestone bore the likeness of his locomotive—bore it proudly, you might say—while the petroglyphs of trainmen occasionally showed cabooses. There were plenty of unheralded Casey Joneses in that era, men who stuck to the throttle in the face of almost certain death. In fact, one of the slang words for "locomotive engineer" is "hero."

Among the heroes was Joseph Sieg of Philadelphia. Joe was a Pennsy passenger engineer. On October 22, 1882, he was speeding toward his home city through the cut at Bergen, New Jersey, when, without warning, flames shot from his firebox under pressure of a strong back draft and filled the wooden cab. Joe and his fireman retreated to the tender, then to the open front platform of the first coach. The express kept running at about thirty miles an hour with no hand on the throttle. Joe ordered his fireman back into the cab to set the brakes, but the coal heaver was halted by a deadly curtain of flame rolling into the coach. For a moment the engineer paused. He must have been thinking that the lives of nearly two hundred passengers depended upon him alone. Then he plunged through fiery smoke over the coal pile into the cab. Passengers waited tensely. Soon the train slackened speed. When it finally stopped on Hackensack River bridge, the blaze was swirling upward instead of being fanned toward them—but nobody cheered. Joseph Sieg, a human torch, had applied the brakes and then crawled into the water tank. Willing hands lifted him out, took him to a hospital. Four days later he died. The Pennsylvania Railroad paid him extraordinary tribute by running special trains from three cities for the funeral.

One of the saddest disasters in Pennsylvania railroad history inspired two railmen to acts of extraordinary heroism on December 23, 1903. The eastbound Duquesne Limited, B. & O., hit a pile of wooden ties that had been jostled off a westbound Nickel Plate freight train on a sharp curve at James Creek, seven and a half miles from Connellsville, and shot down the terreplein to the edge of Youghiogheny River. Among the sixty-five persons killed that night were a couple who had planned to marry the next day, the pastor of a new Italian Catholic church, a past ruler of the Connellsville Lodge of Elks, and a locomotive fireman who had taken the day off for Yuletide shopping and was returning homeward with an armful of gift packages done up gaily in red and green. Both Baggageman Thomas J. Dom and Conductor Helgoth were severely injured. The conductor, crawling out of the wreckage and aware that he was dying, called over to Dom: "I'm scalded to death. For God's sake, get a red lamp and flag 49 or she'll be on us!"

The baggageman dragged himself back to flag the oncoming train. Unable to find a lantern, he struck three matches, one at a time, and halted the train not three feet from the rear end of the wreck, thus preventing additional loss of life. Dom fainted right under the locomotive pilot, but recovered later. Helgoth's dead body lay crumpled beside the track. This type of courage is symbolized by William B. Chisholm's poem "Flag the Train," which concludes:

> Farewell, ye best loved, farewell!
> I've died not all in vain—
> Thank God, the other lives are saved!
> Thank God, they've flagged the train!*

Loyalty of a different sort was revealed in a flagging incident on the morning of October 7, 1904, when a Lehigh Valley passenger train was brought to a quick stop by a red flag at a curve near Delano. The color was slowly wigwagging close to the roadbed; the engineer thought that some employee had come to grief and was unable to rise, possibly a rear brakeman who had fallen from a preceding train with this signal in hand. It seemed strange, though, for the crew had no orders to meet another train at Delano. Walking ahead to investigate, they were surprised to discover that the red flag was being carried in the jaws of a small terrier.

That only heightened the mystery. The engineer took the dog

* Used by permission of *Railroad Magazine*.

into his cab and got under way again, traveling at a slow pace for a mile or so. As the track was clear, the affair continued to be puzzling until they reached the next station. There the agent recognized the terrier as having belonged to an aged trackwalker, Bernard Dougherty. For six years, in blistering sun and driving blizzard, the animal had preceded its master on inspection trips up and down the tracks. That particular morning Dougherty did not appear as usual—he was dead. However, the dog didn't know it. At the regular hour for beginning its daily routine, the terrier, gripping the flag between its teeth as its master had taught it, started off alone down the track, evidently sure that Dougherty was following a short distance behind.

Very few of the rail-dog stories you hear concern boomers, for the boomer was an itinerant railroader who traveled light, skipping at short notice from one road to another, from one job to another. His tenure at any one place was too uncertain to permit his acquiring a pet (except the human female on the love-'em-and-leave-'em basis). His uniform was generally a black "thousand-miler" shirt, so called because he was reputed to wear it on about a thousand miles of rail travel before sending it to the laundry.

The boomer's heyday was the period of national expansion between the Civil War and World War I. He was bred of wander-lust, wars, strikes, depressions, seasonal rushes, liquor, the desire to avoid shotgun weddings, and often just plain bad luck. Most boomers were actuated by a restless desire to see what lay beyond the next hill or to follow the wild ducks northward in the spring and southward in the fall. Others had an irresistible urge to punch some trainmaster on the jaw for a real or fancied insult and then collect their pay. Still others hit the bottle too much, or carelessly let a boxcar roll off the dock, or perhaps caused a wreck by failing to deliver a train order, and flew the coop, leaving the "home guards" (company men) to face the music.

E. T. Mulquin, known as "Mul," who is vice-president of the Morse Telegraph Club of America, recalled the time back in 1902 when he was dispatching Lackawanna trains at Scranton. The track ran down from the yard to the river's edge, and the yard force would coast a cut of cars down there with a boomer switchman on top to set the brakes. One foggy night, as Mul tells the yarn, the crew shoved ten cars down the track, waited for the boomer to return, and then began yelling. Back through the murk a voice drifted faintly: "Cut off ten more! Them ten went into the river!"

Mul also told an anecdote about an eastbound Lackawanna freight that got out of control while descending the grade from Pocono Summit to Stroudsburg. A stockman who happened to be riding the caboose noticed that they were rapidly gaining momentum and asked nervously: "Ain't we runnin' pretty fast?"

The rear brakeman, who was a boomer, rolled a cigarette of Lancaster County leaf. "Hell no!" he yawned. "You should see us go when we are late."

A million railroaders were uprooted by the Civil War, the violent strikes of '77, '86, and especially '94, and a succession of panics and business slumps. They became floaters. Blacklisted as strikers or furloughed when traffic fell off, they roamed to areas where work was to be had, at least temporarily. But the top factor in creating boomers was the seasonal rushes—moving the various crops as soon as they were harvested. Drifters worked while the rails were hot and then rambled on to localities where new rushes were just beginning.

Nowadays the periodic needs of railroad companies for additional help to wheel the seasonal crops is met by recruiting local workers—men on the extra list who are laid off when the feverish activity subsides but who can be depended upon to stick around as long as it lasts. The old-time boomer did not worry about being given the gate. He would leave town in the firm belief that some road, somewhere, was bound to hire a capable man and that he could eat off a "pie-card" (meal ticket) while waiting for his next pay. When a drifter "pulled the pin" (resigned), he would tell his pals that he was "going to the Indian Valley Line," that mythical "pike" (short railroad line) where a good job with ideal working conditions could always be found.

No retired boomer is better known than Harry K. McClintock, nicknamed "Haywire Mac," who landed his first American railroad job in western Pennsylvania in 1902. Around that time the industrial core of the nation, lying within a two-hundred-mile radius of Pittsburgh, was expanding rapidly. New mills were springing up everywhere, and new factory towns mushroomed overnight. As a result, railroads were buried under an avalanche of freight. Shippers fought, bribed, and schemed to get more cars to haul their products; the carriers built, bought, and borrowed all kinds of rolling stock to meet the furious demand. It was this boom that made Haywire Mac a boomer, for he claimed:

I went to work as a yard brakeman at the Pennsy's Wall yard just east of Pittsburgh. The company's policy was to hire only greenhorns as brakemen and firemen, and thus they had the doubtful privilege of training car hands and smoke pushers for other pikes. Officials in those days could not afford to be choosy. Any boomer who wandered into the yard and claimed he'd never had a job except on pap's farm was pretty sure of going to work for the Pennsy after a more or less nominal checkup of his record.

Yard men in the Pittsburgh district toiled from six to six. They served no apprenticeship whatever, but drew full pay from the moment they stepped on a footboard. My first assignment was riding the stake engine. This was a hazardous form of switching whereby locomotives shoved cars ahead with a long pole. If you didn't see the engine coming and brace yourself accordingly, you were almost certain to get knocked off the car roof. So many men were messed up on this job that the Wall yard was known for years as "The Slaughter House." One poor kid had a foot crushed the very first night I worked there. Three nights later, two men were badly injured. That finished me. I walked off in the middle of the night, hired out elsewhere on the Pennsy, and never went near a stake engine again.

Mac's experience recalls the joke, nearly a hundred years old, about an official's saying to an applicant for a brakeman's job, "So you want a berth, eh?" Then, to his clerk: "Mr. Brown, have any brakemen been killed on the road within a day or two?"

Brown (apologetically): "Well, sir, none so far this week."

Official (to applicant): "Ah, well, my man, call next Monday. By that time I guess there'll be a vacancy."

For about forty-eight hours after payday the boomers were plutocrats, but their prosperity rarely lasted longer than that; usually they were broke for at least a week before the pay-car came around again. Haywire Mac recalled:

Some guys were content to get along on what could be procured in the grocery store for cash or credit, while others of us remembered

that Providence was inclined to smile on the hustler. I will say nothing about the time-honored boomer custom of knocking a hoop up
on a whisky barrel and driving a soapy nail through a stave. The
soap made the nail easy to withdraw, and if you happened to have a
bucket or bottle handy, you could catch the resultant stream for future
reference. After that, a broken matchstick plugged the hole up, and
by driving the hoop back into place you covered all signs of tampering. Such tricks I refuse to divulge, but I must mention the savage
nature of barnyard fowls. These birds have been known to attack
unarmed brakemen viciously. A poor shack [brakeman] would have
no recourse but to kill the pugnacious Plymouth Rock or Leghorn in
self-defense, and after that there was nothing to do but cook the
carcass on the caboose stove and eat it.

One of the boomer's most useful possessions was his paid-up
membership card in some railroad brotherhood. During his frequent lean periods he would shove this under the nose of a worthy
brother when he wanted to eat, sleep, ride, or all three, and it
usually achieved the desired result. A typical boomer fireman was
James B. Relyea, known as "Link-and-Pin Relly," now retired
from the road and living in Philadelphia. Link-and-Pin Relly
reminisced as follows:

Did any of you brothers ever leave West Philly with all the freight
cars the Pennsy ever owned or borrowed, and try to get some place?
You're the rathole artist [fireman] and you have a decrepit old hog
[locomotive] that couldn't pull a setting hen off her nest. You take
turns with the hoghead [engineer] and the head brakeman in raising
fog [steam] enough to keep her creeping along. You make Frankford
in about two hours—and Frankford is not even out of the city! You
follow the tramps [slow freights] ahead, over crossovers and back,
dodging the hotshots [fast trains]. Twenty-seven hours later you arrive
at Jersey City—twenty-seven hours for less than ninety miles!

The Philadelphian cited this fond memory of firing a freight
engine on the Reading:

I tried to get her hot, but the clock [gage] wouldn't say 100, no
matter how much I slaved. The hogger tried it, too, and even the head
shack took a crack at firing, but no luck! We lumbered along to
Reading. The engineer was toting sufficient grub for a week. That was
smart, for at Bridgeport we were held up by a car which had turned
over in front of us with a couple hundred tons of pig-iron [the loco-
motive] on top of it. We were delayed so long that the brains [con-
ductor] sneaked over to his home in Norristown just in time to miss

Trainmaster Van Buren, who jumped all over the drag [slow freight train] looking for him. Van asked me, "Where's the conductor?"

"He's around some place," I replied vaguely, trying to cover up.

"You're a liar!" said the T.M.

So, of course, I squared off and socked him on the beak, and then shook the dust of the Reading railway off my feet and boomed around the country.

The life of a boomer was one that only a bred-in-the-bone railroader could love. Starvation cast its shadow ahead of the pay-car. Romance? Sure, romance and adventure, new faces and new towns, but all the while the master mechanics' clerks are laughing at you, and home guards stick up their noses. The few greasy bills the paymaster hands you are no compensation for long hours and aching bones. Our real pay was the call of the rail, two short whistle blasts of a train leaving town. Two short blasts by some fat hoghead on a freight engine would make a boomer postpone his bath, leave his beer half drunk, or his lady waiting at the church.

As railroading lost its pioneering quality and fell into the groove, as locomotives grew heavier, trains longer, traveling safer, and the competition for jobs more keen, the independent order of boomers gradually faded away. Thus passed a rugged era. Boomers were generous, worldly-wise, self-assured often to the point of insolence, humorous, resourceful, and given to braggadocio, but withal a likable lot. They knew railroad operation better, perhaps, than the home guards did, because they circulated widely and were continually picking up new kinks. They took chances and they often thumbed their noses at officials. Many of them chewed tobacco. As they drank too much, the company liked to blame its wrecks on booze rather than on equipment failure. Still, it required plenty of redeye to make some fellows even want to railroad in the rowdy wooden-axle days when the industry was young, hard as steel, and sprinkled with blood.

Boomers were not noted for the classic purity of their diction, but their distinctive lingo did much to enrich the American language. A large portion of this lingo has unfortunately followed the drifting fraternity into the sunset. Link-and-Pin Relly once copied down verbatim some of the actual conversation he heard between a brakeman and a beefy-faced engineer. Here is a choice excerpt:

Brakeman: "An' you'd think Big Head Carroll owned the buggy, he has me go all the distance every stop. Says I can't cook an' growls even if I do all his work. That dirty so-an'-so hoghead Mertz left me in the rain at Frankford Junction. I was there an hour before Ben Hendry came along. I got our buggy at the river bridge. Wonder Carroll don't turn me in for knuckle-dustin'! Some trip, twelve hours! Add for deadheadin' an' what do I get? Railroadin' is hell!"

What the speaker really meant was this:

Brakeman: "My obnoxious conductor, Mr. Carroll, does not like the way I cook meals in the caboose, so he makes life unpleasant for me, even when I do more than my share of work. He is such a stickler for rules that you might think he owned the caboose. Especially the rule that requires a flagman to get off every time the train stops and walk back a certain distance to protect it from any train that might be coming up behind. On one such occasion Engineer Mertz, whom I dislike intensely, pulled out of Frankford Junction before I could return to the caboose, leaving me out in the rain. It was a full hour before another train, with Ben Hendry at the throttle, came along and picked me up. I overtook our caboose on Schuylkill River bridge. It is a wonder that Carroll does not report me to the trainmaster as the kind of flagman who sticks close to the caboose so that the train will not leave him. My average freight run takes twelve hours, to which should be added the time consumed in traveling between its terminus and my home. Railroading is hell."

Although the typical railroad man, in the era before automatic safety devices and the eight-hour day, complained loudly and often to his fellows about working conditions, he preferred his job above all others. He liked to "shoot off steam" about retiring to a chicken farm in Delaware County, a saloon in Manayunk, or some such haven, but those who did, grew homesick for the click of wheels over rail joints.

This state has no rail song comparable in popularity to "Casey Jones," "I've Been Working on the Railroad," or "Life's Railway to Heaven," although "The Wreck of the Old 97" involves a loco-motive built at the Philadelphia Baldwin plant in 1903. The last-named ballad arose from the fact that this engine, No. 1102 of the Southern Railway, plunged off a Virginia trestle with fast mail train No. 97 when she was only a few months old. Surviving the crash for nearly thirty-two years, the Philadelphia-built engine continued to pull Southern trains until she was scrapped in 1935.

The popular song "Where Do You Work-a, John?" which informs us that John is employed at pushing a truck on the "Delaware Lackawan," has some Pennsylvania interest in the fact that Delaware, Lackawanna & Western trackage is sprawled over this state as well as two others.

Haywire Mac's picturesque "Big Rock Candy Mountains" has even more appeal to Pennsylvanians because, as we have seen, the boomer author really got his start near Pittsburgh. This song, which has become famous, portrays the hobos' never-never land of empty boxcars, wooden-legged cops, and rubber-toothed bulldogs, "where they hung the Turk that invented work," where trainmen tip their hats to bums, where handouts grow on bushes and cigarettes on trees, and where "little streams of alcohol come trickling down the rocks."

> Oh, I'm bound to go where there ain't no snow,
> Where the rain don't fall and the wind don't blow—
> In the Big Rock Candy Mountains.*

* Used by permission of the Villa Moret Publishing Company, San Francisco.

Lumberjacks and Raftsmen

by J. HERBERT WALKER

Pennsylvania's lumber era produced a special breed of men. With rugged enthusiasm these untamed incredibly robust men challenged the virgin forests and the treacherous waterways. The lumberjack, raftsman,* and log driver—they were all laborers in the lumber industry—worked, ate, drank, and played with amazing gusto. The logger's steel calks whittled down many a wooden sidewalk and barroom floor. In his lustiest moods he was not averse to jumping on an antagonist who was down, and spiking him in the face; the marks left on an opponent's face by steel spikes came to be known as "logger's smallpox."

Maine, where the lumber industry was born, first bred the race of giant lumberjacks. Their calked boots and picturesque dress followed a long trail. Down through the New England states to New York, stopping for long years in Pennsylvania, the trail led to Michigan and Wisconsin and finally across the country to the

* Old-timers spell it "raftman."

Pacific Coast. That trail of three thousand miles required nearly one hundred years to be completed. The West Coast is the last stand, but modern methods of logging have softened the lumberjacks. The tales and legends are softer, too. There are radios, telephones, bathtubs, central heating plants, automobiles, dieticians, and doctors and nurses in the comfortable camps of today. How different from those days of seventy to one hundred years ago in the Pennsylvania woods!

In the heyday of Pennsylvania lumbering there were fifty thousand workers. In my younger days I knew many of them. I stood in awe of their strength and agility. I listened to their sagas and songs and now, in retrospect, I wish I had made a more systematic collection of them when so many lumberjacks, raftsmen, and log drivers were still alive.

Pennsylvania reached the apex of its lumber production between 1850 and 1870. The chief products were white pine and hemlock, with some oak and other hard woods. All the territory drained by the large rivers of the state was originally forest-clad— and a noble forest it was! One section in north-central Pennsylvania was so dense with dark evergreens that it won for itself the name "Black Forest."

In 1850 the United States produced five billion board feet of lumber, with New York leading, Pennsylvania second. Construction of the famous Susquehanna boom at Williamsport pushed the industry in Pennsylvania until the state led the nation in 1860, a lead it maintained until 1870, when Michigan displaced it as the top producer. But Pennsylvania still had the largest number of sawmills.

Records of the Susquehanna Boom Company at Williamsport show that during the most active years, between 1868 and 1906, the pine saw logs stored there exceeded eight billion feet board measure. That was for logs that came down the tributaries and into the boom. As much as fifty billion board feet of white pine lumber must have been taken from the headwaters of Pennsylvania streams. Likewise, a similar quantity of hemlock must have fallen to the ax of the lumberjack. With oak and other trees felled, it is reasonable to assume the grand total may have been two hundred billion board feet of lumber—a staggering volume.

On a small farm in the center of Potter County rise three streams, one of which eventually flows to the St. Lawrence by way of the Genesee River; another to Chesapeake Bay by way of the Susquehanna; and the third to the Gulf of Mexico by way of the Allegheny. While great quantities of timber were cut on the headwaters of the Allegheny and the Delaware and their tributaries, it is without question that the Susquehanna watershed provided the most. The Susquehanna River system in Pennsylvania drains an area approximately 157 miles long and 161 miles wide. Into this system went the timber wealth of a thousand hills along the Sinnemahoning, the Loyalsock, the Clearfield, the Pine, and other major creeks—trees many of which were so tall, says a tale, that it took two men and a half to see to the top of them; so thick it took years to let the daylight in; so big the fellow who cut them must have been a liar!

But of all the giant trees felled and taken out of Pennsylvania mountains, none attained the stature of the ones cut for spars that were used for masts and yards on sailing vessels. Their length, straightness, and texture placed them above every other species. They were kings. They found their way into shipyards at Philadelphia, Baltimore, Camden, and even Liverpool, England. The pilot of a spar raft was the king pilot of all. While some spars were cut on the headwaters of the Allegheny and the Delaware, those taken from the headwaters of the West Branch of the Susquehanna were supreme. Here stood the finest white pine. Here was the greatness of Pennsylvania's lumbering industry. Here folklore ran its fullest gamut.

"Boys, look at the bubbles on the water. We're going to have a flood."

"Boys, put a tin cup outside the building to catch the rain. When we get an inch of water in the cup, it'll be time to raft in."

Thus would speak men on the headwaters of streams, waiting anxiously for high water so that they could send their rafts of white pine down river to the mills. Rafting was a prosperous business on nearly all the major creeks and rivers of Pennsylvania, but on the Susquehanna it surpassed all the others combined. The great volume of water and the condition of the river bed were favorable to rafting. Just as there are divisions on the railroads today, there were rafting divisions on the Susquehanna: Division I extended on the West Branch from Clearfield to Lock Haven; Division II from Lock Haven to Columbia, Marietta, and Wrightsville; and Division III from Marietta to tidewater in Chesapeake Bay.

Small rafts were made up in small streams. When they got into larger waters, they were combined for the runs downstream to the sawmills. The actual building of a raft gave rise to the term "rafting in." The logs were placed side by side in quiet eddies and joined together with a lash pole. The logs, from twenty-eight to eighty feet long, were attached to the lash pole by U-shaped bows that were held firmly to the logs by pins driven into holes bored in the logs. One section of logs thus attached was called a platform. Usually three platforms were coupled together to make a raft. On small streams these rafts were called colts, pups, or half rafts. In the early days of rafting the logs were squared before being placed in the rafts. Later they were brought down the streams in the round.

When the rafts reached wider waters, two or more of them were coupled together. This reduced the number of men required to guide the rafts down the streams. Heavy oars or sweeps, one at each end of the raft or train of rafts, were used to steer and guide the massive collection of logs. These oars were from forty to sixty feet long and mounted on a head block so that they could be swung back and forth. It took real men to handle them.

Sometimes small platforms were built on the rafts and covered with stones and earth. On these platforms raftsmen made fires over which they cooked eggs and ham or bacon and around which they stood in an effort to dry their clothing soaked from the splashing waters. Some rafts carried shanties in which members of the crew slept and ate; others had tents. Some rafts had only a box of cold food.

Rafting was a hazardous occupation. There were many perilous spots on the West Branch, the Allegheny, the Delaware, and the smaller streams. Rocky Bend and Chest Falls, not far from Mahaffey on the West Branch, were among the most dangerous. Giant rocks, reverse currents, swift water—so swift that the water of the upper Susquehanna drops down at a rate of four hundred feet to the mile—and streams narrow even in floodtime made rafting dangerous, and required almost superhuman deftness and endurance. Every current, every eddy, every rock, every swift channel, and every treacherous bend had to be known by a raft pilot. It was tedious, cautious work. The pilot, supreme in his command of the raft, was stationed at the bow. By swinging the great fore-and-aft oars left or right, he brought the lashed timbers down the winding streams.

The size of rafting crews varied from two to eight men. The raftsmen in their bright-colored woolen shirts, fur caps, multi-colored neckerchiefs, trousers covered with pine pitch, and leather boots were a vivid sight against the harmonious background of river and forest. Often, as they floated down the rivers, their voices could be heard singing this favorite rafting chant:

> Thus drifting to sea on a hick of white pine,
> For grub and the wages we're paid,
> The scoffers who rail as we buffet the brine
> May see us in sun or in shade;
> But true to our course, though the weather be thick,
> We set our broad sail as before,
> And stand by the tiller that governs the hick
> Nor care how we look from the shore.*

Lumbering, especially in the West Branch Valley, took on great momentum when log driving came into existence. The Williamsport boom, consisting of two branches, one at Williamsport and the other extending down river from what is now Linden, was constructed in 1846. The boom was made up of a large number of timber cribs filled with rocks and placed fifty feet apart. The most important boom in the state, it extended for about ten miles down the center of the river diagonally with the current. The upper end of the boom was nearest to the shore; a shear

* From *Mountain Minstrelsy of Pennsylvania*, by Henry W. Shoemaker. Used by permission.

boom* was placed so that it could swing freely to permit the passage of rafts. Boom logs connected the stationary cribs extending down river. These logs rose or fell with the crest of the river and acted as a barrier holding the logs in the boom, from which the logs were selected for the sawmills lining the shore.

Logs for the boom were run free on the waterways. Log drivers rode the logs downstream, their spiked boots aiding them in maintaining their position on the logs. They used heavy peaveys (long pike poles) to keep the logs moving. The log drivers were followed by batteaus (long, covered boats) in which the drivers slept and ate.

The free logs that came downstream in drives were frequently started on many of the smaller waterways by the operation of splash dams, when even spring rains and melting snows provided insufficient water. These dams were contrivances built across streams to impound the water. They were equipped with gates to let the water out. When the dams were filled, the gates were opened and the water was let out with a splash that sent the logs downstream on the artificially created flood. By a series of dams that repeated the splashes at each one, the logs were driven to the larger streams.

Each log was branded at both ends with a branding iron that identified its owner; the brands were registered in county courthouses. Upstream sawmills obtained their logs from the boom. The boom company sorted the logs according to the brands and delivered them to the mill pockets along the river. The actual work was done by workers known as "boom rats," who with agility and courage rode herd on the thousands of logs. A boom rat carried his pike pole under his arm like a knight of old.

As in the cattle country of the West, branding offered a temptation to river rustlers who stole logs, doctored brands, and bootlegged stolen timber to unscrupulous millowners down the river. These rustlers were known as "Algerenes," after the pirates of Algiers, North Africa, who had preyed on American shipping. They stole a negligible proportion of the total production, but

* The shear boom log, extending from the upper end of the boom proper to the shore, could be freed at either end and swung downstream so that rafts could proceed through the opening.

they added spice to the river life and inspired many colorful stories for campfire, shanty, and river ark entertainment.

Log driving and the boom, together with the large number of sawmills, combined to make Williamsport the greatest lumber manufacturing city in the world for many years. Log driving struck a fatal blow at rafting. Because this new method of getting logs downstream cut more rapidly into the forest resources, it hastened the end of the lumbering era.

Log driving introduced mass production methods into the lumber industry. Its hazards were as great, if not greater, than cutting timber or piloting gigantic rafts. Some say the log drivers surpassed the raftsmen in determination, daring, and courage. There was bad blood between the raftsmen and the drivers, which eventually led to the "Log Drivers' and Raftsmen's War." The raftsmen wanted free use of the rivers, unobstructed by log drives. The log drivers maintained they had the right to the waterways.

A group of raftsmen, armed with rifles, shotguns, and axes, met log drivers starting a drive of logs down a stream. Three log drivers fell wounded. The others fled. The raftsmen then proceeded to the log drivers' camp, tore down buildings, wrecked the batteaus, and tossed barrels of meat and other foods, tools, clothing, and numerous articles into the stream. There was a court trial. The raftsmen were found guilty of riot, while the log drivers were found guilty of obstructing the streams. Both sides drew fines.

But court or no court, the war went on. Raftsmen struck at log drivers in their own way. On dark nights, when great piles of logs had been placed along the streams waiting for the spring floods, raftsmen would drive great iron spikes through the bark. Spiked logs found their way into the sawmills where they would break the whining saws and endanger millworkers' lives. To avoid the danger, bark was then removed from all piled-up logs along the streams. The legislature passed a law making log-spiking a criminal offense.

And there was more trouble!

Around the 1870's the Williamsport mills received great demands for lumber. Six hundred million feet of logs were on hand or were on the way. Men were driven to get more work done; a day's work was stretched out to fourteen hours. The men objected. A strike was called even though the millmen and the boom rats were unorganized. Saws didn't turn for three weeks, for concessions made by both sides were rejected. Then it was decided to reopen the mills. The plants were attacked by the strikers. Raftsmen and log drivers came out of the woods and moved downstream. Here was going to be fighting that would put barroom brawls to shame! There was violence and bloodshed, but the state sent troops, and the mills resumed.

Rafting and log driving were done chiefly in the spring when streams were at flood stage, but timber-cutting was a winter occupation. In deep snow and bitter cold, working from dawn to darkness, the lumberjacks labored hard to cut down the giant trees for raftsmen and log drivers to deliver to the sawmills. Timber tracts were operated by contractors or jobbers who hired and boarded their own lumberjacks. Discipline was strong, and the slightest infraction of the rules was cause for discharge. A foreman had to be an iron man to control the unruly lumbermen.

In the early days of the industry, the woods were dotted with shanties that housed only four lumberjacks each. When mass production came in, lumbering required a large number of men. Then logging camps increased in number and grew larger. Some camps boarded a hundred or more men at a time.

A typical shanty was built of logs that were chinked with wood and moss and daubed with mud; it had a plank floor, and a shingle roof. The men slept in double-deck bunks filled with straw. The cookhouse and dining hall were in a separate shack that had a wing for the woman cook, if one was employed. Most of the cooks were men. The buildings were lighted by homemade tallow candles, lard-oil lanterns, and in later years, kerosene.

The absence of sanitary conditions did not bother the men nearly so much as poor food. Operators who furnished the best food in the camps kept the best crews. Woodsmen would travel from camp to camp in search of the best food.

Some camps had only one cook; larger camps would also have an assistant known as a "cookee." Male cooks and cookees could be slovenly, but never women cooks. Rough as they were, the lumberjacks demanded neatness of their women cooks. The cookee washed dishes, waited on the tables, peeled potatoes, and packed food for noonday lunches. He also called the men to their meals. He had many calls: "Come and get it," "Take the bait," "Gobble the hash," "Gulp the soup," "Munch the oats," and "Grab the biscuit." Single-word calls included: "eat," "grub," "hash," "beans," and "mulligan." In later years the meal call was a metallic sound made by striking an iron triangle with a hammer, known as the "gut hammer." It was heard farther than the cookee's voice.

The men of the lumber camps ate their breakfast before daylight and their evening meal long after dark; every possible daylight hour was used for work in the woods. Delay in getting to work in the morning was considered a bad omen. If a man returned to camp at night without his inner shirt being wet with sweat, he was considered lazy. Whenever a lumberjack took another man's regular place at the table, he had a fight on his hands.

Tin plates and tin cups were provided the men for eating. Wheat and corn bread, corn meal mush, molasses cake, buckwheat cakes, potatoes, turnips, sauerkraut, beans, dried corn, rice, smoked ham, beef at times, salt pork, salt fish, and fresh pork were the staples. Sometimes—but not too often—molasses, honey, sugar, prunes, and dried apples were added to the bill of fare. Eggs, fresh milk, and fresh fruit were lacking in their diet. The tea was said to have been strong enough to wash the surface coating off the oilcloth table covering, and sometimes it ate up the whole cloth and the pine table top!

When lumberjacks killed deer and brought them to the cook, venison helped out the camp larder. Wild pigeons were plentiful, so pigeon pie was a favorite. In the nesting season, loggers would find a good nesting ground, knock squabs out of the nests, and have merry feasts. What couldn't be consumed was salted down in hogsheads for use in winter. Sometimes in winter fresh fish could be taken from the streams. When hemlock lumbering began,* fish could be obtained from the streams in summer.

---

* Hemlock trees were first cut to get bark for the tanning of leather; the bark peeled more easily in summer, so hemlock trees were usually cut then.

Victor Brooks, a north-central Pennsylvania lumberman, said, "Thunder an' lightnin', our rafts are safer with Cubagh [a noted pilot] drunk than with some of these self-constituted pilots sober." Lumberjacks, log drivers, and raftsmen were hard drinkers. If some of these men believed that smoking helped to digest their coarse food, there must have been many who held the same opinion about whisky. The heavy food they ate in the camps caused heartburn, bellyache, and water brash. Whisky wasn't used as an appetizer; it was used as an after-dinner tonic! But away from camps, it was something else.

In the Pennsylvania woods there were different kinds of whisky —squirrel, fighting, and sleeping. The names indicate the results of drinking the various brands. If you drank squirrel whisky, you wanted to climb trees! Then there was one other kind that seemed to have quite a following. It was called "Logger's Delight." Five gallons of grain alcohol were placed in a barrel with twenty pounds of fine-cut tobacco. The barrel then was filled with rain water and agitated three times daily. After a month's standing the concoction was strained through a cloth and adulterated with water. Then it was ready!

According to one writer, this was a profitable brand to sell because after the customer became intoxicated by drinking other brands, the drinking of Logger's Delight would hold him in the same degree of intoxication as long as he drank it. The sleeping brand was unprofitable because the customer was soon put to sleep and in this condition was a liability instead of an asset to the barkeeper. Any barkeeper who wanted to make money selfishly would start his customer off in the morning with squirrel whisky and for the rest of the day sell him Logger's Delight.

Heavy drinking led to many brawls among raftsmen, who always took a supply of whisky on board with them; if they ran out of liquor along the way, they could always buy more from peddlers who rowed their boats, loaded with whisky, out to the rafts. Often raftsmen fought among one another merely for sectional honor. Proud of their physical prowess, crews would match one another's champions. Thus, if the Sinnemahone crew had a man they thought could humble the champion of the Chest Creek crew, the two parties arranged for a fist fight in the woods. At the match

the two men went at each other until one or the other went down
for the count. Such a fight might last for hours with no holds
barred as the contenders were cheered on by their respective crews.

Lumbermen, loggers, and raftsmen left tales of their drinking
episodes all the way from the headwaters of the Susquehanna to
Chesapeake Bay, from the upper reaches of the Allegheny to St.
Louis and New Orleans, and from the headwaters of the Delaware
to Philadelphia. After delivering the logs or the rafts at each
destination, the men often passed days and even weeks at a time
in drinking, overeating, and carousing.

George W. Huntley, Jr., tells the story of a notorious drinker
named Guthrie in Emporium who, while intoxicated, was bumped
by a team of horses and believed injured. A doctor said there was
nothing wrong with him physically, but that he was bordering on
a state in which persons are said to see peculiarly colored animals
floating around.

Here was a chance for Guthrie's companions to repay him for
some of the tricks he had played on them. He was taken to a hotel
room and told his leg would have to be amputated. Frank Shives,
a young butcher, soon appeared with knives, a saw, and a large
beef leg bone. Oren Freeman administered an anesthetic—more
whisky! Jacob Swope and Hank Strickland held Guthrie on the
operating table. The butcher knife was run back and forth across
Guthrie's leg as the saw screeched across the old leg bone the
butcher had brought. Shives quit sawing to indicate Guthrie's
leg was off, and the "patient" was given another drink of whisky!

Guthrie was told he was bad off, might die soon, and that
a drunkard couldn't enter the pearly gates. He asked for a
minister, and another jokester came in to play the part. Next day
Guthrie was quite sober. His pals asked him to join them in a
jamboree. "I can't," said Guthrie, "I've lost my leg." Then his
pals yanked him out of bed, dragged him to the barroom below,
and told the whole story, much to Guthrie's chagrin.

Cal Sheppard, known as "The Portage Bard" for his ability to
improvise poetry, once started on a bender. His wife, a great scold,
came with a wagon and team to take him home. On the way home
they had to ford a stream. Cal walked out on the wagon tongue,
pulled a connecting pin, and mounted the nigh ox. Then he

rode off, and left his wife sitting in the wagon in the middle of the stream. A neighbor rescued her. Cal wasn't heard from for two weeks.

Sheppard worked in Wiley's Camp, but when the first snow fell he usually went bear hunting. One winter he came across what he thought were bear tracks, and trailed them to Dan Barr's house. Here he discovered that the bear tracks were really the footprints of Dan Barr, who had hunted in his bare feet!

The truth finally came out one day in a saloon to Sheppard's embarrassment. Sol Ross, a neighbor, astonished the fellows in the saloon by reciting:

> Here's to Cal Sheppard, "The Portage Bard,"
> He is a bear hunter good and hard;
> He pursues the chase sun, moon, and stars,
> But can't tell a bear track from that of Dan Barr's.

To this Sheppard retorted immediately:

> Here's to Sol Ross, good fellow, but shallow,
> Who has no brains, but a head full of tallow;
> He squawked so much the tallow ran away,
> Which made him shallow the rest of the day.

Like all pioneer workers, the lumberjacks, raftsmen, and log drivers were superstitious. White pine lumbermen made it a rule always to cut their timber between the dark of the moon in September and the dark of the moon in the following April, in order, they said, to prolong its life. It was claimed that cutting during these months prevented lumber from weather-staining. They proved their statements by pointing to buildings made of white pine lumber, logged in the wintertime, which were well preserved after having been exposed to the weather from fifty to one hundred years.

But there are exceptions to every rule. When hemlock first took the place of white pine in providing bark for the leather tanneries, the cutting had to be done in summer when the bark would peel easily.

When log camps were constructed, care was taken to make sure that none of the logs came from trees that had been struck by lightning. It was believed that such shacks would attract more lightning.

Isaac Wycoff had an uncanny way of testing a tree's soundness. He would cut both ends of a log, roll it out on skids, and get someone to hold his watch tightly against one end of the log while he placed his ear against the other end. He maintained that if the log was sound, he could hear his watch ticking through its entire length. And some of the logs were more than a hundred feet long!

Medical superstitions resulted from the primitive medicine practiced in the woods. Doctors were few and far between, and dentistry was practiced by itinerants. One dentist from Harrisburg hung out his shingle in Cameron and carried on the then primitive profession visiting near-by lumber camps. One day Dode Lester and Skip Develing, local lumberjacks, had their teeth pulled, after which they invited the dentist to accompany them to a near-by farm on a picnic. The dentist accepted, and the three musketeers, well supplied with whisky, sallied forth. The dentist was less accustomed to whisky than his companions, and after a few drinks he was stretched out in deep sleep under a tree. His mischievous companions, in their drunken stupor, decided to give the dentist a dose of his own medicine: they opened his satchel, took out a pair of forceps, and pulled all the dentist's teeth. Then the pair drained their jugs of whisky. All three were later found under the same tree by a passer-by. The poor dentist was rushed to a hospital in Harrisburg. Upon his discharge a few weeks later, he went back to Cameron and looked up Lester and Develing. After apologies, they all drank to a renewed friendship.

Home remedies, made principally from "yarbs" and roots found in the woods, were applied with superstitious practices in healing the sick and injured.

When Ross Detrick smashed his leg in an accident, he was to have been rushed off to the hospital at Emporium. Meanwhile an old Indian appeared in the camp where Detrick lay. He said the leg would not need to be amputated. The Indian got some herbs and bark, boiled them into a dark salve, and bathed the leg all night. The inflammation went down, and the leg was saved.

Goose grease, pennyroyal, bear's fat, boneset, burdock, scrapings of elder bark made into a salve, and other herbs and plants were widely used. For example, if a tea were made from the leaves of boneset stripped upwards, it was a good emetic; if the leaves were stripped downward, it was a purgative.

A dose of star root, or fawns' tail—a remedy that came down from the Indians—rhubarb tea, or a smart-weed poultice applied to the stomach was good for colic that came from eating too many raw cucumbers or green apples. Rattlesnake oil, camphor, and vinegar liniment were also used. A bottle of hartshorn was in the kit of every woman who helped with the sick. Pokeroot and whisky were good for the "roomatiz," as every variety of rheumatism was called. The root was grated and put into whisky to remain for a few days. Then the concoction was strained and the patient was given spoonfuls at frequent intervals.

Old women who had an intimate knowledge of home remedies and who would walk many miles in response to a call from a sickroom were held in high respect, even awe.

One such woman was Aunt Pop Smith. In the heat of summer, the snows of winter, or in raging storms, she never faltered. Nor was she ever daunted. Faith, hope, and her own remedies were applied equally. Doctor, nurse, maid, and housekeeper all in one, this unlearned woman, typical of many others in the big woods, plied her art. If her remedies failed, she remained to place a cool hand on a fevered brow and say a simple prayer as life passed; frequently she laid out the body in a coffin made by a kindly handyman she had called into service.

Granny Prentice had a reputation as a powwow doctor. She was adept at removing children's warts. Muttering to herself, she rubbed each wart with a bean, put the beans in bags, and hung them up. When the beans rotted, the warts disappeared.

Powwowing was not uncommon and it was practiced by both men and women. Erysipelas set into the leg of Dan McChosen after he had cut it with an ax while peeling spars. Aug Rider, who had won some reputation as a powwow doctor, said he could do nothing with the leg unless McChosen had the blood of a well-bred Spanish chicken. None could be found in the woods. However, an ordinary chicken was obtained and killed; its warm blood was taken to Rider. Rider was told it was a Spanish chicken, but he would have none of it. George Huntley, a lumberman, bathed the inflamed McChosen leg. McChosen said, "By cracky, I'm going to get well." He did!

Huntley had a cow that began to give bloody milk. Powwow doctors said someone in the Huntley family had killed a toad. The only thing to do to heal the cow was to allow her milk to soak into the ground. But some other powwow doctor said this would make the cow go dry. Huntley fed the cow on pumpkins and corn—and killed her for beef!

One of the most interesting legends of the Susquehanna River came out of the days of spar rafting—the story of the White Woman of Montgomery's Bar.

Susan Hilbish was a waitress in one of the taverns along the river not far from where the North and West Branches of the Susquehanna unite. She fell in love with a strong, burly, spar-raft pilot who frequented the tavern in spring-flood time. Once he brought his fiddle, and a dance was arranged. Toward the close of the evening, he got another fiddler to take over while he danced with Susan. They fell madly in love—at least Susan did. He promised to return for a dance on his next trip down the river. He did come back, but this time he fell in love with another girl at the dance. Susan was heartbroken. She went upstairs and drank a bottle of poison. Her body was found next day inside a closet on the second floor. On the inside of the closet door she had scratched:

> O faithless one, how little you can know
> Of heartaches and pains that I endure,
> I loved you, trusted, and in vain did wait,
> For the day when our love would be secure.
>
> But another heart now wins over mine,
> My dreams of hope and love and life are gone,
> Be true to her, I pray, my dying wish,
> I end it all . . .

Young folks no longer gather there to dance and plight their troth. Those dances are now but a haunting memory; the building is in ruins. But on wild, weird nights, villagers still hear the ghost of Susan Hilbish speaking out of the shadows of the past.

When lumberjacks were not felling pine trees, drinking bad liquor, or carousing in town, they amused themselves with song, story, and clog dancing. In the early fall when evenings were still mild, they would sit around punky smudges, smoke, and sing until the very hills seemed to ring with melody. On winter evenings or Sunday afternoons, they would gather around their bunkhouse stove and exchange tall tales, ghost stories, and songs. There was also a good deal of fiddling—the woods were full of fiddlers, right-handers and southpaws. Some church people in the towns regarded the fiddle as the devil's own instrument, but that did not worry the fiddlers. They used to gather at Fiddler's Greens, which were scattered through the woods of Cameron, Elk, Potter, Sullivan, McKean, and other counties. The woodsmen also played banjos, harmonicas, jew's-harps, drums, and rattling bones.

In addition to ballads that sprang up in various Pennsylvania lumber camps, there were the ballads brought into the state by Maine and Canadian lumberjacks who flocked here in the post-Civil War years. Lumberjacks invariably sang solo, almost never in quartets or choruses; the latter were for barber shops and college halls. Singers usually sang unaccompanied in the traditional style. A Nova Scotian sang his native songs, a man from Maine obliged with ballads from his own state, and other transients did likewise. They were a lot of homesick boys in the Pennsylvania lumber camps!

The intermingling of the songs and ballads of different regions aided improvisation. Wood bards borrowed freely from one another—phrases, lines, metrical patterns, and of course tunes. A popular pastime was the improvisation of stanzas for cumulative ballads in which every man in the bunkhouse might offer a verse, and thus extend a ballad's length interminably. The substitution of local names, places, and even a central situation for those of an imported product was a common practice. An example is "The Log Jam at Hughey's Rock," a Pennsylvania variant of the famous ballad "The Jam on Gerry's Rock." In this case, localization was accomplished by the substitution of Hughey's Rock for Gerry's Rock as the place of the tragedy; Billtown for Eaglestown or Eganstown, in the last line of the second stanza; and Young Woman's Town (an obvious corruption) for Saginaw town as the home of Fair Clara, in the third line, sixth stanza.

A better example, perhaps, is that of "The Wild Lumberjack."

This is a variant of the well-known ballad "The Cowboy's Lament," which in turn is an adaptation of an old British ballad. In each case the central situation is the same: a miscreant on his deathbed bemoans his dissolute life. Words, phrases, and whole lines have been borrowed from the original. Yet enough creative effort has gone into the Pennsylvania variant to dignify it as an authentic and distinctive expression of its locale.

When the lumberjacks began deserting Pennsylvania for the brighter prospects offered in the camps of Michigan, Minnesota, Wisconsin, and ultimately Washington, they carried their ballads with them, including those made in our state. Thus one of these, "The Maine-ite in Pennsylvania," was recorded in Michigan:

The Maine-ite in Pennsylvania

(From *Ballads and Songs of the Shanty-Boy*, by Franz Rickaby. Cambridge, Mass.: Harvard University Press, 1926. Used by permission.)

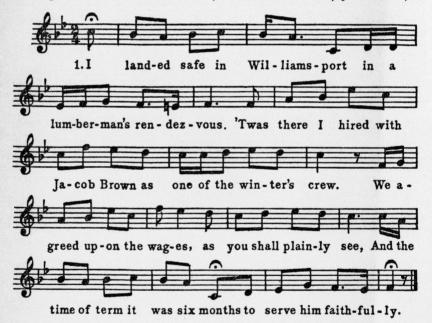

1. I land-ed safe in Wil-liams-port in a lum-ber-man's ren-dez-vous. 'Twas there I hired with Ja-cob Brown as one of the win-ter's crew. We a-greed up-on the wag-es, as you shall plain-ly see, And the time of term it was six months to serve him faith-ful-ly.

2. It would melt your heart with pity, it would make your blood run cold,
   To see the work of Nature did all in her rudest mold,
   And to see those overhanging rocks along the ice-bound shore,
   Where the rippling waters fierce do rage and the cataracts do roar.

3. There's the tomtit and the moosebird and the roving caribou,
   The lucifee and pa'tridge that through the forests flew,
   And the wild, ferocious rabbit from the colder regions came;
   And several other animals too numerous to name.

4. So to conclude and finish, I have one thing more to say:
   When I am dead and in my grave, lying mold'ring in the clay,
   No artificial German text you can for me sustain,
   But simply say I'm a roving wreck right from Bangor, Maine.

The Jolly Lumbermen

(Text from *Mountain Minstrelsy of Pennsylvania,* by Henry W. Shoe-maker. Philadelphia: Newman F. McGirr, 1931. Used by permission. The tune, a variant of the well-known chantey "Canaday-I-O," was sung by L. Parker Temple in the Recording Laboratory of the Library of Congress, 1946; recorded by Rae Korson.)

Moderately fast

1. Come all you jol-ly lum-ber-men and list-en to my song,— I'll tell you all my sto-ry— and I won't de-tain you long,— Con-cern-ing some husk-y lum-ber-men who once a-greed to go— And spend a win-ter re-cent-ly on Coll-ey's Run, i-o.—

2. We landed in Lock Haven
    The year of 'seventy-three;
A minister of the gospel
    One evening said to me:
"Are you the party of lumbermen
    That once agreed to go
And spend a winter pleasantly
    On Colley's Run, i-o?"

3. "Oh yes, we'll go to Colley's Run,
    To that we will agree,
[Then we'll agree to accompany you
    To Colley's Run, i-o.]
Provided you pay good wages,
    Our passage to and fro,
Then we'll agree to accompany you
    To Colley's Run, i-o."

4. "Oh yes, we'll pay good wages,
    Your passage to and fro,
Provided you will sign papers
    To stay the winter through.
But, mind you, if you get homesick,
    And back you swear you'll go
You'll have to pay your own passage down
    From Colley's Run, i-o."

5. 'Twas by that 'tarnel agreement
    That we agreed to go—
Full five and twenty in number,
    All able-bodied men.
The road it was a pleasant one,
    By train we had to go,
Till we landed at McFarling's tavern,
    Full seventeen miles below.

6. But there our joys were ended,
    Our troubles they began;
The captain and the foreman
    Came following up the Run.
They led us in every direction,
    Through some places I did not know,
Among the pines which grew so tall
    On Colley's Run, i-o.

7. Our hearts were clad with iron,
    Our soles were shod with steel,

But the usages of that winter
  Would scarcely make a shield.
For our grub the dogs would laugh at,
  And our beds were wet with snow;
God grant there is no worse hell on earth
  Than Colley's Run, i-o!

8. But now the spring has come again,
    And the ice-bound streams are free;
  We'll float our logs to Williamsport;
    Our friends we'll haste to see.
  Our sweethearts they will welcome us,
    And bid others not to go
  To that God-forsaken gehooley of a place
    Of Colley's Run, i-o!

The Log Jam at Hughey's Rock

(Sung by Bud Smith of Lock Haven. From *A Story of the Sinnema-hone,* by George William Huntley, Jr. Williamsport: The Williamsport Printing and Binding Company, 1936. Used by permission.)

Come all you bold shanty boys and list while I relate
Concerning a young shanty boy and his untimely fate—
Concerning a young riverman, so manly, true, and brave—
'Twas on the jam at Hughey's Rock he met a watery grave.

It was Sunday morning, as you will quickly hear,
Our logs were piled up mountain high, we could not keep them clear;
Our foreman said: "Turn out, brave boys, with hearts devoid of fear;
We'll break the jam at Hughey's Rock and for Billtown we'll steer."

Now some of them were willing, while others they were not;
For to work on jams on Sunday they did not think they ought;
But six of our Yankee boys did volunteer to go
And break the jam at Hughey's Rock, with the foreman, young Monroe.

They had rolled off many logs when they heard his clear voice say:
"I'd have you boys be on your guard, for the jam will soon give way."
These words were scarcely spoken when the mass did break and go,
And it carried off those six brave youths and their foreman, Jack
  Monroe.

When the rest of our brave shanty boys the sad news came to hear,
In search of their dead comrades to the river they did steer;
Some of the mangled bodies a-floating down did go,
While crushed and bleeding near the bank was that of young Monroe.

They took him from his watery grave, brushed back his raven hair;
There was one fair maiden among them, whose sad cries rent the air;
There was one fair form among them, a maid from Young Woman's
  Town,
Whose moans and cries rose to the skies, for her true love who'd gone
  down.

Fair Clara was a pretty girl, the riverman's true friend,
She, with her widowed mother dear, lived at the river's bend;
The wages of her own true love the boss to her did pay
And the shanty boys for her made up a generous purse next day.

They buried him with sorrow deep; 'twas the first of May.
Come all of you bold shanty boys, and for your comrade pray.
Engraved upon a hemlock tree that by the grave did grow
Was the name and date of the sad fate of the shanty boy Monroe.

Fair Clara did not long survive; her heart broke with her grief,
And scarcely two months afterwards, death came to her relief.
And when this time had passed away and she was called to go,
Her last request was granted, to be laid by young Monroe.

Come all of you brave shanty boys, I would have you call and see
Those green mounds by the riverside where grows the hemlock tree.
The shanty boys cleared off the wood by the lovers there laid
  low—
'Twas the handsome Clara Vernon and her true love, Jack Monroe.

Cherry Tree Joe McCreery

(Attributed to Henry Wilson. From *The Last Raft,* by Joseph Dudley
Tonkin. Harrisburg: The Telegraph Publishing Company. Used by
permission.)

The feats of a giant lumberjack and raftsman, Joe McCreery,
known as "Cherry Tree Joe," are legendary in the central Pennsylvania mountains.

You rivermen have surely heard
  About the appropriation
That was made to clear our little ditch
  And benefit the nation.
That we might run through Chest Falls,
  Nor get the least bit weary,
So they raised the stamps and gave the job
  To Cherry Tree Joe McCreery.

There's Bob McKeague and E. B. Camp
   Who held the ready ginger;
Some men of sense said, "Build a dam,"
   But they'd raise not a finger.
"We'll blow the rocks sky high," said they,
   "So Porter don't get skeery."
"But let her rip and she'll go through,"
   Said Cherry Tree Joe McCreery.

Now you all know and I can show
   That fate's a cruel master;
When once you're going down the hill
   He's sure to push you faster.
And that's the way, mind what I say,
   And don't you see, my dearie,
That everything that happens now
   Is blamed on Joe McCreery.

One day this spring, as I came up,
   I met somebody's daughter,
Who held her apron to her eyes
   To catch the salty water.
"Dear girl," said I, "what makes you cry?
   You must be feeling dreary."
"My daddy's stoved in Chest Falls,
   And I'm hunting Joe McCreery."

The other day they had a splash,
   And jammed her tight as thunder,
A circumstance that caused our folks
   To gaze around in wonder.
They prayed and tore and ripped and swore
   Until they grew quite leery.
Sheff cut his bill raft into sticks
   And cursed poor Joe McCreery.

Now Captain Dowler, t'other day,
   He struck a raft of timber,
'Twas hanging up on Sliding Point,
   And tore the rope asunder.
The captain winked and scratched his head
   And said, "It makes me weary,"
Then jumped his oar and went ashore
   And prayed for Joe McCreery.

Our Squire Riddle on the hill,
   Who deals out justice even,

His head is very bald, you know,
   No hair 'twixt him and heaven.
I asked him why his hair came out.
   He answered to my query,
"It just came out thinking 'bout
   Cherry Tree Joe McCreery."

In years to come when no rafts run
   On our dear little river,
And the cheery cry of "Land! Tie up!"
   Is heard no more—forever,
Down Rocky Bend and through Chest Falls,
   On winter nights so eerie,
The phantom raftsmen chase the ghost
   Of Cherry Tree Joe McCreery.

The Shantyman

(Text obtained from M. J. Colcord of Coudersport by George Korson.
Sung in the pine woods of the West Branch.)

The shanty man is the man I do love best,
   Though some think him free from care,
A-swinging of an ax from morning until night,
   In the middle of the forest drear.

At three o'clock our noisy old cook
   Cries out, " 'Tis the break o' day."
In broken slumbers here we do pass
   These cold winter nights away.

When the spring doth come in, double hardships begin,
   The water is so freezing cold;
Dripping wet our clothes and our limbs are almost froze,
   And our pike poles we scarce can hold.

The shanty man is the man I do love best,
   And I ne'er will deny the same,
For my heart doth scorn those few foppish city beaus,
   Who think it a disgraceful name.

Death of Frank Farrel

This version of the ballad, once sung in Sullivan County lumber
camps, was found by D. D. Brown in his family Bible. A former
resident of Lopez, the Sullivan County town where Farrel's death
occurred in the late nineties, Brown moved to Elkins, West Vir-

ginia. From there in 1937 he sent this copy to the *Wyalusing Rocket.*

> I am a lad that's seen trouble and sorrow,
>   Many accidents occurred;
> I will sing to you the latest,
>   No doubt you all have heard.
> It was out in Sullivan County,
>   Where scores of men are found,
> And known to all throughout the land
>   As that famous lumber town.
>
> The robins were a-singing
>   In the merry month of May;
> Frank Farrel left his home
>   So happy and so gay,
> Little thinking of the danger
>   In the forest tall and sound,
> And has swept away many a loving son
>   In that famous lumber town.
>
> It was on a Monday morning
>   He began his daily toil;
> Little did his brother dream
>   He soon would lie beneath the soil;
> Parted from a loving father
>   And laid by his mother's mound,
> Never to hear those stately hemlocks fall
>   In that famous lumber town.
>
> The brothers a tree were cutting
>   Which toward the earth did fall;
> It caught the limb of a maple,
>   Jerry to his brother did call.
> It shot down like an arrow
>   And crushed Frank to the ground,
> And killed there by his brother's side
>   In that famous lumber town.
>
> Now Frank in his grave is sleeping,
>   And the hemlocks creak and wave,
> But little we know which one of us
>   Will next go to our grave.
> Whenever we visit the cemetery
>   Let us stroll by Frank's mound,
> Who met his death at Sweeney's Camp
>   In that famous lumber town.

Song of the Shanty Boys

(From *Mountain Minstrelsy of Pennsylvania*, by Henry W. Shoemaker. Used by permission.)

Now, boys, if you will listen, I will sing to you a song.
It's all about the shanty boys and how they get along.
They are a jovial lot of boys, so merry and so fine,
And spend the pleasant winter months in cutting down the pine.

Some have left their homes and friends they love so dear,
And to the lonely pine woods their pathway they do steer,
There in the pine woods the winter to remain,
And waiting for the spring days to return again.

But spring will soon be here, and bright will be the day:
Some will go to their dear homes, others wander far away,
For farmers and for sailors, likewise mechanics, too;
For it takes all kinds of tradesmen to form a lumber crew.

The choppers and the sawyers, they lay the timber low;
The skidders and the swampers, they haul it to and fro;
Then comes the loaders, just at the break of day,
A-loading up the teams, for the river haste away.

Noontime rolls around; the foreman loudly screams:
"Lay down your saws and axes and haste to pork and beans."
Arriving at the shanty, the splashing does begin—
The rattling of the water pails and banging of the tin.

"Hurry up there, boys, Dick, Tom, Ed, and Joe,
Or you will have to take the pails and for the water go!"
While they all are splashing, "To dinner!" they do cry.
Oh! you should see them jump and run for fear they'll miss their pie.

When dinner it is o'er, to the shanty they do go,
They all load up their pipes and smoke till everything is blue.
" 'Tis time for the woods, boys," the foreman he does say.
They gather up their mitts, for the woods they haste away.

They all go out with cheerful hearts and well-contented minds,
For the winter winds do not blow cold among the waving pines,
And loudly make their axes ring until the sun goes down.
"Shout hurrah! the day is done, for the shanty we are bound."

They all reach the shanty, with cold and wet feet.
"All hands off with your boot-packs, for your suppers you must eat."
The cook calls for supper; they all rise and go,
For it's not the style of one of the boys to miss his hash, you know.

The boot-packs and rubbers are all laid aside,
The gloves, mitts, rags, and socks are all hung up and dried.
At nine o'clock or thereabouts into the bunks they climb,
To dream away the lonely hours while working in the pine.

At four in the morning the foreman loudly shouts,
"Hurrah there, you teamsters, it's time that you are out!"
Up jump the teamsters, all in fright and dismay,
"Oh! where are my boot-packs? My socks have gone astray."

The rest of the men get up; their socks they cannot find;
They lay it to the teamsters and curse them till they're blind.
If any of their acquaintance should happen to be there,
They'd kill themselves a-laughing at the boys' wild career.

When Sunday it is come, they all lounge about:
Some reading novels, others writing to their fairs,
For married men and single in the shanty you will find,
Who've left their homes and dear ones to work among the pines.

But spring will soon be here, and bright will be the day,
"Lay down your saws and axes, boys, and haste to break the way."
For when the floating ice is gone and business it will thrive,
Five hundred able-bodied men are working on the drive.

With their cant hooks and jam pikes, the men they nobly go
To risk their lives on the Muskegon River, or West Branch, oh!
Cold, frosty mornings, they shiver with the cold;
So much ice on the jam pikes, they scarcely can them hold.

The Leek Hook

(Sung by Wes Berfield. From *A Story of the Sinnemahone*, by George
William Huntley, Jr. Used by permission.)

"The Leek Hook" is an example of the cumulative ballad composed of lumberjacks' improvised verses. The leek hook was a
metal barb attached to boots and used to dig up leeks. In Potter
County, it was believed that a good mess of leeks would ward off
illness and injury for a year.

A brave young raftsman dwelt among the Potter County pines.
He had no fruit trees 'round his hut, nor any flowers nor vines;
Yet he had a gallant heart, for when the war began,
He swore he could lick "Old Jeff" or any other man.

So he sold his yoke of steers, likewise his yellow dog,
And left his double-bitted ax a-sticking in the log.

He donned his brightest scarlet shirt, and "Now," said he, "I shall
Just take a hike to Brindlesville and have a chat with Sal."

When gentle Sally saw him come, she dropped her gathered leeks,
Her waterfall came tumbling down, the roses left her cheeks;
"O John," she cried, "you're all dressed up and I know what it's for,
You've 'listed for a volunteer; you're going to the war!"

"O Sally, dry your tears," said John, "and do not be afraid,
But bear thee up as gallantly as should a Potter County maid.
And give to me some trifling thing, some token ere I go—
That I may wear it as a badge in presence of the foe."

Then stooped that lovely, blushing maid, and from her tiny heel,
Unstrapped a wondrous instrument—a shining spur of steel.
And "Wear thou this," the damsel said, "for it shall be thy shield—
A talisman against all harm upon the battlefield."

Oh, many a field in Dixieland and many a Southland stream
Hath seen that fearless volunteer—that leek hook's awful gleam.
And soon the Johnnies learned to say, "There comes that cussed Yank
Who wears a bayonet on his heel and strikes upon the flank."

And wheresoe'er that leek hook flashed, by mountain, lake, or plain,
'Twas there the fiercest fighting was, the biggest heaps of slain.
"For I hold it true," said John, "that any man of nerve
Can kill most Rebs, to go upon an individual curve."

At Malvern Hill, at Gettysburg, and at the Seven Pines,
That leek hook flashed like living fire, along the Rebel lines.
And so for three long years he fought, o'er many a weary mile,
Killing six general officers and scores of rank and file.

All honor to the shining blade that digs the fragrant root,
Yet makes a fearful weapon on a Potter County foot.
All honor to the people, too, who claim this for their bounty:
"We all were raised on lusty leeks and live in Potter County."

The Wild Lumberjack

(From *Mountain Minstrelsy of Pennsylvania,* by Henry W. Shoemaker.
Used by permission. Sung in the Potter County logging camps, where it
was collected by John C. French.)

One day I was out walking on the mountain,
    A wood robin was singing. I happened to spy
A handsome young lumberjack on the banks of the river,
    All dressed in white linen, and laid out to die.

CHORUS

So beat your drum lowly, and play your fife slowly,
   And play the dead march as you carry me along.
Oh, take me to the mountain, and lay the sod o'er me,
   For I'm a wild lumberjack and I know I've done wrong.

Once out in the forest I used to go slashing;
   Once in the big timbers I used to be gay.
I first took to drinking, and then to card playing,
   Was shot in the breast, and I'm dying today.

Go, someone, write to my gray-haired mother,
   And also to my brothers and my sisters so dear;
But there is another far dearer than mother,
   Who'd bitterly weep if she knew I was here.

Go, someone, and bring me a cup of cold water—
   A cup of spring water, the poor woodsie said;
But ere it had reached him his spirit had vanished—
   Gone to the Giver, the poor fellow was dead.

Coal Miners

by GEORGE KORSON

The peculiar concentration achieved by the group of ballads in this chapter reflects the life in the once typical mining communities, termed "mine patches" in the anthracite region and "coal camps" in the bituminous fields of central and western Pennsylvania. Until modern conditions broke down the barriers, the patch or camp was as much a closed town as any feudal village in the Middle Ages. Behind their hills, far from the world's activities, the miners somehow worked out their humble destinies.

Being unincorporated, the mining village and everything in it, including church and school sites, were owned by the coal operators. From the time they were brought into the world by a company doctor to the day of their burial in a cemetery, the ground

of which had been leased from the company, the mineworkers
lived in the shadow of their employers, often absentee owners,
whom they personified as the Coal King. Their feeling toward
this imaginary potentate is epitomized for the ages in the following epitaph engraved on an anthracite miner's tombstone in a
Hazleton cemetery:

> Fourty years I worked with pick & drill
> Down in the mines against my will
> The Coal Kings slave, but now it's passed;
> Thanks be to God I am free at last.

The original workers in both the anthracite and bituminous
mines of Pennsylvania were English, Welsh, Irish, and Scottish.
In the soft-coal counties, especially around Pittsburgh, the Irish-
Scots were among the more articulate miners. Descendants of
Irish emigrants who had settled in the industrial districts of Scotland early in the nineteenth century, they were real Scots down to
the Scottish burr in their speech and love of Scottish traditions and
folk minstrelsy. There were also many German miners and some
Cornish. In the eighties and nineties came the Slavs, Hungarians,
and Italians in large waves to both the anthracite and bituminous
regions. From the South, Negroes migrated to the western Pennsylvania mining counties.

Some patches and coal camps stood out against the tides of
immigration a long time, but ultimately none escaped. Differences
of tongue, race, national origin, and religion led to many conflicts.
In the anthracite region, tension was further increased by a strati-
fication that set the contract miner above his laborer in the social
scale.

The passage of time ultimately resolved differences. Slowly but
steadily, conflicting groups began to understand John Mitchell's
gospel, "The coal you dig isn't Slavish or Polish or Irish coal; it's
coal." The very smallness of the communities threw different
groups closer together. Intermarriage also had its effect on group
relations. In time of strikes and mine disasters there was a sharing
of food and meager worldly possessions, and the exchange of sym-
pathy. These factors, added to the compelling economic necessity
for unity, steadily led to a situation where mineworkers thought
and acted along similar lines.

The original groups—English, Welsh, Scottish, and Irish—had progressed to a common viewpoint before mass immigration from southeastern Europe had reached its peak. Isolation and leisure among English-speaking miners led to a common cultural development. Of leisure they had an abundance; overexpansion of the respective industries, the seasonal character of their work, and constant labor trouble had kept them busy only a few months of the year. They spent their idle time at home because they were too far from built-up towns, and transportation was still primitive. Lacking commercial amusements such as were available to city workers, they fell back on their own inner resources for diversion. From this situation came folklore.

In both the anthracite and bituminous counties the first folk music was a transplanted one. After immigrant mineworkers had gone through a period of orientation they turned to their immediate environment for inspiration and material in the making of indigenous ballads. In both regions they adapted to their uses the bardic and minstrel arts that were part of their heritage. They used the metric patterns and melodies of folk songs, hymn tunes, and current music-hall hits familiar to them. The texts, however, were original. Their local color stamped them indelibly as of the mining scene. The mark of coal dust was upon them. A point of departure was their lack of allusions to earth magic with which so many folk songs are associated. Of course, coal miners also sang other folk songs and ballads of European heritage or of American tradition, a pleasure shared in common with other Americans. But in their own songs and ballads—those that came out of their own hearts—they gave small heed to the natural world. Their whole existence was bound up with coal, and upon it they concentrated their creative efforts.

Improvising or composing songs, ballads, ditties, and doggerel about the hard coal and soft coal industries and the mining life was common in the latter part of the nineteenth century. In the hard coal region, at least, it spread spontaneously like some mysterious fever. Many were its victims. Mineworkers seemed to have gone daft thinking, talking, writing, and singing in metered and rhymed sentences. There was scarcely a mine disaster, strike, or any other event of local significance that did not inspire a poetized effusion. Even little breaker boys and mule drivers lisped home-made doggerel. Molly Maguire passwords were cast in blank verse; making ballads was one of the diversions of condemned Mollies. In 1877, several weeks before their hanging, four doomed Mollies in the Carbon County prison at Mauch Chunk appeared to take their impending fate with mock casualness:

> You may hear them every evening singing a merry song,
> Composing rhymes is their delight; they do it very well.

Carried away by their ability to play with words, men and boys indulged the game inside the mines. In the beginning mine bosses were amused or annoyed by their employees' wooing the muse underground. When these employees did so on company time, however, they took disciplinary action. For instance, one day deep in the Kaska William mine near Pottsville, Superintendent Jack McQuail caught two of his day laborers improvising poetry. After listening to them a few minutes in the darkness and identifying their voices, he intoned as follows in rhythmic syllables:

> Paddy Carr and Mickey O'Neill
> You'll work no more for Jack McQuail—
> And bejabers, that's poetry too!

The Welsh miners in various parts of the anthracite and bituminous regions of Pennsylvania held Eisteddfods, musical and literary tournaments. The featured event was "chairing of the bard," a colorful, stirring ceremony installing the ensuing year's local bard in office. Many a humble mineworker with a meager schooling won the chair with a Welsh ode and bore a bardic name symbolic of his achievement. Outside the Eisteddfods, however, miner bards were not selected by any such formality, but came to the fore by talent or force of personality. An authentic voice made itself heard. All the influences of the mining environment were embodied in a bard's consciousness. There were no restrictions as to color, creed, or national origin; the mantle fell naturally on him who had the "call." Local bards made up ballads about mine disasters, strikes, visits of celebrities, and other special events. At other times they poetized on whatever caught their individual fancies. And their range of interest was truly remarkable.

They took their bardic art without self-consciousness and with casual unawareness of the value of their creations. More often than not it was their fate to be forgotten once their song was launched. Traditionally the story occurred first to a balladist. Not until he had improvised his text or committed it to paper did he seek a suitable tune. As a rule, the tune was determined by the text's meter. Tunes were adapted quite freely to suit specific texts.

Traditional ballad singers sang without pausing between stanzas, and usually without accompaniment. On those rare occasions when they were accompanied, a guitar was the instrument used. The miner audiences showed a preference for a steady rhythm that gave them a chance to tap their feet.

If these ballads make small use of detail, it must be borne in mind that in many cases they were composed right after an event. Like a special edition of a daily newspaper hot off the press, a ballad gave the major facts with which the audience was chiefly concerned. The ballads were quickly learned by heart, and with many variants wove themselves into the community's tradition.

Intersectional circulation was promoted by visitors who went from one place to another, by workers who changed jobs from one county to another, by itinerant peddlers who were to be found in both the hard and soft coal regions, but chiefly by strolling miner minstrels. One type of minstrel is represented in this chapter by John J. Curtis, the blind miner from Morea. There were quite a few of these disabled miners who, rather than go to the poorhouse or depend upon relatives for support, chose minstrelsy as a livelihood. A miner would make a ballad, or have one made for him, about his "sad fate," an allusion to the loss of legs, arms, sight, or some similar permanent disability sustained in a mine accident. Led by a faithful dog or boy, a blind miner shuffled along singing, playing a fiddle, or strumming a guitar, and selling broadsides of his personal ballad. Curtis supported himself in this way for years.

Then there were the other minstrels who for the most part were heaven-sent entertainers. The man who could dramatize a ballad with a gesture, the lift of an eyebrow, or by the intonation of his voice, was indeed fortunate. If in addition to these gifts he had a sense of humor and could play a fiddle or guitar, he was usually found among the tramp minstrels. Vagabonds with a distaste for the mining craft, they preferred to tramp from place to place and spread cheer and laughter in otherwise drab mining communities. They lived by their wits and subsisted on the coins of good will thrown their way after a street-corner or barroom performance. Some of them circulated in their own counties, but others took the whole anthracite region as their stage. They rarely got into the newspapers, their fame being spread by word of mouth.

Wilkes-Barre's Con Carbon enacted the traditional role of court jester to John Mitchell, union president, during the famous 1902 strike. In the darkest hours of that six-months' struggle, Mitchell would summon Carbon with some such plea as "Sing for me, Con," or "Spin me a yarn, Con." Here was minstrelsy dedicated to the cause of labor! Shades of MacLiag and his royal patron, Brian Boru, the Brave! These bards and minstrels of the mining regions deviated from the tradition of ancient minstrelsy in one significant respect. They served not kings and lords and great ladies, but humble American coal miners.

Under a moonlit sky, against the background of colliery buildings and towering culm banks, and in an atmosphere infiltrated with coal dust and brimstone smells, the mineworkers and their families would gather for singing, storytelling, and dancing. A plate of sheet-iron borrowed from the colliery would be laid on the grass as a sounding board for jigs, reels, hornpipes, and breakdowns as the fiddler scraped out his lively tunes. And,

> The man in the moon had charge of the light plant,
>   Our cottage walls were not of bricks;
> Young and old enjoyed the night camp
>   On the green at Number Six.

Another common meeting place, but strictly for men only, was the spacious porch of a company store. One of the best-remembered of these improvised stages was Mackin Brothers' store porch in the East End section of Wilkes-Barre whose fame was spread by a ballad:

> Winter or the summer-time,
> Whether rain or whether shine,
> Every man is there in line
>   Seated on the step.

Minstrelsy took possession of the local barrooms, especially on paydays and Saturday nights. In the coal regions the saloon was a club, an oasis in a desert of wretchedness and oppression, an escape from a harsh environment. It was the only place outside of the union hall where men of diverse origins and clashing nationalities met as social equals. A boisterous welcome was extended to every adult mineworker regardless of race, creed, personal appearance, or previous condition of servitude. There were no qualifications for membership, and the only dues were a nickel for high-collared beer or a dime for a glass of the hard stuff. The saloon satisfied the miner's craving for fellowship and offered balm for wounds suffered in the daily grind. The sense of dignity that he had lost in the mines was momentarily recovered amid alcoholic mists of an evening. In this mellow atmosphere bitterness was forgotten; men laughed without inhibition; and their masculine humor gleamed through the darkness. Only in beaten men does the light of humor die out, and these men were not beaten.

Mingled with humor was song. They sang every type of song, but preferred their own indigenous ballads because they fitted in with the favorite theme of barroom audiences—shop talk. After a schooner or two of beer or a jigger of Scotch, even the most incompetent miner talked big. One evening a mine boss, while passing a saloon, overheard one of his miners boasting of the large amount of coal he could mine in a day, an amount far beyond his powers. The next morning the boss met the same miner on the way to work and stopped him, saying, "Sandy, I'll bet you're not as good a man at digging coal today as you imagined yourself in the barroom last night." To which the miner replied, "I would be as good a man if you gave me the same room I had last night."

Off-hour braggarts were a favorite theme with bards. The anthracite ballad "A Celebrated Workingman" is of this type. Here is a bituminous sample:

In the barroom, in the barroom,
  Where big diggers congregate;
A-shovelin' coal and a-layin' track
And a-pilin' back the slate.

If you want a car of coal,
  You'll never have to wait,

If you call upon the digger
In the barroom, in the barroom.

And minstrelsy throve even in the mines hundreds of feet below
the surface. The miner did not sing at the face, where the work
was far too arduous and hazardous and the air too thick with coal
dust. This accounts for the lack of work songs of the "John Henry"
type among coal mining ballads. A miner, however, might sing
while waiting in a branch entry for the smoke and coal dust to
settle in his room after he had blasted down the coal. Miners often
waited for hours at a time for the delivery of empty cars at their
rooms or chambers and made good use of these idle hours. They
would gather in one another's rooms or chambers, at a switch or
turnout, or in the fireboss' shanty, perhaps with a smuggled
mouth-organ, fiddle, or accordion. An old wooden door formerly
used to control underground ventilation became an improvised
dance floor. And in the eerie darkness of this setting, lighted only
by tiny yellow flames sputtering from teapot-shaped oil lamps,

Many a tale was told in the depths of the darkness,
  Stories repeated not verged on the truth;
Sweet were the songs that were sung with a gladness
  Few not the oaths from the lips of a youth.

Auxiliary mineworkers such as pumpers, chainers, and mule
drivers, however, did sing while at work. This was true particularly of the mule drivers on their long rides through the dingy
entries:

If the mules were in a patient mood,
  And meekly jogged along,
The boys enlivened every hour
  With merry jests and song.

Memorable too were the wakes, some of which were far from
mournful. Wakes were well attended in the mine patches and coal
camps because bereaved families customarily set a bountiful table
and kept on tap an ample supply of liquor. Wakes also brought
about a reunion of friends and relatives from scattered localities.
The long hours of the night were passed with stories, some humorous, some ghostly, mingled with reminiscences and small talk.
To keep mourners awake there were also stunts, tricks, and hoaxes

that in some cases involved taking macabre liberties with the corpse.

Old-timers also recall the fiddling, dancing, and ballad-singing tournaments at which gold medals and cash prizes were awarded. They differed from the Welsh Eisteddfods in that they were in the nature of sporting events on which hard-earned dollars were wagered. Intersectional rivalry was intense, and often bitter personal feuds resulted. The best-known feud was that between Patrick "Giant" O'Neill of Shenandoah and George "Corks" Kramer of Locust Gap Patch. O'Neill's nickname was derived from his towering reputation as an exhibition dancer. It had nothing to do with his stature; actually he was short and slender.

In the early seventies O'Neill had won the anthracite regional jig-dancing championship. The resultant fame got him an engagement with the Welsh and Sands circus. Several years later he had stepped into the role of one of the two Dublin Dans in Howerth's Hibernica, a traveling magic-lantern and vaudeville show that toured the country for the entertainment of chiefly Irish audiences. When Hibernica broke up in the anthracite region in 1894, O'Neill had bowed himself off the professional stage forever to return to his former trade as a blacksmith and tool sharpener at various Schuylkill County collieries.

He was still the anthracite champion in 1896 when he was challenged to a match by Corks Kramer, a tall gangling young mineworker. The challenger's nickname testified to his lightness of foot and skillful interpretations of jigs, reels, clogs, and hornpipes, the most popular dances of the day. O'Neill accepted the challenge, and the contest, preceded by much ballyhoo, was held at Locust Gap. A great crowd turned out for the match, with Kramer's partisans far outnumbering O'Neill's, as it was Kramer's home territory.

Giant O'Neill lost his crown in that match, but many of the spectators felt he should have won, and they expressed their disappointment by jeering as the gold medal was pinned on young Kramer's chest. When it was charged that the judges had been prejudiced against the Giant, one of the local men offered to post a bet of $2,500 that Kramer would outdance the Giant again.

That was a sizable fortune for those days, and whether or not it was a bluff its effect was to silence O'Neill's followers.

The years rolled on, the men grew older, and the chance of another match between them seemed to have passed forever. But in 1935 the long-deferred opportunity came at the Pennsylvania Folk Festival. When an elimination contest was planned in Pottsville, old-timers, remembering this ancient feud, demanded that Kramer and O'Neill be brought together again. Kramer came from his home in Ashland and O'Neill from Atlantic City, where he was then living. After a local sparring they were selected by the Pottsville judges to settle their feud once and for all at the Pennsylvania Folk Festival in Allentown.

Their appearance on the stage of the Allentown High School provided the climax of the festival program. Kramer, tall, gray-haired, proudly wearing the gold medal he had won at Locust Gap in 1896, towered over Giant O'Neill, a stoop-shouldered, white-haired little old man. There was something pathetic about this dancing contest between two veterans of the anthracite industry. The judges sensed it and, grasping an opportunity to put an amicable finish to the ancient feud, decided that it had been a good match in which Kramer and O'Neill had danced equally well. The ancient rivals, still breathless from their vigorous stepping, were brought to the center of the stage and, as the spectators applauded and cheered, they shook hands in renewed friendship.

When, more than twenty years ago, I stumbled upon this rich seam of folklore, the nonmining world was unaware of its existence. There is a simple explanation for this lack of knowledge. The miners' minstrelsy had functioned in a drab, isolated environment beneath the surface of the American social pattern. Illiteracy was common, newspapers and magazines were rare, and the written word itself was suspect. But for the retentive memories of the survivors of the folklore-producing generation, all trace of the miners' social-cultural life might have disappeared. And what a great misfortune that would have been! Then the world would have lost the picture of a submerged people in whom a boundless vitality survived in the midst of a hemmed-in existence.

Down, Down, Down

(From the Archive of American Folk Song, Library of Congress. Sung by William E. Keating at Pottsville, 1946. Recorded by George Korson.)

Starting out in the early twenties as a local barroom ballad, "Down, Down, Down" with its pounding refrain has found its way into folklore anthologies since publication in *Minstrels of the Mine Patch*. Originally the ballad had about forty stanzas, but because it was too long to sing without interruption, it was broken up into groups of stanzas corresponding to the levels of an anthracite mine. At each level, the customers around the bar would shout, "Time out for a round of drinks!" The singer's drinks were on the house. This was his traditional prerogative.

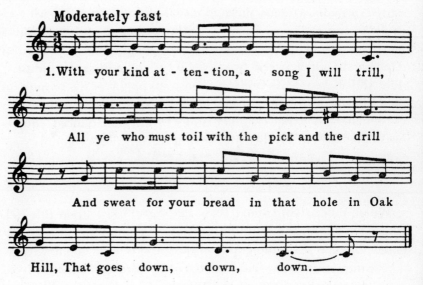

2. When I was a boy, said my daddy to me:
   "Stay out of the mines, take my warning," said he,
   "Or with dust you'll be choked and a pauper you'll be,
   Broken down, down, down."

3. But I went to Oak Hill and I asked for a job,
   A mule for to drive, or a gangway to rob.
   The boss said, "Come out, Bill, and follow the mob
   That goes down, down, down."

4. I was booked the next day to go down in the mine.
   I goes into Tim Harvey's and samples some shine.
   With a real near-beer headache, I reported on time
     To go down, down, down.

5. Said Pete McAvoy, "Here's Bill Keatin' the scamp."
   Just back, Pete supposed, from a million-mile tramp.
   Then he showed me the windie where I'd get a lamp
     To go down, down, down.

6. The lamp man he squints through the windie at me.
   "What's your name and your age and your number?" said he.
   "Bill Keatin', I'm thirty, number twenty-three,
     Mark that down, down, down."

7. With a frown of disfavor, my joke it was met.
   For an argument plainly, Jim Griffiths was set,
   For he told me that divil a lamp would I get
     To go down, down, down.

8. I said, "Mr. Lamp Man, now don't l'ave us fight;
   Can't ye see by me eyes I was boozin' all night?
   Sure the mines will be dark and I'll have to have light
     While I'm down, down, down."

9. With an old greasy apron he polished his speck.
   He declared of the rules he'd be makin' a wreck,
   If he'd give me a lamp without a brass check
     To go down, down, down.

10. Then I found the supply clerk for whom I inquired.
    He was stubborn as blazes, with malice all fired.
    He gave me a lot of red tape and the check I required
      To go down, down, down.

11. I at last had the check that would pacify Jim,
    So into the windie I flung it to him.
    "Now," said I, "quit your grumblin' and give me a glim
      To go down, down, down."

12. A contraption he gave me, a hose on a box,
    'Twas so heavy I thought it was loaded with rocks.
    If a car jumped the road, you could use it for blocks
      While you're down, down, down.

13. By two rusty clamps it's attached to your cap,
    And the box it hangs onto your hip by a strap.
    Oh, the man that transported them lamps to the Gap
      May go down, down, down.

14. Then into the office I sauntered to Sam.
With a cheery "Good mornin'," says I, "Here I am,
With booze in me bottle and beer in me can
    To go down, down, down."

15. He said, "Billy, me bucko, how are you today?"
"Outside of a headache," I said, "I'm O.K.
I've been samplin' the moonshine in every café
    In the town, town, town."

16. "Now, where was this job at?" I wanted to know.
"Was it up in the new drift?" but he shook his head, no.
"When you hit the fifth lift you'll have one more to go,
    So go down, down, down."

17. I asked him what tools would I need in the place.
"Very few," said the boss with a grin on his face.
"One number six shovel and darn little space
    While you're down, down, down."

18. When you're drivin' the gangway you need lots of tools,
And you buy them yourself, it's the anthracite rules,
But a laggin' suffices to drive balky mules,
    When you're down, down, down.

19. At drivin' mules I'm not overly slick
But the plugs in Oak Hill I showed many's a trick,
When I hollered "Yay" if they started to kick,
    They went down, down, down.

20. Then up to the head of the shaft I made haste,
I saluted the top man and stood in my place.
I says, "Give me a cage for I've no time to waste,
    Let me down, down, down."

21. "All aboard for the bottom!" the top man did yell,
We stepped on the cage, and he gave her the bell.
Then from under our feet, like a bat out o' hell,
    She went down, down, down.

A Celebrated Workingman

(From the Archive of American Folk Song, Library of Congress. Sung by Daniel Walsh at Centralia, Columbia County, 1946. Recorded by. George Korson.)

"A Celebrated Workingman" by Ed Foley, one of the most picturesque of the anthracite itinerant minstrels, is a satire on the off-hour braggart of the mines. Foley sang it for the first time at the wedding of a niece at Mount Carmel in October 1892. It has had a steady popularity ever since.

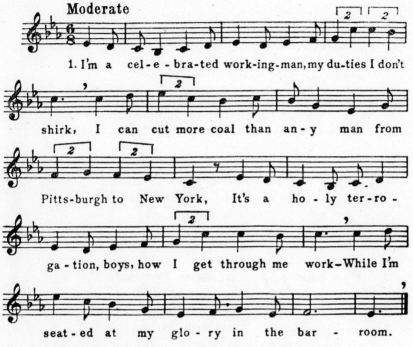

1. I'm a cel-e-bra-ted work-ing-man, my du-ties I don't shirk, I can cut more coal than an-y man from Pitts-burgh to New York, It's a ho-ly ter-ro-ga-tion, boys, how I get through me work—While I'm seat-ed at my glo-ry in the bar-room.

2. I can stand a set of timber, post, and bar or single prop.
I can throw a chain on the bottom or I can throw it up on top.
Oh, give me a pair of engines and be jeepers I'll not stop,
   Till I land me triple wagons through the barroom.

3. I'll go down and work upon the platform or go out and run the
      dump.
I can put in pulleys on the slope or go down and clean the sump.
I can run a 20,000 horse-power steam engine pump—
   That's providing that I have it in the barroom.

4. I'll go down and work the flat vein; I'll go up and work the pitch.
I can work at the Potts or Newside—I don't care the devil which.
I can show the old track layer how to decorate the ditch—
   Now haven't I often proved it in the barroom?

5. Now at driving I'm a daisy; just give me a balky team,
When I'll beat the spots off an evening run, be it water, wind or
      steam,

With your balance planes, and endless chains; they're nowhere to
    be seen,
When I pull me trip of wagons through the barroom.

6. Now at bossing I'm a daisy, and I know I'm no disgrace,
    For I could raise your wages, boys, just twelve cents up the l'ast,
    Now didn't the Reading Company miss me when they didn't make
        their haste,
    And capture me, before I struck the barroom?

7. I can show the boss or super how the air should circulate,
    I can show the boss fireman how the steam should generate;
    Now the trouble at the Pottsville shaft, sure I could elucidate,
    Now haven't I often proved it in the barroom?

8. And now my song is o'er and I haven't any other,
    For heaven's sake don't fire no more or else we'll surely smother;
    The landlord would rather throw us out than go to the bother
        Of putting up a ventilator in the barroom.

9. And now my song is ended and I hope you'll all agree,
    That if you want any pointers you'd better send for me,
    But I'm not worth a good gol darn till I empty two or three
        Of the very biggest schooners in the barroom.

Blue Monday

(Sung by Michael F. Barry at New Kensington, Allegheny County,
    1940. Recorded by George Korson.)

In coal mining regions, paydays and Saturday nights were
customarily given over to Bacchus, and as this bituminous ballad
suggests, penance followed on blue Monday.

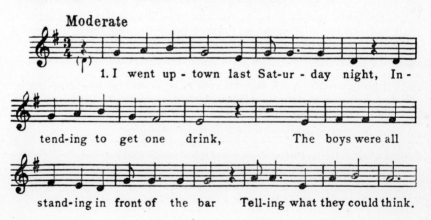

Moderate

1. I went up-town last Sat-ur-day night, In-
tend-ing to get one   drink,   The boys were all
stand-ing in front of the bar Tell-ing what they could think.

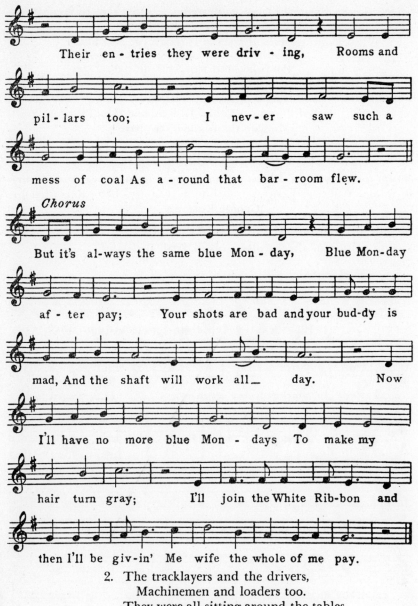

Their en-tries they were driv-ing, Rooms and
pil-lars too; I nev-er saw such a
mess of coal As a-round that bar-room flew.

Chorus

But it's al-ways the same blue Mon-day, Blue Mon-day
af-ter pay; Your shots are bad and your bud-dy is
mad, And the shaft will work all— day. Now
I'll have no more blue Mon-days To make my
hair turn gray; I'll join the White Rib-bon and
then I'll be giv-in' Me wife the whole of me pay.

2. The tracklayers and the drivers,
Machinemen and loaders too.
They were all sitting around the tables
Telling what they could do.
But if they would only stay at home
Their dollars and dimes to save,
When a strike comes on they could sing this song:
"Operator, your work we don't need."

CHORUS
But it's always the same blue Monday,
Blue Monday after pay.
Your shots are bad and your buddy is mad,
And the shaft will work all day.
Now I'll have no more blue Mondays
To make my hair turn gray;
I'll join the White Ribbon and then I'll be givin'
Me wife the whole of me pay.

The Pretty Maid Milking Her Goat

(From the Archive of American Folk Song, Library of Congress. Sung by Daniel Walsh at Centralia, Columbia County, 1946. Recorded by George Korson.)

"The Pretty Maid Milking Her Goat," for all its mocking text, is sung to one of the loveliest of all Irish melodies.

Moderate

1. It was a cold winter's morning As I went to work for my grub, I heard a maid sing most charming As she sat on the heel of a tub; Her mouth was both large and commodious, A small boy might skate down her throat; Her bull-frog bass voice was melodious, As she sat there milking her goat.

2. I stood and I gazed at this cr'ature,
   I was smashed in two halves by surprise—
Thinks I she's some goddess of nature,
   Or the queen of Georgetown in disguise;
I says to her aisy and civil,
   "Do you warble that poem by note?"
I was towld to inquire of the divil
   By the pretty maid milking her goat.

3. Then I said, "Dearest fairy, have patience,
   Till ye hear what I'm going to propose.
Come, leave all your wealthy relations,
   And travel with me, O primrose.
Your everyday dress shall be silken,
   And to show how much on you I dote,
I'll grab howlt of the tail while you're milking,
   And help you to pump the ould goat."

4. She said, "Don't stand there givin' me taffy
   Or think I'm a foolish galoot,
I know I could ne'er be happy
   With you and your No. 9 boots.
You're nothin' but a common railroader;
   I can tell by the mud on your coat,
And to none but a red-ash coal loader,
   Will my pappy give me and the goat."

The Broken Shovel

(From the Archive of American Folk Song, Library of Congress. Sung by Daniel Brennan at McAdoo, Schuylkill County, 1946. Recorded by George Korson.)

I first heard of "The Broken Shovel" in 1925 in Carbondale, Lackawanna County, where a saloonkeeper said he could sing it. When I asked him to do so, he refused. He had given the ballad to another man who failed to keep his promise of rewarding him with a bottle of whisky. It was my misfortune to come along when he was in a recalcitrant mood. After persistent inquiries, however, I finally was directed to Daniel Brennan, who graciously sang it for me.

"Pretta-Moor" (stanza 4) is a corruption of the Gaelic *Prathe-More,* meaning "big potatoes." It is similar to the slang phrase "some punkins." The ballad describes a fist fight that is supposed to have taken place in the little mine patch of Beaver Brook near

Hazleton in 1890. Some believe that Pretta-Moor was a local peddler who got his nickname from calling, "Big potatoes." Others hold that the mediator was really the mine boss.

1. Good Chris-tians all,___ come and lend an ear, Un-to me dit-ty ___ and the truth you'll hear; It's of Bar-ney Gal-la-gher so bold and thrue, Ar-rah that broke me shov-el, Ar-rah that broke me shov-el, Ar-rah that broke me___ fine brand-new shov-el in two.

2. When the whistle blew and the shovel was broke,
   Old Neddy Kearn was the first man spoke,
     Saying, "Barney Gallagher, come tell me thrue,
   Phat for you broke me shovel,
   Phat for you broke me shovel,
     Phat for you broke me fine brand-new shovel in two?"

3. "Oh," said Barney Gallagher in a stuttering way,
   "I'll c-c-crack your jaw if I hang this day,
     To insult a m-m-man so b-b-bold and thrue,
   About your b-b-bloody shovel,
   About your b-b-bloody shovel,
     About your b-b-bloody shovel that was broke in two."

4. Barney and McGlynn, they both pitch in,
   Like Corbett and Mitchell they form a ring;
     The crowd around began to roar

Stanza 2

Phat for you broke me shov-el,

Phan who the divil entered,
Phan who the divil entered,
    Phan who the divil entered but the Pretta-Moor.

5. "Howlt on," sez the Pretta, "we must have fair play.
He's a Ross's man; we will win the day;
    But if you touch him, then I'll touch you."
That was all about the shovel,
That was all about the shovel,
    That was all about the shovel that was broke in two.

Down in a Coal Mine

(From the Archive of American Folk Song, Library of Congress. Sung by Morgan Jones at Wilkes-Barre, 1946. Recorded by George Korson.)

"Down in a Coal Mine," originally a stage song published in 1872 and long popular in the anthracite region, is probably the best-known mining song in the country.

Moderate

1. I am a jov-ial col-lier lad, as blithe as blithe can be, And let the times be good or bad, they're all the same to me; There's lit-tle of this world I know and care less for its ways, And where the Dog Star nev-er glows, I wear a-way the days.

Chorus (slower)

Down in a coal mine, un-der-neath the ground,

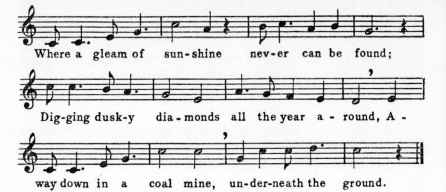

Where a gleam of sun-shine nev-er can be found;

Dig-ging dusk-y dia-monds all the year a-round, A-

way down in a coal mine, un-der-neath the ground.

2. My hands are horny, hard, and black from working in the vein,
   Like the clothes upon my back my speech is rough and plain;
   And if I stumble with my tongue I've one excuse to say,
   It's not the collier's heart that's bad, it's his head that goes astray.

CHORUS
Down in a coal mine, underneath the ground,
Where a gleam of sunshine never can be found;
Digging dusky diamonds all the year around,
Away down in a coal mine, underneath the ground.

3. At every shift, be it soon or late, I haste my bread to earn,
   And anxiously my kindred wait and watch for my return;
   For death that levels all alike, whate'er their rank may be,
   Amid the fire and damp may strike and fling his darts at me.

4. How little do the great ones care who sit at home secure,
   What hidden dangers colliers dare, what hardships they endure;
   The very fires their mansions boast, to cheer themselves and wives,
   Mayhap were kindled at the cost of jovial colliers' lives.

5. Then cheer up, lads, and make ye much of every joy ye can;
   But let your mirth be always such as best becomes a man;
   However fortune turns about we'll still be jovial souls,
   For what would America be without the lads that look for coals?

*Opusceny Banik z Wilks Barroch**
(The Lonely Miner of Wilkes-Barre)

(Sung by Mrs. Mary Rusin at Pittsburgh, 1947. Recorded by Jacob A. Evanson.)

"I don't know who made this song," said Mrs. Rusin, "but it is

---

* Key to Slovakian pronunciation will be found on p. 435.

so sad and beautiful, it almost makes me cry. There were many Slovakians like the man in the song who had left their families in the old country to find work in Pennsylvania's coal mines. My father was a coal miner and we were always so afraid of the danger to him. My parents were great singers and I learned most of my songs from them. I learned this song from friends who had brought it from Wilkes-Barre."

The reference in stanza 3 to "my miner" recalls the custom of anthracite contract miners' employing immigrants as laborers to help them get out the tonnage. The literal translation was supplied by Calvin Bruck and John Rusin, editor and columnist respectively of the *Slovak People's Daily.*

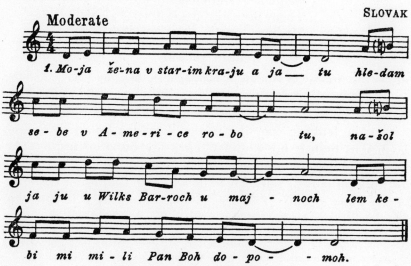

Moderate

SLOVAK

1. Mo-ja že-na v star-im kra-ju a ja __ tu hle-dam se-be v A - me-ri - ce ro - bo tu, na-šol ja ju u Wilks Bar-roch u maj - noch lem ke - bi mi mi - li Pan Boh do - po - - moh.

2. *Každe rano ja še mušim hajsovac,*
   štiri kari na šichtunaladovac.
   Ohlednem še tristo razi v hodzine,
   či me uhle abi rak nezabije.

3. *A jak prišla jedenasta hodzina,*
   už moj majner še do domu odbira
   už ja ňemam vov tej majne nikoho,
   lem mileho Pana Boha sameho.

4. *Ach Bože moj dopomož mi dorobic,*
   a ščešlivo še do domu navracic
   ku tej mojej milej žene i dzecom.
   Višliš žadosc v mojim šercu žalosnom.

1. While my wife is in the old country,
   I am in America seeking work;
   In the mines of Wilkes-Barre I found it—
   And, dear Lord God, help me!

2. Each morning I am hoisted down
   Four cars per shift to load;
   Three hundred times an hour I look about me
   Lest a fall of coal or rock kill me.

3. And at the eleventh hour,
   My miner leaves for home;
   Now there's none but me in the mine—
   I am alone, dear Lord God, except for thee.

4. O God, help me finish my work,
   And safely return home
   To my dear wife and children—
   My heart is so sad—hear my plea!

Jenkin Jenkins

(From the Archive of American Folk Song, Library of Congress. Sung
by Thomas Roberts at Wilkes-Barre, 1946. Recorded by George
Korson.)

"Jenkin Jenkins," popular in the Wyoming Valley, is unique
in that its hero is not a miner but a fireboss, who inspects the
inside workings for accumulations of gas before the miners report
for work; usually he starts his round at 4 A.M. Calling an Irishman
"Patsy Patsy" (stanza 4) is an old joke dating back to the time
when Irishmen doubled their given names like the Welsh to win
favor among Welsh mine bosses.

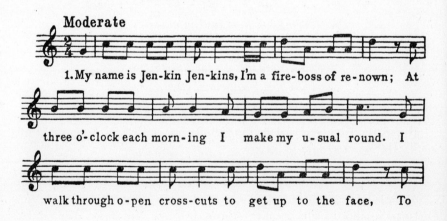

Moderate

1. My name is Jen-kin Jen-kins, I'm a fire-boss of re-nown; At
three o'-clock each morn-ing I make my u-sual round. I
walk through o-pen cross-cuts to get up to the face, To

find how much gas there is   in   ev-ery min-er's   place.

2. My name is Jenkin Jenkins,
    I'm a fireboss of renown;
    I'm known by all the men and boys
       That work down underground.
    I travel over rock and coal
       That fall down in the night.
    I grope my way the best I can
       With my small safety light.

3. At my headquarters at the foot
       When I return from my round,
    The miners all depend on me
       For everything safe and sound.
    For I am the only person
       That dare go in the mines,
    To investigate all dangers
       Before commencing time.

4. In your place, Patsy Patsy,
       I'm sure the roof will drop;
    Don't let your laborers load any coal
       Until you stand a prop.
    In your place, Evan Evans,
       I find a very bad joint.
    You're not arranging your chamber right
       According to the point.

5. Say, Davis, Smith, and Dougherty—
       Where were you yesterday?
    I hear you three have been drinking
       Ever since you got your pay.
    You three cannot deny it;
       I see it in your faces.
    You three can now take out your tools—
       I've got men in your places.

The Old Miner's Refrain

(From the Archive of American Folk Song, Library of Congress. Sung
by Daniel Walsh at Centralia, Columbia County, 1946. Recorded by
George Korson.)

"Once a miner and twice a breaker boy" is an old saying in the
anthracite region. It recalls the custom of employing old miners
to pick slate in the breaker alongside boys. But since mechanical

slate pickers have displaced manual picking, there no longer is any place for old men in the breaker or, for that matter, anywhere else in the industry. "The Old Miner's Refrain," one of the oldest anthracite ballads, sums up a miner's career—his dreams, his hopes, and his thwarted ambitions.

Moderately slow

1. I'm get-ting old and fee-ble and I can-not work no more, I have laid my rust-y min-ing tools a-way; For for-ty years and o-ver I have toiled a-bout the mines, But now I'm get-ting fee-ble, old and gray.

I start-ed in the break-er and went back to it a-
Chorus: Where are the boys that worked with me in the break-ers long a-
gain, But now my work is fin-ished for all time; The
go? Man-y of them now have gone to rest; Their
on-ly place that's left me is the alm's-house for a
cares of life are o-ver and they've left this world of

D. S. for Chorus

home, Where I'm going to lay this wea-ry head of mine.
woe, And their spir-its now are roam-ing with the blest.

2. In the chutes I graduated instead of going to school—
    Remember, friends, my parents they were poor;
When a boy left the cradle it was always made a rule
    To try and keep starvation from the door.
At eight years of age to the breaker I first went
    To learn the occupation of a slave;
I certainly was delighted, and on picking slate was bent—
    My ambition it was noble, strong, and brave.

CHORUS

Where are the boys that worked with me in the breakers long ago?
    Many of them now have gone to rest;
Their cares of life are over and they've left this world of woe;
    And their spirits now are roaming with the blest.

3. At eleven years of age I bought myself a lamp—
    The boss he sent me down the mine to trap;
I stood in there in water, in powder smoke and damp;
    My leisure hours I spent in killing rats.
One day I got promoted to what they called a patcher,
    Or a lackey for the man that drives the team:
I carried sprags and spreaders and had to fix the latch—
    I was going through my exercise, it seems.

4. I next became a driver, and thought myself a man;
    The boss he raised my pay as I advanced.
In going through the gangway with the mules at my command,
    I was prouder than the President of France.
But now my pride is weakened and I am weakened too;
    I tremble till I'm scarcely fit to stand.
If I were taught book learning instead of driving teams,
    Today, kind friends, I'd be a richer man.

5. I next became a miner and laborer combined,
    For to earn my daily bread beneath the ground
I performed the acts of labor which came in a miner's line—
    For to get my cars and load them I was bound.
But now I can work no more, my cares of life are run;
    I am waiting for the signal at the door
When the angels they will whisper, "Dear old miner, you must come,
    And we'll row you to the bright celestial shore."

The Shoofly

(From the Archive of American Folk Song, Library of Congress. Sung by Daniel Walsh at Centralia, Columbia County, 1946. Recorded by George Korson.)

"The Shoofly" appeared during the depression of the seventies. It was made by a village schoolmaster, Felix O'Hare, who put into it the anxiety and despair that followed the closing of the small mine at Valley Furnace in the Schuylkill Valley in 1871. Normally the unemployed miners might have had jobs at the Shoofly, a near-by colliery, but there a bad seam had been struck, causing a shutdown.

Moderately fast

1. As I went a-walk-ing one fine sum-mer's morn-ing, It was
   And when I drew nigh her she sat on her hunk-ers, For to

down by the Fur-nace I chanced for to stroll.— I es-
fill up her scut-tle she just had be-gun——

pied an old la-dy, I'll swear she was eight-y, At the
And to her-self she was sing-ing a dit-ty, And

foot of the dirt banks a-root-ing for coal;——
these are the words the old la-dy did sing:——

Chorus

A— cry-ing, "Och-one! sure, I'm near-ly dis-tract-ed,——

—— For it's down by the Shoo-fly they cut a bad

vein; —— And since they con-demned the old slope at the Fur-nace, —— Sure all me fine neigh-bors must leave here a - gain." ——

2. " 'Twas only last evenin' that I asked McGinley
     To tell me the reason the Furnace gave o'er.
   He told me the company had spent eighty thousand,
     And finding no prospects they would spend no more.
   He said that the Diamond it was rather bony,
     Besides too much dirt in the seven-foot vein;
   And as for the Mammoth, there's no length of gangway,
     Unless they buy land from old Abel and Swayne.

CHORUS

   A-crying "Ochone! sure, I'm nearly distracted,
     For it's down by the Shoofly they cut a bad vein;
   And since they condemned the old slope at the Furnace,
     Sure all me fine neighbors must leave here again."

3. "And as for Michael Rooney, I owe him some money,
     Likewise Patrick Kearns, I owe him some more;
   And as for old John Eagen, I ne'er see his wagon,
     But I think of the debt that I owe in the store.
   I owe butcher and baker, likewise the shoemaker,
     And for plowin' me garden I owe Pat McQuail;
   Likewise his old mother, for one thing and another,
     And to drive away bother, an odd quart of ale.

4. "But if God spares me children until the next summer,
     Instead of a burden, they will be a gain;
   And out of their earnin's I'll save an odd dollar,
     And build a snug home at the 'Foot of the Plane.'
   Then rolling in riches, in silks, and in satin,
     I ne'er shall forget the days I was poor,
   And likewise the neighbors that stood by me children,
     Kept want and starvation away from me door.

5. "And if you should happen to cross the Broad Mountain,
    Step in and sit down on me cane-bottomed chairs;
Take off your fixin's, lay them on the bureau,
    While I in the kitchen refreshments prepare;
And while we are seated so snug at the table,
    Enjoying the fruits of a strong cup of tea,
We'll talk of the quiltin's we had at the Furnace—
    Me heart does rejoice an old neighbor to see."

A Miner's Prayer

(Sung by Mrs. Ralph B. Thompson at Pittsburgh, 1940. Recorded by
George Korson.)

This bituminous ballad makes a pathetic plea for the miners'
children when hunger stalks the coal fields.

Moderately slow

1. I keep listen-ing for the whis-tles in the morn-ing,

But the mines are still; no noise is in the air.

And the chil-dren wake up cry-ing in the morn-ing,

For the cup-boards are so emp-ty and so bare.

And their lit-tle feet are oh! so cold they stum-ble,

And we have to pin the rags up-on their backs.

And our home is brok-en down and ve-ry hum-ble,

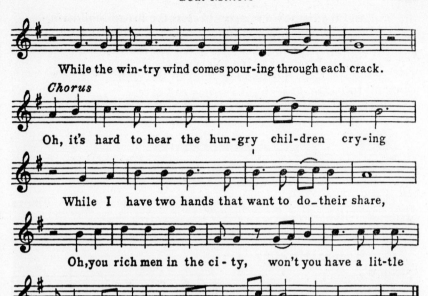

While the win-try wind comes pour-ing through each crack.

Chorus

Oh, it's hard to hear the hun-gry chil-dren cry-ing

While I have two hands that want to do_their share,

Oh, you rich men in the ci - ty, won't you have a lit-tle

pi-ty, And just lis-ten to_ a_ min-er's prayer?

2. Down beneath the frozen ground the coal is laying,
 Only waiting till we seek it from its bed,
 While above the earth with aching heart we're praying,
 While each wife and mother waits with bowed down head.
 Oh, we only ask enough to clothe and feed them,
 And to hear the hungry children sing and play.
 Oh, if we could give these things to those who need them,
 I know that would be a miner's happy day.

CHORUS

 Oh, it's hard to hear the hungry children crying
 While I have two hands that want to do their share,
 Oh, you rich men in the city, won't you have a little pity,
 And just listen to a miner's prayer?

When the Breaker Starts Up on Full Time

(From the Archive of American Folk Song, Library of Congress. Sung by Jerry Byrne at Buck Run, Schuylkill County, 1946. Recorded by George Korson.)

"When the Breaker Starts Up on Full Time" catches the mining folk in a joyfully expectant mood. After prolonged unemployment the miners hear a rumor that their local breaker is to resume production. All the good things sung about represent so much wishful thinking; in the eighties, when this ballad first appeared, such luxuries were beyond reach even when the breakers were working full time.

Moderately slow

1. Me trou-bles are o'er, Miss-is Mur-phy, — For the

Ditch-man next door told me straight, — That the

break-er starts full time on Mon-day, — That's

phat he told me at an-y rate. — Sure the

boss he told Mick-ey this morn-ing, — When

he's 'bout to en-ter the mines, — That the

coal was quite scarce [down] 'bout New York, — And the

break-er would start on full time. —

Chorus

And it's o - ho-ho, my, if the news be true, Me

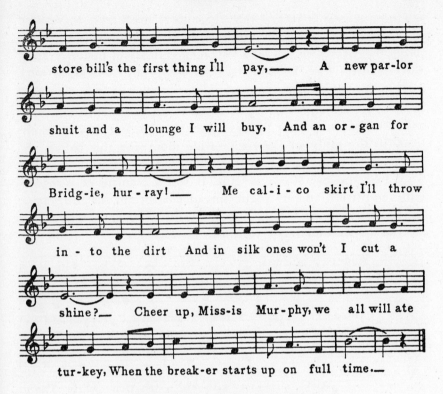

store bill's the first thing I'll pay,—— A new par-lor
shuit and a lounge I will buy, And an or-gan for
Bridg-ie, hur-ray!—— Me cal-i-co skirt I'll throw
in-to the dirt And in silk ones won't I cut a
shine?—— Cheer up, Miss-is Mur-phy, we all will ate
tur-key, When the break-er starts up on full time.——

2. I'll ne'er stick a hand in the washtub,
 The Chinee man he'll get me trade,
 I'll ne'er pick a coal on the dirt bank,
 I'll buy everything ready made.
 I'll dress up me children like fairies,
 I'll build up a house neat and fine,
 And we'll move away from the Hungaries,
 When the breaker starts up on full time.

CHORUS
And it's oh-ho-ho, my, if the news be true,
 Me store bill's the first thing I'll pay,
A new parlor shuit and a lounge I'll buy,
 And an organ for Bridgie, hurray!
Me calico skirt I'll throw into the dirt
 And in silk ones won't I cut a shine?
Cheer up, Missis Murphy, we all will ate turkey,
 When the breaker starts up on full time.

The Avondale Mine Disaster

(From the Archive of American Folk Song, Library of Congress. Sung by John J. Quinn at Wilkes-Barre, 1946. Recorded by George Korson.)

"The Avondale Mine Disaster" tells the story of the anthracite industry's first major tragedy in 1869. When fire swept the primitive Avondale mine near Wilkes-Barre, 110 men and boys lost their lives. In the midst of the region-wide mourning this ballad appeared, seemingly from nowhere. Hundreds of penny broadsides were sold and everybody sang it. It was a favorite of itinerant miner-minstrels, and its vogue spread far beyond the anthracite region. Variants have been found by folk-song collectors as far away as Newfoundland.

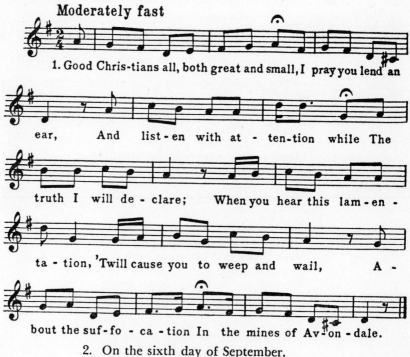

1. Good Christians all, both great and small, I pray you lend an ear, And listen with attention while The truth I will declare; When you hear this lamentation, 'Twill cause you to weep and wail, About the suffocation In the mines of Avondale.

2. On the sixth day of September,
   Eighteen sixty-nine,
   Those miners all then got a call
   To go work in the mine;
   But little did they think that [day]
   That death would soon prevail

Before they would return again from
    The mines of Avondale.

3. The women and their children,
    Their hearts were filled with joy
To see their men go to their work
    Likewise every boy;
But a dismal sight in broad daylight,
    Soon made them turn pale,
When they saw the breaker burning
    O'er the mines of Avondale.

4. From here and there and everywhere,
    They gathered in a crowd,
Some tearing off their clothes and hair,
    And crying out aloud—
"Get out our husbands and our sons,
    Death he's going to steal
Their lives away without delay
    In the mines of Avondale."

5. But all in vain, there was no hope
    One single soul to save,
For there is no second outlet
    From the subterranean cave.
No pen can write the awful fright
    And horror that prevailed,
Among those dying victims,
    In the mines of Avondale.

6. A consultation then was held.
    'Twas asked who'd volunteer
For to go down this dismal shaft
    To seek their comrades dear;
Two Welshmen brave, without dismay,
    And courage without fail,
Went down the shaft, without delay,
    In the mines of Avondale.

7. When at the bottom they arrived,
    And thought to make their way,
One of them died for want of air,
    While the other in great dismay,
He gave a sign to hoist him up,
    To tell the dreadful tale,
That all were lost forever
    In the mines of Avondale.

8. Every effort then took place
    To send down some fresh air;
The men that next went down again
    They took of them good care;
And traversed through the chambers,
    And this time did not fail
In finding those dead bodies
    In the mines of Avondale.

9. Sixty-seven was the number
    That in a heap were found.
It seemed that they were bewailing
    Their fate underneath the ground;
They found the father with his son
    Clasped in his arms so pale.
It was a heart-rending scene
    In the mines of Avondale.

10. Now to conclude, and make an end,
    Their number I'll pen down—
A hundred and ten of brave strong men
    Were smothered underground;
They're in their graves till the last day,
    Their widows may bewail,
And the orphans' cries they rend the skies
    All around through Avondale!

The Miner's Doom

(From the Archive of American Folk Song, Library of Congress. Sung by Daniel Walsh at Centralia, Columbia County, 1946. Recorded by George Korson.)

"The Miner's Doom" is an old Welsh ballad long popular in the anthracite region, where many of the miners are of Welsh descent. It was brought over from Wales by Thomas Jones of Seek, Schuylkill County, who originally sang it for me in 1925.

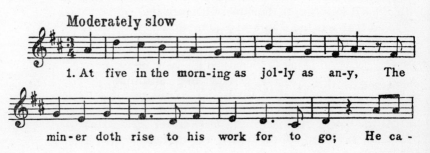

Moderately slow

1. At five in the morn-ing as jol-ly as an-y, The min-er doth rise to his work for to go; He ca-

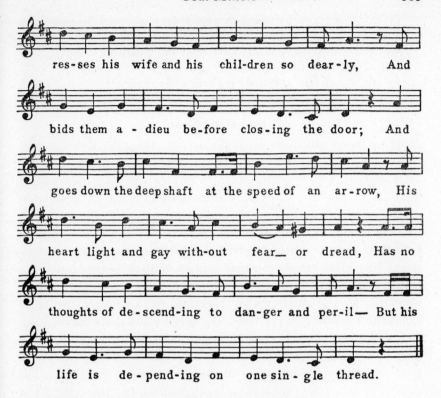

res - ses his wife and his chil-dren so dear-ly, And

bids them a - dieu be-fore clos-ing the door; And

goes down the deep shaft at the speed of an ar-row, His

heart light and gay with-out fear__ or dread, Has no

thoughts of de - scend-ing to dan-ger and per-il— But his

life is de - pend-ing on one sin - gle thread.

2. His wife is his queen and his home is his palace,
   His children his glory, to maintain them he tries;
He'll work like a hero; he faces all danger.
   He'll deprive his own self their bare feet to hide.
Now his day's work is o'er; he's homeward returning,
   He thinks not how the change in an hour will be.
But he thinks how his wife and his children will greet him—
   But his home and his children he'll nevermore see.

3. Now his wife had been dreaming of her husband so dearly;
   She'd seen him in danger—"God help me," she cried;
Too true was the dream of a poor woman's sorrow—
   The rope broke ascending; her dear husband died.
Their home that morning was as jovial as any,
   But a dark cloud came rolling straight o'er their door—
A widow, three children are left for to mourn him,
   The one that they ne'er will see any more.

4. At the day of his funeral the great crowds had gathered,
   He was loved by his friends, by his neighbors, by all.

To the grave went his corpse, by his friends he was followed;
  The tears from our eyes like the rain they did fall.
And the widow, lamenting the fate of her husband,
  Brokenhearted she died on the dear loved one's tomb.
To the world now is left their three little children
  Whose father had met with a coal miner's doom.

Two-Cent Coal

(Sung by David Morrison, 81, at Finlayville, Allegheny County, 1940.
Recorded by George Korson.)

"Two-Cent Coal" commemorates one of the most devastating
disasters in the history of the Monongahela River. During that
winter of 1876 the river was frozen to a depth of fourteen inches.
Because of the ice the mines were idle from Christmas to late in
February, and the miners barely kept alive. Previously, the miners'
wages had been cut from three cents a bushel to two cents, the
equivalent of fifty cents a ton, a rate the miners regarded as sub-
standard. In the disaster that overtook the operators' property
when the ice broke in the river, the miners saw the hand of God.

This tune is closely related to some versions of the come-all-ye
song "Foreman Young Monroe" ("The Jam on Gerry's Rocks").
It is of interest to note that the singer follows the come-all-ye
custom of dropping into speaking voice on the last few syllables of
the last stanza. Samuel P. Bayard thinks this variant of the tune
is quite rare outside the Northeast. "Its recovery in southwestern
Pennsylvania," he writes, "is another bit of evidence that the
commonwealth has been a meeting and mingling ground of northeastern and southern traditions—and a possible center whence these
mingled traditions were diffused westward."*

Moderately slow (*somewhat free*)

·1 Oh, the boss-es' tricks of 'sev-en-ty-six They met with some suc-

cess,   Un - til the hand of God came down And

* *California Folklore Quarterly*, III, No. 2 (April 1944), pp. 161-63.

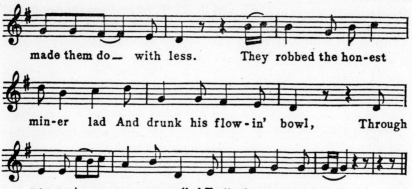

made them do— with less. They robbed the hon-est

min-er lad And drunk his flow-in' bowl, Through

pov-er-ty we were com-pelled To dig them two-cent coal.

2. But the river it bein' frozen—
    Of course, the poor might starve;
   What did those tyrant bosses say?
    "It's just what they deserve."
   But God who always aids the just,
    All things He does control,
   He broke the ice and He sent it down
    And sunk their two-cent coal.

3. Their tipples, too, fled from our view,
    And down the river went.
   They seemed to cry as they passed by:
    "You tyrants, now repent!
   For while you rob the miner lad,
    Remember, you've a soul,
   For your soul is sinkin' deeper
    Than the ice sunk your two-cent coal."

4. It's to conclude and finish,
    Let us help our fellow man,
   And if our brother's in distress
    Assist him if you can,
   To keep the wolf off from his door,
    And shelter him from the cold,
   That he never again shall commit the crime
    Of diggin' two-cent coal.

John J. Curtis

(From the Archive of American Folk Song, Library of Congress. Sung by Andrew Rada at Shenandoah, 1946. Recorded by George Korson.)

John J. Curtis was blinded while at work in the Morea colliery,

Schuylkill County, in 1888. Led by a boy, he roamed the anthracite region singing this ballad, and selling broadsides on which it was printed. The text was made for him by the Lansford bard, Joseph Gallagher, from whom I obtained it in 1925.

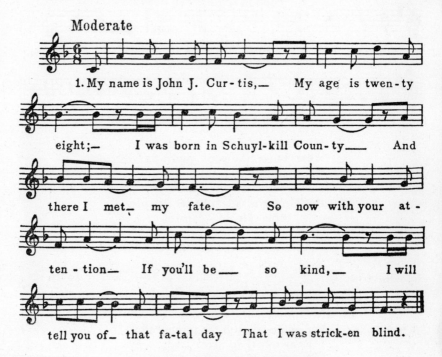

Moderate

1. My name is John J. Cur-tis,— My age is twen-ty eight;— I was born in Schuyl-kill Coun-ty__ And there I met— my fate.__ So now with your at-ten-tion— If you'll be__ so kind,— I will tell you of— that fa-tal day That I was strick-en blind.

2. It was on a bright May morning,
   As the sun peeped o'er the hill,
   The little birds sang loud and sweet,
   And I seem to hear them still;
   My heart was filled with purest joy
   As to the mines I did stray,
   To earn an honest living
   In the colliery of P.A.*

3. At eight o'clock I climbed the pitch,
   And to my work did go,
   I drilled two holes and loaded them—
   Touched one and fled below.
   It soon went off; I then went back
   To the one that did remain,

* Originally "Morea."

When by its mouth it too went off
    And blew me down again.

4. I lay there in the darkness;
        I was buried in the coal.
    The blood in streams ran down my cheeks;
        Great lumps o'er me did roll.
    When I got free, my cap and lamp
        Was all that I could find,
    And when I struck a match,
        'Twas then I knew that I was blind.

5. Now, kind folks, do have pity
        On whom you chance to find
    Wandering through your city,
        That in both eyes is blind;
    You know not when your day will come
        That this same path you'll stray,
    So be kindhearted while you can
            To the miner from Morea.

Union Man

(From the Archive of American Folk Song, Library of Congress. Sung
by Albert Morgan in the Newkirk Tunnel Mine near Tamaqua, 1946.
Recorded by George Korson.)

This short ditty is an excellent example of the way the folk
reflect in their songs the varied phases of their life. Better than
an economist's report, the five stanzas are a satiric comment on
rising wages and rising prices. Composed by the singer, the song
has circulated widely in the lower anthracite region.

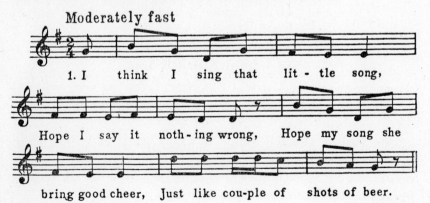

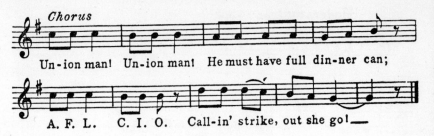

Un-ion man! Un-ion man! He must have full din-ner can;

A. F. L.   C. I. O.   Call-in' strike, out she go!__

2. We all got contract, she expire;
   Mr. Lewis mad like fire;
   Miners strikin' too much time,
   Uncle Sam take over mines.

   CHORUS
   Union man! Union man!
   He must have full dinner can!
   A.F.L., C.I.O.,
   Callin' strike, out she go!

3. We signin' contract, we get raise
   After strikin' twenty days.
   Butcher comes and ringin' bell
   He raises price—what the hell!

4. I'm drinkin' too much beer last night;
   To go to work I don't feel right.
   In my can some bread and meat,
   I'm too dam' sick I cannot eat.

5. I fire shot at ten o'clock,
   Tumble brushes full of rock,
   Timber breakin' o'er my head,
   Jeepers cripes, I think I'm dead!

Me Johnny Mitchell Man

(From the Archive of American Folk Song, Library of Congress. Sung
by Jerry Byrne at Buck Run, Schuylkill County, 1946. Recorded by
George Korson.)

"Me Johnny Mitchell Man," by Con Carbon of Wilkes-Barre,
made its appearance during the 1902 anthracite strike as an expression of the Slavic miners' loyalty to John Mitchell, the miners'
leader.

Moderate, free

1. Oh, you know Joe Sil-o-vat-sky, Dat man is my brud-der; Last

night is come to my shan-ty: "John, I'm come and tell you for, I'm-a

tell you for to-mor-ra, John, Eve-nink dark as night; Lots-a

min - ers all, beeg and schmall, Gon-na have a shtrike.

Dunt be shcab-by fel-la, John, Dat's I'm tell you right," he say

"No sir, Mike, come out on shtrike, I'm John-ny Mitch-ell man."

Chorus

Vell, I'm-a dunt a-fraid for not-tink, Dat's me nev-er shcare,

Come on shtrike to-mor-ra night Dat's de busi-ness, I dunt care.

Right-a here I'm tell you, Me not shcab-by fel-la, I'm a

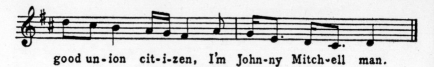

good un - ion   cit - i - zen,   I'm   John - ny   Mitch - ell   man.

2. Vell, me belong for union,
   I'm good citizen,
   Seven, mebbe 'leven year,
   I'm vorkin' in beeg, beeg 'Merica;
   I'm vorkin' fer de Black Heat',
   Down in de Lytle Shaft,
   In de Nottingham, Conyngham
   And every place like dat.
   I'm got lotsa money,
   Nine hoondret mebbe ten,
   And shtrike kin come, like son-of-a-gun.
   I'm Johnny Mitchell man.

   CHORUS
   Vell, I'm-a dunt afraid for nottink,
   Dat's me never shcare,
   Come on shtrike tomorra night—
   Dat's de business, I dunt care.
   Right-a here I'm tell you,
   Me not shcabby fella.
   I'm a good union citizen,
   I'm Johnny Mitchell man.

On Johnny Mitchell's Train

(From the Archive of American Folk Song, Library of Congress. Sung
by Jerry Byrne at Buck Run, Schuylkill County, 1946. Recorded by
George Korson.)

During the 1902 strike, which lasted about six months, many
strikers left for the big cities in search of work to tide them over
until the settlement. Having no fare for regular passenger trains,
they hopped freight trains, jocularly termed "Johnny Mitchell
specials," after the miners' leader.

Moderate

1. I'm   an   hon - est   un - ion   lab-orin'   man,   And   I'll

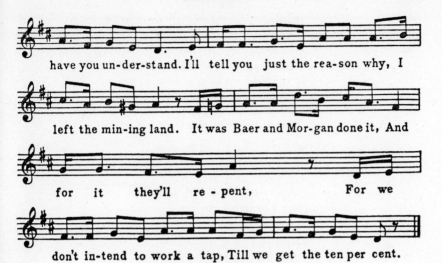

have you un-der-stand. I'll tell you just the rea-son why, I

left the min-ing land. It was Baer and Mor-gan done it, And

for it they'll re - pent, For we

don't in-tend to work a tap, Till we get the ten per cent.

CHORUS*

There's no use for Mr. Durkin,
In the coal mine to be workin';
We were a little shaky,
    But no longer we're in pain.
So what's the use o' kickin',
When the top and bottom's stickin'?
I'll pack me grip and make a trip
    On Johnny Mitchell's train.

2. I struck a place called Coatesville,
        A flourishin' iron town,
    Where politics were very strong,
        And candidates goin' round.
    I was invited to a party,
        He says, "Phat are you doin', Dan?"
    I says, "I'll tell you plumb and plain,
        I'm a Johnny Mitchell Man."

3. When I landed in New York City,
        I a friend of course did meet,
    I axed him if he would show me
        The place they call Wall Street.
    I met several operators,
        Assembled in a mob,
    Along with Morgan's president,
        I think they called him Schwab.

* Sung to the same tune.

4. The small operators they were pl'adin',
  And they wanted to give in,
  And recognize the union—
   But Baer said that's too thin.
  So it broke up in a wrangle,
   Put Baer nearly insane,
  Then I took a side-door Pullman car
   On Johnny Mitchell's train.

5. So I'll bid ye all adieu now,
  Let ye bid me the same,
  The strike is nearly over,
   And with joy I'm near insane.
  Here's health unto the union,
   Which is very strong they say,
  Likewise to the conductor
   On Johnny Mitchell's train.

Muff Lawler, the Squealer

(From the Archive of the American Folk Song, Library of Congress.
Sung by Joseph McCarthy at Shenandoah, 1946. Recorded by George
Korson.)

  Michael "Muff" Lawler was once the "Boss Molly" of Shenandoah. I made this recording in his home town. Lawler acquired his peculiar nickname from breeding mufflers, a strain of fine gamecocks that found their way into many of the cockpits of the region. He was tried in the Schuylkill County courts in 1876 as an accessory after the fact in the murder of Thomas Sanger, a mine foreman, and William Uren, a miner, at Raven Run. When the jury disagreed he was retried and convicted but saved his neck by turning state's evidence. As an informer he drew a storm of jeers upon his head. The ballad "Muff Lawler, the Squealer" appeared to mock him. I first heard it sung at Philadelphia in 1925 by a self-exiled Molly who told me that in the seventies he had fled to escape arrest. I shall never forget the mocking tone and the trembling voice with which that elderly man sang it. I have since then recorded several variants of this song, but none moved me as that original one, the text of which appears in *Songs and Ballads of the Anthracite Miner.*

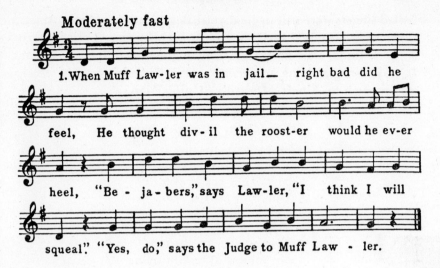

1. When Muff Law-ler was in jail— right bad did he feel, He thought div-il the roost-er would he ev-er heel, "Be-ja-bers," says Law-ler, "I think I will squeal." "Yes, do," says the Judge to Muff Law-ler.

2. It was down in the office the lawyers did meet,
   "Come in, Mr. Lawler"; they gave him a seat.
   "Give us your whole history and don't us deceive."
   "Bejabers, I will," says Muff Lawler.

3. "There are some o' thim near," he says, "and more o' thim far;
   There are some o' thim you'll never catch I do fear."
   "If they are on this earth," he says, "we'll have them I'm sure."
   "Yes, but bejabers they're dead," says Muff Lawler.

4. "It's the live ones we want, not the dead ones at all."
   "If you want the whole history, you'll have to take dead ones and
      all."
   "Come out with your history or quickly we'll plant
   You back in your cell, Mr. Lawler."

5. "Now I'll commence," he says, "me whole story to tell,
   When I go back to Shenandoah, I'll be shot sure as hell."
   "We'll send you to a country where you're not known so well."
   "Bejabers, that's good," says Muff Lawler.

I wish to acknowledge the courtesy of the Library of Congress
in permitting me to include in this chapter some of the anthracite
ballads that I recorded for its Archive of American Folk Song in
1946. I was able to record again most of the anthracite ballads in
my published collections because some of the best traditional

ballad singers were still in good voice despite advanced age. Among them were Dan Walsh, Jerry Byrne, Bill Keating, Tom Roberts, Andrew Rada, Dan Brennan, Morgan Jones, and John J. Quinn. It was also gratifying to record several ballads of more recent origin, such as Albert Morgan's "Union Man."

Oilmen

By HARRY BOTSFORD

In a small area in northwestern Pennsylvania, the science of drill-ing and producing oil had its genesis. Before Edwin L. Drake sank the world's first successful drilled oil well at Titusville in 1859, petroleum production had been dependent on the limited amount that was found in springs, crevices, salt and water wells, and as a greasy scum on rivers and creeks. Oilmen in the section of Pennsylvania around Oil Creek in Venango County and a small segment of Crawford County developed many basic methods of procuring oil in large quantities and utilizing it as a fuel and an illuminant. Consequently, they are responsible for many of the revolutionary changes that the widespread use of petroleum has brought to the world.

The first American prospectors along Oil Creek encountered in the sand a number of oil pits approximately eight feet in diameter and twenty feet deep. Cribbed with oil-soaked logs, the pits had obviously been used for the collection of oil that seeped through the sand into the pits. Little is known of the pits' origin; the Indians who were questioned confessed to ignorance, for there were no legends about the pits in their century-old tribal lore. Some authorities contend that the mysterious race of mound builders, antedating the Indians who inhabited the region, built the pits, but this theory is denied by other experts who believe that the logs were too deftly fitted to have been fashioned by the crude instruments of the mound builders. The questions of who built the ancient oil pits, how and where the petroleum was used, and how it was transported seem destined to remain unanswered.

Indians valued the oil of the region for its curative qualities— quite different from its commercial importance today. Oil seeps into springs on the banks of Oil Creek, which winds crookedly into the Allegheny River. The quantity of oil in the spring water feeding into the creek was not large, but it was sufficient to give the waters of the stream the iridescent film from which it got its name.

To one spring, where all tribes met in amity, came each year Seneca and other Indian tribes. According to legend, the Indians, bringing with them their ailing and wounded, gathered shortly after the spring floods. There were days of fasting while the sick tribesmen were bathed and laid in the sun and while the squaws gathered oil from the creek by spreading blankets on the surface of the water. After they had absorbed oil, the blankets were laboriously wrung out into clay bowls.

On a night when there was a full moon, the climatic event of the pilgrimage took place. The Indians, painted and feathered, lined the banks of the stream, on which burned only one fire. The chief medicine man seized a burning brand from the fire, uttered an incantation, and tossed the torch into the creek at a point where the water was covered with a heavy scum of oil. The oil caught fire, and the leaping flames spread rapidly. Soon the creek was ablaze for a mile downstream. In a few minutes the fire died down, leaving in the air the tangy smoke of burned oil, through which the moon shone dimly. Then new campfires were lighted; venison and fish were cooked. While savory smells drenched the air, the medicine men concentrated on care of the ill and injured. Wounds were bandaged and soaked with oil from the earthen bowls; the ailing members of the tribe were forced to swallow some of the oil. Although the medication seems to have been primitive, the Indians were convinced of its effectiveness. The ritual, followed by feasting and dancing, was carried on for several days. When the celebration was completed, the tribesmen carried those who had not recovered to a new camp ground a few miles away where there flowed a mineral spring. As a last resort the sufferers were forced to drink large quantities of the water.

Years after the 1790's when white men, led by gigantic Jonathan Titus, settled the village of Titusville, the water near Oil Creek was still esteemed by the Indians for medicinal purposes. One tribesman also sensed the commercial value of oil. Alone and somewhat bedraggled, he would go from house to house in Titusville and endeavor to sell bottles of crude oil as a medicine. However, most of the white settlers were skeptical about its benefits and would chase the peddler away.

For years the presence of oil was almost forgotten by the white settlers. A few remembered it as something of a local curiosity. In the early 1840's the lumbering firm of Brewer, Watson & Company erected a sawmill on Oil Creek and built a dam to drive the water wheel. Near the mill was a spring from which the millowners collected oil to lubricate the sawmill machinery; thus, the little mill acquires stature as having the first machinery to be lubricated with crude oil.

During the same decade Samuel Kier, a druggist from Pittsburgh, noticed that drillers of the salt wells around Tarentum often found in their product a greasy fluid that ruined the salt water and spoiled its palatability. Kier conceived the idea of vending the oil as a cure-all and had it retailed in gaudy, fantastically painted wagons. He also experimented to see if the oil was an illuminant and discovered that it burned readily but with an unpleasant odor. Kier marketed his product as "Kier's Carbon Oil," after he had distilled it twice and found that it had practical uses. As his source of raw material depended on the bad luck of salt-well drillers, his expansion was sharply limited. It never occurred to him to drill for oil.

Nevertheless, Kier's interest in securing petroleum with which to make his product provided the impetus for the drilling of the first well. In the mid-1850's, Dr. Francis Brewer of Brewer, Watson & Company was consumed with curiosity as to what the oil was and whether the raw material had any commercial potentialities. He employed J. D. Angier to dig a system of trenches to collect the oil; this project was mildly successful but the expenses consumed the profits. Brewer then took three flasks of the oil to his old mentor, Professor Dixi Crosby at Dartmouth College, asking him to analyze its contents and to give his opinion as to its practical value. The professor deprecated oil's money-making future, and Brewer determined to forget his pipe dream.

After Brewer returned to Titusville, the professor told his son, Albert, and their lawyer friend, George H. Bissell, of Brewer's strange liquid. The two young men were immediately fired with wild plans of making fortunes through large-scale production of oil. They interested Bissell's partner, Jonathan Eveleth, in the plan. With no initial investment of money, they promoted a stock company with a $250,000 stock structure, a neat bit of financing. Eventually this company, the Seneca Oil Company, met with reverses, moved to New Haven, and came under the control of James W. Townsend, a cold-blooded, shrewd banker. Acting on Bissell's theory that oil production could be increased through drilling wells—which he formed allegedly after seeing a derrick in one of Kier's Rock Oil advertisements—Townsend hired Edwin L. Drake to go to Titusville to drill for oil.

In 1858 Drake, an ex-railroad conductor, arrived in the oil country but could not find immediately the equipment or men to drill for oil. As his funds were soon exhausted and his New Haven backers refused further advances, he had to borrow money from a merchant and a druggist in Titusville to continue the project. By May 1859 he had procured the necessary machinery and a driller, Uncle Billy Smith. In late August, Uncle Billy's boring tools suddenly hit a petroleum deposit at a depth of sixty-nine feet, and oil came up the drivepipe. Their success was a remarkable bit of luck, for petroleum was never found at that depth afterward in the area, and if the well had been drilled a few feet in any direction from the spot Uncle Billy had chosen, the deposit would have been missed.

As a result of this fortuitous circumstance, the industry grew apace, and rapidly extended operations down Oil Creek, up and down the little valleys, into the rugged farmland, in an area miles from where Drake had proved that oil could be found by punching a hole down to the oil-producing sands. The volume of oil produced, transported, refined, and marketed the first few years is astonishing. Public acceptance of oil was established in a very short time because the world was waiting for a cheap, dependable illuminant and lubricant. Long before August 1859, more than fifty oil refineries were distilling shale coal for kerosene oil. When a ready volume of crude oil was made available, the refineries shortened their process by using crude oil instead of coal, and thus produced a better illuminant.

Just as in any industry in which there is a spectacular discovery of the raw material, tremendous booms developed whenever there was a valuable strike, and often quickly subsided. Great fortunes were made overnight and almost as rapidly were lost. Just as coal mining did, the oil fields produced some fabulous characters whose greatly embellished exploits will be remembered by their successors in the industry. For instance, there was I. N. Frazer, the tall, laughing wildcatter who opened up the famed Pithole oil fields. No oilman will forget Samuel Van Syckel who built the first successful pipe line for the transportation of crude oil. Van Syckel broke the monopoly held by almost sixteen thousand teamsters who had the oil producers in an economic wringer. The "Pipe Line War" had its casualties, particularly when the enraged teamsters attempted to destroy the pipe line.

Colonel E. A. L. Roberts' fame is an integral part of oil-field history. Roberts invented a system of "shooting" wells with nitroglycerin, a process that revived old oil wells and made newly drilled wells more productive. The industry fought this patent, and the fight probably engendered more court cases than ever ensued from any other patent dispute. Roberts, however, won every case. Infringers, daring men who mixed nitro in wooden tubs under cover of darkness and carried it in jugs to shoot oil wells illegally, were known as "moonlighters." Death walked with these men and often nudged them into a stumble that exploded the nitro. The "Moonlighters' War" also had many casualties.

Finally the industry accepted the mandates of the courts and paid the prices asked by the Roberts organization.

In the background of oil lore is a host of little men—the forgotten individuals who came to the oil fields seeking their fortunes and made substantial but obscure contributions to the development of the industry. These men came from everywhere; some of them were freshly discharged from military service in the Civil War, and were looking for excitement and opportunity. Many came from the cities; they were usually young, and weary of boring jobs and living in a commercial world where there was little opportunity. A few of these hopefuls eventually became oil producers and died wealthy and serene in the knowledge that their dreams had been realized. John Wilkes Booth was one of these background figures in the oil fields.

Most of the men became and stayed drillers, tool-dressers, teamsters, pumpers, rig builders, or roustabouts. Newcomers quickly discovered that the work was rugged and called for great and sustained physical exertion. Those who couldn't stand the gaff were soon weeded out and hastily returned to a safe, placid existence. Drillers and tool-dressers labored for twelve hours straight, whether they worked the "afternoon tour" (the shift from noon until midnight) or the "morning tour" (the remaining twelve hours). The pumper had to be a man of many skills and talents, for his duties included those of an engineer, a fireman, a plumber, a carpenter, a blacksmith, and an ordinary laborer. In theory, he was on duty twenty-four hours a day. He might be paid only $50 a month, but on this small wage he lived comfortably. He was given a house, which was supplied with free gas for heating and illumination, and a generous tract of land. There was an abundance of game and plenty of trout in the streams. He was, and still is, his own boss.

Oil-well shooters rode wagons filled with felt-lined cells in which were packed gallons of nitro; they were paid the highest wage, for a substantial percentage of them died lonely, quick deaths. Even today when they drive specially designed trucks equipped with every possible safeguard, their fatality rate is so unreasonably high that no insurance company will accept them as risks.

Oil-producing was a new industry with no experienced men to

give the answers to mechanical problems. When faced with an unfamiliar situation, every oilman had to rely on a philosophy that made a creed of trial and error, and use all his powers of ingenuity. These men, most of them in the host of forgotten individuals, considered whipping a problem a routine part of the job. Hundreds of unknown oilmen could have become wealthy had they patented the processes they invented. Drake himself was such a man. Had he patented his invention for using a drivepipe instead of a drill when quicksand was encountered, he might have died a rich man instead of a ward of the state, as he actually did. Most of his original backers were also lost in penniless obscurity. A Titusville oil producer, Andrew Fasenmeyer, invented the process of condensing natural gas into gasoline. But he never patented his process. No one knows who invented the system of multiple production of oil wells from one central powerhouse—an important contribution. The Pennsylvania oil fields are still the laboratory of the whole oil industry, where new methods of production are devised by men who can think, reason, and experiment.

From 1859 until January 1864, the expansion of the new industry was quite orderly as it progressed down the valley of Oil Creek. Every well drilled was something of an adventure, but there was a minimum of uncertainty if wildcatters drilled in the valley, where profitable small wells usually resulted. Some oil producers recognized that drilling, as it progressed down the valley, would be sharply constricted when the Allegheny River was reached. They wondered if it would be possible to find oil in paying quantities outside the immediate area of Oil Creek. Drilling in a virgin sector is a sheer gamble, but there are always a few men who have the courage and the money to risk such a venture. I. N. Frazer was one of these reckless individuals; he was also blessed with luck. He leased the Holmden farm in the Pithole Creek area, a bleak, unproductive farm country, and drilled his first well on January 7, 1864. It was a gusher—the first one that had ever been drilled. The flow averaged about six hundred barrels of prime crude oil a day.

It was inevitable that, with such a fantastic flow of wealth, the area would be quickly settled and hundreds of new wells would be drilled almost immediately. To the astonishment of the natives,

Pithole City, a big and rambling community, was built almost over-night. Before the drilling of the Holmden well, one could have bought every farm in the vicinity for a few thousand dollars. When the residents heard that a big hotel, one of about two dozen, was being erected on ground that *rented* for $14,000, they were certain they lived in a crazy world. They were not entirely wrong, for it was, indeed, an era when strange, fantastic things happened. Almost before people realized it, the wilderness with its dozens of rich, flowing oil wells had become a city of over 30,000 inhabitants, a community with a daily newspaper, a waterworks, hundreds of saloons and dives, and many ornate, expensive hotels. In volume of mail received at the local post office, the city of Pithole ranked third in the commonwealth.

Fact and fiction are inextricably mixed in the tales about the picturesque crew of men and women who flocked to the city. Ben Hogan, for example, reputedly had been a spy for both sides during the Civil War—and supposedly had made money at it! He had been a pretty good prize fighter. Given to boasting that he had killed four men, he gloried in his wickedness and placed over his saloon a big sign that shouted: "Ben Hogan—Wickedest Man in the World." Old-time oilmen who knew Hogan insist that the sign was no overstatement. His consort, "French Kate," likewise rumored to have acted as a C.S.A. spy, was a voluptuous redhead of slight morals. Hogan's place had a bad reputation; drunken customers were robbed, slugged, and carried down to the banks of Pithole Creek to recover. Yet, in spite of its ill fame, the Hogan saloon prospered and was filled twenty-four hours a day.

For years, Hogan followed the boom oil towns. When law and order finally took over, he fled to a large river-boat saloon, where he again prospered. In his last days he became an evangelist. Oil-men, suspecting him of the worst, doubted his sincerity when he announced that he would hold a series of meetings in Oil City. Before he could leave his train, he was met by a delegation of grim oilmen who issued a terse ultimatum: Hogan was given a choice of staying in Oil City and being immediately lynched or remaining on his train. Ben wisely accepted the safe alternative.

During his stay in lawless Pithole City, Hogan feuded constantly with another shady character, one "Stonehouse Jack," who was a fellow saloonkeeper and also a pugilist of sorts. This man was possessed with an impish quality; every so often, just for the fun of it, he and his cohorts would stage a raid on Hogan's place and smash it up in a most thorough manner. Hogan took a couple of pot shots at Stonehouse Jack, but his aim was poor.

When Pithole City was still a bright memory, Stonehouse Jack was suspected of a trifle of arson in Titusville. The citizens immediately formed a committee that acted promptly and firmly. Without benefit of trial, Stonehouse Jack was escorted to the railroad station, placed on a Buffalo-bound train, and given a ticket. It was, the committee pointed out, a one-way ticket, and they grimly reminded him that if he returned, they proposed to hang him without ceremony.

A few days later the *Titusville Herald* published a letter from Stonehouse Jack. It was a sort of thank-you letter, impish and puckish, indicative of the strange character of the man. This letter, to the best of my knowledge, is the curtain speech of Stonehouse Jack:

I avail myself of this, my first leisure moment since my return to Buffalo, to convey to your paper my heartfelt thanks to the citizens of Titusville for the very hospitable manner in which I was received and entertained during my late stay in your city.

To the committee of vigilance who so kindly relieved me of every expense during my stay and furnished me with free transportation to Buffalo and to citizens generally who joined in the procession to the cars on my departure, my thanks are especially due. As also to those persons (their names, I regret, being unknown to me) who, in the goodness of their hearts made their arrangements to raise me to a more "elevated" position than I desire to occupy.

In conclusion I wish to say, Messers. Editors, if you or any of the persons above referred to, visit this precious locality, I assure you, you and they will receive a warm reception upon making themselves known to

Yours respectfully,
Stonehouse Jack.

What finally happened to Pithole was inevitable. Flowing wells were not always encountered by the probing drills. The pitifully young industry knew but little of the art and science of keeping oil wells producing. As a result, wells quickly lost their productivity. There were other men like Frazer, daring individuals who explored for new oil fields and often found them. New boom oil towns suddenly loomed on the horizon and beckoned to Pithole City residents anxious for new opportunity and more excitement. With the opening of a new field, there would be a trickle of Pithole inhabitants filtering out to the fresh wells.

In February 1866, just after the daily parade of the painted ladies on their saddle horses, smoke swelled lazily into the clear sky. There was a bad fire at the lower end of Holmden Street. As the buildings were all wooden, the fire spread rapidly before it was stopped. The homeless didn't bother to rebuild; they left, traveling over the twenty-foot-wide plank road that led to Pleasantville and other points.

Then on a blazing hot day in June, another destructive fire created havoc. The volunteer fire department didn't function well. When the smoke cleared away, the wicked little city was no more; only a few dozen buildings remained. No one mourned much. There were many places to go: Red Hot, Shamburg, Cash-Up, Ball Town, Pleasantville. The residents left, most of them without a single backward glance. Many of them were singing. A very few of them had made fortunes; many had earned a good wage; some had lost their wealth. But, from that time on, however, they were bound with invisible ties to the oil industry. Not many of them ever returned to a more placid, less exciting way of life.

A few years after the final fire, only seven people lived in the area, now a Pennsylvania phantom city. The lumber used to build one of the largest hotels sold for a few dollars as kindling wood. All that is left today is a hillside covered with lean scrub oaks and scanty grass. A few dimples in the terrain are the only remains of the cellars of the buildings along famous Holmden Street. The walls of the old reservoir are still solid, but the water is gone. There isn't an oil well in sight. An old-timer may point out the scrubby acres of a farm that was once valued at a million dollars. The owner refused to sell until he had reaped a crop of buckwheat. When the buckwheat ripened, the final curtain had been rung down and the land had reverted to its original value.

As long as there is an oil industry, its men will spin tales of Pithole City and the things that happened in the area within a radius of fifteen miles of what was once the third largest city in the state.

Often they will talk about the Benninghoff robbery. John Benninghoff lived on a farm that fronted Oil Creek and produced oil in a most abundant manner. Distrusting banks, he kept most of his royalty earnings in two safes in his home. Robbers visited his house one cold night, opened one safe, and extracted $260,000. They overlooked the second safe, which was stuffed with almost as much loot. The robbers made a clean getaway, but later several of them were captured and convicted. One man had invested his share in an Ohio brewery. Benninghoff took title after a civil suit—to the delight of oilmen, for Benninghoff had been a most ardent prohibitionist! The leader of the bandits escaped with the major share of the loot, and invested it in a large ranch in Colorado. It is said he prospered there and became a respected citizen.

Oilmen will never forget John Washington Steele, the legendary "Coal Oil Johnny." Steele was brought up by an aunt who owned some very rich oil land near Rouseville. She died suddenly and tragically, and Steele, not yet of legal age, found himself heir to a great fortune with a daily income of nearly $2,800. When he reached the age of twenty-one, his inheritance was turned over to him. Losing his head, he left his wife and child and started a spending spree that lasted about two years.

During his orgy he committed a series of insanities that led to a Philadelphia newspaperman's dubbing him "Coal Oil Johnny." While in his cups—which was most of the time—he would throw money away and sign any document placed before him. In Philadelphia, where he lived for a while, his prodigality made the headlines with great frequency. Once, when a hotel clerk was discourteous, Coal Oil Johnny rented the hotel for a day at a charge of $8,000, fired the clerk, and offered free food and drink to anyone who came near the hotel. The place was a shambles at the end of the day. Coal Oil Johnny had his own carriage, a gaudy affair with a strange coat of arms on the doors; it depicted flowing oil wells, derricks, and tanks. He backed minstrel troupes and lost money in crooked card games.

Inevitably he lost all his inheritance. In two years he spent nearly one and a quarter million dollars. However, he seemed relieved when he realized that the money was gone, for neither he nor his aunt had ever really enjoyed it. When he returned home, he was twenty-three years old. He hunted up his wife and told her that he was ready to settle down. She forgave him and helped him to become a model of industry and a respected railroad employee. Never again did he drink.

Wherever oilmen gather, whether in an exclusive club or in an engine house in eastern Texas, the chances are that the talk will eventually swing to Gib Morgan and his stories. Oilmen tell me that they have heard the stories in the steamy jungles of India, deep in the Malay country, in the arctic cold of Siberia—wherever oil is found. To the younger generation of oilmen, Morgan is a legend. He has been dead many years, but his amazing tales live and grow and appear to have an astonishing vitality and durability. To us of the older generation, the man was very real. As a youngster I saw and heard him, and believed too many of his salty and fantastic tales.

Gib Morgan was the minstrel of the oil fields. If he had a home, he spent most of his time away from it. He was a fiercely proud old vagabond, a tall, angular individual with buttermilk-blue eyes, a sweeping, grizzled mustache, and a mellow, persuasive voice that helped to give a semblance of verity to the stories he told so vividly. There was something distinctive about him, although he dressed as did most oilmen of the day. Perched jauntily on the side of his head was the inevitable, sand-pumping-splashed, black derby hat. He usually wore a blue flannel shirt, open at the throat. His pants were the jeans worn by all oilmen, and he wore high, laced boots of good leather. Possibly his individuality came from the way he walked and the way he would flip a casual and friendly hand in greeting to a drilling crew as he passed.

We never knew when he was going to visit our little town of Pleasantville in Venango County. Often, of a late afternoon, he would be seen plodding up a dusty road, swinging his arms, chewing intently on a gigantic wad of Spearhead eatin' tobacco, and looking straight ahead. His coming was news. Oil-field workers suddenly found that it was necessary for them to go to town that night. In the bar of the Eagle House there would be a private session limited to about two dozen oilmen. To be invited to be present was the equivalent of a royal command. After Gib had been primed with rye, the session would be ready to start, and the door of the long, narrow barroom would be locked. No one could enter or leave until the session was ended, the last story told, and the final drink downed.

Morgan usually stood at the end of the bar, with a tall water glass of whisky at his elbow. Every time he took a swallow, which was often, the bartender would instantly refill the glass, whereupon Gib would gaze at him reproachfully. Until he had absorbed what he considered the requisite volume of alcohol, he would remain somewhat aloof. A good showman, Morgan knew the value of suspense and used it to advantage. Eventually he'd start talking. Maybe someone would be complaining that the production of a certain well was declining sharply. Gib would look at the man, and a toothy smile would momentarily flash behind the heavy mustache.

"Whickles!" he would say, with a slight cough. That was the kickoff, the traditional signal for someone to ask a leading question designed to launch a story from Morgan.

"What in the world are whickles, Gib?" Sam Wilson or some other oil producer would ask.

Morgan would sneer thinly, gloomily note that his glass had been refilled, and drink most of it. His pale eyes would light up, and his deep, resonant voice could be easily heard.

"Whickles!" he would snort. "Mean to tell you ain't heard about whickles? What manner of oilmen are you? Them whickles is what causes your oil production to go down, gents!"

And then would come the story. Morgan told it slowly, persuasively, with dramatic pauses. When he was spinning his tale, it would be as quiet in the bar as a funeral home.

Before the time of any man present, Gib would begin, bachelor Mont Morrison lived in a little shack at Skunk Hollow. Morrison, a pumper, owned two canaries by which he set great store. The male bird, according to Morgan, was a rather delicate creature named Oscar. The bird had a great fondness for dried-apple pie, a weakness shared by his owner.

One day Morrison, partially overtaken with drink, made a dried-apple pie, but neglected to let the apples first stand in water and expand. He gave Oscar a liberal piece that the bird hungrily gobbled. "Gentlemen, that there bird swole up as big as a eagle and exploded forthwith," Gib Morgan related solemnly. Morrison, fortunately, had not tasted the pie, which was rapidly swelling. He did, however, witness what had happened to Oscar and forthwith decided never to drink again.

The unhappy accident left the other canary, a flighty female named Minnie, in a lonely world that she did not relish. Removed from the solace of drink, Morrison had plenty of time on his hands and vainly tried to console Minnie. She became peckish about her food, sang gloomy songs, and generally brooded. One bright spring day Morrison noted that Minnie seemed to have perked up a bit. She took a bath and preened her feathers. She warbled a few gay bars of music and sat perched with her head on one side, her eyes bright with expectancy. The cage had been hung out in the morning sun; pretty soon Morrison noticed a gigantic bumblebee buzzing around the cage in a most amorous manner. The bee was literally strutting in the air, diving, twisting, floating to a dead stop, and fluttering his wings daintily. To such antics Minnie gave feminine encouragement, singing gay trifles of jigs and reels, dancing up and down on the perch, and even uttering silly sounds of endearment.

It burst upon Morrison that he was witnessing a love affair. It was something that touched his heart, and he decided to further the cause by opening the door of Minnie's cage. She stepped out daintily and tried to fly. Years of confinement severely handicapped her, and the first time she tried to do a power dive, she lost control and struck the ground smartly on her stomach. The big bee alighted and solicitously examined the inert canary; she recovered almost immediately. Presently, the two of them flew away, the bumblebee circling the slow-winged Minnie and still stunting.

"It was a right pretty sight," Morgan related. Every morning the two of them would come back for food. Then, after an absence, they returned one morning with a brood of children.

"Them offspring was whickles, a cross between a canary and a bumblebee, embracin' the worst qualities of both parents. They growed fast, intermarried, had terrific appetites. And tempers! One day Mont brushed one of the youngsters outa his hair a little roughlike. The whickle uttered a sort of a banshee war cry, and ten of his brothers and sisters made for poor Morrison and stang him fore and aft. He swore some stingers were over an inch long. Just before he passed out he hollered for mercy to the parents. He swore that Minnie and her husband was sittin' on the kitchen table, titterin' and eggin' the kids on and takin' great joy in his misery."

Morgan would pause, wipe the long mustache with a graceful gesture, and stare unseeingly across the smoky room. Then his eyes would turn solemnly toward the bar and the filled glass of rye. He would start just a little and look very sad. "Me, I'm a temperate man," he would interpolate. "But when I tell this story, it grieves me and a little rye helps.

"Well, gents, Morrison was badly swole when he woke. He hurt considerable. He felt that the only thing that would cure him was plenty of swigs of likker. He went over to Cash-Up and after he had managed to swaller a quart or so, he started to feel better. He tried to tell the bartender about the whickles and got throwed out for his pains. Hurt his feelin's.

"The whickles and the parents never returned to Morrison's shack. But one day Mont was comin' back from Shamburg with a gallon of applejack. He had partook pretty liberal and after he had sung some duets with himself, he laid down to take himself a little nap. He forgot to put the cork back in the jug, which was a bad mistake. He woke up to the sound of a terrible buzzin', and a sound of singin'. He lay there, quiet as a mouse. He told me that he was afraid to move. The whickles, almost a thousand of them by this time, was engaged in drinkin' up that applejack. They enjoyed it, too. They was even good-natured. They had formed a sort of a singin' society and sung songs, very rowdy ones, too, in a sort of a cross between a canary's voice and the buzzin' of a bumblebee. Off-key, the singin' was very loud and kinda wicked.

"Eventually, they flew off without disturbin' Morrison. It was about this time that wells around Skunk Hollow started to dry up. Producers claimed it was due to a lot of things, but Morrison knew better. He discovered that the whickles had acquired a taste for crude oil. They was a new breed of critters, so it was reasonable that they should find food the easiest way. They was millions of them by this time. One day Morrison saw the whole string of them divin' out of the sky into the lead line of one of the best wells on the Benedict farm. Within a week, that well's production fell off terrible. Morrison, being a sensible feller, jacked up his courage with a little redeye and went off to see old man Benedict. He told him about the whickles and outlined a scheme for capturing them. He suggested that Benedict place a dozen jugs of whisky on the ground around the well. Eventually, the whickles would come out and drink the likker and fall down dead drunk. They could then be captured and destroyed. Did old man Benedict foller his advice? He did not! Instead, he heaved a sucker-rod wrench at poor old Mont and danged near hit him.

"Mont died of a broken heart. I was the only other man he took into his confidence. Me, I'm open-minded. Your oil wells are producin' less and less oil, and you don't do nothin' about it. Whickles is robbin' you blind. If you was smart, you'd put whisky—rye whisky—in jugs around your ailin' wells. You could go out in the mornin' and find the ground covered with drunken whickles. Yessir!"

No one dared to laugh aloud, but the crowd would smother its laughter in quiet chuckles. One oil producer, we had heard, had taken Morgan's advice and placed three jugs of whisky around a well. When he returned in the morning, all he found was an empty jug and Gib Morgan sound asleep on the ground. Morgan simply stated that he had come out to watch the experiment and had carelessly fallen asleep. He did not, however, explain why the empty jug was cradled in his arms.

Morgan had other tales, equally wild and improbable. He told the amusing story of the time he had just missed a fortune when he was drilling a deep well on the Dunham farm over Enterprise way. All of a sudden, he explained, the drilling cable had started to throw slack. Then suddenly the cable would straighten with a vicious snap.

"Before we could pull out them tools," he recalled, "the cable was plumb jacked in two. We never could fish out them tools. They just kept bouncin' up and down. We had struck a rubber rock, gents! You can go over there to this day and listen down that casin' head and still hear them tools bouncin'—and that was twenty years come March."

Two other oil-field lads and I tried all one day to find that old casing head. Gullible? Well, you had to hear Gib Morgan tell his stories, and, if you were ten years old, you'd be convinced by the man's tone and earnestness.

He never accepted charity, aside from drink, food, and shelter. He didn't do all of his tale-spinning in bars. Often, he would drop in of an evening in some remote engine house or visit some lonely wildcat drilling well. He was always welcome, and always urged to tell stories, of which he seemed to have an inexhaustible store.

Morgan said that he himself had once built the biggest pipe line in the world, running from Philadelphia to New York City and New Jersey. His partner was a man named Siggins. Siggins received word that his wife in New York was about to elope with a local coal dealer. It was imperative that he should reach New York before the two ran away. He took his problem to Gib, who solved it neatly. "I told Siggins that I'd pump him up there in a jiffy," Gib recounted. "We had a few drinks. Then I wished him Godspeed and gave him a bottle and a couple of sandwiches. He crawled into the line feet first, and I opened the throttles on the pumps and away he went.

"He never reached New York, sad to say. I'd forgot to warn him about the big Y in the line where it branched to New York and New Jersey and I'll be damned if he didn't hit it full speed and it split him right in half. He arrived in sections, too late to stop the elopement. His widdy never forgave me. Always claimed I done it apurpose. Seems she wasn't extry fond of the coal dealer, after all."

Gib Morgan claimed that he had the biggest pipe-line crew on record while he was building the big line. They numbered high into the thousands. "Best-fed men you ever see," Morgan would say.

His cooking and feeding arrangements were a trifle on the unusual side, as they were geared to meet the tremendous traditional appetites of pipe liners. The batter for pancakes was mixed mechanically in a hundred-barrel tank. The boiler-plate griddles were fifty feet square, fired by natural gas. They were

greased by three active colored men who strapped sides of bacon
on their feet and skated hither and yon over the griddles. "These
men had to be spelled right often, as the heat was pretty fierce,"
Morgan would point out.

The batter was piped to the big griddles, and the pancakes
were turned with long-handled snow shovels, and reached the
table on conveyor belts. On the table were ten-barrel tanks,
equipped with swivel-pipe arrangements that made it easy for the
men to put syrup on their cakes.

"Did you make any money on that pipe line?" someone was
sure to ask.

Morgan would look reproachfully at the questioner. Then he
would sadly admit that he had netted around a million dollars.

"Got it in the bank, eh Gib?" the insistent one would inquire.
At this point Morgan would inevitably reach for his glass and
empty it deftly. There would be a look of deep tragedy on his
angular face.

"Lost every cent of it," he would sadly admit. "Invested it in
the polka dot business, had a corner on polka dots, and made a
barrel of money. Pink polka dots, especial, was in great demand.
Then one day a feller come along and invented a square polka
dot. That put me out of business. Public fancy turned to the
square polka dots. I had to go back to work, broken in health
and pocket."

He would pause, wipe a nonexistent tear from the buttermilk-
blue eyes, bite off a healthy chew of eating tobacco, and stand
there, the picture of abject misery.

One of Morgan's favorite stories was about an old tomcat owned
by the Widow McGraw at Oil Center. When questioned as to
the location of Oil Center, he was a trifle vague. This cat, it
seemed, was the undisputed champion of the little oil town. He
had whipped every cat in the area. He was death on dogs and
would claw and bite them, inflicting great injury. Furthermore,
he was naturally a mean cat, a free thinker, and a Populist at
heart. When he roamed the streets, other cats climbed trees and
dogs crawled under porches. Brooked no opposition, did this cat.

His name was Josiah, and the Widow McGraw, who ran a boarding house, set great store by him.

Josiah's one-cat reign of terror was shattered by a mongrel hound dog, a stranger in Oil Center. The dog was owned by a drilling contractor from Bradford, a man named Beach. "The hound was a peaceful critter, but addicted to skunks," Morgan once told us. "He loved to hunt skunks and usually smelt pretty high. Fresh from a successful skunk hunt, he smelt awful, at which times Beach would insist that he walk at least a full hundred yards behind him, greatly to the dog's disgust. The critter couldn't understand why his owner should object to such a delightful perfume as skunk. Matter of fact, the hound brooded a lot about this attitude on the part of his owner."

It appeared that Josiah, fat and filled with a desire to exert himself, became aware of the presence of the hound unexpectedly. He was sunning himself, vainly trying to think up some new deviltry, when he saw Beach coming briskly up the street. He was walking fast, trying to keep the distance between himself and the hound. The dog had managed to flush two adult skunks right on the outskirts of the town and was redolent—and brooding glumly on the unreasonable attitude of Beach, with whom he earnestly and affectionately desired to share the fresh perfume.

Josiah, being a smart cat, noted that Beach was a stranger. His ears picked up, however, as he noted the hound moodily marching along, head down and utterly saddened. The sight of the unchastened dog fired Josiah with ambition, angered him, and awakened his innate sense of superiority. This was a dog to be taught a lasting lesson. Josiah prepared for battle. He was a great believer in the element of surprise, for it had always been effective in the past. Furtively, he climbed a tree and crawled out on a limb that protruded over the plank sidewalk. From this point on, the story is Morgan's:

"Just as the unsuspectin' dog was under him, Josiah leaped from the limb, straight to the hound's back. As he lighted, he spit and let out a bloodcurdlin' howl. Usually, this scared the daylights outa a dog. As a rule, Josiah would set his teeth in the dog's neck and start to scratch, a thing that inflicted great pain on an ordinary dog.

"Well, this time Josiah was in for a surprise. The second he lit, the fresh skunk perfume on the hound hit him right between the eyes; he was paralyzed and indignant, for, with all his faults, he was a clean cat and persnickety. In the split second he lost his sense of battle, the hound, already moody and grouchy, shook him off, took a quick snap, and nipped Josiah's tail mighty painful. The pain of that bite and the stench of the skunk dazed and terrified Josiah. There was only one thing to do and the cat done it. That was to run. He just managed to reach a telegraph pole as the hound took another savage bite at the tail. The dog stood and bayed for a few minutes, while Josiah crouched shamefully on the crossarm of the pole. What made it bad was that when the dog bayed, every cat and dog in Oil Center came out to see what was happening. To their joy, they noted that the champeen cat from whom they had all suffered indignities had been whipped and forced to run.

"It was humiliatin' for Josiah. Maybe he realized that his reign of terror was ended. If he ever tried to explain what had happened to him, no one would understand it. At dusk, he backed down the pole and suffered the crownin' indignity of all. A fat little pug dog, owned by the postmaster, had been one of his first victims and the creature had vowed to even the score. As Josiah's feet hit the ground, he heard a rush of feet and a furious bark. Thinkin' it was the hound that had been lurkin' in the darkness, and wailin' and screamin' for mercy, Josiah lit out for the shelter of the McGraw boardin' house. As the door opened for him to enter, he looked over his shoulder and saw that it was the pug dog who had chased him. That was the time, gents, when Josiah's mind musta cracked. From that time on, the cat was definitely deranged. He held himself aloof, became a sneakin' shadow. It was evident to all of us that he was broodin', calculatin' and plannin' some sort of revenge.

"The hound had the habit of walkin' back and forth in front of the McGraw place and sneerin' at Josiah, who spent most of his days on the porch roof.

"One mornin' a bleary-eyed tool-dresser tried to tell a bartender a strange and fantastic story. The man's hands shook as he raised a big hooker of rye. He said that the night before, a little drunk, he had gone into Button's livery stable for some sleep and was wakened by a gurgling sound. When he opened his eyes and looked, he could hardly believe what he saw. The nitroglycerin wagon used by the local oil-well shooter had been stored in the barn. In the felt-lined cells were three full cans of nitro. The tool-dresser claimed that he saw Josiah worry a cork out of a can and then drink nearly a gallon of it. 'I was scared to death,' the man admitted. 'If I had moved, the damned cat woulda dropped the can and blowed the town to pieces.' The bartender nodded. He knew nitro would explode sometimes with the smallest possible jar. But he suspected the tool-dresser and, tongue in cheek, asked him what had happened when the polar bears and blue elephants started to dance. In his delicate and refined way, he was hinting that the tool-dresser was sufferin' from too much likker—a gross libel, accordin' to the tool-dresser.

"Me, I heard all this when I dropped in for a little morning snifter. I had three fast ones after the bartender had tossed the tool-dresser out. I ran out in the street and tried to reason with people, to tell them that they was in dire danger. The fools, they laughed in my face and said I was drunk.

"Saddened me, the narrow view these citizens took. But I'm no fool! I climbed the hill fast and watched the town of Oil Center through a telescope. Always carried one in them days.

"Well, I hadn't waited very long until I see this man Beach startin' to work. Behind him was the hound, walkin' slow and sad. Beach had no more than passed the McGraw place when out on the sidewalk strutted Josiah. His ears was laid back and his eyes was blazin'. He walked stiff-legged and very careful-like. His belly was all swole out, he was that full of nitro.

"When the dog was thirty feet away, Josiah made his presence felt. He sorta reared up on his hind legs and started talkin' cat language. He called that dog every mean name he could think of; he invited the dog, if he had a speck of courage, to come to grips with the champeen cat of the world. It was a powerful flow of language and no self-respectin' dog could be expected to take it.

"The hound pinned back his ears, opened his mouth, and raced for Josiah. The cat sat down calmly, and just as the dog's body hit him I could hear his horrible laugh of revenge. The next second there was an awful explosion. Josiah had exploded, and his revenge was complete. Trouble was, it blowed up the whole town and everybody in it. Me, I was the only one saved."

As Gib ended the tale, there would be silence, which would finally be broken by furtive chuckles and backslapping. "You ask where was Oil Center?" Morgan would wind up. "The town's no more, gents. All that's left is a big hole in the ground."

Folk Songs of an Industrial City

by JACOB A. EVANSON

Pittsburgh is proud of its musical heritage. From its earliest days the city has been musically enterprising. In 1814, while still a frontier town, it was manufacturing pianos; two years later, a book of music was printed there. Through more than a century there has been built up an important song-literature composed by Stephen Foster, Ethelbert Nevin, Charles Wakefield Cadman, Harvey Gaul, and other western Pennsylvania composers. During this period the world's greatest music was brought to Pittsburgh by its own and visiting orchestras, choruses, and smaller groups and soloists. Forty or more national groups, each with fine musical traditions, have been a colorful part of the city's life.

The nineteenth century's end was the heyday of singing quartets, and many championship contests were held. One of the best groups was the Smoky City Quartet, whose fame is legendary among the city's South Siders.

Pittsburgh's folk-song tradition originated in the frontier days when its settlers carried on the tradition of English and Scottish minstrelsy. Still surviving in the memories of the city's oldest inhabitants are variants of many British and Scottish traditional ballads, among them "King John and the Bishop," "Molly Baun," "Bonny, Bonny Bunch of Roses," "Erin's Green Shore." Hundreds of folk songs of other European countries may be found in living memory in Pittsburgh, but this chapter is concerned primarily with the region's native ballads.

The earliest record of indigenous balladry in Pittsburgh is found in the memoirs of Henry M. Brackenridge (1786-1871) in 1834. Recalling the colorful races held around 1800 at the racecourse located in what is now downtown Pittsburgh, Brackenridge wrote:

The whole town [about 1,500 population] was daily poured forth to witness the Olympian games. . . . There was Crowder with his fiddle and his votaries, making the dust fly with a four-handed or rather four-footed reel; and a little farther on was Dennis Loughy [Loughey], the blind poet, casting his pearls before swine, chanting his masterpiece in a tone part nasal and part guttural.

Brackenridge quotes one stanza, without tune, of Loughey's "masterpiece":

> Come gentlemen, gentlemen all,
> Ginral Sincleer shall remembered be,
> For he lost thirteen hundred men all,
> In the Western Taritoree!

Though this is all we have of the ballad, it clearly was made in the great tradition, and a score of old ballad tunes—the ballad maker's stock in trade—can be found to match the vigor and meter of the words. The reference to "Ginral Sincleer" and his loss of men in the "Western Taritoree" is to General Arthur St. Clair, whom President Washington made governor of "the Territory Northwest of the River Ohio" in 1789, and whose army was defeated by Indians in 1791. As topical ballads are almost always written immediately after the incidents that inspired them, we may assume that Loughey wrote his ballad shortly after the battle.

Even Stephen Foster belongs in this ballad-making tradition. Serving as a local bard and using one of the most famous ballad tunes, "Villikins and His Dinah," in 1856 he wrote the political satire "The Great Baby Show" or "The Abolition Show," which appears in this chapter.

Evidence of vigorous folk hymn-tune making is preserved in the hymn-tune books published in Pittsburgh in 1816 and thereafter. These tunes were largely the work of itinerant preachers and singing-school masters. Though without much formal musical training, these men possessed a background of British folk-song tradition and a practical sense of the musical needs of a frontier people. Reversing the usual process, they made new tunes to fit old texts. The tunes were named after local places, a characteristic practice of hymn-tune makers: "Pittsburgh," "Pennsylvania," "Allegheny," and the famous "Dunlap's Creek," a version of which is in this chapter.

From earliest times on, we catch strains from folk troubadours—singers who accompanied themselves on the fiddle, guitar, banjo, or accordion—roaming Pittsburgh in the tradition of ancient minstrelsy. They entertained any and all listeners on street corners and in saloons, lodges, and homes. It was an informal custom, carried on for the most part in the singers' own neighborhoods and for sheer love of minstrelsy. The minstrels charged no fees, but gratefully accepted any proffered drink or food, or the scattered coins of their appreciative audiences. They sang both current music-hall ditties and Old World folk songs, and circulated topical ballads made up by themselves or by others and expressing the iron- and steelworkers' thoughts and feelings. Such ballads, printed as broadsides or sheet music, were sold during strikes, and the proceeds were used to buy food.

One of the most popular street troubadours was Philip Byerly, known as "The Irish Minstrel Boy," who in the eighties and nineties sang his way into the hearts of fellow steelworkers in Soho, a Pittsburgh district. Possessing a good tenor voice, he sang not only the Irish folk songs beloved of his audiences, but also his own ballads, the most popular of which was "In Soho on Saturday Night," included in this chapter.

According to Miss Mary Means, a music teacher in the Pittsburgh schools:

Byerly played the guitar, and a trio consisting of himself, a fiddler, and a mandolin player made their nightly rounds of the saloons in Soho, then the toughest neighborhood in Pittsburgh. My maternal grandfather, William Henry Cargo, lived on the hill overlooking the Soho Works, now the Jones and Laughlin Steel Corporation. He was one of the "good folks" whom Byerly and his fellow street minstrels would serenade after the saloons had closed at eleven o'clock. (My grandfather was in the wholesale liquor business, which may account for the deference paid him by the minstrels!)

On these occasions Grandfather would invite them to sandwiches, cake, and a "boilermaker and his helper," steelworker slang for a shot of bonded whisky and a beer chaser.

These street minstrels would sing whatever was requested by Grandfather, whom they referred to affectionately as "The Laird o' the Hill." Mother and her sister and brother, who were very young, would sit quietly at the top of the back pantry steps and listen. It is from those childhood days that Mother remembers the song "In Soho on Saturday Night."

In this chapter I am limiting myself largely to the folklore of the steel industry, even though Pittsburgh has other great industries, such as coal mining, glass, aluminum, railway equipment, and similar manufactures. Steel, however, dominates Pittsburgh's economy and community life. Of Allegheny County's million and a half population, one person in every three works in steel or is directly dependent on those who do. Pittsburgh's great power is awe-inspiring, but the city is also friendly. It is smoky, dirty, noisy, and sweaty, as human beings give out their energies to turn iron ore into steel.

In common with other occupational groups, iron- and steelworkers have a folk-song tradition. From the end of the Civil War to the 1900's, ballad making and minstrelsy formed an important part of their social life. Old-time steelworkers enthusiastically tell of this song tradition; their stories are confirmed by the large number of ballad texts buried in the dusty volumes of the *National Labor Tribune* and its successor, the *Amalgamated Journal*, official organs of the Amalgamated Association of Iron, Steel, and Tin Workers.

Virtually every union lodge had its own bard who made up ballads upon request or to mark special occasions, such as strikes, lockouts, and disasters. Billy Jenkins, now an octogenarian, who contributed the song "Amalgamate as One" to this chapter, was one of the noted bards. Sylvester Sullivan, Ed Lambert, and Reese E. Lewis from the seventies and eighties, and the younger Oscar Bennett and Albert Stolpe, were other makers of steel verse, much of which may be found in the back numbers of the union publications.

The best-remembered steelworkers' bard, Michael McGovern, did not suit his rhymes to tunes. He preferred to be known as "The Puddler Poet." Born in Ireland in 1848, he worked for many years in Ferndale, Bucks County, before moving to Youngstown, Ohio, in the nineties. There was hardly a union convention or picnic that "M. McG." did not attend to recite one of his poems. Although he wrote of the homely things familiar to iron- and steelworkers, he stood in awe of the great English classical poets; much of his verse—ornate and diffuse—suffers thereby. He wrote more poetry about the steelworkers than did any other man, and when he died in 1933 his family found more than a thousand unpublished verses among his papers. How sincerely Michael McGovern was appreciated is attested to by the fact that about ten years ago a monument over his grave in Calvary Cemetery, Youngstown, was purchased with funds contributed from seven states by steelworkers and congressmen, preachers, judges, lawyers, national labor leaders, and business and professional men. Upon its face was engraved this self-composed epitaph:

> Just place a rock right over me,
> And chisel there that all may know it;
> Here lies the bones of M. McG.
> Whom people called "The Puddler Poet."

In contrast to coal miners, lumberjacks, farmers, and other rural occupational groups, steelworkers had access to all the commercial amusements of a big industrial city like Pittsburgh. Meager wages, however, kept steelworkers from patronizing them as often as they wished. So there was always the corner saloon where beer and whisky were cheap and where one could drink in the congenial company of one's fellow men on equal terms. Poor men's clubs, as they were termed, with their sawdust floors, swinging doors, and free-lunch counters were all over Pittsburgh, and most numerous perhaps in Soho, where iron- and steelworkers were concentrated.

To be sure, there are many tales to be told of saintly characters and families and of groups of heroic courage and enterprise, but, on the whole, life was raw and elemental. Men drank hard and fought often in saloons and on the streets. It was bare-knuckle fighting with no holds barred.

Steelworkers had their superstitions. Like coal miners, they believed that women visiting the works brought bad luck to the men. That was what Terence Sean O'Shaughnessy believed, as told to Mary Means by an old-time steelworker:

Terence was doin' guard duty at the main gate of the Works. Comin' and goin', he knew every man jack who passed through those gates on the day shift. Only the good St. Patrick himself could get by O'Shaughnessy, the men used to say, and even then, he'd have to prove to Terry that he *did* drive the snakes out of Ireland.

Well, anyway, one rainy day, who drives up to the gate demanding to enter but the wives of three Front Office Boys.

"Ye'd oughta know better, me pretties," chides Terry in his best blarneyin' tone. "It's bad cess to us when ladies are among us here. Old Betsy is a jealous mistress. She will not pour nicely. So, go ye now home, lassies, to your imbroid'ry and cookery. Else your men will go hungry—and *worse*, this very day!"

Then Terence Sean O'Shaughnessy did a strange thing. He spat three times, once toward the Monongahela; once toward the Allegheny; once toward the Ohio. Then, mumbling some spell, he crossed himself and returned to his two-by-four shack out of the rain.

Steelworkers grouped themselves by heritage in their social life. Many were immigrants (even today approximately forty per cent of Allegheny County's residents are either immigrants or second generation of immigrants). There were dances and balls in winter and picnics in the summer; every church and national holiday was celebrated with a party. Even wakes were often an excuse for carousing.

A member of one of these national groups naturally felt most at home in the company of his own kind, who shared memories of a common homeland, spoke the same language, and enjoyed the same folk songs and dances. For example, the Scotch had their gatherings of the clan; the Irish, their Ancient Order of Hibernians; the Welsh, their Eisteddfods; the Polish, their Falcons; the Slovaks, their Sokols. The cultural heritage of thirteen national strains forms the background of the songs in this chapter.

While the song-making process was thinning out among the older steelworkers of British background, minstrels of continental European heritage were making steel songs of power and beauty. Up to the Civil War, Pittsburgh's population had consisted of British, German, and other northern-European peoples, with the Scotch-Irish dominant. With the post-Civil War industrial expansion came our southern Negroes and southern and eastern Europeans. The largest groups of these today are the Italians, Poles, Czechoslovaks, Russians, Yugoslavians, and Hungarians. I count among the happiest experiences of my research for this volume the opportunity to have met some of the makers of these indigenous non-English songs, and to have heard them sing of their experiences in and around Pittsburgh steel mills. In contrast to the Tin Pan Alley orientation of many of the songs of the same period, they drew upon their Old World folk music for tunes. Consequently, their songs are fresh, strong, and expressive, though their foreign languages form a barrier to their general use. Those included here are full of pathos and compassion, reflecting the new environment's emotional impact upon immigrants trying desperately to adjust themselves to American mores.

Menas Vardoulis, one-time steelworker, who contributed "The Immigrant's Heartbreak," said:

Many of us Pittsburghers of Greek heritage have always made up new songs to old Greek tunes. We think no more of it than telling a story. In fact, the songs are stories. They are simple and easily learned and pass from one to another just like stories. We never gave much thought to the author. We learned to make songs back on the Karpathos Islands where about a thousand of us in Pittsburgh came from. Our people there have an ancient tradition of song making.

Axel Simonen, who wrote "Song of Steel," explained,

I have had no musical training, but I know a great many Finnish songs, and I make songs for my pleasure and that of my friends who came from Finland.

Andrew Kovaly, who supplied the songs "I'm a Labor Man" and "I Lie in the American Land," recalled:

We who came from Slovakia sang much in those days [the 1900's], in saloons, and in church and Sokol halls. We would make up songs of our own about our life in McKeesport and sing them to old Slovak folk-song tunes we had known in the old country.

From the very beginning of the city's history, hostility toward newcomers was felt by some members of the native population partly out of fear that the former threatened their economic security. Among most immigrants there was a pathetic eagerness to shed their old-country ways and quickly conform to the customs of the new country. This was especially true of the second generation. Only in the privacy of their homes or in the company of their countrymen did they carry on the Old World traditions that marked them for the older groups' derision. In the past quarter century a more friendly climate has developed. With self-confidence has come a realization among these newer Americans that their patriotism is not tainted by singing ancestral folk songs, doing folk dances, wearing colorful costumes on festive occasions, and enjoying favorite Old World dishes. There is a new pride in the possession of this culture and in sharing it with their neighbors.

The Twenty-Inch Mill

(Text from the *National Labor Tribune,* April 26, 1894. Used by permission.)

The oldest iron-steel song in this chapter, its salty lines tell of the two-fisted, lusty rolling-mill men who made Pittsburgh's iron and steel back in the early seventies. The ballad was probably inspired by Carnegie's twenty-inch mill on Thirty-third Street where the first Pittsburgh-rolled beams were made around 1870. The ballad presumably had had a decade or two of oral circulation before it was printed in the April 26, 1894, issue of the *National Labor Tribune.*

The ballad is in the come-all-ye tradition. As the original tune is unknown, I have adapted a version of "Canaday-I-O."

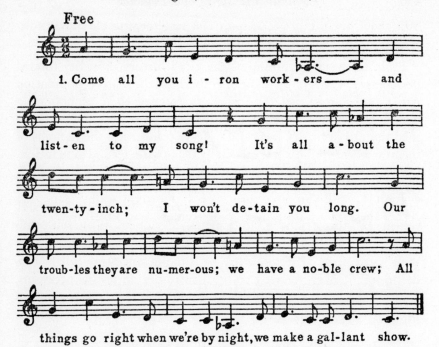

Free

1. Come all you i - ron work - ers ____ and list - en to my song! It's all a - bout the twen - ty - inch; I won't de - tain you long. Our troub - les they are nu - mer - ous; we have a no - ble crew; All things go right when we're by night, we make a gal - lant show.

2. We have roughers built like elephants, and others thin and spare;
   Our catcher says it's all the same—our roller seldom there.
   We have hookers, they're all skillful men, while our straight'ners
       number five,
   And when we go to changing rolls all nature seems alive.

3. We have helpers; we have heaters that sometimes burn the steel;
   We have pilers too, and chargers that help to ram the peel.
   Our buggy man's a daisy; he's a man that takes no sass
   But he always helps big Jumbo to drive them in the pass.

4. When we are on the night turn they come well filled with beer;
   It takes a big supply, you know, to put them in good cheer.
   They try like men to work again; you may look on with pride;
   The bar at last goes through the pass, but sticks fast in the guide.

5. And when we are changing rolls and the second set is in,
   Jake starts to charge up and thinks it is no sin.
   And when the bloom is heated all ready to draw,
   He's plainly told to sit awhile and give them time to thaw.

6. Now we can't do much on iron rails, on slap-jacks or tees;
   We're no great hands on channel bars, on posting rounds or zees;
   But we're expert hands on 6 x 6; your orders we can fill,
   And for your life don't let them go to any other mill.

In Soho on Saturday Night

(Sung by Mrs. Julia Means at Pittsburgh, 1947. Notated by Miss Mary
Means.)

This ballad is a satire on the way of life in Soho, Pittsburgh's
rowdiest neighborhood, in the nineties. Steelworkers living there
went about their roistering, fighting, carefree way without much
interference from the police. Millwork was mere child's play
compared to the strains and hazards of a policeman's beat in Soho.
Pounding its sidewalks was an ordeal that required the power of
a John L. Sullivan, the agility of a tightrope walker, and the
recklessness of a stunt flyer. No wonder that Pittsburgh's cops
regarded an assignment there as equivalent to exile in Siberia!

They tell us in So-ho on Sat-ur-day night,

Most ev-'ry per-son you meet they are tight; The

men with their bot-tles, their wives with a can, And young girls go

prowl-in' a-round like a man. One wom-an I

met, I'll niv-er for-get, She fell in a sew'r and she

got soak-in' wet. The crowd gath-er'd 'round her all

think-in' her dead, But then she got up, and quick-ly she

said: "Oh, is-n't it queer how some wom-en drink beer? They

drink and they drink and get tight."___ And the new li-cense

plan, it ain't worth a damn In So-ho on Sat-ur-day night!

Faster

Oh, they all toss'd the drinks, Mis - ter

_____† did the same, As fast as they could fill them up, a -

Slower

round the drinks they came; Mis - ter

_____ got blind drunk, Mis-ter _____ could-n't see;

I was bad, but Mis-ter _____ was a

Much slower

damned sight worse than me. Oh, the new li-cense plan, it

ain't worth a damn in So-ho on Sat-ur-day night!

* The new license plan was part of a drive to clean up Soho.
† Names of prominent Pittsburghers in the nineties were inserted in these blanks.

Where the Old Allegheny and Monongahela Flow

(Sung by J. J. Manners at Pittsburgh, 1947, and used by his permission. Notated by Jacob A. Evanson.)

The source of this song has been only partially identified, but there is no question of its popularity. Manners said he wrote the verse, but learned the chorus from the Smoky City Quartet in the 1900's. Fred Schmidt, who wrote down the chorus for me in 1942, said, "I've sung it all my life. I can sing all four parts just the way they are always sung. A lot of people here on the South Side sing it. I've heard gangs sing it in beer places on corners down on Sarah Street."

George J. Schwartz, an elderly steelworker, added, "I don't know where the song came from, but I learned it about 1910 when I was top tenor of the old Montouth Quartet before Montouth Borough became part of Pittsburgh. Boy, the smoke really rolled over the hills in those days from a hundred puddling mills down on the river!"

Peter Diebold, only surviving member of the Smoky City Quartet, recollected that "Where the Old Allegheny and Monongahela Flow" was a favorite number in its repertoire.

The Allegheny and Monongahela rivers meet at the Point in downtown Pittsburgh to form the Ohio River.

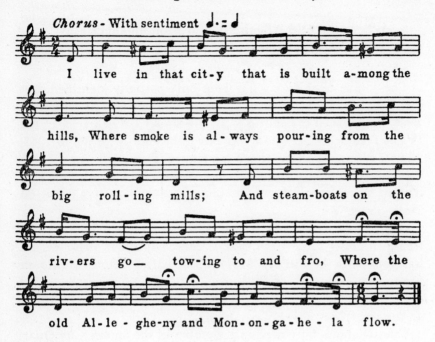

Chorus - With sentiment ♩. = ♩

I live in that cit-y that is built a-mong the

hills, Where smoke is al-ways pour-ing from the

big roll-ing mills; And steam-boats on the

riv-ers go— tow-ing to and fro, Where the

old Al-le-ghe-ny and Mon-on-ga-he-la flow.

Aja Lejber Man
(I'm a Labor Man)

(Sung by Andrew Kovaly at McKeesport, 1947. Notated by Jacob A. Evanson.)

"I came to McKeesport from Slovakia in 1899," said Andrew Kovaly. "I was only fourteen years old and life was hard for immigrants. But my father, brother, and friends who had come here ahead of me helped me. I got a job in a steel mill and have worked there ever since. I don't know who made 'I'm a Labor Man,' but it was very popular in the early 1900's."

Key to Slovakian pronunciation. Vowels: *a* as in *father; e* as in *met; i* as in *machine; o* as in *morn; u* like *oo* in *bloom; y* like *ee* in *meet*. Consonants: *c* like *ts* in *cats; č* like *ch* in *chin; ch* like German *ch; h* like *kh* or German *ch; j* like *y* in *yet; ň* like *ny* in *canyon; š* like *sh* in *shin; ž* like *z* in *azure*. All other consonants are pronounced as in English, except that all *r*'s are trilled.

In words of three syllables or less, the accent falls on the first syllable. In words of four or more syllables, the accents fall on the odd-numbered syllables, i.e., first, third, fifth, etc.

W. S. Platek, John Rusin, and Victor Polansky contributed to the translation of Slovakian songs.

Moderate SLOVAK

1. A - ja lej - ber man, ro - bim ka - zdi den,

vše se - be ra - hu-jem ke - lo zo-spo-ru-jem,

ke - lo zo-spo - ru-jem na - ti - dzen.

2. Pride petnasti,
   ta i šesnasti,
   talara nabaru,
   "daj nam po poharu,
   naj še napijeme napedu."

3. S kraju list dostal,
   bim daco poslal,
   šedňem za stoliček,
   napišem listoček,
   poslem žene stovku napedu.

1. I'm a labor man,
   I work every day.
   To myself I always figure,
   "How much am I saving,
   How much am I saving each week?"

2. Comes the fifteenth,
   And also the sixteenth.
   I put a dollar on the bar.
   "Give everybody a glass,
   Let us drink on payday!"

3. From the old country I received a letter
   Asking me to send something.
   So I sit down behind the little table,
   I write a little letter—
   I send my wife a hundred dollars on payday!

*Odpočívam v Americkej pôde**
(I Lie in the American Land)

(Sung by Andrew Kovaly at McKeesport, 1947, and used by his permission. Notated by Jacob A. Evanson.)

This ballad, dating back to the early 1900's, tells of a tragedy once common in the steel industry. Andrew Kovaly recalled the song's making:

I was a young foreman in a Bessemer mill here in McKeesport. A very good friend of mine, a member of my crew, had saved enough money to send to Slovakia for his family. While they were on the way to America, he was killed before my eyes under an ingot buggy. I tried to grab him but it was too late. It was terrible. I felt so bad that when I met his wife and little children at the railroad station I hardly knew how to break the sad news to them. Then I made this song. My friend was very proud of America and it was with pride and happiness that he had looked forward to raising his children as Americans. The song made me feel better and also my friend's wife. But she cried very hard. I have never forgotten it.

2. *Jaše vracim kecme nezabije,*
   lem ti čekaj odomňe novinu.
   Jak ot domňe novinu dostaneš,

* Key to Slovakian pronunciation will be found on p. 435.

šicko sebe doporjatku prines,
sama šedneš navraneho koňa, *
atak pridzeš draha dušo moja.

3. *Ajak vona do McKeesport prišla,*
   to uš muža živoho nenašla;
   lem totu krev co znoho kapkala
   atak nadnu, prehorko plakala.

4. *"Ej mužumoj co žeši učinil,*
   žesi tote dzeci osirocil!"
   "Povic ženo tej mojej siroce,
   žeja ležim utej Americe;
   povic ženo najme nečekaju,
   boja ležim v Americkim kraju."

1. Ah, my God, what's in America?
   Very many people are going over there.
   I will also go, for I am still young;
   God, the Lord, grant me good luck there.

2. I'll return if I don't get killed
   But you wait for news from me.
   When you hear from me
   Put everything in order,
   Mount a raven-black horse,
   And come to me, dear soul of mine.

3. But when she came to McKeesport,
   She did not find her husband alive;
   Only his blood did she find
   And over it bitterly she cried.

4. "Ah, my husband, what did you do,
   Orphaned these children of ours?"
   "To these orphans of mine, my wife, say
   That I lie in America.
   Tell them, wife of mine, not to wait for me,
   For I lie in the American land."

* Stanzas 2 and 4 have six lines each. The last two phrases of the music are repeated to accommodate the two additional lines of these stanzas.

O Kăïmós tou Mĕtanásti
(The Immigrant's Heartbreak)

(Sung by Menas Vardoulis at Pittsburgh, 1947. Notated by Jacob A. Evanson. Transliteration and translation by Vardoulis and Rudolph Agraphiotis.)

Menas Vardoulis learned this song in 1920 when he was in the steel mills. "I don't know who made it," he said, "but my fellow steel workers of Greek heritage sang it."

The half-expressed, soul-searing tragedy of this song very likely has been experienced by countless thousands of immigrants to this country. According to Vardoulis, "It is almost impossible to exaggerate the fantastic ideas the Greeks have had about America. I know of one man who, on getting off the boat in New York, actually picked up a five-dollar bill in the street, but threw it away disdainfully, in expectation of picking up hundred-dollar bills!"

1. Φεύγω, γλυκειά, φεύγω, γλυκειά, φεύγω,
    γλυκειά μανοῦλά μου, "Α!
    Feúgo, glikiá, feúgo, glikiá, feúgo, glikiá manulá mu, Ah!
    φεύγω γλυκειά, μανοῦλά μου, μὴ βαρυαναστενάζῃς·
    feúgo, glikiá, manulá mu, mi varianastenázis;
    καὶ τὴ φτωχή, καὶ τὴ φτωχὴ καρδοῦλά μου, "Α!
    ke ti ftochí, ke ti ftochí kardulá mu, Ah!
    καὶ τὴ φτωχὴ καρδοῦλά μου μὴ μοῦ τὴν κομματιάζῃς.
    ke ti ftochí kardulá mu mi mu ti kommatiássis.

2. Θά πάγω στήν, θά πάγω στήν 'Αμερική, "Α!
   Tha págo stin, tha págo stin Ameriki, Ah!
   θά πάγω στήν 'Αμερική, γρήγορα νά πλουτίσω·
   tha págo stin Ameriki, grígora na plutísso;
   Τά δάκρυά σου, τά δάκρυά σου, μάννα μου, "Α!
   ta dákriá sou, ta dákriá sou, mána mu, Ah!
   τά δάκρυά σου, μάννα μου, έγώ νά τά σφογγίσω.
   ta dákriá sou, mána mu, egó na ta sfonghísso.

   . . . .

10. Τί μ' ώφελεῖ, τί μ' ώφελεῖ ή 'Αμερική, "Α!
    Ti m'ofeli, ti m'ofeli i Ameriki, Ah!
    τί μ' ώφελεῖ ή 'Αμερική καί δλα τά καλά της,
    ti m'ofeli i Ameriki ke óla ta kalá tis,
    ποὺ μάρανε, ποὺ μάρανε τῆς μάννας μου, "Α!
    pu márane, pu márane tis mánas mu, Ah!
    ποὺ μάρανε τῆς μάννας μου τά φύλλα τῆς καρδιᾶς
    της;
    pu márane tis mánas mu ta fílla tis kardiás tis?

1. I leave, sweet, I leave, sweet mother of mine,
   Ah, I leave, sweet mother of mine, don't sigh painfully;
   And poor, and poor heart of mine.
   Ah, poor heart of mine, don't break.

2. I will go, I will go to America,
   Ah, I will go to America soon to get rich;
   Those tears of yours, those tears of yours, mother of mine,
   Ah, those tears of yours, mother of mine, wipe them away.

   . . . .

10. Of what benefit, of what benefit is America,
    Ah, of what benefit is America and all her wealth;
    After I have withered, after I have withered,
    Ah, after I have withered the leaves of my mother's heart?

Pittsburgh Is a Great Old Town

(Sung by Matt Gouze at Pittsburgh, 1947. Notated by Jacob A. Evanson.
Used by permission of People's Songs, Inc.)

According to Peter Seeger, ballad singer, this song was inspired
by the spectacle of Pittsburgh during the war boom:

The song was made pretty much by Woody Guthrie, the Oakies' balladist. That was back in the summer of 1941 when he and I and two
other fellows—The Almanac Singers, a jalopyful of modern troubadours—stopped in Pittsburgh on a country-wide junket. The early war

boom was on, and Pittsburgh was an awesome sight. This song, with a somewhat different text, was the result of communal effort, but mostly Woody Guthrie's.

Its popularity increased when Alan Lomax used it in 1943 on his C.B.S. broadcast "Trans-Atlantic Call—People to People." At least four different versions are now in circulation. Pittsburgh public-school children sing one form in which the stanzas are telescoped into one:

> Pittsburgh is a river town, Pittsburgh!
> Pittsburgh is a hilly old town, Pittsburgh!
> Pittsburgh is a smoky old town,
> Solid steel from McKeesport down.
> Pittsburgh is a great old town, Pittsburgh!

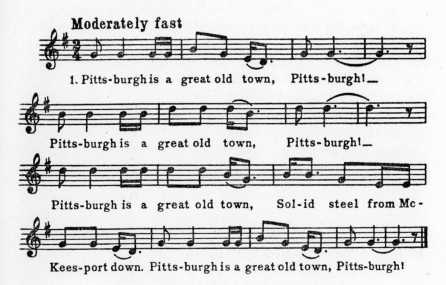

2. Pittsburgh is a smoky old town, Pittsburgh!
   Pittsburgh is a smoky old town, Pittsburgh!
   Pittsburgh is a smoky old town,
   Coal piled high in great big mounds.
   Pittsburgh is a smoky old town, Pittsburgh!

3. Pittsburgh is a river town,
   Two rivers meet at the Point downtown.

4. Pittsburgh is a hilly old town,
   Her streets and roads go up and down.

Joe Magarac

(Text and tune by Jacob A. Evanson, 1946. Based on the famous legend.)

After learning the many stories about Joe Magarac, steelworkers' folk hero, I wrote this ballad in our folk-song tradition. Joe is a legendary superman who performs incredible feats of strength and skill, as great as the steelworkers' imagination can invent. He is the Paul Bunyan of the steel mills. They say he makes horseshoes and pretzels out of iron ingots with his bare hands. From cooling steel he makes cannon balls as easily as boys make snowballs. He's so tough he can spit right into a Bessemer, and it doesn't dare to spit back at him.

And the way he can work! Everybody wants him on his crew, for the tonnage then shoots right up, and likewise wages. Moreover, it's more comfortable when he's around. For instance, there was the time he caught a ladle with fifty tons of hot "soup" in it when the crane chain broke right above his crew. Not a drop splashed on anybody. And there was the time the dinkey engine with a whole train of loaded ingot-buggies broke loose and headed full steam downhill, right into the front office full of people. Fortunately, Joe caught the last buggy just in the nick of time and pulled the whole train back up hill. No doubt about it, Joe Magarac is the greatest steelworker that ever lived.

The Hungarians pronounce his name "Mah-zhe-rahk," the Slovaks, "Mah-geh-rahts," but there are some in Pittsburgh who hold that he is really Joseph Patrick McGarrick! This apparently is the first time the Irish got into the dispute. After a diligent search to determine Joe Magarac's origin, I must acknowledge that the evidence is inconclusive.

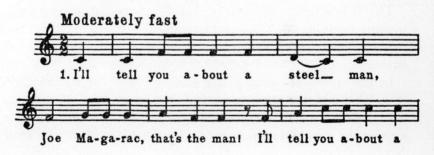

Moderately fast

1. I'll tell you a-bout a steel— man,

Joe Ma-ga-rac, that's the man! I'll tell you a-bout a

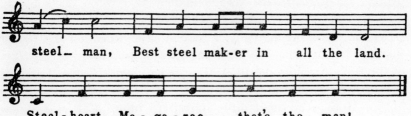

steel_ man,   Best steel mak-er in   all the land.

Steel-heart Ma - ga - rac,   that's the man!

2. He was sired in the mountain by red iron ore,
     Joe Magarac, that's the man!
   He was sired in the mountain by red iron ore,
     Raised in a furnace—soothed by its roar.
       Steel-heart Magarac, that's the man!

3. His shoulders are as big as the steel-mill door,
   Hands like buckets, his feet on half the floor.

4. With his hands he can break a half-a-ton dolly,
   He stirs the boiling steel with his fingers, by golly.

5. He grabs the cooling steel—his hands like wringers,
   And makes eight rails between his ten fingers.

6. Joe can walk on the furnace rim,
   From furnace to furnace—just a step for him.

7. Joe never sleeps, but he's got to eat,
   Hot steel soup, cold ingots for meat.

8. Now, if you think this man's not real,
   Then, jump in a furnace, see him cook the steel.

The Homestead Strike

(Sung by Peter Haser at New Kensington, 1940. Recorded by George
Korson. Variant sung by John Schmitt at Pittsburgh, 1947. Notated by
Jacob A. Evanson.)

The first attempt to organize the Pittsburgh iron- and steelworkers came in 1849, when four hundred puddlers rioted un-
successfully against strikebreakers. Nine years later the ironworkers
established a secret order called the Sons of Vulcan.

In the rapid expansion of the steel industry during the Civil
War, labor and management clashed frequently. In 1865 the Sons
of Vulcan came out into the open and negotiated the first wage
scale in the iron and steel industry; and in 1876 the various craft

unions merged into the Amalgamated Association of Iron and Steel Workers.

As the mills became bigger and more powerful, the struggle increased in intensity, culminating in the Homestead Strike—one of the bloodiest episodes in American industrial history.

Before dawn on the foggy morning of July 6, 1892, the whistle of the Homestead steel mills started to blow. This was a pre-arranged signal to warn the workers of trouble, and was reinforced by a horseman who galloped through the streets to call them out. Hugh O'Donnell, the steelworkers' leader, had received a telegram from the lookout on the Smithfield Street bridge in Pittsburgh, seven miles down the Monongahela River; it read: "Watch river. Steamer with barges left here."

Before long, O'Donnell and most of the 3,800 workers, armed with rifles, shotguns, pistols, and clubs, reached the mill in time to see the tugboat *Little Bill* emerge from the fog with two barges in tow. Their worst fears were realized when armed men in the uniform of the hated Pinkertons prepared to embark. These uni-formed strikebreakers had been hired by the Carnegie Steel Com-pany, which on June 20 had locked out the workers as the result of a wage dispute. Then the employees, backed by the Amalga-mated Association, had retaliated by organizing on a military basis, and for five days had succeeded in preventing anyone from entering the plant.

The stage was set for an epic battle. The company and the union were both powerful. Each had taken the law into its own hands. "This was no ordinary strike or lockout. It was revolution, sheer, stark, elemental." The *Little Bill* steamed away, leaving three hundred Pinkertons in the two barges, but opposed to them were thousands who now swarmed over the mill property to points of vantage. An all-day battle was on, mainly with small arms, but also with dynamite, burning oil and gas, and even obsolete cannon. When the Pinkertons finally surrendered, the toll on both sides was ten men dead and over sixty wounded.

The Homestead Strike inspired much verse and song. One of the most popular sheet-music songs of the year was "Father Was Killed by the Pinkerton Men," a sentimental ditty typical of the melodramatic nineties. The real folk song of the bloody episode was "The Homestead Strike." It was sung everywhere, and old-timers still sing it when a nostalgic mood takes possession of them. John Schmitt, from whom I obtained the tune, said he learned the ballad during the strike when he was sixteen. The text was taken from George Korson's book *Coal Dust on the Fiddle*.

Moderately fast

1. We are ask-ing one an-oth-er as we

pass the time of day, Why work-ing men re-sort to arms to

get their prop-er pay,   And why our la-bor un-ions they must

not be rec-og-nized, Whilst the ac-tions of a syn-di-cate must

not be crit-i-cized.   Now the

trou-bles down at Home-stead were brought a-bout this way, When a

grasp-ing cor-po-ra-tion had the au-dac-i-ty to say: "You must

all re-nounce your un-ion and for-swear your lib-er-ty And

we will give you a chance to live and die in slav-er-y."

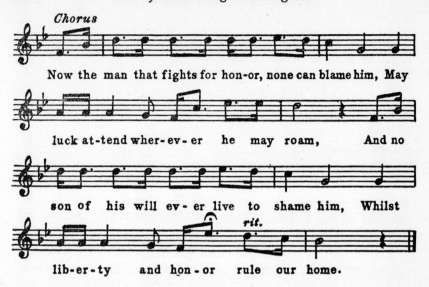

Now the man that fights for hon-or, none can blame him, May luck at-tend wher-ev-er he may roam, And no son of his will ev-er live to shame him, Whilst lib-er-ty and hon-or rule our home.

2. Now this sturdy band of workingmen started out at the break of
      day,
   Determination in their faces which plainly meant to say:
   "No one can come and take our homes for which we have toiled so
      long,
   No one can come and take our places—no, here's where we belong!"
   A woman with a rifle saw her husband in the crowd,
   She handed him the weapon and they cheered her long and loud.
   He kissed her and said, "Mary, you go home till we're through."
   She answered, "No, if you must fight, my place is here with you."

CHORUS

Now the man that fights for honor, none can blame him,
   May luck attend wherever he may roam,
And no son of his will ever live to shame him,
   Whilst liberty and honor rule our home.

3. When a lot of bum detectives came without authority,
   Like thieves at night when decent men were sleeping peacefully—
   Can you wonder why all honest hearts with indignation burn,
   And why the slimy worm that treads the earth when trod upon
      will turn?
   When they locked out men at Homestead so they were face to face
   With a lot of bum detectives and they knew it was their place
   To protect their homes and families, and this was neatly done,
   And the public will reward them for the victories they won.

March of the Rolling-Mill Men

(Text by Reese E. Lewis, in the *National Labor Tribune*, March 30, 1875. Used by permission.)

Here is a song of iron and steel's craftsmen when the industry was just getting under way, and before the pride of individual skill and craftsmanship had been killed by mass production machines. Those "lusty lads, with souls of fire" have here made a battle song keyed to their fierce pride as men and workers. Even their craft names sound wonderfully rough-and-ready in this marching song that calls upon Vulcan's sons to unite and "Stem the tide of evil practice, Mammon's sordid might and avarice," that was coming in with the new industrialism.

The rousing words, full of mouth-filling vowels and hammering consonants, are in an ancient bardic tradition, and so is its Welsh tune, "March of the Men of Harlech." The text's call for a union of all iron and steel crafts was answered in the following year, when they were united in the Amalgamated Association of Iron and Steel Workers.

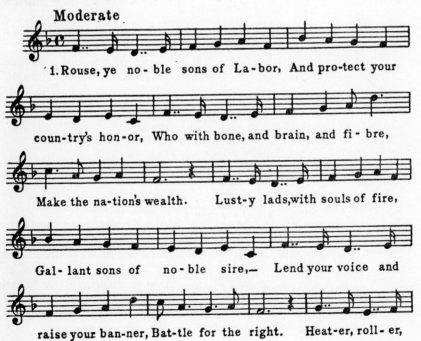

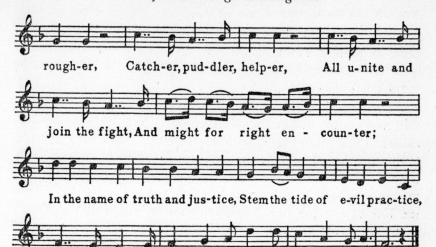

rough-er, Catch-er, pud-dler, help-er, All u-nite and

join the fight, And might for right en - coun-ter;

In the name of truth and jus-tice, Stem the tide of e-vil prac-tice,

Mam-mon's sor-did might and av-'rice, Our land from ru-in save.

2. Ye who aid our locomotion,
Wield the "cord which binds the nation," *
Honest types of God's creation,
Honor to your names.
Hearts of oak and arms of metal,
Who by dint of skill and muscle,
Fashion bridge and iron vessel,
Ever true and brave.
Heater, roller, rougher,
Catcher, puddler, helper,
All unite and join the fight,
And might for right encounter;
Let's be firm, with soul unbending,
'Mid the flash and sparks ascending,
Vulcan's sons are now arising,
Comrades, all unite.

Amalgamate as One

(Sung by William Jenkins at Canonsburg, 1947, and used by his
permission. Notated by Jacob A. Evanson.)

The theme of this ballad is as old as American labor itself. One
big union has always been labor's ideal hope. Billy Jenkins made
it in 1894, and it was widely sung, especially during strikes. It

* The railroads.

was the unofficial song of the 1909 strike. "We were out of work for months and months," recollected Jenkins. "Those were bad days for steelworkers. But we did what we could. We printed thousands of copies of 'Amalgamate As One,' and sold them in the steel towns."

What Billy Jenkins did not mention was that he did not personally profit from the sale of this song. The proceeds went for strikers' relief. Immigrating from Wales in 1881, Billy Jenkins was a steelworker around Pittsburgh for forty years before retiring to become a successful toymaker. He made up many songs and ballads about work in the steel mills and the life of the workers. "Amalgamate As One" contains much of the sentimentalism of Victorian America, and was Jenkins' most popular song.

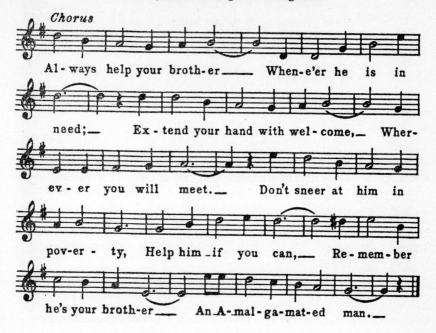

Al-ways help your broth-er____ When-e'er he is in
need;___ Ex-tend your hand with wel-come,___ Wher-
ev-er you will meet.___ Don't sneer at him in
pov-er-ty, Help him_if you can,___ Re-mem-ber
he's your broth-er___ An_A-mal-ga-mat-ed man.___

2. Always treat union men as you find them,
      Where'er in this world you may roam,
   And if ever you meet a true brother,
      Do not turn him away from your home;
   Remember he may have been cast out
      Through fighting for Honor and Right;
   And compelled to leave home in starvation,
      With no place of shelter at night.

      CHORUS

   Always help your brother
      Whene'er he is in need;
   Extend your hand with welcome,
      Wherever you will meet.
   Don't sneer at him in poverty,
      Help him if you can,
   Remember, he's your brother—
      An Amalgamated man.

3. If we part, let us hope not forever,
      But my plea is the same to the end;

Have courage to help one another,
   In pledges we took to defend;
Trades unions should all band together,
   And I hope that the day will soon come,
That we shall not be so divided,
   Amalgamate now all as one.

Teräksen Soitto
(Song of Steel)

(Sung by Axel Simonen at Glassport, 1947, and used by his permission. Recorded by Eero Davidson and Jacob A. Evanson. Translated by Davidson.)

"I made up the words of 'Song of Steel' about 1930," said Axel Simonen. "I was a steelworker then. On a visit to Detroit I recited the song to my friend Edward Pylkäs, another steelworker, who gave me the tune."

Key to Finnish pronunciation. Vowels: *a* as in *father; e* as in *met; i* as in *din; o* as in *open; u* as in *put; y* like French *u* or German *ü; ä* like *a* in *bat; ö* like *e* in *herb*. Consonants: *g* is hard; *j* like *y* in *ye; r* is always trilled; *t* almost like *d*. Double vowels mean a longer duration of the vowel sound. Repeated consonants must be pronounced. Each letter is pronounced. The accent in all cases is on the first syllable.

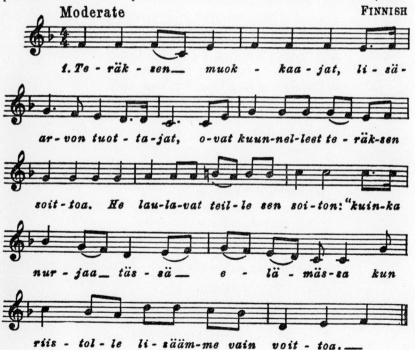

2. *Tehtaissa riistetään;*
    osingoista kiistetään.
    Voitot täytyis saada aina suuremmat.
    Kun terrori kiihtyy niin nurisee orjat
    että on: "Kyllä olot nämä kurjat,
    siksi työ olot pitäis saada paremmat."

3. *Teräs on soittanut,*
    laulunsa laulanut
    heille jotka terästä ain' muokkaavat:
    "Tunne sun voimasi, työn joukko suuri;
    murtuvi varmasti vahvinkin muuri,
    joukkovoimaan työläiset luottavat!"

4. *Teräs se soittaapi;*
    laulunsa laulaapi
    aina kun työmaalla työskennellään.
    Sen soitossa suuressa orjatkin herää;
    voimiaan alkavat yhteen jo kerään
    Ken syrjähän jäiskään nyt nöyrtymään?

5. *Teräs se soittaapi;*
    lauluaan laulaapi:
    "Työläiset liittykää, järjestykää!
    Siinä on vainen se voima mi voittaa,
    taistellen joukolla vapaus koittaa,
    ja saapuvi onnekas keväinen sää!"

1. Makers of steel,
    Producers of wealth,
    Have heard the music of steel.
    They sing the song of steel:
    "How wrong it is in this life
    To add more to the riches of the greedy."

2. In the mills there is scheming;
    The greedy are grasping for power.
    Always they want more profits.
    When aroused, their slaves murmur
    Like this: "Sure, our living is wretched,
    That's why we should have better working conditions."

3. Steel has its own music,
    Its song has a message
    To those who shape the steel:
    "Know your strength, working masses;

Even the strongest wall can crumble,
If the workers trust their mass power!"

4. Steel plays a song;
It sings its own song
In the mill where we are working.
Even slaves bestir themselves;
They are beginning to gather strength.
Who would now remain timidly on the sidelines?

5. Steel plays a song;
It sings its own song:
"Workingmen, unite, organize!
Therein lies the strength to win.
Union aids the fight for freedom,
And ushers in the joyful spring of life!"

Dunlap's Creek

(Text by Isaac Watts. Tune attributed to Samuel McFarland.)

"Dunlap's Creek" is one of the best-known American folk-hymn tunes. The hymn was first printed in 1816 in *The Pittsburgh Selection of Psalm Tunes,* a compilation by John Armstrong, and the source of the present text.

Dunlap's Creek rises in Fayette County near Uniontown and empties into the Monongahela River at Brownsville; Dunlap's Creek Presbyterian Church dates from 1774.

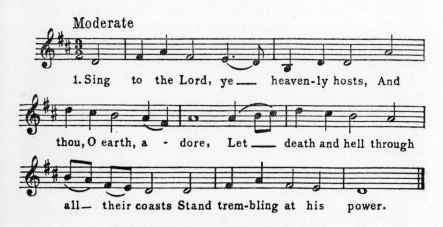

2. His sounding chariot shakes the sky,
He makes the clouds His throne,

        There all His stores of lightning lie,
          Till vengeance dart them down.

3. His nostrils breathe out fiery streams,
      And from His awful tongue
    A sovereign voice divides the flames,
      And thunder roars along.

4. Think, O my soul, the dreadful day
      When this incenséd God
    Shall rend the sky, and burn the sea,
      And fling His wrath abroad.

5. What shall the wretch, the sinner do?
      He once defied the Lord,
    But he shall dread the Thunderer now,
      And sink beneath His word.

6. Tempests of angry fire shall roll
      To blast the rebel-worm,
    And beat upon his naked soul
      In one eternal storm.

The Great Baby Show or The Abolition Show

(Text by Stephen Foster. Air: "Villikins and His Dinah.")

This little-known political satire by Stephen Foster refers to a procession that took place in Pittsburgh on September 17, 1856, during the Frémont-Buchanan Presidential campaign and was in honor of Frémont, the Republican nominee. The "border-ruffians" from Missouri were so called by the Free State men (supported by Republicans) in the bloody dispute in "Poor Bleeding Kansas" over the slavery issue. "Ohio Yankees of Western Reserve" refers to the fact that the Western Reserve, a tract of land in Ohio, belonged to the Connecticut Yankees. The convention of western Pennsylvania Republicans, of which the parade was a part, was often referred to as "a council of freemen" because it was opposed to slavery in any form. "Both of our towns" were Pittsburgh and Allegheny.

Moderate

1. On the sev-en-teenth day of Sep-tem-ber, you know, Took

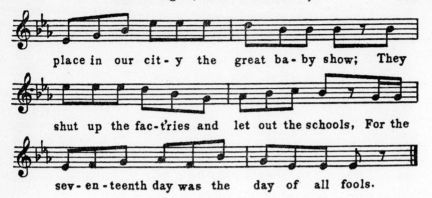

place in our cit-y the great ba-by show; They

shut up the fac-t'ries and let out the schools, For the

sev-en-teenth day was the day of all fools.

CHORUS*

Sing tu ral lal, lu ral lal lu ral lal lay. *(Four times)*

2. They made a procession of wagons and boats,
   Of raccoons and oxen (they all have their votes),
   Sledge hammers, triangles, and carpenters' tools,
   One thousand and eight hundred horses and mules.

CHORUS

Sing tu ral lal, lu ral lal lu ral lal lay. *(Four times)*

3. They had minstrel-show gem'men to join in their games,
   And jokers and clowns of all ages and names;
   They had popguns and tin pans and all kinds of toys,
   And a very fine party of women and boys.

4. They had young men on horseback, so nice and so gay,
   Aged seventeen years on this seventeenth day;
   And the ladies all thought they were bold cavaliers,
   These bright-looking lads aged seventeen years.

5. They had grim border-ruffians, I'll bring to your mind,
   And they've plenty more left of the very same kind;
   They all were so happy, played cards on the way,
   And the children looked on, on this seventeenth day.

6. They had Ohio Yankees of Western Reserve
   Who live upon cheese, ginger cake, and preserve;
   Abolition's their doctrine, their rod, and their staff,
   And they'll fight for a sixpence an hour and a half.

7. Now was it not kind in these good simple clowns
   To amuse all the children in both of our towns,

* Sung to the same tune.

> To shut up their workshops, and spend so much money
> To black up their faces, be gay, and be funny?

> 8. They called it a council of freemen, you know,
>   But I told you before 'twas a great baby show,
>   For when they had met they had nothing to say
>   But, "Poor Bleeding Kansas" and "Ten Cents a Day."

In 1856 the *Pittsburgh Morning Post,* opposed to the young Republican party, printed the ballad in a form different from the one I have given. Stanza 6 of the above version was missing and the following two stanzas, numbered 6 and 7, were attributed by Foster to a person called "Mit." In the first stanza "Old Buck" is James Buchanan. "Ten-Cent Jimmy" also is Buchanan, so named because it was believed that his proposal to manipulate the currency would reduce a laborer's wage to ten cents a day. The 1845 fire destroyed much of Pittsburgh, and Buchanan, a resident of Mercersburg, apparently came to the financial rescue.

> Then their ship *Constitution* was hauled through the street,
> With sixteen small guns she was armed complete;
> But the brave ship of state, by which Democrats stand,
> Carries thirty-one guns, with Old Buck in command.

> In the year '45 when the fire laid us waste,
> Old Buck gave us five hundred dollars in haste.
> They then took his money, and lauded his name,
> But he's now "Ten-Cent Jimmy," their banners proclaim.

The Johnstown Flood

(Text supplied by Edwin Hartz. Sung by Mrs. Clara Bell Delaney, 71, 1947. Notated by Miss Mary Means.)

No other tragedy touched the American people as did the Johnstown flood. It produced many a legend and inspired much poetry and song. The ballad given here, author unknown, is the most popular in the region's oral tradition about the flood.

This version is a composite. Hartz had learned the words from his mother, Mrs. Etta Woods Hartz, a lifelong Pittsburgher, who was eighteen years old at the time of the flood. Miss Means wrote down the tune from the singing of Mrs. Clara Bell Delaney, another Pittsburgher.

On May 31, 1889, the South Fork Dam, four hundred feet above and sixteen miles beyond Johnstown, broke. A roaring, forty-foot "ball" of water, a twenty-million-ton Niagara, rushed with incredible fury upon the city; it tore along with everything in its path— human beings, animals, trees, bridges, buildings; tossing locomotives around like cockle shells; piling up a mountain of debris at the railroad bridge below the town, which at once caught fire to become a funeral pyre for the living and dead trapped in it. Within a few hours thirty-five thousand people were homeless, and twenty-two hundred had been crushed, drowned, or burned to death in "the worst peacetime disaster of the nation's history."

Pittsburgh, eighty miles down the Conemaugh and Allegheny rivers, was the first to come to the rescue. Johnstown was an old steel town and thousands of its steel-mill "graduates" were in the Pittsburgh mills. The flood disaster struck them with special force and they made substantial contributions to Johnstown's relief. The Pittsburgh Relief Committee was in official charge of the stricken people of Johnstown for the twelve days before the state took over.

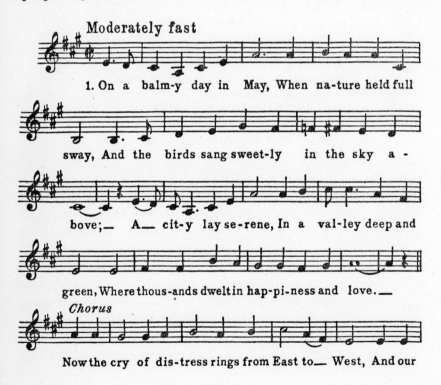

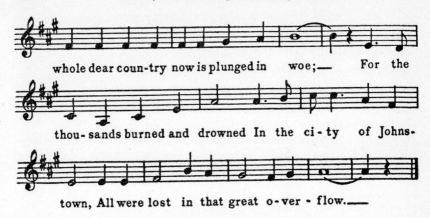

whole dear coun-try now is plunged in   woe;—   For the

thou- sands burned and drowned In the ci - ty   of Johns-

town, All were lost in that great o - ver - flow.——

2. Ah! but soon the scene was changed;
   For just like a thing deranged,
   A storm came crashing thru the quiet town;
   Now the wind it raved and shrieked,
   Thunder rolled and lightning streaked;
   But the rain it poured in awful torrents down.

CHORUS

Now the cry of distress
Rings from East to West,
And our whole dear country now is plunged in woe;
For the thousands burned and drowned
In the city of Johnstown,
All were lost in that great overflow.

3. Like the Paul Revere of old
   Came a rider brave and bold;
   On a big bay horse he was flying like a deer;
   And he shouted warning shrill,
   "Quickly fly off to the hills."
   But the people smiled and showed no signs of fear.

4. Ah! but e'er he turned away—
   This brave rider and the bay
   And the many thousand souls he tried to save;
   But they had no time to spare,
   Nor to offer up a prayer,
   Now they were hurried off into a watery grave.

5. Fathers, mothers, children all—
   Both the young, old, great, and small—

They were thrown about like chaff before the wind;
When the fearful raging flood
Rushing where the city stood,
Leaving thousands dead and dying there behind.

6. Now the cry of fire arose
   Like the screams of battling foes,
   For that dreadful sick'ning pile was now on fire;
   As they poured out prayers to heaven
   They were burned as in an oven,
   And that dreadful pile formed their funeral pyre.

The Trolley

(Sung by John S. Duss at Ambridge, 1947, and used by his permission.
Notated by Jacob A. Evanson.)

The city's first horse-drawn streetcar started rolling in 1859.
Complete with candle lights and straw-covered floor, this "rapid
transit," as it was called, rumbled along Penn Avenue to Bayard's
Town, just beyond the present site of the Pennsylvania Railroad
station. In 1888 Pittsburghers rode on their first cable car. Two
years later the electrically driven trolley car was introduced.

Coming a generation before the automobile, the trolley car was
an important mode of local and intercity transportation and
inspired many songs throughout the country. Here is Pittsburgh's
own version made up in 1900 by John S. Duss, who is now in his
eighties.

He is the only surviving member of the Harmony Society, which
was dissolved at the end of a century's existence in 1905. Composed
of German immigrants under the leadership of George Rapp, the
society carried out one of the most successful experiments in
communal living in American history. Their town, Economy (now
Ambridge), stood on the Ohio River seventeen miles below Pittsburgh. After religion, music was the Harmonists' greatest joy.
They considered it a necessary part of their life. According to
Duss, they sang at work and play, as well as at worship. They sang
favorite Old World folk songs and American tunes. It was out of
this atmosphere that Duss's trolley song emerged.

Moderately fast

1. Heigh ho, a - way we skim o'er the cit-y high-ways;

Wak-ing the qui-et by-ways, clang goes the gong! Like a

flash to and fro, on the trol-ley we go; While the

swift wheels make mu-sic all a - long.

"Ding, ding," the bell says, "let's all be jol-ly, jol-ly!"

Joy reigns a-board the trol-ley, speed-ing a - far! And all

care flies a - way, and we're gay night and day, When we

ride up-on the jol - ly trol-ley car.

2. Onward, the car sweeps, onward with force vulcanic!
   Merchant and staid mechanic sit in the throng;
   Seizing each one his chance o'er the papers to glance,
   While the swift wheels make music all along.
   Granddames and grandsires, babies awake and squawky,
   Soldiers in suits of khaki fresh from the war!
   Rich and poor, high and low, they are all on the go;
   And they're happy on the jolly trolley car.

The Mouse's Courting Song

(Sung by Grantison Farrish at Pittsburgh, 1942. Notated by Mrs. Gladys
Lentz Zeiler and Jacob A. Evanson.)

This song is a modern variant of the famous classic "A Frog He
Would A-Wooing Go," which was printed as early as 1549. In the
traditional form it is Mr. Frog who woos Miss Mouse, but Pittsburgh Negro children took the names of their version's hero and
heroine from Walt Disney and the hero's character from Western
thrillers. Baseball and a democratic land made their contributions, too. Mrs. Zeiler's Miller School first-grade pupils learned the
song from the Farrish boy, who, in turn, had learned it from
neighborhood children.

Moderately fast

1. There was a lit-tle mouse who lived on a hill, Hm-hm, Hm-

hm, There was a lit-tle mouse who lived on a hill, He was

rough and tough like Buf-fa-lo Bill, Hm-hm, Hm-hm.

2. One day he 'cided to take a ride,
   Hm-hm, hm-hm.
   One day he 'cided to take a ride,
   With two six-shooters by his side,
   Hm-hm, hm-hm.

3. Then Mickey rode till he came to a house,
   And in this house was Minnie Mouse.

4. He strutted right up to the kitchen door,
   And bowed and scraped his head on the floor.

5. O Minnie, Minnie, Minnie, will you marry me?
   Away down yonder in the orchard tree!

6. Without my Uncle Rat's consent,
   I would not marry the Pres-eye-dent!

7. Her Uncle Rat gave his consent,
   The Weasel wrote the publishment.

8. Oh, what you gwina have for the wedding feast?
   Black-eyed peas and hogshead cheese.

9. The first one came was Uncle Rat,
   Head as long as a baseball bat.

10. Second one came was Mr. Snake,
    He wrapped himself 'round the marble cake.

11. The next one came was a little moth,
    To spread on the tablecloth.

12. The next one came was a big black bug,
    Carrying 'round a little brown jug.

13. The next one came was a bumblebee,
    With a broken wing and a crooked knee.

14. The next one came was a nimble flea,
    Saying, Minnie, Minnie Mouse, will you dance with me?

15. The next one came was Mr. Cow,
    He wanted to dance but he didn't know how.

16. Last one came was Mr. Cat,
    He ruffled and tuffled and ate Uncle Rat.

17. And that was the end of the wedding feast,
    Black-eyed peas and hogshead cheese.

Monongahela Sal

(Sung by Robert Schmertz, the copyright holder, at Pittsburgh, 1947, and used by his permission. Recorded by Jacob A. Evanson.)

For some years past, people have asked me, "Do you know 'Monongahela Sal'?" I finally caught up with the man who made it, Robert Schmertz, an architect and a member of the faculty of Carnegie Institute of Technology.

"I'm nuts about hillbilly," said Schmertz. "Years ago somebody left a long-neck banjo at my house. I don't know anything about music, but I figured out how to play a few chords on it, and I've been making up songs ever since."

These songs were made to be rendered tongue-in-cheek, as it were, and Schmertz sings them with a straight face. He plays the

banjo in perfectly steady rhythm but sings the melody with such
free and intricate rhythms and pitches that only by writing out
each stanza can justice be done. Only the basic melodic structure,
which is a variant of "Red River Valley," is given here, together
with the rolling chorus-tune and a special tune for stanza 8. I have
included all stanzas and choruses of the long narrative song, which
is in the rootin'-tootin'-shootin' "he done her wrong" tradition.
Schmertz has a grand sense of the place names of this region that
"roll on the tongue with venison richness": Monongahela, Mones-
sen, Ohio, Aliquippa (Alliquippi for a rhyme with Mississippi),
Emsworth, Sewickley, Dravo.

Moderate

1. She was born in an old Mon-es-sen al-ley,— And her
2. She was smart, she was pert, she was pret-ty,— And the

maw and her paw, they called her Sal; She grew
bloom of health was on her cheeks, But she

up to be the pride of the val-ley,— A—
bought it in Mo-non-ga-he-la Cit-y,— And the

typ-i-cal Mo-non-ga-he-la gal.
drug-gist said that it would last for weeks.

Chorus

Roll on,— Mo-non-ga-he-la,— Roll

on to the O-hi-o, Roll on, past Al-li-quip-pi, Down

to the Mis-sis-sip-pi, Clear to the Gulf of Mex-i-co.

3. She wandered one day by the river,
    And she watched the *Jason* steaming by;
    And her heart gave a leap, and a quiver,
        As she caught the handsome pilot's roving eye.

4. His name, so they say, was Moat Hanley,
    And he wore a fancy sparkin' coat;
    He was tall, dark and handsome and manly,
        And the best durn pilot ever steered a boat.

SECOND CHORUS

Roll on, Monongahela,
Where the catfish and the carp left long ago;
You used to be so pure,
But now you're just a sewer,
Messin' up the Gulf of Mexico.

5. Moat gave a toot on his whistle,
    And the *Jason* churned the water at her stern;
    And Sal steppin' light as a thistle,
        Reached up and took Moat Hanley's hand in her'n.

(Stanza 6 sung to tune of "Careless Love")

6. It was love, careless love, on the river,
    It was love, careless love, by the shore;
    And I know that the Lord will forgive her,
        'Cause she never knew what love was like before.

THIRD CHORUS

Roll on, Monongahela,
Away from the ice and snow;
I think you're mighty lucky,
To roll past old Kentucky,
Clear to the Gulf of Mexico.

(Return to the regular tune)

7. He swore that he always would love her,
    As they locked through the old Emsworth dam;
    But that night overboard he did shove her,
        And then Moat Hanley took it on the lam.

FOURTH CHORUS

Roll on, Monongahela,
And lap the waters gently at Dravo;
Where they're back to making barges
At much more normal charges,
Than the L.S.T.'s they made a year ago.

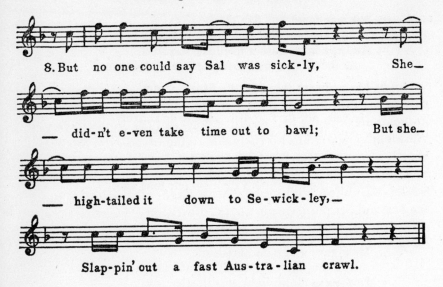

8. But no one could say Sal was sick-ly, She—

— did-n't e-ven take time out to bawl; But she—

— high-tailed it down to Se-wick-ley,—

Slap-pin' out a fast Aus-tra-lian crawl.

(Return to the regular tune)

9. So she hopped a fast freight by Rochester,
   She swore she'd have Moat Hanley's gore;
   From a yard-bull who tried to molest her,
   She up and swiped a great big forty-four.

10. Now Sal hit the grit, right at Beaver,
    And the *Jason* was a-comin' 'round the bend;
    In the pilot house stood Moat, the gay deceiver.
    Says Sal, "I'm sure to get 'im in the end."

FIFTH CHORUS
Roll on, Monongahela,
And blow, gentle breezes, blow;
'Cause it's getting mighty smoggy,
And the folks are getting groggy—
I've lived here all my life and I should know.

11. She raised up that big shootin' iron,
    She banged six shots right into Moat;
    And when she had fin'ly ceased firing,
    She'd sure messed up that fancy sportin' coat.

12. Now Sal to the judge said, "Good mornin'!"
    The jury foreman said, "Not guilty, gal";
    So let all you pilots take warnin',
    Don't mess around Monongahela Sal!

River Go Down

(Sung by the pupils of Daniel Webster Public School at Pittsburgh,
1945. Notated by Miss Margaret Bailey.)

Floods have always haunted Pittsburgh. Adequate controls are
now in the making, but there have been more than one hundred
inundations since the first recorded flood in 1753, in which George
Washington nearly lost his life while trying to cross the Allegheny.
Shortly after the 1945 flood when six blocks of Pittsburgh's business district were inundated and the basement of Daniel Webster
School was filled with water, Miss Bailey, the school's music
teacher, and her pupils made up this prayer-song. The song's Negro
melodism may be traced to the presence of Negro children in
the school.

List of Songs and Ballads

Index